ATOMIC TUNES

ATOMIC TUNES

The Cold War in American and British Popular Music

TIM AND JOANNA SMOLKO

INDIANA UNIVERSITY PRESS

This book is a publication of

Indiana University Press
Office of Scholarly Publishing
Herman B Wells Library 350
1320 East 10th Street
Bloomington, Indiana 47405 USA

iupress.org

Manufactured in the United States of America

First printing 2021

Library of Congress Cataloging-in-Publication Data

Names: Smolko, Tim, author. | Smolko, Joanna R., author.
Title: Atomic tunes : the Cold War in American and British popular music / Tim Smolko, Joanna Smolko.
Description: Bloomington : Indiana University Press, 2021. | Includes bibliographical references and index.
Identifiers: LCCN 2020042418 (print) | LCCN 2020042419 (ebook) | ISBN 9780253056160 (hardback) | ISBN 9780253024466 (paperback) | ISBN 9780253056177 (ebook)
Subjects: LCSH: Popular music—United States—History and criticism. | Popular music—Great Britain—History and criticism. | Cold War—Music and the war. | Popular music—Political aspects—United States—History—20th century. | Popular music—Political aspects—Great Britain—History—20th century.
Classification: LCC ML3477 .S67 2021 (print) | LCC ML3477 (ebook) | DDC 782.4216409/045—dc23
LC record available at https://lccn.loc.gov/2020042418
LC ebook record available at https://lccn.loc.gov/2020042419

CONTENTS

ACKNOWLEDGMENTS

WE'D LIKE TO THANK THOSE who read portions of the manuscript, gave encouragement, provided us with precious writing time, or simply educated us in subtle but invaluable ways: Dan and Doris Cush, Deane Root, Mariana Whitmer, Kathryn Miller Haines, Julie Darken, Kelly Holt, Rachel Cabaniss, Erin Leach, Simon Hunt, Bart Lemahieu, Neil and Marty Hughes, Greg Kelso, Jimmy Brown, Susan Clay, Jen Wolf, Stacey Piotrowski, Lora and Solomon Smothers, Taryn and Myles Magloire, David and Nicole Bryan, Lee and Amy Moody, Hillary and Mike Thompson, Ana and David Durling, Jim Kenaston, Adelle and Parker James, Beth and Brett Jamieson, Emily and Bradley Shadrix, Betsy and Kevin Weinrich, Wayne Crotts, Craig Duncan, Joel Doerfel, David Haas, David Schiller, Christy Desmet, Jean Kidula, Susan Thomas, Sujata Iyengar, Richard Menke, Josh and Corazon Bedford, Steve Valdez, Carolyn Brunelle, Reba Wissner, Russell Reising, Lisa Kraus, and Jeannette and Chris Jones.

Thanks to our family members for the encouragement and support.

Thanks to Susan, Jessica, Cindy, and others in the UGA Interlibrary Loan department, who procured dozens of books and articles for us.

Thanks to the committee of the Hampsong Fellowship in American Song for awarding us the 2016 grant, which helped us pay for research materials and song licenses.

Thanks to Felicia Miyakawa and Andrew Dell'Antonio for publishing portions of the book on *The Avid Listener.*

Thanks to Thierry Noir, John Holmstrom, Paul Research, Peggy Seeger and Nancy Schimmel for interviews and correspondence.

Thanks to David Miller, Rachel Rosolina, Allison Chaplin, Janice Frisch, and Kate Schramm, and to all the fine people at Indiana University Press. Thanks to Carol McGillivray for overseeing an excellent copy edit.

Thanks to Ian and Elanor and Ringo and Buster for love and laughter.

ATOMIC TUNES

INTRODUCTION

Cold War History in Music and Lyrics

FROM 1945 UNTIL 1991, THE United States and the Soviet Union engaged in a nuclear-arms race for military supremacy, an ideological battle between capitalism and communism, and a series of proxy wars that cost the lives of at least five million people.[1] Although tension between the two countries can be traced back to the Bolshevik Revolution in 1917, many historians mark the atomic bombings of Hiroshima and Nagasaki in 1945 as the beginning of the Cold War. The forty-six-year conflict vacillated between mild anxiety and rampant paranoia and introduced for the first time in history the possibility of man-made global catastrophe. The escalation of the arms race and a host of other technological, political, social, and military developments made the Cold War among the most globally significant events in recent times.

Although the two superpowers never directly engaged in a full-scale military battle, the Cold War was the most ominous occurrence of brinkmanship in human history. Its disturbing legacy remains with us. In 1986, the number of nuclear weapons in the world reached a peak at over seventy thousand.[2] Over the next twenty years, the number was slowly reduced to approximately twenty-six thousand by 2006.[3] In more recent times, the number has been reduced even more to approximately thirteen thousand five hundred, with eighteen hundred of these considered to be on "high alert, ready for use on short notice."[4] While this reduction is hopeful and encouraging, the effects of the Cold War continue to loom over us. We still live in its aftermath. The Cold War forged many of the ideologies and principles that shape our politics today. The conflict played a significant role in forming our current notions of what constitutes left wing or right wing in politics, liberal or conservative in ethics, communist or capitalist in economics, and universalist or Christian in religion.

As would be expected, the arts and culture of the period reflected the Cold War, especially in films (*Dr. Strangelove, Red Dawn, WarGames*); television (*The Prisoner, The Day After, Threads*); editorial cartoons (Herblock's "Mr. Atom" and Bert Dodson's "Nuke"); and novels (George Orwell's *Nineteen Eighty-Four*, John le Carré's *The Spy Who Came in from the Cold*, and Tom Clancy's *The Hunt for Red October* and *Red Storm Rising*). Geopolitics even affected sporting events, such as the Olympics with the American and Soviet boycotts of the 1980 and 1984 summer games. All genres of music showed the influence of the Cold War. Some of the most famous jazz musicians, such as Louis Armstrong, Benny Goodman, and Dave Brubeck, made highly publicized tours in the Eastern Bloc in the 1950s and 1960s. The Texan classical pianist Van Cliburn gained worldwide fame for winning the first International Tchaikovsky Competition in Moscow in 1958. Musicals (*Chess*) and operas about the Cold War have been composed, including two well-known works by John Adams, *Nixon in China* and *Doctor Atomic*. Among the most famous of the many classical works about the Cold War are Alfred Schnittke's oratorio *Nagasaki* and Krzysztof Penderecki's *Threnody to the Victims of Hiroshima* for string orchestra.

There have been many books written on Cold War film, television, and literature and on the role that jazz and classical music played in the conflict. Scholarly studies have been published about the popular music from World War I and World War II.[5] Yet the American and British popular music written specifically about Cold War topics has yet to be fully explored. Between 1945 and 1991, well over five hundred songs were written about various aspects of the conflict: nuclear weapons, fear of the Soviets, the proxy wars, civil defense, uranium mining, the space race, McCarthyism, espionage, the Berlin Wall, and glasnost.[6] Some songs were written to bring an issue to light, some to persuade listeners to a particular point of view, still others to simply entertain and amuse. Songs ranged from the serious to the comical, to the morbid, to the tasteless and covered all points in between. Like uranium in a bomb, the songs themselves are the core element in this study, but popular musicians did much more than just write songs about the Cold War; they spoke of the conflict extensively in interviews, participated in protest movements, designed their stage shows on it, depicted it visually in their music videos, plastered it all over their album covers and T-shirts, and even named themselves after it. Some of popular music's biggest stars, such as Pete Seeger, the Rolling Stones, Elton John, ABBA, John Denver, Bruce Springsteen, and Billy Joel, played concerts in the Eastern Bloc. In some ways, as we will show, popular music played a role in ending the Cold War.

What can a study of these songs add to the ever-growing body of literature on the Cold War? These songs give deep and substantial insight into the social history of the conflict, capturing the thoughts and emotions of everyday people who lived under the shadow of Stalin, *Sputnik*, mushroom clouds, and missiles.

They can surprise listeners by revealing and communicating aspects of these world-changing events in ways that documentaries and history books cannot. They grapple with controversial geopolitical issues of the time in concise, three-minute packages: Is the Soviet Union an "evil empire?" Is communism at our doorstep? Are nuclear weapons more of a danger or a deterrent? Could World War III actually take place? What constitutes a just war? Can we trust our leaders? Rarely has popular music addressed such weighty questions as the ones in these songs. Like fossils in our collective memory, they have preserved Cold War events that have been forgotten, or half-remembered, and bring them back to life again. Although popular songs cannot give a detailed understanding of the conflict, they can communicate something that is perhaps just as important as the historical facts: a visceral sense of what it was like to live through the Cold War. Many of these songs are just as relevant today since we continue to live in a world of nuclear weapons, suspicious superpowers, proxy wars, and walls being constructed. In some ways, the Cold War never ended.

The Cold War, and popular music about it, can be divided into three eras. The "Atomic Age" lasted from the mid-1940s to the mid-1960s. Songwriters wrote about atomic and hydrogen bombs, uranium mining, civil defense, bomb shelters, radiation poisoning, the space race, and McCarthyism. The scare of the Cuban Missile Crisis in 1962 brought about the second era, commonly called détente, from the mid-1960s to the late 1970s. This period produced fewer songs about the Cold War since the superpowers were pursuing disarmament treaties thereby reducing the threat of nuclear war. Popular musicians in this period were voicing their political concerns about the civil rights movement, the Vietnam War, the economy, and second-wave feminism. Although the Vietnam War, the greatest military conflict of the Cold War, generated many songs, it did not escalate into a crisis of global proportions, and the United States never seriously threatened to use nuclear weapons. Détente ended in 1979–1980 with the Soviet invasion of Afghanistan, and the renewal of the arms race. This second wave of atomic anxiety lasted into the latter years of the 1980s—sometimes called the "Second Cold War." Several songs from this period charted highly and became part of the cultural landscape. Music throughout history has always been a mirror of cultural change, and the songs written about Cold War topics mirrored the degree of tension in geopolitical affairs. But before introducing the music, it would be helpful to provide a summary of the major events of the Cold War.

OVERVIEW OF THE COLD WAR

The Cold War, like the two world wars, was a war of technology. When the twentieth century began, the centuries-old techniques of cannon-fire exchange and cavalry charge by armies facing each other on a battlefield were still practiced. Hand grenades, land mines, warplanes, tanks, submarines, aerial bombs, and poisonous gas were used only sparingly in warfare or had not yet been invented. Machine guns were a relatively new technology. Combatants kept, for the most part, to the chivalric codes of the Geneva and Hague Conventions, which sought to minimize military and civilian deaths. Civilian deaths were far fewer than military deaths since battles were often fought on static battlefields, in rural areas, or at sea.

By the middle of the twentieth century, as the result of mobilization, industrialization, scientific discovery, and two world wars, human warfare had completely changed. War could be waged not only on land and at sea, but underwater and in air. War had appalling dimensions—weapons could now obliterate large cities and kill millions of people in minutes. Atomic bombs and saturation bombing resulted in civilian deaths far outnumbering military deaths. War could be fought remotely with the push of a button and could bring an end to human life on earth. The Cold War was a struggle between continuing the trajectory that science and technology had set forth for modern warfare and avoiding its catastrophic consequences.

Although the Cold War encompassed a variety of interrelated historical events, the three major aspects of the conflict were the nuclear-arms race, the ideological battle between capitalism and communism, and the proxy wars. A brief review of the first topic, the arms race, shows how rapidly it escalated.[7] The bombs dropped on Hiroshima and Nagasaki in 1945 inaugurated the Atomic Age. In 1949, the Soviet Union successfully tested its first atomic bomb. In 1952, America exploded its first hydrogen bomb, "Ivy Mike," which was approximately seven hundred to one thousand times more powerful than the Hiroshima bomb. The Soviet Union detonated their first hydrogen bomb in 1955. The next generation of weapons was the intercontinental ballistic missile (ICBM), which could travel thousands of miles and detonate a nuclear warhead. The Soviet Union tested the first ICBM in 1957, and in the same year, they launched the first satellite, *Sputnik*. These successes led to the false assumption that the USSR was far ahead of the United States in its conquest of space and had a great number of ICBMs at its disposal. This perceived "missile gap" contributed to the massive increase in nuclear weapons produced during the Eisenhower and Kennedy administrations in the late 1950s and early 1960s. By the mid-1960s, other countries such as Great Britain, France, and China had developed and successfully tested atomic bombs, and there were over thirty thousand nuclear weapons in the world. An alliance between Nikita Khrushchev and Fidel Castro caused the Cuban Missile Crisis in 1962, which resulted in Soviet nuclear weapons being based in Cuba, just ninety miles from the coast of Florida. The dilemma was peacefully resolved, but it was the closest the world had come to nuclear war. After this brush with catastrophe, the superpowers began pursuing nuclear disarmament treaties in the mid-1960s to reduce the threat of nuclear war.

This period of détente ended in 1979–1980 when Russia invaded Afghanistan, and Presidents Jimmy Carter and Ronald Reagan greatly increased military spending. By the mid-1980s, the superpowers boasted a dizzying array of nuclear-war technology. The arms race raged on until General Secretary Mikhail Gorbachev was convinced that military spending was suffocating the Soviet economy. He, along with Reagan, England's Margaret Thatcher, and Germany's Helmut Kohl brought the Cold War to an end, resulting also in the end of the communist era in Russia and most of the Eastern Bloc countries.

The second major aspect of the Cold War, fear and mistrust between the superpowers as a result of the ideological battle between capitalism and communism, had its origins well before 1945. It all started with the Bolshevik Revolution in 1917.[8] This event, which made Russia a communist country, spread anxiety across America that bolshevism would infiltrate and spread communism, radicalism, and anarchy. When this didn't happen, anxiety died down, but relations between the two countries were still strained in the 1920s and 1930s. During World War II, when the Nazis invaded the Soviet Union in June 1941, President Roosevelt provided the country with massive quantities of aircraft, tanks, and supplies under the Lend-Lease Act. The defeat of Germany and Japan at the end of World War II left just two countries as world superpowers, the United States and the Soviet Union. Although allies during the war, their relationship soon soured due to mistrust over their opposing political ideologies and strained mutual occupation of Berlin. While the United States encouraged democratic elections and freedom of speech in their occupied countries, West Germany and Japan, Joseph Stalin forced his brand of oppressive communism on East Germany, Poland, Hungary, Romania, Czechoslovakia, Bulgaria, and others.

Reports of mass executions, forced labor camps in Siberia, and widespread famine caused by agricultural collectivization convinced most Americans that communism's utopian ideals were illusory. The US government spoke of the Soviet Union, and communism in general, in the harshest and frankest of terms because of their threat. In the late 1940s and early 1950s, the House Un-American Activities Committee (HUAC) and Senator Joseph McCarthy separately conducted numerous investigations and accused hundreds of Americans of being communist spies and sympathizers. Even after the government admonished the HUAC and McCarthy in the late 1950s for overstepping, the red scare lingered for decades. As with the reduction in the arms race, Mikhail Gorbachev played a large part in repairing the relations between the two countries. He loosened the Soviet Union's grip on the Eastern European countries in the late 1980s, granted civil liberties to Soviet citizens with glasnost, encouraged government transparency with perestroika, and did nothing to stop the Berlin Wall from being dismantled. Although Reagan called the USSR an "evil empire" during his first term, his cooperation and good faith dealings with Gorbachev during his second term ended the decades of ill will between the superpowers.

The last major aspect of the Cold War was the proxy wars.[9] To view the Cold War merely as a nuclear-arms race and an ideological struggle between capitalism and communism is insufficient. The term "Cold War" is a misnomer since it implies nonviolent confrontation. Even though war was never waged directly between the armed forces of the two superpowers, there were many violent confrontations, which resulted in over five million civilian and military deaths. Bethany Lacina and Nils Petter Gleditsch write that "the Korean War and the Vietnam War were massive Cold War confrontations, and the Chinese Civil War was also fed by superpower military assistance. The wars between Iran and Iraq and the Soviet invasion of Afghanistan were also driven in part by the logic of Cold War politics and the parties were armed by the US and USSR."[10]

As developing countries in Asia, Africa, Central America, South America, and the Middle East emerged from under colonial occupation, the two superpowers sought to steer them toward capitalism or communism, foisting a new brand of colonialism on them. In some cases, developing countries sought the aid of a superpower to bolster their political revolutions. Robert J. McMahon states that "the Third World emerged as early as 1950 as the Cold War's principal battlefield. Conflicts with local roots . . . became exponentially more costly because the superpower conflict became superimposed upon them."[11] The major wars in Korea and Vietnam—and smaller ones such as the Angolan Civil War, the Nicaraguan Civil War, the Salvadoran Civil War, the Yom Kippur War, and the Soviet War in Afghanistan—were enmeshed in Cold War politics. Historians often refer to these wars as "proxy wars" because they were fought with the aid of, or under the auspices of, the United States or the Soviet Union. They were the result of the fear that nuclear weapons might be used if the superpowers engaged directly in war. If one country used nuclear weapons, the other would inevitably use theirs in turn, and the war could escalate to global proportions, rendering the earth uninhabitable. This doctrine of mutual assured destruction (MAD) prompted the two superpowers to gain ground for their ideologies by engaging smaller countries in localized, conventional warfare.

The Cold War had many battlegrounds and was fought with many unconventional weapons. It was fought in the propaganda mills, on the athletic fields of the Olympic Games, in space with *Sputnik* and Apollo 11, in the sea with nuclear submarines, in underground uranium mines, and in dark alleyways, where spies waited with miniature cameras. It was fought with science, art, architecture, literature, television, and film. As we will show in this book, it was also fought with popular music. But before turning to particular songs about the Cold War, it is necessary to determine the role that these songs played. What impact did they have in shaping public opinion or government policy regarding the conflict? Protest songs have had an impact on government policy in certain cases, such as the role that "We Shall Overcome" played in the civil rights movement. Even if songs don't change people's minds, they surely can bring nationwide attention to those already committed to causes. What about the Cold War songs? Did they have any influence on the decision-making of those with political power? To answer these questions, the broad dimensions of political popular songs should be considered in order to place them in context.

GEOPOLITICS IN A SONG

Like film, television, literature, and other arts, popular music has had an enormous impact on global culture in the last century. Shirley Fedorak writes that popular music is "a reflection of a culture's values, ideals, and patterns of behavior, while also providing commentary on social, political, economic, and religious issues."[12] The academic journal *Popular Music & Society* and books by scholars such as Simon Frith and Reebee Garofalo have investigated how popular songs both reflect and shape mainstream society and thereby become central repositories of social history.[13] The American and British popular songs about the Cold War do the same. They reveal the perspectives and opinions of the general populace, adding deep insight into the social history of the conflict.

While popular songs reflect the culture from which they arise, the extent to which they actually shape society or affect the political viewpoints of listeners is less apparent. The political aspects of popular music have been explored by numerous scholars.[14] Several musicologists have examined whether or not popular songs with a political dimension, or protest songs, can add anything worthwhile to political discourse. Elizabeth J. Kizer believes they cannot, writing that "protest lyrics are creative expressions designed to elicit an emotional response rather than being polemics for cognitive examination. They do not call for intellectual processing from the auditors [listeners] to whom they are directed; the treatment of topics, and the topics themselves, appeal to the emotions."[15]

Jeffrey J. Mondak takes a more middle-of-the-road perspective saying, "While many protest songs encourage emotional response, emotion-stirring content is not a necessary feature of protest music. Most protest songs do have some lyrics that are specifically intended to provoke intellectual response; protest songs typically include a balance of emotional and intellectual appeals."[16]

More recent scholars, such as John Street, have taken a much stronger position stating that popular musicians have more political power than they realize. He maintains the political power of music is much more than just the lyrical content. He writes that "from the earliest days of rock 'n' roll, priests, parents and politicians have warned of the dangers inherent in the rhythms, the voices, the words and the images of the music.... Censorship has been a constant feature of the music's history.... [Priests, parents and politicians] have made popular music into a political issue, and they have invested it with the potential to endanger and disrupt the established order."[17]

In his book *Give Peace a Chant,* Dario Martinelli sees protest songs (he prefers to call them "songs of social protest") as being of such importance that they should be considered a genre in themselves.[18]

Popular musicians strongly believe that a political viewpoint expressed through music can be as powerful as the spoken or written word. E. Y. "Yip" Harburg, the lyricist who penned the song that epitomized the Great Depression, "Brother Can You Spare a Dime?," said, "Words... make you think a thought. Music makes you feel a feeling. But a song makes you feel a thought. Together, they stand ready to soothe not only the savage breast, but the stubborn mind. Barriers fall, hostilities melt, and a new idea can find a soft spot even under a hard hat."[19]

Woody Guthrie, Pete Seeger, Phil Ochs, John Lennon, Bob Marley, and U2's Bono all believed that music has the power to seriously address political issues and change people's minds individually and collectively. Bob Dylan has also been closely linked with social protest, yet he steered away from writing songs with strong political import in 1964 beginning with *Another Side of Bob Dylan.* Just two years after his first album, he refused to be pigeonholed as a "protest singer." Did he lose faith in the ability of music to impact politics? Dylan has always been sly with interviewers, especially in the mid-1960s, yet he seems to have been sincere when he told Nat Hentoff in a March 1966 interview, "I don't believe songs can change people."[20] Sting, who wrote one of the most well-known Cold War songs, "Russians," takes the middle ground. He says that songs can't change people's minds the instant they are heard but may in the long term. "I believe in the power of music. I think you can plant seeds in people's minds about issues that you care about.... Those seeds obviously won't bear fruit for a long time. You play to a young person... [who]... could quite easily become part of a political class... that will make decisions and that seed will have borne fruit."[21]

Politicians often use popular songs during their campaigns to appear cool and hip, but do songs have any place in political discourse? Political leaders are responsible for making difficult decisions on complex affairs that require objective arguments, detailed exposition, lengthy dialogue, precise fact-checking, and reasoned debate. Popular songs are well suited to express idealistic notions and critique the actions of politicians, but they rarely offer objective, pragmatic solutions. Popular songs are brief and rarely present two sides of the story. The overwhelming majority of Cold War songs were from the left-wing perspective. James E. Perone wrote of the Vietnam War songs, "Very few musical works even acknowledged the fact that there might be some legitimacy to another viewpoint."[22] Songs that expressed right-wing viewpoints existed, but few of them made an appearance on the record charts. Nevertheless, popular songs can have a tangible influence on politics. They can crystalize an issue and make cogent arguments filled with passion and fervency. Like a razor-sharp editorial cartoon, they can change a person's mind for good or for ill, sometimes in a heartbeat.

The best example of a successful political protest song would have to be "We Shall Overcome." In the late 1950s and early 1960s, protest movements began to reach the nation at large through radio reports and, especially, television news. In news reports on civil rights marches, one would often see a large crowd singing "We Shall Overcome," making the song an integral part of the event. In a speech to the US Congress on March 15, 1965, President Lyndon B. Johnson invoked the song in denouncing the violence against African Americans during the Selma to Montgomery marches, one of the defining events of the civil rights movement. The speech was broadcasted live to the nation and has become known as his "We Shall Overcome" speech.[23] Suddenly, the President of the United States quoted a song from the street. "We Shall Overcome" is a textbook example of an effective protest song. It has all the components Dario Martinelli identifies in successful songs of social protest: a common instrumentation, a simple harmonic and rhythmic structure, a catchy hook, and a culturally connoted, recognizable sound.[24] It struck a nerve and will be forever linked with that cause.

Yet few of the Cold War songs were this type, where a group of protesters would collectively sing and draw attention to their cause. Would the nuclear-arms buildup have been reduced and the Cold War itself ended earlier if an anthem on par with "We Shall Overcome" had been written and sung by millions in Washington, DC, making the issue impossible for politicians to ignore? Possibly, but no such song arose. The Aldermaston Marches in England in the late 1950s and early 1960s were filled with songs against nuclear weapons, but none were powerful and universal enough to become an anthem. Folk musicians in the 1950s and 1960s, and reggae, rock, punk, and heavy metal musicians in the 1980s wrote many antiwar songs, but none became the touchstone of a movement. Protest songs like Country Joe and the Fish's "I-Feel-Like-I'm-Fixin'-to-Die Rag" brought attention to the atrocities of the Vietnam War, but they did not offer any concrete solutions to the larger problems of the Cold War in general. On those occasions where musicians put on antinuclear concerts, the crowd had few anthems to sing. The five No Nukes concerts organized by MUSE (Musicians United for Safe Energy) in September 1979 attracted hundreds of thousands of people and featured well-known performers such as Bruce Springsteen, Jackson Browne, Graham Nash, Carly Simon, and James Taylor. The concerts showed that popular musicians wished to voice their concerns about nuclear power and weapons, but only a few songs directly addressed the issues ("Power" and "Plutonium Is Forever" by John Hall, "Before the Deluge" by Jackson Browne, and "We Almost Lost Detroit" by Gil Scott-Heron). The majority of songs performed were simply the current hits of the artists, or covers of older hits.

R. Serge Denisoff is helpful in assessing the Cold War songs by distinguishing between two types of protest songs: "those on the top forty and those of the streets." He writes, "Popular protest songs [those on the top forty charts like *Billboard*] are not collective statements of discontent, but rather individualized sentiments as to what is wrong with society. Solutions are not offered, social action is not advocated and, most important, the songs are impersonal statements sandwiched in between other Top Forty selections of a totally apolitical nature, not to mention commercials."[25]

Protest songs that made the Top 40 usually were not the sing-along type, "those of the streets," and therefore didn't play much of a part in galvanizing the populace or spurring them into political action. What Denisoff says of the 1965 number one hit "Eve of Destruction" (sung by Barry McGuire and written by P. F. Sloan) applies to the majority of the songs about the Cold War: "'Eve' was not written to be used in a protest movement or a demonstration. Rather, it was an expression of intellectual discontent cast in a symbolic form."[26] The rise of the singer-songwriter in the mid-1960s was crucial in creating this new type of protest song, which was personally introspective rather than outwardly communal. Rather than writing songs of a jingoistic, "sing-along" nature, they cast their viewpoints in a more confessional, poetic, individualistic type of expression. Many of the Cold War songs from the mid-1960s to the late 1980s fit this category. Another good example is "Wooden Ships" (written by Paul Kantner of Jefferson Airplane, and David Crosby and Stephen Stills of Crosby, Stills and Nash in 1969), a song that expresses strong antinuclear sentiments but is hardly conducive to being sung communally at a rally.

Since there are well over five hundred songs written about the Cold War, it is impossible to cover them all. We have selected songs to analyze based on three criteria: they give insight into the historical events of the Cold War; they reflect public opinion on Cold War issues; and they are stimulating and creative in their own right. We have focused on those songs that make direct references to the people, places, and events of the Cold War and have avoided giving "Cold War interpretations" to lyrics that are vague and general. We have covered just a few of the Vietnam War songs since several fine scholarly books have already been published about them by other authors.[27] We have little to add about the well-known antiwar anthems, such as "Give Peace a Chance" by John Lennon or "War" by Edwin Starr (written by Norman Whitfield and Barrett Strong) since much has been written about them already. On the other hand, we have analyzed dozens of obscure songs that few general readers would know about. They deserve more attention, fit the three criteria above, and, thanks to YouTube, iTunes, and Spotify, are easily accessible online. Let us turn to some general characteristics of the songs, and how the Atomic Age differed from the 1980s.

CHARACTERISTICS OF ATOMIC AGE SONGS

The Cold War songs from the mid-1940s to the mid-1960s are sometimes shocking in their candor, often ridiculous, frequently insightful, and always entertaining. Although they give insight into the conflict and reflect the widespread concern over communism and nuclear weapons, the majority are inane and campy. Since many of these songs were recorded on small, regional record labels, music critics and executives at major labels did not scrutinize them. Not surprisingly in an era that saw the rise of rock and roll and the sexual revolution, the bomb is used repeatedly as a metaphor for love and sex, as in "Atom Bomb Baby," "Atomic Baby," "Atomic Love," "Your Atom Bomb Heart," and "You Hit Me Baby Like an Atomic Bomb." Some songs portrayed bomb shelters not as protection from radioactive fallout, but as the ultimate make out pads.

The public reacted to the atomic bomb with a strange mixture of fear, fantasy, and frivolity. This reflected the public's uneven knowledge of what nuclear warfare actually entailed. Several scholars, such as Paul Boyer, have shown that the general public understood well the magnitude of atomic explosions and that a great new elemental power had been unleased.[28] At the same time, the US military had made sure that the public knew little about the effects of radiation on the human body. Boyer writes, "The long history of official lying and misrepresentation on the issue of radiation . . . dates from the very beginning of the atomic era."[29] The cultural output of the period reflects this spotty understanding. Many Atomic Age movies were made about the effects of radiation (*Them!* and *Godzilla*, both from 1954) but they were often viewed as fantastical entertainment rather than an actual threat. Peter Parker did not suffer from radiation sickness when he was bitten by a radioactive spider; he gained amazing powers and became the superhero Spider-Man. Even the songs with a dire and serious message about communist aggression and nuclear annihilation have their edge taken off through their humorous lyrics, major keys, or bright musical accompaniment. Apart from some folk and country songs, almost every song from the Atomic Age has an element of humor to some degree. The pleasantness and easygoing nature of a song like "Bert the Turtle (The Duck and Cover Song)" muffles the grim reality of nuclear war. Doris Day's "Tic, Tic, Tic" compares the beating heart of someone in love to the ticking of a Geiger counter. These early songs about nuclear war have a naiveté and innocence that is sometimes astonishing.

Yet it was not all fun and games. A few songwriters effectively convey the horrors of nuclear warfare with grim lyrics, impassioned singing, and dark musical accompaniment, such as Sammy Salvo's "A Mushroom Cloud" (1961). Country songwriters from the Bible Belt invoke the wrath of God on communists and use biblical images of hell to depict the postapocalyptic earth. "Old Man Atom" by Vern Partlow (1945) portrayed atomic power as an unpredictable force that scientists cannot control. Folk musicians wrote most of the serious songs from the Atomic Age. They range from the hopeful ("Last Night I Had the Strangest Dream" by Ed McCurdy), to the sorrowful ("What Have They Done to the Rain?" by Malvina Reynolds), to the vitriolic ("Masters of War" by Bob Dylan).

CHARACTERISTICS OF THE 1980S COLD WAR SONGS

As the Atomic Age continued into the early 1960s, the wonder and excitement that accompanied the harnessing of atomic energy and the naiveté about its effects slowly dissipated. By the 1980s, only the fear and dread of a full-scale nuclear war remained. Weariness of living in a world with an unimaginably large stockpile of nuclear weapons became the most prevalent theme of songs in the 1980s. The enthusiasm for building bomb shelters in the late 1950s and 1960s, which represented hope in surviving a nuclear attack, is largely absent from the Second Cold War.

What are the characteristics of the 1980s songs? First, as we mentioned in the section "Geopolitics in a Song," many songwriters voice their opinions through quiet personal reflection and inner conviction rather than outward communal expression. Second, the Russian people are often portrayed as a menace, such as in "So Afraid of the Russians" (1983) by Made for TV, a group produced by John Cale of the Velvet Underground. It isn't until the late 1980s, when the arms race begins to slow down, that the tone changes and becomes more hopeful. Billy Joel portrays Russians as ordinary and approachable in his 1989 song "Leningrad." Third, like the Atomic Age songs, most are quite specific in topic and theme. Few simply protest the war in general. The songs are about specific types of bombs and missiles, world leaders by name, as well as specific events and specific places. Because of this, they are veritable time capsules, capturing and preserving Cold War history in detail. Fourth, many songs refer to earlier Cold War events from the 1940s to the 1960s, recounting them, putting them in perspective, and highlighting their significance. XTC's "Living through Another Cuba" recalls the Cuban Missile Crisis. A popular subject in the songs from 1984–1985 is the fortieth anniversary of the Hiroshima bombing, when the Cold War began. Examples are Rush's "Manhattan Project," Gary O's "Shades of '45," and Midnight Oil's four song EP *Species Deceases*. Songs like these confirm how long the Cold War lasted, showing a protracted, multigenerational war. Lastly, few of the 1980s nuclear songs have the frivolity and comedic nature of the Atomic Age songs. As mentioned before, dozens of songs from 1940s and 1950s make trite parallels between love, sex, and bombs. Songs in the 1980s that use atomic themes as a filler for sexual passion are rare. Three examples we could find are "Atomic" by Blondie, "You Dropped a Bomb on Me" by the Gap Band, and "Radioactive" by the Firm. Some songs advocate partying, dancing, and a general attitude of carpe diem to relieve the pressure of the apocalypse (like Prince's "1999"), but the majority are dark, serious, and solemn.

Since the 1980s was the decade of the music video, inevitably the medium of television would make an impact on how songs were received and interpreted. Some songs' lyrics have no overt connection to the Cold War, but their videos make the connection explicit. A good example of this is "Let's Go All the Way" (1986) by Sly Fox. The phrase "going all the way" was commonly understood in the 1980s as a metaphor for sexual intercourse. The persistence of the phrase in the chorus leads one to believe the song is simply about the urge to have sex. Popular songs and music videos from the 1980s were filled with sexual euphemisms. Yet the lyrics and the video have no sexual content whatsoever. Along with the two singers, African American Gary "Mudbone" Cooper and Puerto Rican Michael Camacho, the video focuses on two boys, one Black and one White, destroying plastic models of machine guns, tanks, and fighter jets using a hammer and anvil. This seems to be a visual representation of arms reduction treaties. A brief section of the video shows an atomic bomb exploding in reverse. At the end, the two boys carry a beach ball–sized globe together, as if they hold the earth in their hands. Perhaps the video and title of the song express a hope, however unlikely, that the number of military weapons can be reduced "all the way" to zero.

ORGANIZATION AND SCOPE OF THE BOOK

As shown by the table of contents, we have organized the book according to musical genre with a general chronological trajectory, rather than taking a strict chronological approach or structuring the book according to lyrical subject matter. Each chapter, for the most part, focuses on a specific genre of popular music. Some songs can fit into more than one category since popular music styles are malleable. Nevertheless, we have found in each particular genre a commonality of lyrical sentiment, musical accompaniment, and mood in the songs. As Eric Drott writes, "genre . . . serves as one of the major organizing principles of musical life, and generic classifications frame our expectations by situating musical works within a context of shared conventions, values, and practices."[30] Thus, folk songwriters appeal to reason and common humanity as the foil against the inhumanity of nuclear war. Country artists almost always espouse conservative viewpoints, show patriotism, and cite biblical passages. Comedy songwriters attempt to diffuse fear of nuclear war by making light of it. Heavy metal and hardcore punk bands write about the grim consequences of nuclear destruction and the fearmongering by the superpowers. New wave bands write about the loss of a lover because of war or focus on the general feeling of anxiety brought about by the Cold War.

The first five chapters cover the Cold War–themed popular music from 1945 to the mid-1960s, commonly referred to as the Atomic Age, from the bombing of Hiroshima and Nagasaki to the Cuban Missile Crisis (1962). There are chapters on folk, country, novelty/comedy songs, early rock and roll, and other genres. The last half of the book discusses the songs about the resurgence of the nuclear-arms race in the 1980s. It follows the same pattern, with chapters on the prominent genres of music in the 1980s: mainstream rock, heavy metal, punk rock, and electronic/new wave. The final chapter shows how Western rock musicians played a role in events surrounding the dismantling of the Berlin Wall in 1989 and the dissolution of the Soviet Union in 1991.

Some chapter sections are devoted to particular bands or individual musicians, exploring their Cold War songs and how the conflict shaped their lives and music. Some sections are devoted to a particular issue of the war, such as bomb shelters or uranium mining, showing how multiple songwriters addressed an issue from different perspectives. All sections contain in-depth lyric analysis, and most of them integrate musical analysis, concert performance, instrumentation, album-cover artwork, and biographical information into the discussion.

We have confined the scope of the book to English language popular music about the Cold War. Much could be written about the European protest songs that came out of the antinuclear movements and demonstrations. These songs had much to say about Cold War topics but did not necessarily reach mainstream American or British audiences, or the music charts. The songs we are considering are, for the most part, by American and British popular musicians and to a lesser extent Irish (U2), German (Kraftwerk, Scorpions, and Nena), and Canadian (Rush). An important part of the book will be gauging how the British, Irish, German, and Canadian songwriters differed from their American counterparts both in the number of songs they wrote on Cold War topics and in their attitudes and opinions about geopolitical affairs.

In the 1940s and 1950s, most of the popular songs about Cold War topics were from American, rather than British, songwriters. The size of the two countries played a major part in this. America is so much larger and heterogeneous, with more songwriters and performers, more styles of music, and more centers of music production. A second reason is that the folk movement, where antinuclear sentiments and left-wing viewpoints were most prevalent, developed earlier in

America than it did in England. Songwriters such as Vern Partlow and Woody Guthrie were writing songs about the atomic bomb as early as 1945. Of course, folk music has existed in England for centuries, but it wasn't until the 1950s that songwriters such as Ewan MacColl began to grapple with Cold War topics.

A marked shift in this balance occurred in the 1980s. The majority of songs about nuclear weapons and the Soviet Union were from British, rather than American, songwriters for two reasons. The first and most important is that England felt much more threatened by the escalation of the arms race. The United Kingdom and the rest of Europe felt they were the "piggy in the middle," threatened on both sides by America and the Soviet Union. In the early years of the Reagan administration, Americans viewed their nuclear arsenal as a security blanket. Many Britons viewed it as a burial shroud. Second, the British artists dominated the pop music charts on both sides of the Atlantic during the Reagan/Thatcher era. This was due largely to the Second British Invasion (the "new wave"), which occurred roughly between 1980 and 1986. New wave music garnered massive mainstream success because listeners had grown weary of American mainstream rock and the all-consuming influence of disco. The greatest factor in new wave's success was MTV, which provided a perfect platform for the sleek fashion sense and slick music videos of British bands like the Human League, Duran Duran, WHAM!, and Culture Club. Thus, American songwriters wrote most of the Cold War songs in the Atomic Age, and British songwriters wrote most of the 1980s songs.

Like East Germans unseen behind by the Wall, much of the popular music about the Cold War has been unheard for many years. While numerous books and journal articles have addressed how the Cold War influenced popular culture—especially films, television shows, and literature—a much smaller number have addressed music. In his article "Introduction: Music in the Cold War," Peter J. Schmelz reports that "the recently initiated, increasingly active musicological engagement with the Cold War [is] long overdue."[31] Yet his article, an overview of the writings on music about the Cold War, makes almost no mention of popular music. The books and articles that have addressed the music about the conflict have focused mostly on classical music and jazz. There have been articles and books written about the popular music concerning the Atomic Age and the Vietnam War, but little about the many Cold War–themed songs from the 1980s.

In 1996, Bear Family Records released a ten-CD box set of political songs, many about the early years of the Cold War, titled *Songs for Political Action: Folk Music, Topical Songs and the American Left, 1926–1953*.[32] Then in 2005, Bear Family Records released a five CD/one DVD set, *Atomic Platters: Cold War Music from the Golden Age of Homeland Security*, with over 120 songs from the 1940s to the 1960s about the Cold War.[33] In 2010, a thirteen-CD set on Vietnam War music was released, and in 2018 a four-CD set on Korean War music came.[34] The producers of the *Atomic Platters* set have also created an expansive website *CONELRAD*, a valuable resource for studying the popular culture of the Cold War.[35] In 2003, Russell Reising wrote an article with insightful analyses of many Cold War songs, laying a foundation for this book.[36] More recently, Reba Wissner wrote an article about how Cold War popular music is used in the *Fallout* video game series.[37] We are hoping *Atomic Tunes* will add to these endeavors, bringing a new perspective to Cold War research and generating more interest in these songs, which reveal much about humans and the wars we wage.

NOTES

1. This figure of five million is a conservative estimate of the number of military and civilian deaths as a direct result of the proxy wars in Korea, Vietnam, Angola, Afghanistan, El Salvador, and other countries. The figure increases by many millions if one also considers as Cold War deaths those who perished as a result of mass killings by Joseph Stalin and Mao Zedong, forced disappearances (especially in Latin American countries), human radiation experiments, and nuclear bomb tests.

2. Robert S. Norris and Hans M. Kristensen, "Global Nuclear Stockpiles, 1945–2006," *Bulletin of the Atomic Scientists* 62, no. 4 (July 2006): 66, http://bos.sagepub.com/content/62/4/64.full.pdf+html.

3. Ibid.

4. Hans M. Kristensen and Matt Korda, "Status of World Nuclear Forces," Federation of American Scientists website, updated September 2020, http://fas.org/issues/nuclear-weapons/status-world-nuclear-forces/.

5. John Roger Paas, ed., *America Sings of War: American Sheet Music from World War I* (Wiesbaden: Harrassowitz, 2014); Christina L. Baade, *Victory through Harmony: The BBC and Popular Music in World War II* (Oxford: Oxford University Press, 2012).

6. The number of Cold War songs reaches into the thousands if the parameters are broadened to include those with just passing references to the conflict, those used in war films or television shows, and those not specifically about the war but have become linked with it.

7. James P. Delgado, *Nuclear Dawn: The Atomic Bomb, from the Manhattan Project to the Cold War* (Oxford: Osprey, 2009).

8. Deborah Welch Larson, *Anatomy of Mistrust: U.S.-Soviet Relations during the Cold War* (Ithaca, NY: Cornell University Press, 1997).

9. Robert J. McMahon, ed., *The Cold War in the Third World* (New York: Oxford University Press, 2013).

10. Bethany Lacina and Nils Petter Gleditsch, "Monitoring Trends in Global Combat: A New Dataset of Battle Deaths," *European Journal of Population* 21, no. 2–3

(June 2005): 155, http://www.prio.org/Global/upload/CSCW/Data/Monitoring%20trends%20in%20global%20combat%20EJP.pdf.

11. McMahon, *Cold War in the Third World*, 9.

12. Shirley Fedorak, *Pop Culture: The Culture of Everyday Life* (Toronto: University of Toronto Press, 2009), 38.

13. Simon Frith, *Taking Popular Music Seriously: Selected Essays* (Aldershot: Ashgate, 2007); Reebee Garofalo, *Rockin' the Boat: Mass Music and Mass Movements* (Boston: South End, 1992).

14. Dorian Lynskey, *33 Revolutions per Minute: A History of Protest Songs, from Billie Holiday to Green Day* (New York: Ecco, 2011); Jonathan C. Friedman, ed., *The Routledge History of Social Protest in Popular Music* (New York: Routledge, 2013).

15. Elizabeth J. Kizer, "Protest Song Lyrics as Rhetoric," *Popular Music and Society* 9, no. 1 (1983): 5.

16. Jeffrey J. Mondak, "Protest Music as Political Persuasion," *Popular Music and Society* 12, no. 3 (Fall 1988): 28.

17. John Street, "Rock, Pop and Politics," in *The Cambridge Companion to Pop and Rock*, ed. Simon Frith, Will Straw, and John Street (Cambridge, UK: Cambridge University Press, 2001), 243–244.

18. Dario Martinelli, *Give Peace a Chant: Popular Music, Politics and Social Protest* (Cham, Switzerland: Springer, 2017), 3–6.

19. E. Y. Harburg, "Yip at the 92nd Street YM-YWHA, December 13, 1970," typed transcript 1-10-3, p. 3, cassette 7-2-10 and 7-2-20, YHF, quoted in Harriet Hyman Alonso, *Yip Harburg: Legendary Lyricist and Human Rights Activist* (Middletown, CT: Wesleyan University Press, 2012), x.

20. Jonathan Cott, ed., *Bob Dylan: The Essential Interviews* (New York: Wenner, 2006), 105, from an interview by Nat Hentoff.

21. Sting, interviewed by Vladimir Vladimirovich Pozner, December 2010 (38:17–38:50), http://www.youtube.com/watch?v=GHcsGZzJWds.

22. James E. Perone, *Songs of the Vietnam Conflict* (Westport, CT: Greenwood, 2001), 10.

23. For a transcript and video of this speech, see "President Johnson's Special Message to the Congress: The American Promise" on the Lyndon Baines Johnson Library and Museum website. Johnson's uses of "We Shall Overcome" occur at twenty-five and twenty-nine minutes into the speech, http://www.lbjlibrary.org/lyndon-baines-johnson/speeches-films/president-johnsons-special-message-to-the-congress-the-american-promise/.

24. Martinelli, *Give Peace a Chant*, 9–10.

25. R. Serge Denisoff, "Protest Songs: Those on the Top Forty and Those of the Streets," *American Quarterly* 22, no. 4 (Winter 1970): 820.

26. Denisoff, "Protest Songs," 822.

27. James E. Perone, *Songs of the Vietnam Conflict* (Westport, CT: Greenwood, 2001); Michael J. Kramer, *The Republic of Rock: Music and Citizenship in the Sixties*

Counterculture (New York: Oxford University Press, 2013); Doug Bradley and Craig Werner, *We Gotta Get Out of This Place: The Soundtrack of the Vietnam War* (Amherst: University of Massachusetts Press, 2015).

28. Paul Boyer, *By the Bomb's Early Light: American Thought and Culture at the Dawn of the Atomic Age* (Chapel Hill: University of North Carolina Press, 1994), xx–xxi.

29. Boyer, *By the Bomb's Early Light*, 188.

30. Eric Drott, *Music and the Elusive Revolution: Cultural Politics and Political Culture in France, 1968–1981* (Berkeley: University of California Press, 2011), 81.

31. Peter J. Schmelz, "Introduction: Music in the Cold War," *Journal of Musicology* 26, no. 1 (Winter 2009): 3.

32. Ronald D. Cohen and Dave Samuelson's liner notes for the ten-CD box set *Songs for Political Action: Folk Music, Topical Songs and the American Left, 1926–1953* (Hambergen, Germany: Bear Family Records BCD 15720 JL, 1996).

33. Bill Geerhart and Ken Sitz's liner notes for the five-CD, one-DVD box set *Atomic Platters: Cold War Music from the Golden Age of Homeland Security* (Hambergen, Germany: Bear Family Records BCD 16065 FM, 2005).

34. Hugo A. Keesing, Lois T. Vietri, Doug Bradley, and Craig Werner's liner notes for the thirteen-CD box set *Next Stop Is Vietnam: The War on Record, 1961–2008*. Foreword by Country Joe McDonald (Hambergen, Germany: Bear Family Records BCD 16070 MS, 2010); Hugo Keesing and Bill Geerhart's program notes for the four-CD box set *Battleground Korea: Songs and Sounds of America's Forgotten War* (Hambergen, Germany: Bear Family Records BCD 17518, 2018).

35. The *CONELRAD* website, created by Ken Sitz, Bill Geerhart, and Curtis Samson, is available here: http://www.conelrad.com/index.php.

36. Russell Reising, "Iron Curtains and Satin Sheets: 'Strange Loves' in Cold War Popular Music," *Cultural Logic* 10 (2003), https://ojs.library.ubc.ca/index.php/clogic/article/view/191911/188872.

37. Reba A. Wissner, "Pop Music and the Bomb," *Bulletin of the Atomic Scientists*, December 14, 2018, https://thebulletin.org/2018/12/pop-music-and-the-bomb/.

ONE

FOLK

From Paul Robeson to Bob Dylan

AT THE YALTA CONFERENCE IN early February 1945, Winston Churchill and Franklin D. Roosevelt met with Joseph Stalin to discuss what Eastern Europe would look like after the war. On February 27, 1945, regarding Stalin and the Soviet Union, Churchill said, "The impression I brought back from the Crimea, and from all my other contacts, is that Marshal Stalin and the Soviet leaders wish to live in honourable friendship and equality with the Western democracies. I feel also that their word is their bond. I know of no Government which stands to its obligations, even in its own despite, more solidly than the Russian Soviet Government."[1] Just over a year later on March 5, 1946, Churchill gave a speech at Westminster College in Fulton, Missouri. He had clearly changed his mind about the Soviets, saying, "From Stettin in the Baltic to Trieste in the Adriatic, an iron curtain has descended across the Continent. . . . The Communist parties, which were very small in all these Eastern States of Europe, have been raised to preeminence and power far beyond their numbers and are seeking everywhere to obtain totalitarian control."[2]

Russia was an ally during World War II, but by the time Churchill gave his 1946 speech, Russia had become the enemy. In America, as McCarthyism began to influence public thought, any connection with Russia—no matter how ancillary—was viewed with suspicion. Musicians also found themselves among new alliances and conflicts. Bob Dylan's grandfather emigrated from Odessa, and his uncles served in World War II, fighting on the same side as the Russians. In his 2004 memoir, *Chronicles: Volume One,* he wrote about his elementary school days in the late 1940s and early 1950s, saying, "One of the things we were trained to do was to hide and take cover under our desks when the air-raid sirens blew because the Russians could attack us with bombs. We were also told that the Russians could be parachuting from planes over our town at any time. These were the same Russians that my uncles had fought alongside only a few years earlier. Now they had become monsters who were coming to slit our throats and incinerate us. . . . The Reds were everywhere, we were told, and out for bloodlust."[3]

To understand the impact of these events on popular musicians, in particular folk musicians, we must turn back to the 1930s and 1940s. In response to the privations of the Great Depression, President Roosevelt enacted the New Deal, a wide-ranging series of federal programs, public works projects, and banking reforms. The New Deal did not just benefit farmers and blue-collar workers. As songwriter Earl Robinson wrote, "The government decided to pay artists to sculpt and paint. They paid writers to write. They paid dancers to dance, composers to compose, and musicians to make music."[4] Thus, unsurprisingly, many musicians placed themselves on the Left since the US government supported artistic endeavors in a way unparalleled in American history. Musicians who valued the New Deal and the ideals of the Left, such as Paul Robeson, Woody Guthrie, Earl Robinson, and Pete Seeger, felt they got a raw deal a decade later during the McCarthy era. They saw positive features in communism and felt they had a right to voice their opinions without harassment, no matter how unpopular their opinions might have been. They were not looking to fight a cultural Cold War against communism, and they were also not part of an international conspiracy to overthrow capitalism. Instead, they saw the primary battle as one to be waged against fascism. They believed that not only were the politicians fighting the wrong war, they were using the methods of fascist regimes. By suppressing free speech and political dissent, musicians believed politicians were using enemy tools to subdue Constitutional rights.

To trace out these connections, we will focus on three musicians whose careers spanned from the time of Roosevelt's New Deal through World War II and into the Cold War era: Paul Robeson, Woody Guthrie, and Pete Seeger. The mounting tension between communism and capitalism became a battleground on which patriotism, civil rights, fear, betrayal, and music making were hotly contested. The dynamics of this battle can be revealed more deeply due to recently declassified governmental records and recently released documentaries, interviews, and memoirs of the musicians. The remainder of the chapter is devoted to Vern Partlow and Bob Dylan, who anticipated issues the atomic bomb would raise in later years, issues that remain with us today.

PAUL ROBESON

One of the most complex and controversial figures in twentieth-century popular music is Paul Robeson (1898–1976). Though Robeson often performed folk music from African American and other traditions, to simply call him a folk musician would hardly do him justice. He had immeasurable talent. His world-renowned bass range encompassed the classical repertoire, musical theater, spirituals, folk songs, and labor songs. He was a college football star. He earned a degree from Columbia Law School and briefly practiced as a lawyer. He was a Shakespearean actor famous for his characterization of Othello. He spoke and sang in multiple languages and traveled the world. Lastly, he was a political radical. He had an admiration for the Soviet Union and communism during the height of the McCarthy period, which was a dangerous time to have such a view. Even after Premier Nikita Khrushchev in 1956 exposed and denounced the atrocities Joseph Stalin had carried out on his own people, Robeson continued to hold up communism as a solution to colonialism and oppression. In his illuminating book *Paul Robeson: A Watched Man*, Jordan Goodman summarizes his significance as an artist and a political figure: "There has never been another popular entertainer with so much political impact. Robeson was also unique in the extent to which his politics and his art were inseparable. He was at the center of the most urgent political issues of the period—racism, colonialism, and the looming threat of nuclear war. He didn't just sing and speak his ideals; he put them into direct action."[5]

Robeson began recording songs in the 1920s, many of them drawn from African American traditions and Anglo-American folk ballads. His left-wing political identity began to emerge while working in London during the 1920s, where many organizations introduced him to new ideas. As Goodman notes, "In the 1920s and 1930s, London, like Paris, was the center of a rich and vibrant anticolonial, radical intellectual community, drawing its membership mainly from the Caribbean and Africa but also from the Indian subcontinent."[6] Here we can see the seeds of his concern for civil rights for colonized peoples. This concern led to subsequent trips around the world, including several visits to Moscow. During his first trip to the Soviet Union in 1934, he received a warm welcome and became drawn to ideas about racial equality.[7] Here Robeson drew on his fame as a stage and screen actor to garner platforms to speak out on issues of politics and justice. By the 1940s, he advocated for labor rights, spoke for world peace and against nuclear armament, and worked to bring attention to civil rights for people of color, not just in the United States but also those affected by colonization globally.

Though the FBI, CIA, and the British MI5 and MI6 had had him under surveillance for communist activity since the 1930s, his participation in the World Congress for Peace in Paris on April 20, 1949 crystalized his standing as a political radical. Robeson's appearance at this event was portentous for at least three reasons. First, many of the participants and leaders of the conference identified themselves as communists. Second, many in the United States viewed working toward world peace as a communist activity in itself. And third, Robeson gave a speech that the US press intentionally misquoted and misinterpreted in which he highlighted the irony of expecting African Americans and others in the African diaspora to fight for freedoms abroad that they did not experience at home.[8]

There was no nuanced reaction to Robeson in 1949. A *New York Times* article labeled him "Black Stalin."[9] He was thought of as a criminal, although he had not committed any crime. Many African Americans shunned him. On August 27, he was scheduled to perform an outdoor concert in Peekskill, New York, where he had sung the previous three summers. When Robeson arrived, a white supremacist, anticommunist mob attacked the crowd of concertgoers, injuring over a dozen people. Friends whisked Robeson away.[10] He still wanted to perform, so the concert was rescheduled for September 4. Various left-wing unions joined together to form a barrier around the concert grounds. Men stood around him on the stage during his performance because snipers had been found on the surrounding hillsides. Although effigies of Robeson were hanged the night before the concert, it went off peacefully.[11] Robeson gave no speeches; he just sang and left immediately. He was shuffled between cars and driven out of town. Others, including Pete Seeger, who also performed, were not so lucky. Local police intentionally directed those leaving the concert to a road flanked by people throwing rocks. In Seeger's Jeep was his wife, Toshi, their infant daughter, Mika, three-year-old son, Dan, and others. It had all ten of its windows smashed by stones.[12] Over 150 people were injured, and several cars were overturned. After lengthy hearings, a Peekskill grand jury concluded that communists deliberately provoked the violence and the police handled it well.[13]

In 1950, the FBI canceled Robeson's passport. The purported reason for this was Robeson's correlation between civil rights for African Americans and Cold War issues. Tony Perucci elaborates, "As justification for their containment of Robeson, the federal government cites not only Robeson's promotion of African American rights, but also his linking of the Cold War crisis with capitalist investments in colonialism."[14] The blacklisting led to a decade of canceled engagements and limited opportunities for performance.

In 1956, Robeson was brought before the House Un-American Activities Committee (HUAC). Created in 1938, the HUAC's objective was to investigate persons suspected of participating in communist activities. Robeson was not intimidated and used his training as a lawyer to interrogate his interrogators. An excerpt follows:

> MR. ROBESON: In Russia I felt for the first time like a full human being. No color prejudice like in Mississippi, no color prejudice like in Washington. It was the first time I felt like a human being. Where I did not feel the pressure of color as I feel [it] in this Committee today.
>
> MR. SCHERER: Why do you not stay in Russia?

MR. ROBESON: Because my father was a slave, and my people died to build this country, and I am going to stay here, and have a part of it just like you. And no Fascist-minded people will drive me from it. Is that clear? I am for peace with the Soviet Union, and I am for peace with China, and I am not for peace or friendship with the Fascist Franco, and I am not for peace with Fascist Nazi Germans. I am for peace with decent people.

MR. SCHERER: You are here because you are promoting the Communist cause.

MR. ROBESON: I am here because I am opposing the neo-Fascist cause which I see arising in these committees.[15]

Utterly frustrated, the committee closed the meeting before Robeson could read his written testimony.

It is clear that Robeson found himself in the middle of Cold War politics and events, but what of his music? How does Robeson's role as a singer connect with the Cold War? This is a book mainly about songwriters, but Robeson was not one. His importance as a musician during the Cold War is found in *where* he was singing, to *whom* he was singing, and *how* he adapted the songs he sang. The song "Joe Hill" (lyrics by Alfred Hayes) and the cantata "Ballad for Americans" (lyrics by John La Touche) are crucial junctures in which Cold War matters, civil rights, and labor issues come together. The music for both was written by Earl Robinson (1910–1991), himself blacklisted during the Cold War.

On the surface, a union song like "Joe Hill" doesn't seem like a Cold War ballad. Yet unions have always been caught up in the national debate between capitalism and communism. During the first red scare in the late 1910s and early 1920s, many Americans feared bolshevism would infiltrate labor unions and cause an anarchist revolution. Tension between workers and business entrepreneurs died down in World War II with both entities pursuing the common goal of out-producing the Germans and Japanese. But after the war, many business owners saw unions as breeding grounds for communism. Union songs were viewed as communist songs.

"Joe Hill" was written in memory of the union leader and songwriter Joe Hill (1879–1915), who was wrongly executed after being convicted of murder. Because of his work on behalf of unions during his lifetime, he became a folk hero of the union movement after his death. The song was published in 1938 and became well known in the labor movement of the 1930s and 1940s. Robeson began to sing it in the 1940s, and it quickly became an iconic song for him. It tied together his efforts on behalf of workers and his pursuit for international justice. For example, in 1949, before the travel ban, he went to Scotland and sang "Joe Hill" for a group of Scottish coal miners. Henry Foner said, "He always emphasized this need for unity between the Black people and the unions. Neither, he felt, could advance without the help of the other."[16]

Robeson is also associated with the populist folk cantata "Ballad for Americans." In 1940 Robeson recorded it for Victor Records with the American People's Chorus and the Victor Symphony Orchestra. It sold over forty thousand copies by the end of the year. The ten-minute song begins with a full orchestra, setting the scene for the "birth" of Uncle Sam while the founding of the United States is narrated through song. Paul Robeson's narration alternates with a chorus that frequently interjects to ask the narrator who he is. After listing the Founding Fathers and incorporating a long excerpt from the Declaration of Independence, the song moves into the Civil War with the brief quotation, "let my people go," from the spiritual "Go Down Moses." After the chorus repeatedly inquires the identity of the narrator, he finally answers: "Well, I'm the everybody who's nobody, I'm the nobody who's everybody," and lists out the multitudinous jobs performed by ordinary people, sixteen countries from which Americans emigrated, and a dozen religions into which he has been "baptized." The song ends on a climax with the narrator finally revealing his identity: America.

Bing Crosby and other singers recorded versions in the early 1940s, and the song was popular all through World War II. It espoused universal American ideals, highlighting the country as a haven in which immigrants have made a new life. Amazingly, both the Republican and Communist parties employed it during the 1940 presidential campaign. After the war, the song was forgotten. The unity within diversity it praised would increasingly be at odds with the rising xenophobia of the McCarthy era. As Robeson continued to praise Stalin and the Soviet Union and the song's composer, Earl Robinson, was brought before the HUAC for being a communist, "Ballad for Americans" was viewed as inauthentic at best and communist propaganda at worst.[17] Victor Records deleted it from its catalog in the late 1940s.[18]

The song that is most pertinent to Robeson's view of the Cold War is "The Four Rivers" (1944) composed by Jay Gorney, Edward Eliscu, and Henry Myers. Though the song was written during World War II, Robeson sang it often in the 1950s. The four rivers are the Thames, the Mississippi, the Yangtze, and the Don. The song is a call for peaceful coexistence between the citizens of England, America, China, and the Soviet Union. In the 1950s, many Americans regarded utopian ideals such as "peaceful coexistence" as communist propaganda, a ploy used to advance a worldwide communist revolution. The first stanza entreats the four countries to pursue a common goal of peace, using the metaphor of the four rivers uniting and flowing together to the sea. The second stanza personifies each country as John, Tommy, Mao, and Ivan, who, though raised on different rivers, sail together to the sea. The final stanza implores the people on the four rivers to "discover how to work together." In a 1965 speech, Robeson echoed the sentiment of the song when he said,

> Yes, our languages, our idioms, our forms of expression may be different, the political, economic and social systems under which we live may be different, but art reflects a common humanity. . . . While we become aware of great variety, we recognize the universality, the unity, the oneness of the many people in our contemporary world. . . . The large question as to which society is better for humanity is never settled by argument. The proof of the pudding is in the eating. Let the various social systems compete with one another under conditions of peaceful coexistence, and the people can decide for themselves.[19]

In connecting the dots between Paul Robeson's work for civil rights and international peace, it appears the US government was less concerned about Robeson *actually* being a communist and more concerned about the public image the United States wanted to present on the international stage. Pulling back the curtains of the African American experience in the United States, from slavery to the civil rights era, tarnished the image of America as the beacon of freedom, equality, and morality around the world. Robeson's voice—his political and musical voice—was so strong that multiple government agencies attempted to silence him. He paid a heavy price for standing up for his beliefs and principles. Arnold Lubasch sums up Robeson's connection to communism in this way:

> On civil rights, colonialism, and peace, Robeson stood in the forefront of the struggle, a generation ahead of his time. With regard to communism and the Soviet Union, however, he was on the wrong side of history. Even his admirers understood that his most serious fault was a steadfast refusal to criticize the Soviet Union when its actions clearly called for censure. . . . The tragedy for our country was not that one of its noblest sons believed in communism but that our democracy could not tolerate political dissent. We allowed the hysteria of McCarthyism to trample on freedom of speech.[20]

PETE SEEGER, WOODY GUTHRIE, AND THE OTHER ALMANACS

Pete Seeger's life and music are inextricably tied to Cold War history. From his early work in the Almanac Singers in the 1940s, his blacklisting in the 1950s, his Vietnam War protests in the 1960s, to his 2007 song "Big Joe Blues," the winds of history have blown Seeger along by the changing directions of political division. Yet he himself also shaped American history, having others join in his journey by inviting his audience to sing along with his songs.

It is easy to view Seeger as a looming figure, a tall man with a banjo, gently towering over American folk music in a career that spanned an amazing seventy-five years. But here, we will look at his legacy as a polyphonic one in which his voice harmonized with many others across the twentieth century. We won't have space to discuss all his associations and influences here, but we will survey some of the intersecting lines.

Born into a deeply musical family, Seeger followed his own path, dropping out of Harvard in 1938 as he became more involved with folk music. He moved to Washington, DC, to begin work with Alan Lomax in the Archive of American Folk Song at the Library of Congress. Here he was exposed to an immense variety of music, both through recordings that he helped to organize and meetings with musicians that Lomax commissioned to make new recordings. Through Lomax's work he connected with Woody Guthrie, Lee Hays, Millard Lampell, Cisco Houston, and Bess Lomax Hawes, among many others. This loose conglomeration soon came to be known as the Almanac Singers, who were active between 1940 and 1943. They worked as a collective, sharing both an apartment in Greenwich Village and oftentimes songwriting credits. Their personal relationships and musical collaborations were complex and sometimes fraught. Will Kaufman summarizes, "During a dizzying life span of less than three years, the Almanac Singers would remain in a constant state of flux, both ideologically and in terms of its membership."[21] As a result of World War II, the musicians were tossed on the rapidly shifting waves of global events and international alliances.

The Almanac Singers released their first album, *Songs for John Doe*, in May 1941. The songs were pacifistic and isolationist. They reflected a shared orientation that America's focus should be on domestic injustice, such as workers' rights, rather than on international entanglements. Caustic rhetoric characterized the songs, and their stridency came back to haunt the band members in future years. An example of this isolationism is "The Ballad of October 16th," penned by Millard Lampell and set to the tune of "Jesse James." Its narrative centers on the perceived incongruity between Franklin D. Roosevelt's rhetoric of peace and his enactment of the military draft. The chorus concludes with "I hate war, and so does Eleanor, but we won't be safe 'till everybody's dead."

The isolationism of *Songs for John Doe* was outdated almost as soon as it was released. On June 22, 1941, Hitler launched Operation Barbarossa, the Nazi invasion of Russia. On December 7, the Japanese attacked Pearl Harbor. In a rapid about-face, the Almanac Singers wrote and performed prowar songs like "Round and Round Hitler's Grave" (1942). The Almanac Singers all had credit on this collaborative song. Set to the lively tune of "Old Joe Clark," the song's lyrics feature a gleeful violence rarely found in the singers' overall output. The first verse climaxes with wishing they had Hitler "with a rope around his neck." Others envision him being shot with a forty-four or being boiled in a pot of oil.

Some of the Almanacs entered active service in World War II, including Pete Seeger and Burl Ives, who joined the army, and Cisco Houston and Woody

Guthrie, who joined the merchant marine. Woody also served a few months in the army.[22] Lee Hays applied but was rejected because he had tuberculosis earlier in his life. The fact these musicians were World War II veterans has often been overlooked in the reception of their work. However, their service is vitally important in light of Cold War politics to understand how their lives were affected, especially with the political affiliations formed during World War II with the Soviet Union and other countries. During this time period, many viewed Russia as heroic since they sacrificed the most to win World War II. The Soviets suffered over 25 million military and civilian deaths—compared to approximately 420,000 American deaths—and the Nazis had laid to waste large portions of their western lands between the Polish border and Moscow. As historical vistas are sometimes flattened out when viewed at a distance, it is important to understand how powerful the American political rhetoric was during this time in presenting the Soviets as invaluable allies. What Will Kaufman writes of Woody Guthrie could be said about the other folk musicians who served in the military yet later became antiwar protestors, those who admired the Soviet Union yet were patriotic Americans: "[Woody's] relationship to warfare was so conflicted that it presents one of the muddiest threads in his biography, but it must be recognized as at least partly the result of the enormous and sometimes rapid-fire technological and political changes that marked the mid-twentieth century in the United States and abroad."[23]

The FBI investigated Pete Seeger for the first time 1943 while he was serving in the military. He wrote a letter to the California American Legion in 1942 criticizing their resolution that advocated "deportation of all Japanese, citizens or not, and barring all Japanese descendants from citizenship."[24] Seeger's wife, Toshi, his fiancé in 1942, was half-Japanese. "We're fighting precisely to free the world of such Hitlerism, such narrow jingoism," Seeger wrote.[25] At the time Japanese-Americans, many of them living in California, were forcibly moved to government internment camps because the United States had deemed them a security risk.

Because of the dispersal of the group, as well as financial and personality difficulties, the Almanac Singers dissolved between 1942 and 1943. However, members such as Pete Seeger, Woody Guthrie, and Lee Hays joined together with others like Alan Lomax, Earl Robinson, Waldermar Hille, and Irwin Silber to form People's Songs late in 1945.[26] This organization had the two-pronged goal of creating songs to support progressive causes and song styles that would be alternatives to Tin Pan Alley and Hollywood film songs.[27] Their endeavors included concert series, quarterly bulletins, educational outreach, and, its capstone work, several editions of *The People's Song Book*.[28] This songbook brought together traditional folk and protest songs from the United States and around the world. In historical retrospection, the final section, "Topical-Political Songs," is of primary importance since these songs reflect issues that grew in prominence over the next decades: civil rights for African Americans ("Strange Fruit," "Jim Crow," and "Hallelujah, I'm A-Travelin'"), world peace ("Walk in Peace"), and rising concerns about Cold War issues ("Old Man Atom," discussed in-depth later in this chapter). Another song of Cold War interest is "The Investigator's Song," which foreshadows the HUAC and FBI investigations that Seeger, Robeson, and several other folk musicians would endure in the 1950s. It has the humorous line, "Who's gonna investigate the man who investigates the man who investigates me?"

Concerning Cold War issues, the members of the Almanac Singers and People's Songs were not just writing about the debate over capitalism and communism; they were also writing about the atomic bomb. Just as soon as the two atom bombs fell on Japan in August 1945, Woody Guthrie began to voice his opinions, both in letters and songs. As with most Americans at the time, he applauded the bombings since they brought about the surrender of Japan and the end of World War II.[29] He changed his mind about the bombs once he learned how destructive they were. In an August 1950 letter to his friend Stetson Kennedy, he wrote, "Well, I've been reading about the atombomb that hit Hiroshima and Nagasaki, and I've been to a whole string of movie shows that tried to show how bad it was, and none of them can come within ten miles of telling you how terrible bad that atombomb and its blasts and its burns were in real life."[30]

"Dance Around My Atom Fire" (1948) warns the world against erupting into a massive conflagration as a result of atomic warfare. Guthrie poses two alternatives in the song, "brotherhood or a world of ashes." "Come When I Call You" is an innocent children's song about a "pretty little baby that's born, born, born and gone away." Like "The Twelve Days of Christmas" it is a cumulative song that adds a line to each verse. It ends darkly though. Why the baby has "gone away" becomes clearer with each new line added. Starting with verse three, references to warships, guns, warplanes, wrecked cities, blown-up continents, crippled and blind people, and, last but not least, atomic bombs emerge. Woody's letter to President Truman, which he most likely never sent, about the bomb is just as unsubtle as these two songs.

> My dear Mr. Truman
>
> If you ever so much as lay a small claim to be a human with a brain, a soul, a heart, a mind, a feeling you could call the warmth of the blood of man, please, good sir, take a good look at these bills you are signing to make more high explosives to blow us all off of the map. Your face will look a whole lot blanker if the little atoms blow our world away and all of your pals and kinfolks along with the rest of us.
>
> I'm not ready to blow just yet. Your old buddy,
>
> Woody Guthrie[31]

While the restless Woody went his own way after the Almanac Singers, Pete Seeger started a new group. As People's Songs was being established, he came together with his old Almanac friend Lee Hays and recruited Ronnie Gilbert and Fred Hellerman to form the Weavers in 1948. Decca Records soon offered them a recording contract, and they rose to commercial success. Gordon Jenkins arranged the songs for their recordings, creating a fusion between the straightforward folk style familiar to those attending hootenannies in earlier years and a more "pop sound," featuring strings and occasionally a choir. The group consciously worked toward maintaining the authenticity and conviction behind their songs within the new environment. This effort allowed them to reach a wider audience. The Weavers sold millions of records and were popular all over the country and internationally. They influenced many of the most famous folk groups and singers, such as Peter, Paul & Mary, Arlo Guthrie, and the Kingston Trio.

Even as People's Songs as a company and the Weavers as a singing group began to achieve success, they found themselves thrust into the maelstrom of Cold War politics. Musicians who actively participated in People's Songs or who had been associated with the folk movement in the 1940s were listed in *Red Channels,* like Earl Robinson, Pete Seeger, Burl Ives, Alan Lomax, Tom Glazer, and Josh White. *Red Channels* was a book released in June 1950 by the American Business Consultants, an anticommunist organization led by former FBI agents and supporters of the John Birch Society, which also published the weekly anticommunist newsletter *Counterattack.* Like the HUAC, American Business Consultants' objective was to expose communists and communist sympathizers. The tone of *Red Channels* is black and white, leaving little room for gray. The introduction states plainly that the 151 persons listed should be regarded as either communists or hapless dupes of them.[32] Thus, unsurprisingly, when copies of the book were sent to radio stations, television studios, and Hollywood film studios, the people listed therein were thought of as having a scarlet-red *C* embroidered on their garments.

Being listed in *Red Channels* could effectively end one's career. Even more threatening was being called before the HUAC. Among the musicians who appeared before the committee were Paul Robeson, Pete Seeger, Josh White, and Lee Hays. Others, such as Burl Ives, came before the Senate Internal Security Subcommittee (SISS). Because Seeger's name appeared in *Red Channels,* the Weavers as a group were also blacklisted. Ronnie Gilbert said, "It's funny to realize that this huge, important career of ours only really lasted two years before we got the ax. . . . I felt that it happened almost overnight. The moment we were headlined with 'Weavers called Reds,' that was the end of that. Bookings got cancelled, the State Fair got cancelled, all the major dates got cancelled."[33]

On August 18, 1955, the HUAC called Pete Seeger to appear. Near the beginning of his testimony, he asserted he loves his country deeply, had never done anything conspiratorial against it, and served for three-and-a-half years in the armed forces.[34] He also asserted his constitutional rights: "I am not going to answer any questions as to my association, my philosophical or religious beliefs or my political beliefs, or how I voted in any election, or any of these private affairs. I think these are very improper questions for any American to be asked, especially under such compulsion as this. I would be very glad to tell you my life if you want to hear of it."[35]

Effectively, Seeger pleads the First Amendment rather than the Fifth, the latter of which was more commonplace for those brought before the HUAC. Anita Silvey explains,

> Most of those who appeared before the Committee declined to answer questions, citing the Fifth Amendment of the Constitution, which says that Americans cannot be forced to incriminate themselves. Although this is a legitimate defense, many of these citizens were described by the press as "Fifth Amendment" Communists. But Pete was attracted to a different stand. He wanted to claim First Amendment rights. He felt that he had a right to his personal beliefs and that he was being punished without reason. By bringing in the First Amendment, Pete would be declaring that this committee of Congress had no right to ask anyone questions about their personal beliefs. The Hollywood Ten, a group of screenwriters and movie directors, had tried this approach earlier, had spent time in jail, and had been on the blacklist for years.[36]

By claiming the rights of the First Amendment and refusing to answer certain questions, Congress charged Seeger with contempt.[37] Yet he never criticized those who pleaded the Fifth.[38] He was sentenced to one year in jail but successfully appealed. He was finally acquitted in 1962. Natalie Maines of the Chicks, formerly the Dixie Chicks, said, "He's a living testament to the First Amendment. You can't just say you have rights. You have to use them to prove that you have them."[39] In 1957, Seeger wrote that it was "tragic that in our country with so many fine traditions of freedom, it is still possible to be penalized for opinions."[40]

After the Weavers disbanded in 1952, Pete Seeger was able to record and tour but rarely appeared on television. He was not asked to perform on the popular folk music program *Hootenanny* (1963–1964) because of his controversial viewpoints. He hosted his own folk music program *Rainbow Quest* (1965–1966), but it was made on a small budget, filmed in grainy black and white, and broadcast on just a few stations. He was not to appear on a national television broadcast until 1968, when he sang his antiwar song "Waist Deep in the Big Muddy" on *The Smothers Brothers Show*. Seeger explained the song in this way, "It was a story song, kind of an allegory, describing a bunch of soldiers training during World War II and the captain tells them to ford a muddy river. But as it gets deeper the sergeant urges they turn around. The Captain says 'Don't be a Nervous Nelly, Follow me.' But the Captain is drowned and they find his body stuck in the old quicksand.[41]

Even though the song never mentioned the Vietnam War or President Johnson, it was censored. The producers at CBS did not welcome its message of America getting too enmeshed in the affairs of countries halfway around the world. Seeger's performance was recorded for an episode of the show in September 1967, but the CBS producers cut the song out of the broadcast at the last minute. After complaints of censorship by the Smothers Brothers and the public, the song was allowed on the show in February 1968.

Although Seeger considered himself to be a communist, he became disenchanted with the Communist Party U.S.A. in the 1950s and expressed mixed feelings about the Soviet Union throughout the Cold War.[42] In his 1993 songbook, *Where Have All the Flowers Gone*, he wrote, "At any rate, today I'll apologize for a number of things, such as thinking that Stalin was merely a 'hard driver' and not a supremely cruel misleader."[43] In 2007 he wrote "Big Joe Blues," which has lines such as "he put an end to the dreams of so many in every land." When Pete Seeger died on January 27, 2014, some journalists seized on the opportunity to portray him not only as a hapless communist stooge but as an active proponent of Stalin's totalitarianism.[44] He was neither, and such characterizations are grossly unfair. His enthusiasm for communism arose from his concern about aid to the needy, racial equality, workers' rights, and justice for minorities and the oppressed. He believed capitalism was not the answer. Like Paul Robeson, whom Seeger greatly admired, he cannot be faulted for his ideals and principles; he can only be faulted for his misguided belief that communism alone could bring about positive change. Seeger believed in communistic principles but claiming he was Stalinist is hyperbolic. How can someone who risked his well-being for his right to speak freely, owned his own land, built his own house, favored gradual change through nonviolent protest rather than revolution, valued multiculturalism, and worked for the rights of oppressed peoples be pegged as a Stalinist? Seeger felt it was patriotic to protest when necessary, and he always protested nonviolently. He was instrumental in popularizing the ultimate nonviolent protest anthem, "We Shall Overcome," which played a large factor in the civil rights movement. Dan Seeger said of his father, "In a sense, my father was a very iconoclastic American, total patriot, absolutely unrecognized for this by many people, and it's his patriotism that was terribly misunderstood."[45]

VERN PARTLOW'S "OLD MAN ATOM"

While *The People's Song Book* contains several songs that anticipate political struggles of the Cold War in the 1950s and 1960s, there is one that is especially revelatory: Vern Partlow's "Old Man Atom." It is among the first songs to be written about the atomic bomb. Partlow wrote it in late 1945, when he was working as a reporter for the *Los Angeles Daily News*. He recounts how this job brought about the idea for the song:

> I was assigned to interview various atomic scientists who visited the city to speak about the atom bomb. . . . I met with them and talked with them and I became a little alarmed, too, at what they were saying. And I agreed with them that something new had happened in the world—something that would be with us a long time. . . . And so one evening I decided maybe there could be a song about the atom bomb—a folk song about the atom bomb. This is a rather ambitious folk song, but I thought it might be done. . . . The song was written in 1945 and in 1950 it was published by a Hollywood commercial music publisher. It was recorded in six or eight different versions on records. It was being played on radio stations throughout the country and was the subject of rave interviews in various trade magazines. And then it suddenly disappeared from all the networks.[46]

It disappeared because it asked too many probing and disquieting questions about something in which the US government was heavily invested—the bomb. In the late 1940s and early 1950s, the HUAC, Senator Joseph McCarthy, and various anticommunist organizations were on the hunt for leftists, communists, socialists, Marxists, and union organizers. They were also on the hunt for people writing songs warning against the atomic bomb. Such sentiments implied the songwriter was on the wrong side of the Cold War. Sam Hinton (on Columbia Records) and Sons of the Pioneers (on RCA Victor Records) both released versions of Partlow's song in 1950. It had the potential to be a hit before it was banned in August. As the *New York Times* reported on September 1, 1950, RCA Victor and Columbia both caved from the pressure of anticommunist organizations and pulled the records from the shelves.[47] Many AM radio stations also stopped playing it.

Partlow recorded his song sometime between when he wrote it in 1945 and 1950, calling it "Atomic Talking Blues."[48] *The People's Song Book* from 1948 first published the song as sheet music with the title "Talking Atomic Blues."[49] It is best known by the title "Old Man Atom." The lyrics are shown below.

> Lyrics to "Old Man Atom" ("Atomic Talking Blues") from recording by Vern Partlow on *Songs for Political Action*, Bear Family Records, BCD 15 720 JL, 1996, CD 6, track 28.

Verse 1: Well, I'm gonna preach you a sermon 'bout Old Man Atom,
I don't mean the Adam in the Bible datum.
I don't mean the Adam that Mother Eve mated,

I mean that thing that science liberated.
Einstein says he's scared,
And when Einstein's scared, I'm scared.

Refrain 1: Hiroshima, Nagasaki, Alamogordo, Bikini.

Verse 2: Here's my moral, plain as day,
Old Man Atom is here to stay.
He's gonna hang around, it's plain to see,
But ah, my dearly beloved, are we?
We hold this truth to be self-evident
All men may be cremated equal.

Refrain 2: Hiroshima, Nagasaki—here's my text
Hiroshima, Nagasaki—Lordy, who'll be next.

Verse 3: The science guys, from every clime,
They all pitched in with overtime.
Before they knew it, the job was done,
They'd hitched up the power of the gosh-darn sun,
They put a harness on Old Sol,
Splittin' atoms, while the diplomats was splittin' hairs

Refrain 3: Hiroshima, Nagasaki—what'll we do?
Hiroshima, Nagasaki—they both went up the flue.

Verse 4: Then the cartel crowd put on a show
To turn back the clock on the U.N.O.,
To get a corner on atoms and maybe extinguish
Every darned atom that can't speak English.
Down with foreign-born atoms!
Yes, Sir!

Refrain 4: Hiroshima, Nagasaki.

Verse 5: But the atom's international, in spite of hysteria,
Flourishes in Utah, also Siberia.
And whether you're white, black, red or brown,
The question is this, when you boil it down:
To be or not to be!
That is the question.
Atoms to atoms, and dust to dust,
If the world makes A-bombs, something's bound to bust.

Refrain 5: Hiroshima, Nagasaki, Alamogordo, Bikini.

Verse 6: No, the answer to it all isn't military datum,
Like "Who gets there the fustest with the mostest atoms,"
But the people of the world must decide their fate,
We got to stick together or disintegrate.
World peace and the atomic golden age or a push-button war,
Mass cooperation or mass annihilation,
Civilian international control of the atom, one world or none.
If you're gonna split atoms, well, you can't split ranks.

Refrain 6: Hiroshima, Nagasaki.

Verse 7: It's up to the people, cause the atom don't care,
You can't fence him in, he's just like air.
He doesn't give a darn about politics
Or who got who into whatever fix—
All he wants to do is sit around and have his nucleus
bombarded by neutrons.

Refrain 7: Hiroshima, Nagasaki, Alamogordo, Bikini.

Verse 8: So if you're scared of the A-bomb, I'll tell you what to do:
You got to get with all the people in the world with you.
You got to get together and let out a yell,
Or the first thing you know we'll blow this world to . . .

Refrain 8: Hiroshima, Nagasaki,
Moscow, too,
New York, London, Timbuktu,
Shanghai, Paris, up the flue,
Hiroshima, Nagasaki.
We must choose between
The brotherhood of man or smithereens.
The people of the world must pick out a thesis:
"Peace in the world, or the world in pieces!"
Whoosh!

Old Man Atom (A Talking Atomic Blues)
By Vern Partlow

Partlow approaches the subject of nuclear warfare from as many angles as he can, creating a song capturing the salient points of the debate. Partlow evidently did in-depth research on his own, besides interviewing atomic scientists for the *Los Angeles Daily News.* The lyrics are thick with meaning and full of allusion. There are references to atomic science, such as the atom wanting his "nucleus bombarded by neutrons" (verse 7). This bombardment creates the fission chain reaction that makes the bomb explode. There are also allusions to historical events, such as the bombings of Hiroshima and Nagasaki and the bomb tests in Alamogordo, New Mexico, and the Bikini Atoll. There is wordplay, like "atom"/"Adam" in the first two lines and "peace"/"pieces" in the penultimate line. There is mock biblical prophecy ("I'm gonna preach you a sermon"). There is a quote from William Shakespeare's *Hamlet* ("To be or not to be. That is the question."), which is used to show atomic warfare confronts humankind with the possibility of self-slaughter (verse 5). Also, in verse 5, Partlow changes the phrase "ashes to ashes, dust to dust" (a paraphrase of Genesis 3:19 from the Anglican *Book of Common Prayer* funeral service) to "atoms to atoms, and dust to dust." In refrain 8, he lists cities all over the world, making the point they all could be destroyed if World War III ever takes place. Verse 2 contains a twisted reference to the US Declaration of Independence: "We hold this truth to be self-evident, all men may be cremated equal."

Lastly, Partlow makes it clear that America is naive to believe it alone has the ability to create and control the atomic bomb ("Down with foreign-born atoms!"). Partlow felt the Soviets would inevitably develop their own ("the atom's international . . . flourishes in Utah, also Siberia"), which they did in 1949. Partlow saw the solution to the arms race as "civilian international control of the atom" and "mass cooperation or mass annihilation" (verse 6). Atomic energy and weapons should come under the control of a supranational organization, the newly formed United Nations. Partlow most likely based his ideas on the 1946 book *One World or None,* which he alludes to in verse 6.[50] The book is a collection of essays from leading atomic scientists, such as Albert Einstein (whom Partlow name-drops in verse 1), J. Robert Oppenheimer, Leo Szilard, Hans Bethe, and Niels Bohr. Some of these men worked on the Manhattan Project but later had mixed feelings about their involvement when they realized how deadly the Hiroshima and Nagasaki bombings were and how dangerous a future arms race could become. Although President Truman signed the Atomic Energy Act of 1946, which put the bomb in the hands of civilian scientists instead of military generals, he thought that "international control of the atom" was unrealistic and foolhardy. He did not want to share America's nuclear secrets with the rest of the world, especially the Soviets. In 1949, he said, "I am of the opinion we'll never obtain international control. Since we can't obtain international control we must be strongest in atomic weapons."[51] The arms race was on, and in 1950 Truman gave the go-ahead for scientists to develop the hydrogen bomb. In the Cold War climate of 1950, many considered Vern Partlow's views to be scandalous, especially when

Julius Rosenberg was found guilty of passing classified US information about the atomic bomb to Soviet agents. Such controversial lyrics led to the record being pulled from the shelves.

The two most well-known versions of the song are by Sam Hinton and Sons of the Pioneers. The version by Sons of the Pioneers is the more interesting of the two. Singer Hugh Farr personifies the atom by singing from the first-person perspective ("I'm gonna preach you all a sermon about old man atom, that's me!"). Unfortunately, Vern Partlow's original recording is not as well-known as the versions by Pete Seeger, Sam Hinton, and Sons of the Pioneers. "Old Man Atom" shows how rich, prophetic, and provocative a song about the Cold War can be.

BOB DYLAN

In his memoir *Chronicles: Volume One*, Bob Dylan writes about immersing himself in literature in his early days in New York City in 1961. He was staying with Ray Gooch and Chloe Kiel, two friends in Greenwich Village whose apartment was filled with books.[52] One book that caught his attention was the famous treatise *On War* (*Vom Kriege*) by Prussian general and military theorist Carl von Clausewitz (1780–1831).[53] Dylan writes he had a "morbid fascination with this stuff" and that "some of the stuff in his book can shape your ideas. If you think you're a dreamer, you can read this stuff and realize you're not even capable of dreaming."[54] In some of his songs, Dylan was an idealist and a dreamer ("When the Ship Comes In," "Chimes of Freedom," "I Shall Be Released," "Forever Young"), but in other songs, especially his songs about war, one can sense the point-blank realism of Clausewitz.

Dylan wrote several songs about the Cold War in his early years. Two songs from his second album, *The Freewheelin' Bob Dylan* (1963), demonstrate the wide range of his treatment of the subject: one is extremely comical, the other extremely caustic. In "Talkin' World War III Blues," Dylan imagines himself on a psychiatrist's couch trying to explain a strange dream in which he lived through World War III. The deadpan, stream-of-consciousness narrative is full of hilarious circumstances, such as him lighting a cigarette on a radioactive parking meter and driving down 42nd Street in a Cadillac, a "good car to drive after a war." It ends with him discovering his doctor, and everyone else, is also having strange dreams about World War III. "Masters of War" is a scathing critique of the military-industrial complex. Written from the point of view of a soldier, it is directed at military analysts and war profiteers who extend their wealth and power while he is on the front line sacrificing his life. President Eisenhower, in his farewell address to the nation on January 17, 1961, stressed both the necessity of and the potential for corruption in the military-industrial complex. Eisenhower stated, "Until the latest of our world conflicts, the United States had no armaments industry. . . . But now we can no longer risk emergency improvisation of national defense; we have been compelled to create a permanent armaments industry of vast proportions. . . . In the councils of government, we must guard against the acquisition of unwarranted influence, whether sought or unsought, by the military-industrial complex. The potential for the disastrous rise of misplaced power exists and will persist."[55]

The song ends with the soldier imagining the death of one of the profiteers, following his casket, and standing over his grave to make sure he's dead. In the liner notes on the *Freewheelin'* album, Dylan wrote, "I've never really written anything like that before. I don't sing songs which hope people will die, but I couldn't help it with this one. The song is a sort of striking out, a reaction to the last straw, a feeling of what can you do?"[56] Dorian Lynskey described the song as "a vehicle for all those dangerous, unpacifistic emotions that antiwar movements rarely allow themselves to express—that feeling of hating violence so much that all you want to do is match it with violence of your own."[57] In contrast to Joan Baez, whose pacifism is addressed in the next chapter, Dylan was no pacifist. In a 2001 interview he said of "Masters of War," "Every time I sing it, someone writes that it's an antiwar song. But there's no antiwar sentiment in that song. I'm not a pacifist. I don't think I've ever been one. If you look closely at the song, it's about what Eisenhower was saying about the dangers of the military-industrial complex in this country. I believe strongly in everyone's right to defend themselves by every means necessary."[58]

In the remainder of this section we will closely examine three other Cold War songs by Dylan, "Let Me Die in My Footsteps," "Talkin' John Birch Paranoid Blues," and "With God on Our Side." They grapple with the subjects of bomb shelters, the influence of communism in the United States, and the use of religion to justify warfare.

"Let Me Die in My Footsteps" was among Dylan's first compositions. He was deeply immersed in studying the music and life of Woody Guthrie when he wrote the song in early 1962. He intended it to be included on *The Freewheelin' Bob Dylan*, but it was replaced by "A Hard Rain's A-Gonna Fall." The song expresses the typical Midwestern attitude in his hometown of Hibbing, Minnesota, about fallout shelters.[59] A shelter was a symbol of isolationism, something that contradicted a core value in his town—neighborliness. He recounts in *Chronicles: Volume One*, "No one liked thinking that someone else might have one and you didn't. Or if you had one and someone else didn't. . . . It could turn neighbor against neighbor and friend against friend. . . . There wasn't any honorable way out. . . . Salesmen hawking the bomb shelters were met with expressionless faces."[60] For the song's liner notes on the *Freewheelin'* album (before the song got pulled), he wrote about the early 1960s shelter craze, "It struck me sort of funny that they would concentrate so much on digging a hole underground when there were so many other things they should do in life."[61] The lyrics to three of the song's seven verses are below.

Verse 1: I will not go down under the ground
'Cause somebody tells me that death's comin' 'round
An' I will not carry myself down to die
When I go to my grave my head will be high.
Let me die in my footsteps
Before I go down under the ground.

Verse 6: Let me drink from the waters where the mountain streams flood
Let the smell of wildflowers flow free through my blood
Let me sleep in your meadows with the green grassy leaves
Let me walk down the highway with my brother in peace.
Let me die in my footsteps
Before I go down under the ground.

Verse 7: Go out in your country where the land meets the sun
See the craters and the canyons where the waterfalls run
Nevada, New Mexico, Arizona, Idaho
Let every state in this union seep down deep in your souls
And you'll die in your footsteps
Before you go down under the ground.

The song opens by treating a fallout shelter as a metaphor for death. To voluntarily go underground out of fear is to give up on life itself. To stay aboveground, even in the event of nuclear war, gives life dignity and meaning. The second verse puts the Cold War in the context of wars that continually come and go. To frame one's life around the ever-present reality of war is "learnin' to die" rather than "learnin' to live." He builds on this theme in verses three through five, pointing the finger at those who breed fear and pursue war for their own purposes. Verse six marks a shift in the narrative, changing the frame from antiwar statements to resonant affirmations of life. Its imagery is Edenic, with vivid descriptions of nature and peace between men. It reflects the profound influence Woody Guthrie had on Dylan as he developed his own singing and songwriting voice. In its use of nature and travel imagery, it echoes the walk down the highway that characterizes Guthrie's "This Land Is Your Land."

Verse seven continues in this vein but expands from the individual "I" into a collective "you." This brings the listener into the song and into the experience of traveling across the country, a fundamental part of American identity. Curiously, Dylan calls out four states (Nevada, New Mexico, Arizona, Idaho) in the final verse. Unlike Guthrie, who binds together the entirety of the United States ("from California to the New York island"), Dylan concentrates on one area, the Southwest desert country. In a verse that also celebrates the beauty of "every state," why would he draw attention to these four? Perhaps because these are the states whose people and environments were most endangered by atomic bombs and radioactive fallout. All four states carried out uranium mining that adversely affected local citizens and the ecology. Nevada is home to the Nevada Test Site, where over nine hundred bomb tests were conducted. New Mexico is home to Alamogordo, where the first atomic bomb was detonated during the Trinity test, and Los Alamos, America's primary facility for nuclear bomb production during the Cold War. This reading gives the phrase "craters and canyons" an ironic twist. The Nevada Test Site is strewn with massive craters produced by aboveground and belowground bomb tests. Dylan's song was not the first, nor the last, written about fallout shelters. For more on the shelter craze of the late 1950s and early 1960s, and the songs it produced, see chapters 4 and 5.

Along with the bomb, the greatest fear among many Americans in the early years of the Cold War was the spread of communism. This fear was certainly justified. Soviet spies, as well as British and American double agents, infiltrated the US government at uncomfortably high levels. As noted earlier, Julius and Ethel Rosenberg passed US nuclear-weapons designs to Soviet agents. This resulted in Russia joining the nuclear club in 1949. Besides Senator Joseph McCarthy and government agencies like the HUAC, the CIA, and the FBI, citizens established several nongovernmental organizations to stop the red menace. "Talkin' John Birch Paranoid Blues" is Dylan's impression of perhaps the best known of these nongovernmental, anticommunist groups, the John Birch Society.

Robert W. Welch Jr., an American businessman and political activist, founded the JBS in 1958. Welch named the organization after John Birch, a missionary and intelligence officer who was shot in August 1945 by communists in China. Welch claimed Birch was the first American casualty of the Cold War and deserved the honor of having the society named after him.[62] Founded in Indianapolis, with its first local chapters around the Boston area, the JBS soon had chapters spread across the United States. The society supported the work of Senator Joseph McCarthy and situated its headquarters in the city of Appleton, Wisconsin, where he was buried. As part of its extreme anticommunist stance, it also took an anti–civil rights stance during the 1950s and 1960s.[63] In his book, *The Politician,* written in the late 1950s and self-published in 1963, Welch went so far as to assert that communists planted presidents Franklin D. Roosevelt, Harry Truman, and Dwight D. Eisenhower.[64] He writes, "It is to me inconceivable that under all the circumstances which prevailed, and with so many able and experienced generals available, Lt. Colonel Eisenhower could have been shot up all the way to Supreme Commander Eisenhower in so short a time, and with so obviously little military ability, without the Communist push behind him every step of the way."[65]

After such ludicrous claims, most republicans and conservatives shunned the group. Dylan lampoons Welch's view on US presidents being communists in verse nine of the song: "Now Eisenhower, he's a Russian spy, Lincoln, Jefferson and that Roosevelt guy."

Dylan wrote this song early in 1962 and published it the same year in the first issue of *Broadside,* a magazine that featured the lyrics of songwriters from the 1960s folk revival.[66] Dylan recorded it in April 1962 during the sessions for *The Freewheelin' Bob Dylan* with the intention of including it on the album. He was scheduled to perform the song on *The Ed Sullivan Show* on May 12, 1963, then one of the most popular television variety programs. Ed Sullivan himself liked the song. However, CBS executives did not allow Dylan to perform it. They feared the JBS might file a lawsuit against the station. Dylan got up and left the show. CBS executives who owned Dylan's label, Columbia Records, also objected to the inclusion of the song on *The Freewheelin' Bob Dylan.* "Talkin' World War III Blues" was put on the album in its place.[67] Since Dylan was still in the early stage of his career, having released only one album, he was not in a position to fight the executives. He relented, and the song was not officially released until 1991 when a version from a 1963 Carnegie Hall concert was included on the three-CD set *The Bootleg Series, Volumes 1–3.*

In "Talkin' John Birch Paranoid Blues," we hear the clear influence of Woody Guthrie's talking blues style. In this tradition, the text often varies widely in different performances, incorporating elements of improvisation throughout. Like Guthrie and Pete Seeger, Dylan employed the talking blues to offer a cultural critique on a weighty topic using a humorous, eccentric narrative, as in "Talkin' World War III Blues" discussed above. His critique in this song is the way organizations, like the John Birch Society, promote xenophobia, racism, and unfounded suspicion. Dylan imagines himself a member of the JBS and commences his hunt for communists. Written in a first-person narrative, the song consists of ten verses. Four are shown below.

Verse 1: Well, I was feelin' sad and feelin' blue
I didn't know what in the world I was gonna do
Them Communists they was comin' around
They wus in the air

They wus on the ground
They wouldn't gimme no peace . . .

Verse 4: Well, I wus lookin' everywhere for them gol-darned Reds
I got up in the mornin' 'n' looked under my bed
Looked in the sink, behind the door
Looked in the glove compartment of my car
Couldn't find 'em . . .

Verse 5: I wus lookin' high an' low for them Reds everywhere
I wus lookin' in the sink an' underneath the chair
I looked way up my chimney hole
I even looked deep down inside my toilet bowl
They got away . . .

Verse 6: Well, I wus sittin' home alone an' started to sweat
Figured they wus in my T.V. set
Peeked behind the picture frame
Got a shock from my feet, hittin' right up in the brain
Them Reds caused it!
I know they did . . . them hard-core ones.

The narrator begins by expressing his frazzled emotional state caused by the menace of communists who, apparently, are everywhere. The cure is not to visit his doctor or psychiatrist but to join the John Birch Society. In verse three he argues that despite the fact Hitler murdered six million Jews, at least he wasn't a communist. The following verses articulate the narrator's frantic search for them—under his bed, in his sink, behind his door, in the glove compartment of his car, under his chair, up his chimney, and even down his toilet bowl.

By verse six, he has worked up a sweat. When he looks behind his TV set, he gets shocked and suspects it was caused by communists, "them hard-core ones." He quits his job so he has more time to hunt. He suspects Betsy Ross was one because the American flag has red stripes. He calculates that 90 percent of books are communist and should be burned and that 98 percent of his friends are communists and should be imprisoned. Presidents are communists too, as noted above in reference to Welch's claim about Eisenhower. However, the founder of the American Nazi party (George Lincoln Rockwell) is okay since he, like Hitler, hated communists. In the last verse, there's only one person left that he hasn't investigated, "so now I'm sittin' home investigatin' myself!" The dark humor of the song slices through the paranoia of the red scare during the 1950s and early 1960s, showing its tendencies toward obsessive suspicion and isolation.

The last Dylan song we will closely examine is "With God on Our Side," a critique of how American history was taught in schools when he was growing up in the 1940s and 1950s. Until the social history approach emerged in the 1960s and 1970s, American history textbooks generally treated the perspectives of minority groups and conquered peoples in a cursory way. The social history movement sought to recover the voices of ordinary and disenfranchised peoples by providing an alternative to the top-down or "great man" approaches frequently employed in American histories.[68] Reading "With God on Our Side" as a social history document demonstrates the way Dylan challenges standard narratives of American history. It undermines some of the primary tenets of American civil religion held by citizens in the 1940s and 1950s, and by many today. One of which is that America is morally exceptional and always fights just wars. Dylan said of his high school education, specifically his history classes, "The teachers in school taught me everything was fine. That was the accepted thing to think. It was in all the books. But it ain't fine, man. There are so many lies that have been told, so many things that are kept back."[69]

Dylan saw no morality in warfare, no just cause for assuming God is always on the side of America. Reflecting the point-blank realism in Clausewitz's *On War,* he writes in *Chronicles,* "Don't give me that dance that God is with us, or that God supports us. Let's get down to brass tacks. There isn't any moral order. You can forget that. Morality has nothing in common with politics. It's not there to transgress. It's either high ground or low ground. This is the way the world is and nothing's gonna change it."[70]

Bruce T. Murray puts it this way, "The issue of God and war raises a central conundrum of American civil religion: How can you tell if God is on your side? How can you be sure? . . . In the Civil War, civil religion collided into its ultimate dilemma, with both sides claiming that God was on their side."[71]

"With God on Our Side" was released in 1964 on Dylan's third album, *The Times They Are A-Changin'*. In the lyrics, he comments on most of the major wars the United States had engaged in after the Revolutionary War: the American Indian Wars, the Spanish-American War, the Civil War, the two world wars, and the Cold War. The lyrics to five of its nine verses are shown below.

Verse 2: Oh the history books tell it
They tell it so well
The cavalries charged
The Indians fell
The cavalries charged
The Indians died

The country was young
With God on its side

Verse 5: When the Second World War
Came to an end
We forgave the Germans
And then we were friends
Though they murdered six million
In the ovens they fried
The Germans now too
Have God on their side

Verse 6: I've learned to hate the Russians
All through my whole life
If another war comes
It's them we must fight
To hate them and fear them
To run and to hide
And accept it all bravely
With God on my side

Verse 7: But now we got weapons
Of chemical dust
If fire them we're forced to
Then fire them we must
One push of the button
And a shot the world wide
And you never ask questions
When God's on your side

Verse 8: Through many a dark hour
I've been thinkin' about this
That Jesus Christ
Was betrayed by a kiss
But I can't think for you
You'll have to decide
Whether Judas Iscariot
Had God on his side

The ballad opens in a formulaic way: "Oh my name it is nothin', my age it means less." As with "Let Me Die in My Footsteps" and other early songs, Dylan seems to be channeling stylistic elements from Woody Guthrie. Here, Dylan creates a narrator who is reflecting on all he was taught about America in school. He dutifully learned the laws and history of his country and was told the land he lives in "has God on its side."

In the second verse, he begins questioning the veracity of what he was taught. He specifically takes on manifest destiny. White Anglo-Saxons had a noble calling to move westward and conquer the lands and people. The "savages" there needed to be civilized. It is impossible to know what history books Dylan was taught from in school, but a good representative example is David Saville Muzzey's *An American History*.[72] It was first published in 1911 and used in high schools into the 1950s.[73] Muzzey states, "The Indian tribes north of the Gulf of Mexico had generally reached the stage of development called 'lower barbarism,' a stage of pottery making and rude agricultural science."[74] He continues, "There were probably never more than a few hundred thousand Indians in America. Their small number perhaps accounts for their lack of civilization."[75] For Muzzey, the civilizing mission goes beyond the westward trails of the nineteenth century and should be carried into the twentieth. "The surviving Indians . . . are rapidly learning the ways of the white men. It is to be hoped that their education will be wisely fostered."[76] Dylan calls out such narratives in the verse, focusing on the loss of life that Native Americans suffered in the conquest of the West. But perhaps, he sardonically suggests, this can be excused because of the youth of the country.

The third verse begins with the Spanish-American War and also addresses the Civil War, where both sides declared God to be on their sides. Dylan recounts that in his school days, he had to memorize the names of war heroes, a common characteristic of the "great man" approach. The fourth verse, overviewing World War I, shifts the tone. From this point on, Dylan uses increasingly grim and visceral lyrics: "For you don't count the dead when God's on your side." When considering the starkness of verse five, about the Holocaust, it is important to remember Dylan's own heritage as a child of Jewish immigrants. "Never again" rings out through its stomach-churning imagery. And yet, since the Germans were made into American allies following the conclusion of World War II, they are depicted as having God on their side.

The song's structure creates a sequence of World War I (verse four) leading into World War II (verse five) leading into the Cold War framed as a nascent World War III (verses six and seven). These two verses explore Cold War politics and the use of civil religion as a justification for national policies. Fear and hatred of the Russians is expressed in verse six, as well as protective measures—fallout shelters and ducking and covering. Verse seven focuses on the drastic shift in weaponry during the twentieth century. In contrast to verse three, where Civil War heroes fought with guns, World War III will be fought with radioactivity ("chemical dust") produced by nuclear weapons. The destruction will not be confined to battlefields, or even entire countries, but will be worldwide. The movement toward atomic warfare and worldwide destruction is depicted as inevitable. Once either country pushes the button, there will be no time for questions or deliberation. It was the policy of both the United States and the Soviet Union to respond to a nuclear attack with an equal or greater one. Dylan wrote the song sometime in the early months of 1963, so it is likely a response to the Cuban Missile Crisis in October 1962, the closest the world has come to nuclear war.[77] Since the song was written before the United States sent troops to Vietnam, the Vietnam War is not mentioned. Yet in the 1980s when he played the song in concerts, Dylan added an extra verse questioning why America entered the war and if God was on its side.

The first seven verses present an unbroken narrative of war as a God-ordained activity. In the final two verses, Dylan as narrator steps back to reflect on, and restructure, the relationship between God and America's wars. What if instead of enacting God's justice in its wars, America has been performing the work of the ultimate betrayal? Has America played Judas in some of its wars, casting off Christ's gospel of peace? Dylan raises these questions but leaves the answers to the listener.

Verse nine acts as an outro, "So now as I'm leavin' I'm weary as Hell." The consideration of the costs of war, as well as the energy spent reframing his American identity, has left him exhausted. But he ends the song with a tiny flicker of hope, "If God's on our side, He'll stop the next war." Perhaps through examining the traditional structuring of historical narratives and dismantling the view that America is God's anointed warrior, the next war can be avoided.

Despite its ominous lyrics, the song is sung in a major key—unlike, for example, the minor-keyed "Masters of War," which shares much of the same lyrical themes. The slow, ponderous pace of the seven-minute song adds to the gravity of its subject matter. Dylan plays and sings with a heavy dose of weariness and foreboding, as if he is loath to confront the bleak reality of each war he enumerates.

Armed only with a guitar or banjo, folk musicians boldly spoke out against the bomb, McCarthyism, and warmongering politicians around the globe. Writing incisive lyrics, they appealed to reason and common humanity as a foil against the inhumanity of nuclear war. In the next chapter, we investigate how female folk musicians viewed the conflict and shed light on issues, such as the detrimental effects of nuclear testing on the environment, how the threat of nuclear war impacts children, and the rising political power of women.

NOTES

1. Winston Churchill, *Never Give In! The Best of Winston Churchill's Speeches* (New York: Hyperion, 2003), 378.

2. Ibid., 420.

3. Bob Dylan, *Chronicles: Volume One* (New York: Simon and Schuster, 2004), 29, 30.

4. Earl Robinson with Eric A. Gordon, *Ballad of an American: The Autobiography of Earl Robinson* (Lanham, MD: Scarecrow, 1998), 66.

5. Jordan Goodman, *Paul Robeson: A Watched Man* (London: Verso, 2013), xii.

6. Ibid., 9.

7. Arnold H. Lubasch, *Robeson: An American Ballad* (Lanham, MD: Scarecrow, 2012), 78–80.

8. Goodman, *Paul Robeson*, 46–52.

9. "'Black Stalin' Aim Is Laid to Robeson: Ex-Red Official Says Singer, a Communist, Suffered 'Delusions of Grandeur,'" *New York Times*, July 15, 1949.

10. Martin Duberman, *Paul Robeson* (New York: New Press, 2005), 367.

11. Ibid., 368.

12. David King Dunaway, *How Can I Keep From Singing? The Ballad of Pete Seeger* (New York: Villard, 2008), 10–14.

13. Duberman, *Paul Robeson*, 370–372.

14. Tony Perucci, *Paul Robeson and the Cold War Performance Complex: Race, Madness, Activism* (Ann Arbor: University of Michigan Press, 2012), 39.

15. Eric Bentley, ed., *Thirty Years of Treason: Excerpts from Hearings before the House Committee on Un-American Activities, 1938–1968* (New York: Viking, 1971), 784.

16. Henry Foner in *Paul Robeson: Here I Stand* (WinStar Home Entertainment, Fox Lorber Home Video WHE71177, 1999, VHS), 1:02:04–1:02:14.

17. Robinson, *Ballad of an American*, 251–252.

18. Ibid., 101–102, 219.

19. Paul Robeson, *Paul Robeson Speaks: Writings, Speeches, Interviews, 1918–1974* (New York: Brunner/Mazel, 1978), 479.

20. Lubasch, *Robeson*, 208–209.

21. Will Kaufman, *Woody Guthrie, American Radical* (Urbana: University of Illinois Press, 2011), 67.

22. Will Kaufman, *Woody Guthrie's Modern World Blues* (Norman: University of Oklahoma Press, 2017), 25–26.

23. Ibid., 140.

24. Michael Hill and George M. Walsh, "FBI Files: Military Questioned Pete Seeger's Wartime Loyalty," *AP News*, December 19, 2015, https://apnews.com/dc9d717fba864fef80ba36fe224d6846/fbi-files-military-questioned-pete-seegers-wartime-loyalty.

25. Ibid.

26. Robbie Lieberman, *"My Song Is My Weapon": People's Songs, American Communism, and the Politics of Culture, 1930–1950* (Urbana: University of Illinois Press, 1989), 68–69.

27. Richard A. Reuss with JoAnne C. Reuss, *American Folk Music and Left-Wing Politics, 1927–1957* (Lanham, MD: Scarecrow, 2000), 186–187.

28. *The People's Song Book*, foreword by Alan Lomax, preface by B. A. Botkin (New York: Boni and Gaer, 1948).

29. Kaufman, *Woody Guthrie's Modern World Blues*, 139.

30. Woody Guthrie to Stetson Kennedy, August 15, 1950, Woody Guthrie Archives, Woody Guthrie Center, Tulsa, Oklahoma, Correspondence 1, Box 1, Folder 32, quoted in Kaufman, *Woody Guthrie's Modern World Blues*, 148–149.

31. Woody Guthrie to Harry Truman, July 31, 1949, Woody Guthrie Archives, Woody Guthrie Center, Tulsa, Oklahoma, Correspondence 1, Series 1, Box 3, Folder 27, quoted in Kaufman, *Woody Guthrie, American Radical*, 166–167.

32. American Business Consultants, *Red Channels: The Report of Communist Influence in Radio and Television* (New York: American Business Consultants, 1950), 1–7.

33. Ronnie Gilbert, in booklet from the Weavers' four-CD set *Wasn't That a Time*. Liner notes by Mary Katherine Aldin (Vanguard VCD4-147/50, 1993), 21.

34. Bentley, ed., *Thirty Years of Treason*, 687–688.

35. Ibid., 688.

36. Anita Silvey, *Let Your Voice Be Heard: The Life and Times of Pete Seeger* (New York: Houghton Mifflin Harcourt, 2016), 60.

37. Pete Seeger, *Pete Seeger in His Own Words*, ed. Rob Rosenthal and Sam Rosenthal (Boulder, CO: Paradigm, 2012), 104–106.

38. Bentley, ed., *Thirty Years of Treason*, 689.

39. Natalie Maines in *Pete Seeger: The Power of Song* (Weinstein Company and Live Nation Artists 81411, 2007, DVD), 1:15–1:25.

40. Seeger, *Pete Seeger in His Own Words*, 106.

41. Pete Seeger, *Give Peace a Chance: Music and the Struggle for Peace: A Catalog of the Exhibition at the Peace Museum, Chicago*, ed. Marianne Philbin (Chicago: Chicago Review, 1983), 71.

42. The best presentation of Seeger's viewpoints on communism is in *Pete Seeger in His Own Words*, 85–114.

43. Pete Seeger, *Where Have All the Flowers Gone: A Singer's Stories, Songs, Seeds, Robberies*, ed. Peter Blood (Bethlehem, PA: Sing Out, 1993), 22.

44. Michael Moynihan, "The Death of 'Stalin's Songbird,'" *Daily Beast*, January 29, 2014, https://www.thedailybeast.com/the-death-of-stalins-songbird.

45. Dan Seeger in *Pete Seeger: The Power of Song* (Weinstein Company and Live Nation Artists 81411, 2007, DVD), 4:58–5:12.

46. Vern Partlow, from an interview by Ronald D. Cohen and Dave Samuelson in the liner notes for the ten-CD set *Songs for Political Action* (Bear Family Records, BCD 15 720 JL, 1996), 134.

47. "Ban Is Put on Song about the Atom: Record Companies Withdraw Disk after Complaints It Follows Communist Line," *New York Times*, September 1, 1950, 4.

48. Partlow's recording is included in the ten-CD set *Songs for Political Action: Folk Music, Topical Songs and the American Left, 1926–1953* (Bear Family Records, BCD 15 720 JL, 1996), CD 6, track 28.

49. *The People's Song Book*, 114–116.

50. Dexter Masters and Katharine Way, eds., *One World or None* (New York: McGraw-Hill, 1946).

51. S. David Broscious, "Longing for International Control, Banking on American Superiority: Harry S. Truman's Approach to Nuclear Weapons," in *Cold War Statesmen Confront the Bomb: Nuclear Diplomacy since 1945*, ed. John Lewis Gaddis, Philip H. Gordon, Ernest R. May, and Jonathan Rosenberg (Oxford: Oxford University Press, 1999), 36.

52. Bob Dylan, *Chronicles: Volume One* (New York: Simon and Schuster, 2004), 26. Some Dylan scholars have proposed that Gooch and Kiel are not real but composites of people Dylan met in his early days in Greenwich Village. See Mike Marqusee, *Wicked Messenger: Bob Dylan and the 1960s; Chimes of Freedom* (New York: Seven Stories, 2005), 325.

53. Karl von Clausewitz, *On War*, trans. O. J. Matthijs Jolles (Washington, DC: Combat Forces, 1953).

54. Dylan, *Chronicles*, 41, 45.

55. Dwight D. Eisenhower, "Farewell Address, Reading Copy," Dwight D. Eisenhower Presidential Library, Museum, and Boyhood Home, https://www.eisenhowerlibrary.gov/sites/default/files/research/online-documents/farewell-address/reading-copy.pdf.

56. Bob Dylan, quoted in Nat Hentoff's liner notes from back cover of *The Freewheelin' Bob Dylan* (Columbia CS 8786, 1963, LP).

57. Dorian Lynskey, *33 Revolutions per Minute: A History of Protest Songs, from Billie Holiday to Green Day* (New York: Ecco, 2011), 57.

58. Robert Hilburn, "How Does It Feel? Don't Ask," *Los Angeles Times*, September 16, 2001, https://www.latimes.com/archives/la-xpm-2001-sep-16-ca-46189-story.html.

59. David Pichaske, *Song of the North Country: A Midwest Framework to the Songs of Bob Dylan* (New York: Continuum, 2010), 44.

60. Dylan, *Chronicles*, 271.

61. Bob Dylan, quoted in John Bauldie's liner notes for the three-CD set *Bob Dylan: The Bootleg Series, Volumes 1–3 (Rare & Unreleased), 1961–1991* (Columbia C3K 65302, 1991), 9.

62. Terry Lautz, *John Birch: A Life* (New York: Oxford University Press, 2016), 4.

63. *The Blue Book of the John Birch Society* (Boston: Western Islands, 1959), 19.

64. Robert Welch, *The Politician* (Belmont, MA: Robert Welch, 1963), 279.

65. Ibid., 17.

66. Bob Dylan, "Talking John Birch," *Broadside #1*, February 1962, 3, https://singout.org/downloads/broadside/b001.pdf.

67. John Bauldie, liner notes for the three-CD set *Bob Dylan: The Bootleg Series, Volumes 1–3 (Rare & Unreleased), 1961–1991* (Columbia C3K 65302, 1991), 16.

68. Sara L. Schwebel, *Child-Sized History: Fictions of the Past in U.S. Classrooms* (Nashville: Vanderbilt University Press, 2011).

69. Chris Welles, "The Angry Young Folk Singer," *Life*, April 10, 1964, 114.

70. Dylan, *Chronicles*, 45.

71. Bruce T. Murray, *Religious Liberty in America: The First Amendment in Historical and Contemporary Perspective* (Amherst: University of Massachusetts Press in association with Foundation for American Communications, 2008), 58.

72. David Saville Muzzey, *An American History* (Boston: Ginn and Company, 1911).

73. Eric P. Kaufmann, *The Rise and Fall of Anglo-America* (Cambridge, MA: Harvard University Press, 2004), 215.

74. Muzzey, *An American History*, 23.

75. Ibid., 25.

76. Ibid.

77. Dylan performed "With God on Our Side" for the first time on April 12, 1963, at New York's Town Hall. See Clinton Heylin, *Bob Dylan: A Life in Stolen Moments; Day by Day: 1941–1995* (London: Book Sales, 1996), 42.

TWO

FOLK

Women's Voices

IN TRACING THE TRAJECTORY OF American women's lives in the middle decades of the twentieth century (the 1940s–1960s), a common narrative has been that women worked for the war effort in World War II, raised the baby boomers in the early years of the Cold War, and then became politically active in the 1960s with second-wave feminism.[1] Along with raising children during World War II, the war effort fully engaged women as truck drivers, mail deliverers, clerics, laboratory assistants, and telephone and radio operators. Hundreds of thousands of women entered the factories and served in the military in noncombat roles. After the war ended, women retreated to the suburbs to raise their children, host Tupperware parties, and make Jell-O mold desserts in their push-button kitchens.[2] In the 1960s, women became more politically active and brought attention to issues such as reproductive rights, rape, and inequalities in the workplace and divorce law.

But for many women during the early Cold War years, this narrative is too sharply defined and misleading. After World War II, many women continued to work, were politically active, and refused to be bound by traditional gender roles. Until recently, the accomplishments of these women have been neglected. As Joanne Meyerowitz writes, "For historians, women of the postwar era, it seems, were less captivating than women workers during World War II or political activists of the 1960s. Postwar women provided a coda to the saga of Rosie the Riveter or a prelude to the story of 1960s feminists.... Historical accounts stress the postwar domestic ideal, the reassertion of a traditional sexual division of labor, and the formal and informal barriers that prevented women from fully participating in the public realm."[3]

This chapter is about four women who operated outside the prevailing narrative: Peggy Seeger, Malvina Reynolds, Joan Baez, and Janet Greene. The first three were politically active in left-wing organizations, pursuing international peace and nuclear disarmament. Janet Greene was active in right-wing organizations preventing the spread of communism to America. They all reached out to other women to bring attention to women's issues connected with the Cold War. All four were mothers who wanted to see their children inherit a better world. All four were singer/songwriters and used their songs as an active form of political participation.

Post–World War II, women who actively participated in antiwar organizations and demonstrations met with significant resistance. In fact, women who actively participated in politics in any capacity were regarded as suspicious since many men thought a woman's place was in the home. Those identifying themselves as socialists or communists were immediately branded as unpatriotic. Women who worked for international peace and nuclear disarmament were thought of as "communist dupes" and suspected of collaborating with the enemy. *Peace* became a contested word in America since the US government believed that communists used that word for no other reason than to push their own agenda.[4] In the 1950s, members of the Women's International League for Peace and Freedom (WILPF) were suspected of being communists and compelled to prove that peace between nations was a "good" thing. The leaders of the WILPF wrote to their members, "We must insist that because we are espousing a cause which the Communists are also working on, does not mean we are communists, fellow-travelers, communist-infiltrated, etc. Our work must be judged by what we stand for, and the reasons for this stand, not by who else is also working for a similar purpose."[5] The HUAC brought Women Strike for Peace, an American women's organization that lobbied against aboveground nuclear bomb testing and other issues, in for questioning in 1962 because of supposed communist subversion. Yet women who worked for world peace would not be silenced. As we will see, the persistence of women's peace organizations contributed to the decline of McCarthyism in the early 1960s and the enactment of the 1963 ban on aboveground nuclear testing.

PEGGY SEEGER

Peggy Seeger (1935–) wrote over a dozen songs about the Cold War from the mid-1950s to the early 1990s. Few songwriters addressed the conflict for such a long span of their career. The first Cold War song in her most comprehensive songbook, *The Peggy Seeger Songbook*, is "There's Better Things to Do" from 1956.[6] When the Cold War ended in 1989–1991, she was still writing about it with

"Sellafield Child" (1989) and "A Good War" (1991). Half sister to Pete Seeger, Peggy's family's political positions and networks highly influenced her. She grew up in the nexus of the folk revival and had met Woody Guthrie, Lead Belly, and Alan Lomax by the time she was ten.[7] In 1956 she met British folksinger Ewan MacColl, who fell in love with her and wrote "The First Time Ever I Saw Your Face" about her. Roberta Flack's 1972 cover version became a number one hit. Her relationship with and later marriage to him brought her into new vistas as she moved to London in the late 1950s and became part of the folk music scene there.

In 1957, Seeger was one of two hundred American musicians, dancers, and athletes who participated in the Sixth World Festival of Youth and Students in Moscow.[8] The festival's objective was to celebrate the cultures of the world (over thirty thousand people attended representing 130 countries) and foster a peaceful, antiwar stance among the youth. Seeger sang folk songs, spoke in Russian with other participants, and generally felt welcomed. The US State Department was suspicious of Americans traveling to Moscow but did not forbid it. Seeger and other American performers were then invited to travel to China, which brought harsh warnings of fines, loss of passports, and even incarceration from the State Department. Seeger took the risk and traveled to several cities in China. She wrote in her memoir, "We went because we came from liberal, progressive families reared on union songs and the Henry Wallace presidential campaign; we went because we were exercising our right to travel; we went for adventure for its own sake."[9] She was there for forty days. She walked on the Great Wall, had Zhou Enlai sign her banjo, and even met Mao Zedong.[10] In the years before the Great Leap Forward, the Great Famine, and the Cultural Revolution, which would result in deaths numbering in the tens of millions, American socialists regarded Mao as a great leader. Seeger was struck by the humility of the Chinese people, writing in her diary, "Americans, remember and learn this humility, for this is one of the aspects of this 'backward' country that is more forward than in our technically advanced age."[11] This trip to Moscow and China would play an instrumental role in her pursuit of cross-cultural understanding. It would also play a role in her inability to make an impact in the commercial music industry since she was labeled as a "fellow traveler." A *Life* magazine article called the World Festival of Youth, "Communism's sugar-coated device for mass brainwashing of youngsters from everywhere."[12] The article included a photograph of Peggy and fellow folksinger Guy Carawan with a caption that read, "Plugging 'peace,' Guy Carawan and Peggy Seeger strum banjos at Russian party for Americans. They sang 'Going to lay down that atom bomb.'"[13]

In 1953, England became the third country after the United States and the Soviet Union to successfully detonate an atomic bomb. In 1957, England successfully detonated their first hydrogen bomb. In 1957–1958, two British antinuclear organizations formed: Direct Action Committee (DAC) and Campaign for Nuclear Disarmament (CND). They organized the first Aldermaston March, which took place in April 1958. Peggy and Ewan participated. It began in Trafalgar Square and concluded fifty miles and three days later at the Atomic Weapons Research Establishment (AWRE) in Aldermaston, Berkshire, a massive facility where nuclear research was conducted and atomic and hydrogen bombs were assembled. Peggy recalls the experience: "As you topped the rises, you could see the procession snaking ahead, hyphenated by jazz bands, folk music groups, and companies of dancers. . . . We ate and slept in school halls, town halls, and gymnasiums, gathering ranks as we marched along. Ten thousand peacemongers walked past the barded-wire fence of Aldermaston in total silence."[14]

Peggy and Ewan wrote their first antibomb song in this period. Peggy recorded "There's Better Things to Do" and "March with Us Today," while Ewan recorded "Ballad of the Five Fingers," "Brother Won't You Join in the Line?," "That Bomb Has Got to Go," and "Song of Hiroshima." Most of these songs, which paired newly written antiwar lyrics with traditional melodies, were sung on the march and then included on the 1959 British LP *Songs Against the Bomb*.[15]

"There's Better Things to Do" is based on the gospel song "He's Got Better Things for You," a song performed in 1929 by Bessie Smith with the Memphis Sanctified Singers and released on the influential Folkways Records collection *Anthology of American Folk Music* (1952). Peggy's rewrite takes the focus off of divine intervention ("He's got better things for you, more than your friends can do") and instead focuses on work people should be doing *instead* of working toward war: raising children, living to old age, walking for peace. Another song from that period, "March with Us Today," lists people from all walks of life who had joined in the march to Aldermaston; men, women, children, lawyers, preachers, and singers joined the march to "ban the bomb! End the war!"

From the 1960s onward, feminism, parenthood, and environmentalism influenced Peggy's songs. Like Malvina Reynolds, her songs often urged parents to consider the future world they were bequeathing their children. "We Are the Young Ones" (1970) is a diatribe that exposes certain hypocrisies she saw in the education system. We teach children it is wrong to kill "face-to-face," yet it is okay to bomb civilians with aircraft "from above." The last verse ends with a bleak indictment, "From you we learned that power grows from the barrel of a gun."[16]

"The Invader" (1978) focuses on the production of fissionable materials for energy and bombs and the local transportation of nuclear waste near London. Peggy recalls, "I wrote 'The Invader' after discovering that consignments of these lethal materials passed by rail within a half a mile of my home in Beckenham, heading for west London where they sat overnight in a shunting yard."[17] Jean Freedman, Peggy Seeger's biographer, adds, "The trains ran on ordinary railway lines, close to suburban houses and less than a mile from Kitty's [Peggy and Ewan's daughter] school."[18] This led Peggy to form a study group and an organization, the Beckenham Anti-Nuclear Group (BANG). The analogy throughout "The Invader" is a reframing of the biblical creation narrative: the first six days were days of innocence, but "on the seventh day our kith and kin welcomed the dread invader in." In subsequent verses, the silent killer is revealed to be radiation from the production of nuclear energy and its subsequent toxic waste. After risking lives and environments for nuclear energy, "They pack him away into glass and steel . . . as if they were hiding their own black souls." The tonality of the song underpins its bleakness, drifting between the minor and Dorian modes.[19] Seeger also uses scordatura (in this case, drop D tuning) to tone paint the song: "When I sing this, I tune the sixth string of the guitar down to the low D. Throughout the whole song, I never play that D until the starred point in the last verse."[20] In this final verse, Seeger reminds listeners that the silent killer can always find its way out, and we always run the risk of transforming the earth into a "nuclear dustbin." The resolution to the low D happens at the phrase "a fitting end," emphasizing the finality and irreversibility of the effects of nuclear destruction, whether through warfare or by accident.

Peggy's songwriting about the Cold War intensified at the end of détente in the late 1970s. From 1978 until the end of the 1980s, Peggy condemned nuclear warfare incisively. She roundly criticized Margaret Thatcher and Ronald Reagan, whose rhetoric, she felt, could lead to World War III and the permanent devastation of the planet. In her introduction to "Plutonium Factor" (1980) in *The Peggy Seeger Songbook*, she outlines peaceful and creative protests she and others enacted to voice their objections to nuclear energy and nuclear waste.[21] Just as Joan Baez refused to pay the amount of taxes that went to the American military-industrial complex, recounted later in this chapter, Peggy and fellow objectors in England refused to pay the amount of their electrical bills that went to nuclear power. When the debt built up to the point their electricity would be cut off, they would pay in outrageously creative ways. One man from Dorset literally wrote out his check on a cow and led the cow into the bank. Peggy once wrote out her check on a rotten egg and, on another occasion, a piece of cake. Freedman explains, "British law did not require that checks be written in checkbooks; so long as all the appropriate information was supplied, any method could be used, a policy that Peggy exploited with wicked humor."[22] The rotten egg was "*very* gently presented" back to her on her doorstep. The cake was never seen again.[23]

Peggy describes "Plutonium Factor" as a "production piece," unfolding as a minidrama.[24] No longer reusing older folk songs or spirituals, she wrote both words and music. The song's form is highly original and complex, with odd, unexpected rhythms and frequent shifts in time signature, tempo, dynamics, and key. Some lines are spoken, some are sung, some include the harmonies of Ewan MacColl. The lyrics are rich in detail, showing Seeger's knowledge of the subject. Her chief source of information was Anna Gyorgy's 1979 book, *No Nukes: Everyone's Guide to Nuclear Power.*[25] The lyrics outline the production of nuclear energy from excavation, atom splitting, and the challenges of safely storing toxic waste. Much of the song consists of short phrases that deliver potent messages. For example, in the three-word phrase "plutonium never dies," she crystalizes the fact nuclear waste remains radioactive—and therefore deadly to humans—for tens or hundreds of thousands of years. There is no way, the song argues, to control the materials, either within their active use or by preventing them from being stolen by those intending to use them for evil purposes. She also invokes three accidents at nuclear facilities: the Kyshtym disaster in the Soviet Union in 1957 (Seeger has 1958 in her lyrics), the partial meltdown at the Three Mile Island Nuclear Generating Station near Harrisburg, Pennsylvania, in 1979, and the partial meltdown of the Fermi I reactor near Detroit in 1966. The song builds to a haunting children's chant of the locations of nuclear power plants across Great Britain. She gives instructions to chant "like a children's counting-out game."[26] The final verse is a call to action. We have the choice to shut down the nuclear plants or become "a unit in the body-count, a citizen of the Plutonium State."

Perhaps Seeger's most chilling Cold War song is "Four-Minute Warning" (1980). It refers to a public alert system used in England during the Cold War to warn of an imminent nuclear attack. Four minutes would have been the approximate length of time between the confirmation of an approaching Soviet missile and the explosion. Seeger's song consists of eighteen verses, each a rhyming couplet. Seeger sings it as a plaintive, unaccompanied, modal-melody chant. She invites the listener to imagine being at the top of a rotating tower in the center of London. From the tower, the listener can view the city and surrounding area as a hydrogen bomb explodes and winds carry radioactive fallout "way beyond Dover." Seeger got the idea from reading an article in *The Guardian* that "used concentric circles drawn around the centre of London to show what one nuclear bomb would do to our capital city and its environs."[27] The lyrics describe the devastation in brutal detail: most people die in the area from ground zero to six miles out in all directions. Further on, the explosion and fallout do not cause instant death, but this is no consolation. Many eventually perish from radiation poisoning, as verse 11 says, "The ones who are left may take ten years to die." As the song continues, so does the spread of fallout, which causes "12 million" fatalities, the approximate number of people in the London metropolitan area in 1980.

Not only does the song depict the geographical effects of the bomb, it describes the temporal effects as well. In verse 16, Seeger sings that future generations may be affected by genetic mutations. Another unique characteristic of "Four-Minute

Warning" is that it is to be sung in four minutes. Seeger makes this explicit in her songbook, where she writes, "Music note: The song should last exactly four minutes."[28] The listener experiences the visceral reality of how short four minutes feels and how inadequate it is to prepare oneself for a hydrogen bomb explosion. Regarding the warning, the British commonly jested, "Just enough time to boil an egg!"

Few songwriters addressed issues about the Cold War with such depth and incisiveness as Peggy Seeger. She wrote in her memoir, "Senator McCarthy & Co. were right to suspect folk musicians. . . . The bottom line: once released like a dove into the air, a song cannot be controlled. The singing of it can be forbidden or discouraged . . . but, unlike a dove, it cannot be shot down. . . . Music passed on via memory is a political and cultural weapon. Guarding a wondrous body of traditional music is a radical act—a political duty. A most pleasurable one."[29]

MALVINA REYNOLDS

Like Peggy Seeger, Malvina Reynolds (1900–1978) was a prolific songwriter and activist on Cold War issues. Yet unlike Seeger, who as a young girl knew Lead Belly, Woody Guthrie, and, of course, her half brother, Pete, Reynolds labored in relative obscurity for many years until she was recognized as an insightful and fearless political songwriter. Political songwriting came as naturally to her as breathing air. She once said, "When folk music came to the front, when I heard it I knew that was where I belonged. Here was my head full of poetry and music and they came together into songs so that everything I thought began to turn into songs. And because my thinking was social and political, quite a few of the songs had this character because that was the nature of my thinking."[30]

She is best-known for her song "Little Boxes" (1962), which explores the uniformity of suburban life. Pete Seeger made it famous with his 1963 cover, the first song on his album *Broadside Ballads, Vol. 2.*

Reynolds was born and raised in San Francisco. Lowell High School denied her diploma because her parents, David and Abagail Milder, who were Jewish socialists, opposed US participation in World War I. Nonetheless, she got into the University of California at Berkeley with the help of teachers, earning bachelor's and master's degrees in English. She later earned a PhD in romance philology in 1938.[31] While taking a course on ballads, she suggested they ought to be sung in class, not just read, and the professor asked her to sing them in class.[32] Like her father, she was blacklisted because of her writings in communist newspapers. She was never able to teach in her field. She had no qualms about the US entry into World War II in 1941 and worked on the assembly line of a bomb factory.[33]

In 1932, Reynolds and her family hosted a fundraiser for the Scottsboro boys, nine African American teenagers falsely accused of raping two white women in Alabama in 1931. During this fundraiser, the Ku Klux Klan attacked Reynolds and her family by burning a cross in their yard, breaking into their house, beating them, and attempting to kidnap them before police intervention.[34] This appears to be a galvanizing moment for Reynolds as she entered into her role as a political folksinger. Reynolds studied guitar with Earl Robinson in the 1940s and began performing songs, many of which she had written at left-wing political functions.[35] Because of her activism, she became involved with other musicians, including the network associated with People's Songs. She met Seeger in 1947, and he quickly came to appreciate her talent saying, "I had a lot to learn. Pretty soon she was turning out song after song after song!"[36] He covered her songs in performances. They also collaborated on songwriting; Reynolds wrote the lyrics and Seeger wrote the music. For Seeger's album *God Bless the Grass,* she wrote three of the songs and cowrote two with him. By the mid-1950s, Reynolds's politics had come under the scrutiny of the FBI.[37] In 1960, at the age of sixty, Folkways Records released her first album, *Another County Heard From.*

Her first song specifically about a Cold War issue is "RAND Hymn" from 1961. It is a scathing critique of the RAND Corporation. RAND was founded in 1945 as a think tank to inform and shape US policy regarding national security, health care, computing, space exploration, and other issues through research and analysis. RAND scientists and analysts in the 1950s and 1960s played a large role in formulating the doctrines of nuclear deterrence, which are still in use today. Reynolds focused her critique on RAND chief strategist, Herman Kahn, and his theories on nuclear warfare. Kahn's massive book, *On Thermonuclear War,* was released in 1960, a year before the song.[38] Reynolds cites Kahn and his book in the notes section of her 1964 songbook, *Little Boxes and Other Handmade Songs,* which includes "RAND Hymn."[39]

Much of Kahn's book concerns nuclear deterrence, but his other interests include: exploring how America could realistically prepare for, fight, and "win" a nuclear war; how many deaths (in millions or tens of millions) would be acceptable as long as the United States prevailed; and what the postatomic world might be like. In one section he postulates in detail how World War III might play out.[40] He does not stop there. He proceeds with great vigor for almost one hundred pages imagining what World Wars IV, V, VI, VII, and VIII (all of which involve hydrogen bombs) might look like.[41] Thoroughly engrossed in such speculation, he writes in one part, "The most exciting developments of World War VI will have occurred in the new missiles and satellites first seen in World War V."[42] One wonders while reading that if multiple nuclear wars can be considered, analyzed, and planned for with such vim, why peace and nuclear disarmament cannot be considered, analyzed, and planned for with the same vigor.

Reynolds's lyrics focus on how RAND analysts, such as Kahn, treat those dying in a nuclear war as merely numbers and not real people. The analysts transform people into "counters," "numbers," and "zeros." In the fourth verse, Reynolds addresses the protection that nuclear strategists will receive compared to ordinary citizens. Since they have "superior genes," they will be safe in underground bunkers, while the rest of the populace is "doomed to die." The last verse questions which is worse: the Soviets or the RAND analysts, who have so little regard for preserving human life and the planet. Three years after Reynolds's song, Kahn would also be targeted in Stanley Kubrick's 1964 film, *Dr. Strangelove or: How I Learned to Stop Worrying and Love the Bomb*. The titular character is partly based on Kahn. Strangelove commissions a feasibility study from analysts at the "BLAND Corporation"—an obvious play on RAND—about a "doomsday machine," a term for a device that would trigger a world-ending nuclear cataclysm. Kahn uses the term in his book.[43]

The topics of Reynolds's songs were wide-ranging. She wrote songs for children as well as songs from a child's or parent's perspective. Many songs focused on environmental issues, justice for the oppressed, and women's rights. All of these themes come together in her songs about Cold War issues, especially "What Have They Done to the Rain?" from 1962. After "Little Boxes" and "Morningtown Ride," it is perhaps her most well-known and frequently performed song. On her 1962 live album, *Joan Baez in Concert*, Baez introduced her cover of the song by saying it was "the gentlest protest song I know. It doesn't protest gently, but it sounds gentle."[44] "What Have They Done to the Rain?" has a lullaby quality, slow and lilting. The lyrics open with an idyllic scene. Gentle rain falls on the grass and a little breeze blows. A boy enters the scene, but then he and the grass eventually disappear as the rain continues to fall "like tears." Charles H. Smith and Nancy Schimmel (Malvina's daughter) write of the song,

> People now think of this as a song about acid rain, but it was originally written as part of a campaign to stop above-ground nuclear testing, which was putting strontium-90 in the air, where it was washed down by the rain, got into the soil and thence to the grass, which was eaten by cows. When children drank the cows' milk, the strontium-90, chemically similar to calcium but radioactive, was deposited in their bones. Mothers saved their children's baby teeth and sent them in to be tested by scientists who indeed found elevated levels of strontium-90 in their teeth. A year after this song was written, President Kennedy signed the treaty against above-ground testing.[45]

The boy in the song is an unfortunate "downwinder," someone unknowingly exposed to radioactive fallout carried by the rain and wind. Aboveground nuclear testing in the United States caused strontium-90, the toxic isotope in fallout damaging to humans and animals, to enter the food chain by going from air and rain to grass, to cows, to humans. Women passed on radiation to their babies through breast milk.[46] The song addresses the long-term effects of fallout from continuous bomb tests (rain that falls "for years") rather than a world-ending nuclear war, the subject of practically all other antibomb songs. Downwinders typically lived in the Great Basin area, mostly Nevada and Utah, where the jet stream blew fallout from the Nevada Test Site in a northeast direction. Thousands of downwinders suffered or died prematurely from cancer.[47] Crops, trees, and animal life were also affected. A 1952 government report stated that rainstorms intensify the effects of nuclear fallout: "It has been shown that rain is exceedingly effective as a means of producing the downward transport [of radioactive fallout] . . . rain which occurs in and over a newly formed atomic cloud might wash down a very large fraction of the debris to the ground and produce a major hazard."[48]

The hazards posed by fallout first came to the attention of citizens in the Great Basin in the mid-1950s. By the late 1950s, it was a nationwide concern, as evidenced by a two-part feature article in the *Saturday Evening Post* in 1959 titled "Fallout: The Silent Killer."[49] "What Have They Done to the Rain?" puts a human face, a child's face, on the threat Americans encountered from their own country's bombs.

"What Have They Done to the Rain?" was part of the movement against nuclear testing that unfolded from the Women for Peace and Women Strike for Peace (WSP) marches. Reynolds organized and participated in several marches and demonstrations, singing songs to the crowds and writing about her observations. On November 1, 1961, approximately fifty thousand women marched in over sixty cities to protest nuclear testing. As Catharine Stimpson summarizes, "Their goal was nothing less than peace on earth and the control of nuclear weapons."[50] In addition to the march, the women participated in a plethora of political activities, including contacting their congressmen and writing letters directly to both Jacqueline Kennedy and Nina Khrushchev, Nikita's wife.[51]

By 1962, the WSP had drawn the attention of the HUAC, still on the hunt for communist sympathizers. Over a dozen women from the New York chapter received summons in November 1962 to appear at a hearing scheduled for December. The organization presented a unified front. Amy Swerdlow recounts, "The WSP response to the HUAC summons was so ingenious in its exploitation of traditional domestic culture in the service of radical politics that it succeeded in doing permanent damage to the committee's image."[52] At an emergency meeting, the women decided that "the WSP would embrace, as its own, every woman summoned before HUAC, regardless of her past or present political affiliations, even if she had not been a WSP activist."[53] They affirmed in a distributed pamphlet that, in Swerdlow's summary, "the WSP was saying, as it had since its inception, that traditional male-defined politics, either of the Right or of the Left, were obsolete in the nuclear age, as was the Cold War and hence the [HUAC] committee itself."[54] Dagmar Wilson (1916–2011), one of the cofounders of WSP, was among those summoned to testify. HUAC made a mistake with this move because it galvanized the solidarity of the WSP that was already in place. Further, like Paul Robeson interrogating his interrogators, the WSP women began to investigate their investigators and found they had "voted against all peace and civil rights legislation."[55] This led to women all across the country to write to the HUAC to volunteer their testimony.

The investigation into Dagmar Wilson in particular inspired Malvina to pen her song "The H.U.A.C." (1962).[56] It was printed in *Broadside* (an influential folk music magazine) alongside a *Philadelphia Inquirer* article recounting Wilsons's testimony.[57] Set to a rollicking melody, "The H.U.A.C." depicts the committee as a tired, outdated group that "pester the women who work against war" so that it can make headlines, thereby showing its importance and ensuring further funding from Congress. After Senator Joseph McCarthy was discredited in 1954 for overreaching in his hunt for communists, many Americans were tired of the HUAC's "stale hoop-dee-dee" and had little interest in their accusations.

The clear, witty, and nuanced responses of the WSP confounded the HUAC's lines of questioning. The press reception—and from that the reception of the general public—was brutal. The press recounted it as a farce, and this contributed to the collapse of the committee's reputation in the eyes of the American public. As Eric Bentley colorfully summarizes, "It was the fall of the HUAC's Bastille."[58] Further, the WSP march on November 1, 1961, in sixty cities, along with subsequent political efforts, caught the attention of President John F. Kennedy. Recognizing the role women played in the antinuclear movement, Kennedy met with editors of influential women's magazines to express his support for the continued involvement of women in foreign policy decisions.[59] Cooperation between Kennedy and Khrushchev eventually led to the Partial Nuclear Test Ban Treaty, which banned all testing of nuclear weapons in the atmosphere, in outer space, and underwater. Weapons could only be detonated underground, producing a marked reduction in the amount of strontium-90 in the environment. The treaty went into effect on October 10, 1963, six weeks before Kennedy was assassinated in Dallas. The WSP and other groups continued their political pressures throughout the early 1960s, and following the Cuban Missile Crisis in October 1962, public opinion supported de-escalation of the nuclear-arms race. Oregon senator Maurine Neuberger stated, "There is, indeed, a mother's vote, but it is not a sentimental vote. It is a vote that flows from the rational concern of any mother for the welfare of her children, and her natural and acute sensitivity to the survival of future generations in recognizable form. It is a vote cast for the genetic future of mankind."[60] Reynolds's songs document these milestones.

A year before she died in 1978, Reynolds summed up herself and her music this way,

> I don't think of myself primarily as a writer of children's songs. In fact, I tend to avoid that title, because the first thought is, you know, this nice old grandma who makes cookies and sings for kids, and that's not my character at all. I have a very acid edge toward many aspects of modern life, and I'm pretty outspoken about it. I don't mind crossing swords with people when I disagree with them, and I'm not your nice old grandma. However, I always make it clear that the reason I have this sharp cutting edge is because I do care for people. I care about children, and I think the world is ripping them off, taking away their natural environment and much more than that—the natural progression of their tradition—and leaving them stripped, uneasy, uncomfortable, and in deep trouble, and it's because of that that I'm so sharp.[61]

Malvina continued to perform until her death. Her legacy of protest songs continues with her daughter, Nancy Schimmel, who is a founding member of the organization Occupella, a group of five women songwriters who lead singing at marches, meetings, and demonstrations in the Bay Area.[62] Their website, occupella.org, has political songs and parodies they have written and collected, as well as advice on how to start local Occupella groups.

JOAN BAEZ

While the Cold War affected most of the early folk singers after they reached adulthood, Joan Baez (1941–) confronted it in her youth. Her father, Albert Baez (1912–2007), was a brilliant scientist, who earned a PhD from Stanford University in 1950. He coinvented the x-ray reflection microscope. During the early years of the Cold War, his physics research in the defense industry gave him an understanding of the destructive power of the atomic bomb. While many of his colleagues went off to work at Los Alamos, he had a crisis of conscience.[63] After joining a Quaker fellowship, Albert chose to reject the lucrative positions offered to him and instead became a professor. Joan writes, "As for my father, whose struggles of conscience had drawn us to Quaker Meetings in the first place, in that austere silence he became a pacifist. Rather than get rich in defense work, he would become a professor. We would never have all the fine and useless things little girls want when they are growing up. Instead we would have a father with a clear conscience. Decency would be his legacy to us."[64]

Her father's example, as well as her exposure to Quaker teachings on pacifism, shaped Joan's core values. In fact, Joan's first "protest" was against one of the Cold War rhythms, the air-raid drill. In 1958, when she was seventeen, her high school in Palo Alto, California, planned a drill.[65] Rather than ducking and covering, as the younger kids did, high school students were to call their parents, walk calmly home, and go to the basement. She already knew from her father that "the time it took a missile to get from Moscow to Paly High was not enough time to call our parents or walk home."[66] Joan did the math and quickly realized the pointlessness of the exercise. When the drill came, she refused to leave the classroom. Word of her action got out, and a news reporter came to the school that afternoon. The February 7, 1958, issue of the *Palo Alto Times* included an article about her protest. She told the newspaper reporter, "I don't see any sense in having an air raid drill. I don't think it's a method of defense. Our only defense is peace."[67] In following days, "letters to the editor streamed in, some warning that Palo Alto had communist infiltrators in its school system."[68] During her high school years, she discovered not only her social conscience but also her beautiful, vibrato-rich voice. Singing at first to entertain her friends, and often accompanying herself on the ukulele, she soon began to explore the music of folk musicians like Odetta, Harry Belafonte, and Pete Seeger.[69]

At a Quaker event, Baez heard Martin Luther King Jr. speak and subsequently saturated herself in the teachings of nonviolence. She carefully studied the writings of Mahatma Gandhi, Henry David Thoreau, and other proponents of nonviolence, preparing herself for a life of activism.[70] At the ripe old age of twenty-two, she sang "We Shall Overcome" in front of two hundred and fifty thousand people at the March on Washington for Jobs and Freedom on August 28, 1963, during which King gave his famous "I Have a Dream" speech. Fighting for civil rights for African Americans became a seminal pursuit in her life, yet she saw it as a strand within her work for justice around the world.

Joan's commitment to pacifism sometimes put her at odds with both the right and the left. Both extremes, in her view, embraced militarism as a core value. Pacifism, she believed, would undercut both extremes. The reception of her work has sometimes framed her as "not left enough." Avital H. Bloch, for example, frames her as a feminist who has not fully matured, writing,

> True to her leftist politics and her rather unexamined gender stance, Baez developed the most powerful weapons in her own arsenal toward the goal of peace. She had, by the end of the 1960s, learned to direct the "feminine" qualities that had once defined and sometimes limited her, to the very

> causes that the movement had deemed "masculine": war resistance and unequivocal condemnation of U.S. foreign policy. Like many woman [*sic*] of the pre-feminist or bridge generation, Baez held on to traditional gender notions, in her politics as in her music, even as she in fact lived the life of a radicalized, indeed liberated, woman.[71]

Bloch frames the transitional period in which Baez came to maturity well. However, Baez herself would take issue with both being categorized as a "leftist," as well as the idea that any political stance—left or right, even the intricacies of gender politics—should take precedence over the ultimate goal of world peace. Baez was not afraid to protest war and spoke out against abuses from either side, whether right or left, capitalist or communist.

Beginning in 1964, she drew the attention of the US government, through her public letter to the IRS in which she refused to pay the percentage of her taxes that would go to the military.[72] Her popularity—and perhaps her gender—protected her from certain consequences, such as blacklisting, experienced by some of the preceding generation of musicians like Paul Robeson and Pete Seeger. However, her wages were garnished, and she did spend time in the San Rita Rehabilitation Center in 1967 for protesting the draft.[73] Her husband, David, was also incarcerated for refusing his draft and was in jail when Joan played at the Woodstock Festival in August 1969. She was six months pregnant with their son, Gabriel, at the time.

Baez also experienced direct Cold War–related censorship when she toured in Japan in 1967 to promote her albums. She went to raise support for peace groups and for the families of the victims of the Hiroshima and Nagasaki bombings. She did not speak Japanese, nor did the other members of her entourage. She hired a translator, Ichiro Takasaki, to interpret during her tour but was puzzled by the response of the audience during moments when she would speak about her songs and politics—they would often laugh or look amused at moments when she spoke with great seriousness.[74] During the tour, Baez traveled to Hiroshima to perform at a concert and on a television show. During the Hiroshima concert, she spoke about the devastation of the atomic bomb there and in Nagasaki. Takasaki simply said, "The show would be televised." When Baez spoke of the dangers of atomic bomb testing as an introduction to Malvina Reynolds's song "What Have They Done to the Rain?," again Takasaki simply muttered, "The show would be televised." She soon realized that Takasaki was not translating her speeches. She had to hire another translator. After she returned to the United States, Baez found out what was going on. In the February 21, 1967, issue of the *New York Times*, Peter Braestrup reported that Takasaki intentionally garbled Baez's words because an American man identifying himself as "Harold Cooper" pressured him to do so.[75] Takasaki assumed Cooper was a CIA agent because Cooper knew the name of his child and threatened to revoke his US travel visa. According to an article in the *Washington Star,* Takasaki said that Cooper told him, "If Joan Baez says something political, don't translate it correctly, but say something else."[76] At the time, the CIA and the American Embassy in Tokyo denied Takasaki's allegation or the existence of any such "Harold Cooper."

Although our research does not cover many Vietnam War songs, since much has been written on them already, we're choosing to make an exception here for Baez's underappreciated 1973 song "Where Are You Now, My Son?" Although her 1967 song "Saigon Bride," cowritten with Nina Dusheck, has received attention, "Where Are You Now, My Son?" has not.[77] Charles J. Fuss calls it "an underrated relic of the U.S. anti-war movement."[78] The song is a personal snapshot of Baez's time in Hanoi, North Vietnam, in December 1972, two weeks that crucially shaped her life and music. She was invited to Hanoi to deliver Christmas mail to American POWs and wound up in the middle of Operation Linebacker II, the largest bombing raid since World War II. Baez arrived in Hanoi on December 16, and the bombing campaign took place between December 18–29, using B-52 "Stratofortress" bombers.[79] This raid counts as one of the largest in the history of warfare, with over seven hundred individual nighttime sorties dropping over fifteen thousand tons of bombs on Hanoi and the surrounding area.[80] This amount of explosive energy is equivalent to the fifteen kiloton atomic bomb that destroyed Hiroshima. Although Baez did deliver the Christmas mail to the American POWs, she spent most of her days going back and forth between her room in the Hoa Binh Hotel and the basement bomb shelter, trying to help people in need on the streets.[81] Among those who shared the experience with her (and whose voices are on the recording) were Episcopal minister Michael Allen, Vietnam veteran Barry Romo, Cuban sailor Monti, and Columbia law professor, ex-Brigadier General, and prosecutor at the Nuremburg Trials Telford Taylor. One tragic incident haunted her. One morning in the Kan Thiem section of the city after a night of extensive bombing, she heard a Vietnamese woman crying out as she walked back and forth over a small patch of ground. The words she sang translate as, "My son, my son. Where are you now, my son?" Baez wrote in her memoir, "Oh, heaven and earth. Such depths of sadness cannot exist. I crumpled to the ground and covered my face and sobbed. That woman's boy lay somewhere under her feet packed into an instantaneous grave of mud, and she, like a wounded old cat, could only tread back and forth over the place she'd last seen him, moaning her futile song. *Where are you now, my son?*"[82]

Baez and her companions finally escaped Hanoi on a Chinese plane and eventually made it back to San Francisco on New Year's Day. After she recovered from the harrowing experience, she wrote the twenty-two-minute song, which takes up the second half of her 1973 album of the same title.[83]

To create the song, she utilized portions of the fifteen hours of audio she and Michael Allen recorded on cassette tapes during the trip. Interspersed between sections of spoken-word poetry and a sung chorus, both in rhyming couplets, she weaves together sounds of "the sirens, the bombs, Phantoms [supersonic fighter-bombers], B-52's, anti-aircraft, the children laughing, Monti talking, the Vietnamese singing, myself singing in the shelter."[84] The quick cuts between the audio clips accentuate the chaos of war. There are even moments of laughter. A melodic piano underscores the spoken word and sung sections. In the choruses the first line varies across iterations, but the second is always, "Where are you now, my son?" There are also fragments of songs, such as Baez singing "Kumbaya" and "The Lord's Prayer" and a group singing "Silent Night," bringing attention to the fact the bombing took place during Christmas. She quite literally created a soundtrack of war. The alternation between moments of normalcy—conversation, song, friendship—with the sounds of chaos and death brings the listener into the scene and creates a space of empathy for any who have experienced such devastation. There is no enemy or "other" in this space, only the shared experience of loss, fear, and love and a plea for forgiveness for the "rows of tiny coffins we've paid for with our souls." See table 2.1 for an analysis of the song.

Since Baez is known for her vibrato-rich singing style, her spoken-word recitation comes as a bit of a surprise. Perhaps the recitation is meant to be a poetic field report of the battle, as if she is a journalist there on the front lines. Although the spoken word sections relate experiences from Baez's point of view, they feel like a news report, cold and objective. The choruses, with her emotive singing, provide contrast. These are warm and subjective from the perspective of the mother who has lost her son. Baez sums up the piece on the back cover of the LP: "I am passing on to you, as clearly and as powerfully as I can, this gift which was extended to me by the sheer chance of being somewhere at the right time in history and living through it. The war in Indochina is not yet over, and the war against violence has barely begun."[85]

Six years later in 1979, she stirred up controversy about the war by writing an open letter that criticized the Socialist Republic of Vietnam. It appeared in four major US newspapers. She condemned the government's incarceration of political dissenters, forced disappearances, and use of humans to clear live minefields. The letter surprised many Americans, who viewed Baez as a strident left-winger, since she was a key figure in the folk music scene, sung at Woodstock, traveled to Hanoi during the Vietnam War, and protested against America's actions in the war. Liberals called her a "CIA rat," while conservatives like William F. Buckley Jr. and California governor Ronald Reagan praised her.[86] Regardless of political affiliation, Baez once again reinforced her stance for human rights and against violence.

Table 2.1 Analysis of "Where Are You Now, My Son?" by Joan Baez

Timing	Section	Content
0:00–2:22	Recorded audio	Sounds include an air-raid siren, voice of Episcopal priest Michael Allen, aircraft, bombs exploding, and cries of a Vietnamese mother who has lost her son.
2:22–3:09	Spoken-word stanza 1	Sounds of suffering civilians are heard.
3:09–3:31	Spoken-word stanza 2	Sorrow and weeping of the mother who has lost her son can be heard.
3:31–3:53	Sung chorus	
3:53–4:17	Spoken-word stanza 3	Baez helps an elderly man walk amid the rubble. He thanks her in German.
4:17–4:38	Spoken-word stanza 4	Reaction of Hanoi children to American visitors and Vietnamese mourning those who died in the previous night's raid.
4:38–5:00	Sung chorus	
5:00–5:23	Spoken-word stanza 5	Siren prompts the civilians in Hanoi to go to an air-raid shelter.
5:23–10:13	Recorded audio	Cuban sailor Monti says that civilians in the shelter feel that time passes faster when they are being bombed rather than when they are waiting for the attack. He says he is not fearful, since you only have to die once. He and Baez sing and quote Doris Day's song "Que Sera, Sera (Whatever Will Be, Will Be)." Baez and the others in the shelter make jokes and laugh to pass the time. Explosions and antiaircraft fire are heard. Baez leads a singing of "Kumbaya," altering the lyrics to fit the occasion ("No more bombing, Lord, Kumbaya"). More jokes and laughter take place in the shelter.
10:13–10:38	Spoken-word stanza 6	Those in the villages have no access to the shelters in Hanoi. With no air-raid sirens to warn them of danger, some die out in the open or in their beds as they are sleeping.
10:38–11:01	Sung chorus	
11:01–11:23	Spoken-word stanza 7	Six American B-52 pilots are shot down and become prisoners of war.
11:23–12:47	Recorded audio	Baez describes the pilots and their injuries.
12:47–13:10	Spoken-word stanza 8	A short Christmas service is held at the prison camp. The prisoners ask Baez to sing her 1971 hit, the Band's "The Night They Drove Old Dixie Down."

Timing	Section	Content
13:10–13:32	Sung chorus	
13:32–13:54	Spoken-word stanza 9	Back at the Hoa Binh Hotel, Baez and the others celebrate Christmas. Prayers are drowned out by the bombs.
13:54–18:34	Recorded audio	A recording of "Silent Night" is played. Baez leads a singing of The Lord's Prayer. An air-raid siren, bombs, aircraft, and antiaircraft guns are heard.
18:34–18:52	Spoken-word stanza 10	Baez and others listen to two Vietnamese women singing, filling the shelter with merriment.
18:52–20:00	Recorded audio	Two Vietnamese women sing a lively song accompanied by an accordion player.
20:00–20:22	Sung chorus	
20:22–20:46	Spoken-word stanza 11	Baez praises those in the shelter for their bravery and humanity. Humbled by their kindness, she asks their forgiveness.
20:46–21:08	Spoken-word stanza 12	Baez likens the Bac Mai hospital in Hanoi, which was accidentally bombed, to the lotus, the national flower of Vietnam. Both will "blossom once again."
21:08–21:39	Sung chorus	

As her work continued through the 1970s, Baez became involved with Ginetta Sagan (1925–2000), an activist who helped establish many chapters of Amnesty International. Sagan's parents were both killed under Mussolini, and she escaped imprisonment and torture by emigrating to the United States. Together, Sagan and Baez raised awareness of Amnesty and traveled the world to protest human rights abuses, many caused by Cold War confrontations. Later on, Baez participated in Amnesty's A Conspiracy of Hope tour in 1986 and Human Rights Now! tour in 1988, which will be discussed in more detail in chapter 6.

Baez's protests against nuclear warfare were a natural extension of her stance against all warfare—a stance she developed in her youth and galvanized through experiences such as her time in Vietnam. Perhaps her most famous cover of a specifically nuclear song is her frequent performance of Malvina Reynolds's ballad "What Have They Done to the Rain?" Baez released it on her 1962 album, *Joan Baez in Concert*. Like Malvina Reynolds and Peggy Seeger, Baez's work with protest spanned decades and addressed multiple issues. Out of the three, Baez was the most involved in a global perspective on Cold War issues, reaching beyond the United States and the United Kingdom and working toward direct involvement on the international stage. She said in 1970, "Music alone isn't enough for me. If I'm not on the side of life in action as well as in music, then all those sounds, however beautiful, are irrelevant to the only real question of this century: how do we stop men from murdering each other, and what am I doing with my life to help stop the murdering?"[87]

JANET GREENE

One might expect that all folk singers writing about the Cold War would espouse liberal, left-wing ideas since a distinctly left-wing political environment fostered the 1940s folk revival. Yet conservative, right-wing folk singers existed as well, especially in the 1960s. The Goldwaters (named after conservative senator Barry Goldwater) released an album in 1964 humorously titled *The Goldwaters Sing Folk Songs to Bug Liberals*. Their song "Down in Havana" criticizes the Kennedy administration's failed Bay of Pigs invasion of Cuba. It contends Castro's regime could have been defeated if the ground troops had been supported by air cover. In 1965, the Spokesmen recorded the optimistic "Dawn of Correction," a response to P. F. Sloan's pessimistic antiwar song "Eve of Destruction." It argues, among other things, that the nuclear-arms race prevented nuclear war ("the buttons are there to ensure negotiation"). Tony Dolan's album of right-wing folk songs *Cry the Beloved Country* came with a ringing endorsement on the back cover from conservative intellectual William F. Buckley Jr. Two decades later, in the 1980s, Dolan became one of President Ronald Reagan's chief speechwriters. Tired of the left-wing monopoly on popular music, these musicians sought to counter the counterculture.[88] The most noteworthy of the conservative folk singers was Janet Greene.

Little has been written about Greene in scholarly literature. The team of researchers at *CONELRAD* laid the groundwork, however, in their box set *Atomic Platters* and on their extensive website.[89] Born in 1930, Greene sang brilliantly even as a child. She studied music at the Cincinnati Conservatory of Music throughout her teenage years.[90] In her early twenties, a local television producer hired her to perform Cinderella in a children's television series. Greene acted for three years but quit in 1958 after a station manager, Mortimer C. Watters sexually harassed her. She went the following day to retrieve her guitar and personal effects, and he had her arrested for disorderly conduct. Infuriated, she refused bail and remained in jail. She was embarrassed, however, that the press compared this to a sit-in since her mind associated that term with left-wingers. When her case was tried, the charges were dismissed. She followed up by suing for wrongful termination of employment. Fairly surprising—for a female employee at the time—she won. In an interview she stated, "If it had been later on I could have sued him for sexual harassment. He did everything he could possibly do wrong."[91] She found employment again as Cinderella on another television network, this time in Columbus, Ohio. In 1964, she gained the attention of Fred Schwarz of the Christian Anti-Communism Crusade (CACC).

Fred Schwarz, a physician from Australia, believed that communism was a global conspiracy that threatened all democratic, Christian nations, especially America. He left his medical practice, founded the CACC in 1953, and moved to California in the early 1960s. During his over forty-year tenure as chairman of this nonprofit organization, he authored books, gave lecture tours, and published newsletters.[92] In 1964, he hired David Greenroos, Janet's Greene's husband, to work for the Crusade. Schwarz then recruited Greene to write anticommunist songs to bring a musical element into his talks and rallies. Greene agreed that communism threatened America, once saying, "Our American heritage and Christian religion are in great jeopardy. The enemy is Communism. Communism denies the existence of God, the individual right to freedom of choice and [a] woman's right to raise her own family as God intended."[93] Yet she was somewhat reluctant to embark on this new venture: "My husband was the one who wanted me to do it. . . . He was the one who was the most driven."[94] On how she wrote her songs, Greene said, "Well, I sang, of course, at all of the meetings. What I would do is, I would listen to his [Schwarz's] speeches from office recordings and I wrote all of these songs. I got the gist for most of them from his speeches and then I'd set them to music."[95] Schwarz oftentimes directed Greene's career as an anti-communist folk singer, a fact she later acknowledged; however, her songwriting was born from a sincere love for the values she believed defined America: faith, family, and freedom.

Greene was often contrasted with Joan Baez and was sometimes called the "anti-Baez." At the core of Joan Baez's songs is an antithesis between violence and peace. At the core of Janet Greene's songs is an antithesis between communism and freedom. She felt deeply uncomfortable, however, being framed as against Baez, as she greatly admired her musicianship and had attended one of her concerts.[96] Like Baez, Greene combined a flexible and deeply expressive singing voice with an imaginative, and sometimes humorous, lyrical style.

Greene is credited as sole songwriter for four of her eight anticommunist songs: "Poor Left-Winger," "Hunter and the Bear," "Fascist Threat," and "Commie Lies." Fred Schwarz wrote the words to "Comrade's Lament" and "Run." Poet Vincent Godfrey Burns wrote the words of "Termites." The words to "Inch by Inch" are credited to Janet and her husband, David. Greene wrote all the music but borrowed the melody for "Commie Lies" from "The Blue-Tail Fly," also known as "Jimmy Crack Corn." The eight songs were released in 1966 on four

45 singles.[97] Schwarz also included the eight songs on his four LP set of lectures titled *What Is Communism?*[98] Although Schwarz paid Greene and her husband $500 a week for the work they were doing, she received no remuneration or royalties from sales of her records since all the money went to the Crusade.[99] In 1967, she and Schwarz parted ways due to friction between him and her husband. She continued singing as a lounge act for the next three decades.

Greene was a talented singer-songwriter, but her songs bear the mark of her previous career as a performer on a children's show. Although her lyrics contain thoughtful content, the eight songs sound as if they were written for children. This perhaps hindered them from garnering more serious consideration. She presents her viewpoints clearly and directly, using simple metaphors and catchy melodies. This approach was perhaps intentional. David Noebel (a friend and associate of Fred Schwarz) claimed that communists attempted to lure young listeners, even children, into their camp by using simple folk songs with communistic messages. In his 1965 pamphlet, *Communism, Hypnotism and the Beatles,* he writes that the record label Children's Record Guild is nothing more than a communist front. He warns that "the communists have not entered into the children's recording field for any humanitarian purpose. Just the opposite is the truth. . . . These Children's Record Guild records were . . . scientifically calculated to nerve-jam the minds of our children."[100] Perhaps Schwarz and Greene took this approach to counteract what they believed the communists were doing with children's songs.

Janet Greene's work with CACC was emblematic of a larger movement among conservative women to rid the United States of communism. Conservative wives and mothers had been convinced that communists could prey on the minds of impressionable children and young adults and convert them with propaganda and sophistry. Michelle M. Nickerson writes, "Adapting long-standing ideas about women's natural gifts of patience, intuition, and common sense to McCarthy-era necessities, female activists undertook red hunting as a political contribution that they saw themselves well suited to make to the nation. The new 'brainwashing' discourse unleased in the post-World War II era also deepened the involvement of women, who felt it was their maternal duty to protect the delicate minds of children from those who would use their position in the education or psychology fields to politically program youngsters."[101]

Several of Greene's songs make this endeavor to protect children's minds explicit, especially "Commie Lies."

"Commie Lies" (1964) is one of Greene's earliest songs and a favorite of Schwarz.[102] Based on the song "The Blue-Tail Fly," which in its early guises was associated with blackface minstrelsy in the mid-nineteenth century, the acoustic guitar and banjo accompaniment suggest a lightness and humor that contrasts with the heavy warning embedded in the song. An example of this is communism being Satan's new disguise. However, these same qualities would help embed the song in a listener's memory to remember the warnings when presented with communist temptations. The chorus enjoins, "Be careful of the commie lies, swallow them and freedom dies."

"Hunter and the Bear" is a jaunty rock and roll song. It uses the proverbial understanding of Russia as a "bear." Russia has been symbolized as a bear by Western Europe and America for hundreds of years. Both Stalin and Khrushchev were often referred to as "the Russian bear" throughout the Cold War. The hunter is a naive American who just wants to get along and peacefully coexist with the bear. The twist at the end comes when the hunter puts down his gun and offers his hand in friendship. The bear gets what he wants, a full stomach, while the hunter is "on the missing persons list, since he tried to coexist."

In contrast to the jolly quality of "Hunter and the Bear," "Termites" is a dark and heavy-handed ballad. Greene sets the tone with a slow tempo, minor key opening, and a melody that gradually arches up before tumbling back into her voice's low registers. In its brooding narrative, communists are depicted as an unseen swarm of termites who chew through the foundations of the American democratic system with "murderous malice."

"Comrade's Lament" is based on Bavarian folk music with guitar and zither-like accompaniment. It paints a picture of a stereotypical communist as someone who sheepishly follows Stalin, unhappily works, and generally leads a miserable life. In "Fascist Threat," Greene employs a calypso rhythm. The lyrics sketch out the basic elements of a fascist state—a small political party that dominates, a dictator, and a centralization of power—and then equates communism with fascism. She warns of both ideologies, saying, "Freedom dies if either wins." "Inch by Inch" addresses both the Vietnam War and the domino theory. Even though small and far away, Vietnam must be defended militarily to stop the gradual encroachment of communism. "Run" is about Cuban refugees fleeing from Castro's regime and seeking freedom in America.

"Poor Left Winger" is Greene's most well-known song. The protagonist is a *dupe*, a frequent term (like *fellow traveler*) used by right-wingers for naive individuals lured by the false hope of communism. Beguiled by a plaintive communist folk song, she follows a ragged left-wing radical to college and participates in violent protests. Believing his rhetoric for a while, she eventually realizes that "hidden behind that beard beat the heart of a frustrated heel." Set in a country style, the story echoes the common country music cliché of a woman who follows a man only to realize he has done her wrong.

It's also possible to see this as an inverted image of her relationship with Fred Schwarz and David Greenroos. Pressured into singing songs for the right-wing circuit, she eventually realizes they also treated her wrongly. After three years, she pulled out of her association with Schwarz. She and Greenroos divorced in 1977.[103] Just as she had little patience with the on-the-job harassment she experienced during her television career, Janet Greene quickly tired of the pressures put on her by Greenroos and Schwarz. After trying unsuccessfully to restart her television career, she settled into singing at local restaurants and nightclubs. After divorcing Greenroos, she met and married a billboard painter named Jose Nieto. In her *CONELRAD* interview, she recounted how Jose had the opportunity to paint a portrait of a well-known celebrity. Later on, Jose sent the man a copy of the portrait. Jose and Janet were quite thrilled to receive a personal letter from the man and his wife, who happened to be Ronald and Nancy Reagan. In retrospect, exploitative and misogynistic men had, at times, manipulated Greene, but her clear voice—as she fought for her career and the right to express her own viewpoints—ultimately sounded like a descant above the currents of her time.

CONCLUSION

Peggy Seeger visited the Soviet Union and China. Joan Baez visited North Vietnam in order to promote peace and make human connections with those on the other side of the Cold War. Given the opportunity, Malvina Reynolds most likely would have traveled to "enemy territory" as well. Janet Greene saw her role as defending the American ideals of faith, family, and freedom. Summarizing two streams of female activism during the Cold War, Tarah Brookfield writes, "Some activists restricted their international connections to other Western nations or to those fighting the good fight against communism. To do otherwise, they believed, threatened their patriotism. . . . Other activists purposely extended open arms and made it a point to find common interests with 'enemy' women in the Soviet Union, mainland China, and North Vietnam."[104]

Most of the women who wrote songs about the Cold War were in the folk idiom. Why was this so? First, folk music provided a forum for political debate, so songs with political content naturally fit the genre. Second, folk music during the Cold War was a seedbed for leftist, progressive politics, feminism being one of those components. Susan J. Douglas writes, "That young women could be political, even radical—and be admired for it—was becoming accepted on the fringes of American popular culture and powerfully reinforced through the huge folk music revival of the 1960s. . . . [Female folksingers] showed that being female and being political were not mutually exclusive; in fact, they were complementary. And they made this critically important, if subtle, link: that challenging norms about femininity itself was, in fact, political."[105]

Women musicians in other styles, such as rock and pop, often had to conform to the roles assigned by male record producers and executives. The four women discussed in this chapter were simply themselves. As much as possible in a world dominated by white men, female folk musicians sought to be appreciated on the merits of their singing and songwriting alone. As a result they produced some of the most insightful songs about the Cold War—and warfare in general.

NOTES

1. Joanne Meyerowitz, "Introduction," in *Not June Cleaver: Women and Gender in Postwar America, 1945–1960*, ed. Joanne Meyerowitz (Philadelphia: Temple University Press, 1994), 1–2.
2. Elaine Tyler May, *Homeward Bound: American Families in the Cold War Era*. 20th anniversary ed. (New York: Basic, 2008), 1–6.
3. Meyerowitz, "Introduction," 2, 3.
4. Robbie Lieberman, "'Does That Make Peace a Bad Word?': American Responses to the Communist Peace Offensive, 1949–1950," *Peace and Change* 17, no. 2 (April 1992): 198–228.
5. "Materials for Discussion, Not for Distribution," Women's International League for Peace and Freedom, US Section Papers, Swarthmore College Peace Collection, Swarthmore, Pennsylvania, n.d. [c. 1952], quoted in Harriet Hyman Alonso, *Peace as a Women's Issue: A History of the U.S. Movement for World Peace and Women's Rights* (Syracuse, NY: Syracuse University Press, 1993), 169.
6. Peggy Seeger, *The Peggy Seeger Songbook: Warts and All: Forty Years of Songmaking* (New York: Oak Publications, 1998), 38–39.
7. Peggy Seeger, *First Time Ever: A Memoir* (London: Faber and Faber, 2017), 23–24.
8. Jean R. Freedman, *Peggy Seeger: A Life of Music, Love, and Politics* (Urbana: University of Illinois Press, 2017), 97–103.
9. Seeger, *First Time Ever*, 127.
10. Ibid., 130, 140.
11. Peggy Seeger, China diary, 7, privately held. Quoted in Freedman, *Peggy Seeger*, 100–101.
12. "Youth from 102 Lands Swarms over Moscow: U.S.S.R. Teaches—and Is Taught," *Life* 43, no. 7 (August 12, 1957): 22.
13. "Youth from 102 Lands Swarms over Moscow," 26. "Going to lay down that atom bomb" is a verse Guy and Peggy added to the spiritual "Down by the Riverside," also known as "Ain't Gonna Study War No More."
14. Seeger, *The Peggy Seeger Songbook*, 45.
15. *Songs Against the Bomb* (Topic 12001, 1959, LP).
16. Seeger, *The Peggy Seeger Songbook*, 99.
17. Ibid., 142.
18. Freedman, *Peggy Seeger*, 223.

19. The Dorian mode is similar to the natural minor (Aeolian) scale but with a raised sixth scale degree. "Greensleeves" is a familiar song in this mode.

20. Seeger, *The Peggy Seeger Songbook*, 143.

21. Ibid., 166.

22. Freedman, *Peggy Seeger*, 223.

23. Seeger, *The Peggy Seeger Songbook*, 166.

24. Ibid., 167.

25. Anna Gyorgy, and friends, *No Nukes: Everyone's Guide to Nuclear Power* (Boston: South End, 1979).

26. Seeger, *The Peggy Seeger Songbook*, 167.

27. Ibid., 164.

28. Ibid., *The Peggy Seeger Songbook*, 165.

29. Seeger, *First Time Ever*, 410–411.

30. *Love It Like a Fool: A Film About Malvina Reynolds*. Directed and edited by Susan Wengraf (Red Hen Films, [200-?], 1977, DVD), 3:18–3:50, https://www.youtube.com/watch?v=BvOscTN_354.

31. Malvina Reynolds: Song Lyrics and Poems website, created by Charles H. Smith and Nancy Schimmel, http://people.wku.edu/charles.smith/MALVINA/homep.htm.

32. Gabriel San Roman, "The Life and Times of Malvina Reynolds: Long Beach's Most Legendary (and Hated) Folk Singer," *OC Weekly*, August 31, 2016, http://www.ocweekly.com/music/the-life-and-times-of-malvina-reynolds-long-beachs-most-legendary-and-hated-folk-singer-7474438.

33. Nancy Schimmel, "Let's Go Dancing Til the Break of Day: A Remembrance of Malvina Reynolds," Harvard Square Library, http://www.harvardsquarelibrary.org/biographies/malvina-reynolds/.

34. Roman, "Life and Times of Malvina Reynolds."

35. Ibid.

36. "Pete Seeger describes his first visit with Malvina Reynolds," letter to Charles H. Smith dated February 13, 2006, Malvina Reynolds: Song Lyrics and Poems, http://malvinareynolds.com/.

37. Roman, "Life and Times of Malvina Reynolds."

38. Herman Kahn, *On Thermonuclear War* (Princeton, NJ: Princeton University Press, 1960).

39. Malvina Reynolds, *Little Boxes and Other Handmade Songs* (New York: Oak Publications, 1964), 94, 21.

40. Kahn, *On Thermonuclear War*, 417–428.

41. Ibid., 428–522.

42. Ibid., 478.

43. Ibid., 297.

44. *Joan Baez in Concert* (Vanguard VRS-9112, 1962, LP).

45. Charles H. Smith and Nancy Schimmel, notes to "What Have They Done to the Rain?," Malvina Reynolds: Song Lyrics and Poems, http://people.wku.edu/charles.smith/MALVINA/mr183.htm.

46. Joseph J. Mangano and Janette D. Sherman, "Elevated In Vivo Strontium-90 from Nuclear Weapons Test Fallout among Cancer Decedents: A Case-Control Study of Deciduous Teeth," *International Journal of Health Services* 41, no. 1 (2011):137–158.

47. Janet Burton Seegmiller, "Nuclear Testing and the Downwinders," https://historytogo.utah.gov/downwinders/.

48. Philip W. Allen and Lester Machta, *Transport of Radioactive Debris from Operations Buster and Jangle* (Washington, DC: US Department of Commerce, Weather Bureau, Armed Forces Special Weapons Project, 1952), 109.

49. Steven M. Spencer, "Fallout: The Silent Killer," *Saturday Evening Post* 232, no. 9 (August 29, 1959): 26–27, 87, 89–90; Spencer, "Fallout: The Silent Killer: How Soon Is Too Late," *Saturday Evening Post* 232, no. 10 (September 5, 1959): 25, 84–86.

50. Catharine R. Stimpson, "Foreword" in Amy Swerdlow, *Women Strike for Peace: Traditional Motherhood and Radical Politics in the 1960s* (Chicago: University of Chicago Press, 1993), ix.

51. Swerdlow, *Women Strike for Peace*, 21.

52. Ibid., 97–98.

53. Ibid., 98.

54. Ibid., 100.

55. Ibid., 104.

56. Charles H. Smith and Nancy Schimmel, notes to "The H.U.A.C.," Malvina Reynolds: Song Lyrics and Poems, http://people.wku.edu/charles.smith/MALVINA/mr218.htm.

57. Malvina Reynolds, "The H.U.A.C.," *Broadside #18* (Late December 1962): 1, https://singout.org/downloads/broadside/b018.pdf.

58. Eric Bentley, ed., *Thirty Years of Treason: Excerpts from Hearings before the House Committee on Un-American Activities, 1938–1968* (New York: Viking, 1971), 951.

59. Swerdlow, *Women Strike for Peace*, 95–96.

60. Ibid., 94.

61. Malvina Reynolds at the Pied Piper music festival in 1977, quoted in Schimmel's "Let's Go Dancing Til the Break of Day: A Remembrance of Malvina Reynolds," Harvard Square Library, http://www.harvardsquarelibrary.org/biographies/malvina-reynolds/.

62. Occupella website, http://www.occupella.org/.

63. Joan Baez, *And a Voice to Sing With: A Memoir* (New York: Simon and Schuster, 2009), 22–23.

64. Baez, *And a Voice to Sing With*, 24.

65. "Joan Baez in Palo Alto: Her First Protest," Palo Alto History.Org, http://www.paloaltohistory.org/joan-baez-in-palo-alto.php.

66. Baez, *And a Voice to Sing With*, 41.

67. "'Conscientious Objector' Stays at School during Test," *Palo Alto Times*, February 7, 1958, 1.

68. Baez, *And a Voice to Sing With*, 42.

69. Ibid., 43.

70. Markus Jäger, *Popular Is Not Enough: The Political Voice of Joan Baez: A Case Study in the Biographical Method* (Stuttgart, Germany: Ibidem, 2010), 46–67.

71. Avital H. Bloch, "Joan Baez: A Singer and Activist" in *Impossible to Hold: Women and Culture in the 1960s*, ed. Avital H. Bloch and Lauri Umansky (New York: New York University Press, 2005), 143.

72. Baez, *And a Voice to Sing With*, 120–121.

73. Ibid., 146.

74. Ibid., 135–137.

75. Peter Braestrup, "Joan Baez and the Interpreter, or What Japanese Didn't Hear," *New York Times*, February 21, 1967, 1, 34.

76. "Did CIA Seek to Change Quotes of Folk Singer?" *Washington Star*, February 21, 1967. Sanitized and released on the Central Intelligence Agency website, https://www.cia.gov/library/readingroom/document/cia-rdp75-00001r000300040002-9.

77. James E. Perone, *Songs of the Vietnam Conflict* (Westport, CT: Greenwood, 2001), 50.

78. Charles J. Fuss, *Joan Baez: A Bio-Bibliography* (Westport, CT: Greenwood, 1996), 20.

79. Tim Cahill, "Joan Baez in Hanoi: 12 Days under the Bombs," *Rolling Stone*, February 1, 1973, 1, 18–19.

80. James R. McCarthy and Robert E. Rayfield, *Linebacker II: A View from the Rock* (Washington, DC: United States Air Force, Office of Air Force History, 1985), 171.

81. Baez, *And a Voice to Sing With*, 193–225.

82. Ibid., 218.

83. Joan Baez, *Where Are You Now, My Son?* (A&M Records SP-4390, 1973, LP).

84. Baez, *And a Voice to Sing With*, 224–225.

85. Baez, liner notes from *Where Are You Now, My Son?*

86. Baez, *And a Voice to Sing With*, 273–281.

87. Joan Baez, "Playboy Interview: Joan Baez," interview by Nat Hentoff, *Playboy*, July 1970, 55.

88. Bill Geerhart of *CONELRAD* compiled a collection of right-wing folk songs on the CD titled *Freedom Is a Hammer: Conservative Folk Revolutionaries of the Sixties*. Liner notes by Bill Geerhart (Australia: Omni Recording Corporation OMNI-167, 2012, CD).

89. Bill Geerhart and Ken Sitz's liner notes for the five-CD, one-DVD box set *Atomic Platters: Cold War Music from the Golden Age of Homeland Security* (Hambergen, Germany: Bear Family Records BCD 16065 FM, 2005); *CONELRAD* website created by Ken Sitz, Bill Geerhart, and Curtis Samson, http://www.conelrad.com/index.php.

90. "Anti-Baez: The Ballad of Janet Greene," *CONELRAD*, http://www.conelrad.com/greene/index.php.

91. Janet Greene, "The Freewheelin' Janet Greene: The CONELRAD Interview," *CONELRAD*, April 24, 2004 and May 2, 2004, http://www.conelrad.com/greene/interview.php.

92. The Schwarz Report website, "About," https://www.schwarzreport.org/about.

93. Greene, "Anti-Baez."

94. Greene, "The Freewheelin' Janet Greene."

95. Ibid.

96. Greene, "The Freewheelin' Janet Greene."

97. The songs are accessible on the podcast "CONELRAD Cafe: Anti-Baez: The Ballad of Janet Greene," *CONELRAD*, http://www.conelrad.com/about/faces.php?faces=10.

98. Fred Schwarz, *What Is Communism?* (Cantico Records, 1966), four LP set.

99. Greene, "The Freewheelin' Janet Greene."

100. David Noebel, *Communism, Hypnotism and the Beatles* (Tulsa, OK: Christian Crusade, 1965), 4.

101. Michelle M. Nickerson, *Mothers of Conservatism: Women and the Postwar Right* (Princeton, NJ: Princeton University Press, 2012), 170.

102. "Anti-Baez: The Janet Greene Songbook," *CONELRAD*, http://www.conelrad.com/greene/janetgreene_songbook.php.

103. "Anti-Baez."

104. Tarah Brookfield, *Cold War Comforts: Canadian Women, Child Safety, and Global Insecurity, 1945–1975* (Waterloo, Ontario: Wilfrid Laurier University Press, 2012), 8.

105. Susan J. Douglas, *Where the Girls Are: Growing Up Female with the Mass Media* (New York: Times Books, 1994), 145, 148.

THREE

COUNTRY

The Conservative Stance

IN THE AFTERMATH OF WORLD WAR II, the Soviet Union rose as a superpower on par with the United States. While Americans in general viewed this as disturbing, most Southerners considered it to be downright revolting. Southerners, who valued a small federal government, states' rights, congregationalist church governance, and a healthy dose of individualism saw the Soviet Union's large government as a dangerous behemoth. Evangelicals in the Bible Belt, where church attendance was the highest in America and Christian morality guided everyday behavior, detested the Soviet Union's atheism. Southern preachers declared Stalin and Khrushchev to be the devil's henchmen. The Soviet Union's planned economy, controlled by government regulation and collectivization, was the opposite of the South's heritage of free market capitalism, antiunionism, and private ownership. Southerners, rooted in tradition and conservatism, viewed both communism and socialism as radical and revolutionist. Lastly, Southerners felt the Soviet Union was not fit to have a nuclear arsenal, since only America had the moral bearing to be a superpower and watchdog for the world.

All of this comes out in the plain folk language of Cold War country songs.[1] Country musicians were, for the most part, the only songwriters expressing right-wing, conservative, patriotic, religious, prowar viewpoints. Unlike other popular musical styles, where Soviet and American Cold War policy alike come under fire, the country songs are almost unanimous in commending America and condemning the Soviet Union. They issue warnings, make stern judgments, denounce opposition to US foreign policy, plead for conversion to Christ, and pray for God to preserve America from the evils of communism. America and the Christian church become one entity, while the Soviet Union is demonized. As a result, many of the Cold War songs from country performers sound like short musical sermons. This tight connection between country music and religious expression is no coincidence. Nashville, often referred to as "the buckle of the Bible Belt," is the nexus of both country music production and Southern Christianity.

This chapter begins by exploring the many country songs about atomic weapons and how their power points to the magnitude, and sometimes manifestation, of God's power. The following section explores songs about America's obsession with uranium mining in the mid-1950s. The remainder of the chapter groups together all the anticommunist songs by country songwriters and discusses how they expressed Southerners' opinions about McCarthyism, the Korean and Vietnam Wars, Soviet atheism, and the counterculture's flirtation with socialism.

THE ATOMIC BOMB AND GOD

In the early years of the Cold War, many songs were written about the atomic bomb, but no group wrote more than the country songwriters. Fred Kirby wrote the first song conceived about the subject, "Atomic Power," the day after the August 6, 1945, Hiroshima bombing. He did not release it until the summer of 1946.[2] The first song released was "When the Atom Bomb Fell" by Karl & Harty in early 1946.[3] From 1945 to 1963, at least thirteen country songs were written about the relationship between the bomb's power and God's power. See table 3.1.

Why did so many country musicians write about the atomic bomb? In short, the sheer destructive power of the bomb made Americans confront ultimate questions, and Southern songwriters, with their firmly held Christian beliefs, quickly answered them with the Bible. Charles K. Wolfe writes that "the country music audience—still heavily rural in 1946, still lower and middle class, still the product of southern Protestant values—must have seen in the atomic bomb a phenomenon for which no superlative in their vocabulary, no metaphor in their folk speech, was adequate. . . . Their natural response was to turn to the most effective superlative they knew: religion."[4]

In his 1948 book *This Atomic Age and the Word of God,* theologian Wilbur M. Smith shows that atheistic professors, nuclear physicists, congressional leaders, and President Truman quoted biblical passages in order to illustrate the impact of atomic weapons on human civilization.[5] Southern country songwriters unsurprisingly turned to the Bible as well since they believed it was divinely inspired and the final authority in all matters of life and doctrine. These songs show country musicians searching the scriptures for answers to the moral, political, and eschatological questions that the atomic bomb generated.

To get to the heart of these songs, it is necessary to survey the religious culture of the Southern states from which these songwriters arose. As it is today, the South during the Cold War hosted numerous conservative Christian denominations,

Table 3.1 Country Songs Comparing Atomic Bombs to God's Power

Song	Songwriter
"Atomic Power"	Fred Kirby
"When the Atom Bomb Fell"	Karl Victor Davis and Connecticut "Harty" Taylor
"There's a Power Greater Than Atomic"	Arval Hogan and Roy Grant (Whitey-Hogan)
"When They Found the Atomic Power"	Hawkshaw Hawkins and Big Slim
"When That Hell Bomb Falls"	Fred Kirby
"Jesus Hits Like an Atom Bomb"	Lee V. McCollum
"Brush the Dust from that Old Bible"	Bradley Kincaid
"Weapon of Prayer"	Ira and Charles Louvin
"The Great Atomic Power"	Ira and Charles Louvin and Buddy Bain
"The Song of the Atom Bomb"	S. C. McElhannon and M. A. Mayes
"Atomic Sermon"	Billy Hughes
"The Hydrogen Bomb"	Street Sawyer and Angus MacDonald
"God Guide Our Leader's Hand"	Tex Climer, Paul William, and Jimmy Martin

the largest being the Southern Baptist Convention. For the sake of simplicity, we'll be referring to these groups collectively with the term *Southern evangelicals*. The belief systems of fundamentalism, Pentecostalism, and dispensationalism, which were formulated in the late nineteenth and early twentieth centuries, heavily influenced many Southern evangelicals. While conservative values were by no means limited to the Southern states and musicians with conservative values came from all over the country, the South had a religious identity distinct from the rest of the country, hence the name "Bible Belt" from the 1920s to the present day. Most of the Southern evangelicals in the 1940s and 1950s, and by extension most of the country musicians who wrote songs about the atomic bomb, held the following generalized beliefs.

The first characteristic of Southern evangelicalism appearing in songs is the belief in God's omnipotence, his almighty power. The lyrics of "Atomic Power" say that since the bomb is so powerful, it could only have been "given by the mighty hand of God." "There's a Power Greater Than Atomic" warns that God's power is far greater than atomic power. "When That Hell Bomb Falls" and "The Song of the Atom Bomb" treat nuclear weapons as a warning from God of his might. In "Jesus Hits Like an Atom Bomb," the bomb is a sign of the second coming of Christ. Country songwriters saw in the atomic bomb evidence of God's

Performer	Year
Fred Kirby, the Buchanan Brothers, and others	1945–1946
Karl & Harty	1945–1946
The Buchanan Brothers	1947
Hawkshaw Hawkins	1947
Fred Kirby	1950
Lowell Blanchard and the Valley Trio, the Pilgrim Travelers, and the Soul Stirrers	1950–1951
Bradley Kincaid	1950
The Louvin Brothers	1951
The Louvin Brothers	1952
Dexter Logan and Darrell Edwards	1952
Billy Hughes and His Rhythm Buckaroos	1953
Al Rogers and His Rocky Mountain Boys	1954
Jimmy Martin	1963

supernatural power, and such a frightening device should cause one to "brush the dust from that old Bible," as the title of the Bradley Kincaid song says.

Second, the songs show the substantial influence preachers had on what Southerners believed and how they lived their lives. Charles H. Lippy writes, "Clergy have indeed long been near mythic figures in the Southern religious landscape. Arbiters of the divine will and catalysts of conversion, they have exercised a powerful influence in shaping Southern religious and cultural life."[6] Since many Southern churches held to a congregationalist polity, in which individual congregations ruled themselves rather than being under the authority of a larger ecclesiastical body, preachers had greater freedom to interpret scripture in their own manner. A common subject in sermons in the post-Hiroshima years was the atomic bomb. George Marsden posits that "nearly every preacher in the country preached a sermon on the bomb in the years following Hiroshima."[7] Preaching is mentioned in "The Song of the Atom Bomb," which warns that fire from an atomic explosion awaits unrepentant sinners who do not "heed the warning that's been preached far and near." The role of the preacher is made explicit in the appropriately titled "Atomic Sermon" by Billy Hughes, which warns the bomb is a sign of the end of the world. It begins, "Every Sunday mornin', the preacher gave his warnin'. . . . We're gettin' close to that great day."

Third, Southern evangelicals, especially fundamentalists, tended to take a literal interpretation of scripture, linking biblical prophecies and judgments directly to America's possession of atomic bombs.[8] Charles P. Roland writes that fundamentalists "interpreted literally the apocalyptic prophecies that were treated symbolically if not ignored by the major denominations."[9] "Brush the Dust from that Old Bible," "When That Hell Bomb Falls," and "The Song of the Atom Bomb" all express the view that the atomic bomb is an instrument of God's final judgment on sinful humanity. America's preeminent position in world politics is stressed in "When They Found the Atomic Power." It singles out America by saying the Manhattan Project scientists discovered atomic power with the help of God's "mighty hand" while the "Star-Spangled Banner" was playing in the background. "Atomic Power" and "When the Atom Bomb Fell" state that America and its bombs acted as God's instruments of divine judgment on Japan and describe the scorched landscapes of Hiroshima and Nagasaki like the Bible describes hell: "smoke," "fire," "brimstone," and "dust." Kevin S. Fontenot writes, "The fact that America had the bomb indicated that the nation was God's chosen instrument of destruction."[10]

Yet these songs do not reflect the opinions of all country songwriters or Southern evangelicals. Jimmy Martin's "God Guide Our Leader's Hand" pleads for God to assist "all nations" in refraining from using nuclear weapons. Rather than asserting America's favored position in the nuclear race, Martin wishes for a "great worldwide revival" to Christ. A similar sentiment can be found in the Louvin Brothers' "Weapon of Prayer," a song written at the end of World War II but not recorded and released until 1951 during the Korean War.[11] Although Charlie and Ira Louvin are remembered today mostly for the kitsch of their album cover of *Satan Is Real* (1959), country fans consider them among the best duos in the history of country music. The lyrics of "Weapon of Prayer" argue that prayer is a crucial weapon, as essential to winning a war as man-made weapons. The song lacks the vitriol and vengeance found in the other atom bomb songs and in the anticommunist songs studied later in this chapter. Charlie Louvin did a tour of duty in Korea in 1953, two years after the song was released. The lyrics wish for America to win the war but remind the listener of the cost of victory with lines like "someone shed their blood today." Instead of invoking God's wrath on the enemy, they remind the listener that God has provided a "weapon made of love," namely prayer. Nevertheless, most of the songs in table 3.1 express the view that the United States' actions with the bomb are not to be questioned, since God is clearly on America's side.

Finally, Southern evangelicals had a keen focus on Christian eschatology, the sequence of events surrounding Christ's return to earth. They saw the atomic bomb as a sign of the end of the world, an end God would bring about by fire.

Four of the songs ("Jesus Hits like an Atom Bomb," "Brush the Dust from that Old Bible," "The Great Atomic Power," and "The Song of the Atom Bomb") explicitly link atomic explosions to the fire that will destroy the earth on the last day, spoken of most clearly in 2 Peter 3:10, "But the day of the Lord will come like a thief, in which the heavens will pass away with a roar and the elements will be destroyed with intense heat, and the earth and its works will be burned up."[12] Two songs, "The Great Atomic Power" and "The Song of the Atom Bomb," proclaim that the saved will be protected from the bomb blast by ascending and meeting Christ in the air. This is the belief in the pretribulation rapture held by most dispensationalists. Concerning this, Wayne Flynt writes, "War, horrible atrocities, horrific fatalities, atom bomb, cold war, creation of the nation of Israel—all seemed to portend the end of history and to confirm dispensational premillennialism."[13] A primary passage cited for this belief is 1 Thessalonians 4:16–17: "For the Lord Himself will descend from heaven with a shout, with the voice of the archangel and with the trumpet of God, and the dead in Christ will rise first. Then we who are alive and remain will be caught up together with them in the clouds to meet the Lord in the air, and so we shall always be with the Lord."[14] This belief in the rapture explains the absence of country songs about fallout shelters, a hot topic among songwriters in other styles of popular music. Southern evangelicals who believed in the rapture would have little use for fallout shelters since they would have already ascended into the arms of Jesus before the tribulation—when bombs would be exploding.

In Lee V. McCollum's "Jesus Hits Like an Atom Bomb," the atomic firestorm that brings the end of the world is linked with another biblical event with eschatological significance, the great flood. Lowell Blanchard's recording of the song has this curious line: "He [God] told brother Noah by the rainbow sign, there'll be no water but fire in the sky." This reflects the mistaken belief God informed Noah of the great fire that would destroy the earth. This belief is a conflation of two separate biblical passages, Genesis 9:11 and 2 Peter 3:4–13. God never told Noah he would end the world with fire. He only told him, and signified it with the rainbow, he would never again cause a catastrophic flood. The pre–Civil War spiritual "Mary Don't You Weep" also conflates these two separate passages. The line in this song goes, "God gave Noah the rainbow sign, no more water, the fire next time."[15] The reference to Noah in "Jesus Hits Like an Atom Bomb" shows McCollum using the flood catastrophe to give an idea of what a world-ending nuclear catastrophe might be like.

President Harry Truman, the man who gave the order to use the atomic bomb in warfare for the first time and jumpstarted the Cold War, held many of these beliefs and principles. Truman himself was a Southern Baptist raised in Missouri. He believed the Bible was the Word of God and, like many Southern evangelicals, interpreted apocalyptic prophecies literally. In a diary entry on July 25, 1945, nine days after the Trinity test of the first atomic bomb, Truman wrote, "We have discovered the most terrible bomb in the history of the world. It may be the fire destruction prophesied in the Euphrates Valley Era, after Noah and his fabulous Ark."[16] Like many Southern evangelicals, he turned to apocalyptic events in the Bible to describe the magnitude of the bomb. Just as in the lyrics of "Jesus Hits Like an Atom Bomb," he seems to be conflating Genesis 9:11 and 2 Peter 3:4–13, presuming God told Noah the world would end not with flood but with fire. Truman also saw the bomb as a responsibility given to America by God to use "in His ways and for His purposes." In a radio announcement on August 9, 1945—the day of the Nagasaki bombing and three days after the Hiroshima bombing—Truman told the American people, "Having found the bomb we have used it. . . . It is an awful responsibility which has come to us. We thank God that it has come to us, instead of to our enemies; and we pray that He may guide us to use it in His ways and for His purposes."[17] Like the country songwriters, Truman turned to the Bible and his Christian faith to try to understand the conundrums generated by the atomic bomb.

One of the most peculiar features of these songs is that the music rarely reflects the dire and disastrous messages in the lyrics. The only song in table 3.1 with a musical accompaniment that comes close to reflecting the dark lyrics is "When That Hell Bomb Falls," which has a descending figure on pedal steel guitar depicting either falling bombs or the cries of victims. "When the Atom Bomb Fell" and "Weapon of Prayer" are somewhat somber, but the rest of these songs have bright, hummable melodies, lively rhythms, and a cheerful mood that clashes with the foreboding lyrics. Perhaps musicians employed the cheerful music to alleviate the foreboding tone of the lyrics, or perhaps it reflected the trust the songwriters had in God's plan and protection, no matter how fiery the apocalypse might be. This practice of accompanying dark lyrics with cheerful music, atypical in many other styles of popular music, can be traced to country music's origins. In Jimmie Rodgers's "Blue Yodel No. 1 (T for Texas)" from 1928, the protagonist yodels cheerfully about shooting down Thelma—the woman who wronged him—"just to see her jump and fall." In "T.B. Blues" (1931) and "Whippin' That Old T.B." (1932), Rodgers sings and yodels about having tuberculosis, the disease that would soon kill him. In line with this tradition, the song in this group with the gloomiest lyrics, "The Song of the Atom Bomb," has the brightest musical accompaniment of them all. Much like the heavy metal songs about nuclear warfare that we'll explore in chapter 7, the lyrics pummel the listener with images of atom bombs exploding, the world in flames, God's terrible wrath, Satan's malevolent power, blood flowing like water, and people dying in despair. Yet the singing has a blithe and jovial tone, and the accordion accompaniment makes the listener feel as if she or he is riding on a carousel or listening to a merry calliope at the fairgrounds. The clash between word and music is unnerving.

In this respect, these atomic apocalypse songs have an affinity with the tragedy and disaster songs of the early twentieth century, many of which have been collected in the three-CD set *People Take Warning! Murder Ballads & Disaster Songs, 1913–1938*.[18] These old-time, blues and country songs often have a bright melody and instrumental accompaniment to lyrics that recount tragic events, such as murders, tornados, coal-mine explosions, train wrecks, Mississippi River floods, and the sinking of the Titanic. Charles K. Wolfe's and James E. Akenson's edited volume *Country Music Goes to War* surveys the tragic country songs about the Civil War, the Spanish-American War, and the two world wars. Many of these war songs also have peppy rhythms and spirited singing. With the advent of nuclear warfare in the mid-1940s, songwriters had the ultimate potential disaster to recount, and they took to the subject quickly.

In summary, Southern evangelicals and country songwriters in the aftermath of World War II saw in the atomic bomb a manifestation of God's power, evidence of God's judgment on humankind (Japan in particular), and a vivid sign of the end of the world. But by 1955, country songwriters began changing their attitudes about the relationship between God's power and nuclear weapons as a result of several developments. In 1949, the Soviet Union successfully tested their first atomic bomb. Suddenly, the atheistic enemy had access to what Southerners viewed as America's exclusive God-given weapon. Second, the hydrogen bomb—one thousand times more powerful than the atomic bomb—had been successfully tested by the United States in 1952 and the Soviet Union in 1955. Third, three years of battle and over thirty-six thousand deaths in the Korean War made Americans weary of warfare in general. As a result, songs about nuclear bombs being evidence of God's judgment were few and far between. Abject fear of the bomb became common. "The Hydrogen Bomb" by Al Rogers and His Rocky Mountain Boys from 1954 reflects this attitude. In this country song, the bomb does not seem to be under God's control anymore, as it was in the immediate years after World War II. It seems to have a power and will all its own. The lyrics offer no hope of pretribulation rapture into the safe arms of Jesus, just a desperate plea of "God have mercy on me."

URANIUM FEVER

The use of the earth's fossil fuels has generated numerous technological breakthroughs in recent human history. Coal was the fuel of the Industrial Revolution in the eighteenth and nineteenth centuries. Petroleum was the fuel of the automotive revolution in the early twentieth century. Uranium ore was the fuel of the nuclear revolution in the mid-twentieth century. The discovery that uranium could be extracted, enriched, and detonated made nuclear weapons a reality. Tom Zoellner captures the significance of this discovery when he ominously writes, "A mineral lying in the crust of the earth . . . was the home of one of the most violent forces under human control. A paradox there: *from dust to dust*. The earth came seeded with the means of its own destruction, a geologic original sin."[19]

German chemist Martin Klaproth first identified uranium in 1789 and named it after the newly found planet Uranus. French scientist Henri Becquerel detected uranium's radioactive properties in 1896. A team of scientists led by Enrico Fermi discovered nuclear fission in the late 1930s and staged the first nuclear chain reaction in 1942, leading to the construction of the first atomic bomb in Los Alamos, New Mexico. The Manhattan Project scientists fully realized the potential of uranium as fuel for nuclear weapons, and the hunt was on. Large mines in the former Belgian Congo (now the Democratic Republic of the Congo) shipped most of the uranium, but the American West and Canada also had a rich supply of the valuable ore. While large mining companies were at the vanguard of the uranium hunt, the US government's Atomic Energy Commission (AEC) encouraged everyday citizens to join in the quest as well. In 1946, articles began coming out in popular magazines about how to locate and mine uranium, such as "How to Hunt for Uranium" in *Popular Science*.[20] In 1949, the AEC published a lengthy tome called *Prospecting for Uranium*.[21] By the early 1950s, thousands of amateur miners were taking weekend trips to the West, hoping to strike it rich. A ten-page article about uranium mining in the May 23, 1955, edition of *Life* magazine reported that "along with thousands of full-time uranium prospectors in the U.S. and Canada, some 10,000 people spend weekends tramping the hills for uranium. The amateur prospector's minimum reward is an exciting—if sometimes dangerous—outdoor adventure and there is always the chance he will make that rare, bonanza discovery."[22]

Like Hula-Hoops, poodle skirts, sock hops, and Davy Crockett coonskin hats, the uranium hunt was a fad of the fifties. Kids learned how to hunt for the precious ore by playing the board game *Uranium Rush*. Films like *The Atomic Kid* (1954), *Dig That Uranium* (1956) and cartoons like the Popeye episode "Uranium on the Cranium" (1960) reflected the craze. Even Lucille Ball and Ricky Ricardo got into the act. In the 1958 episode "Lucy Hunts Uranium" from *The Lucy–Desi Comedy Hour* (the successor to *I Love Lucy*), America's favorite couple heads out to the desert to strike it rich.

Four country and western songs about the uranium rush were released in 1954–1955. Three of them portray uranium mining as an incurable obsession, a quest for an elusive fortune. In some of the songs, the uranium rush is compared to the California gold rush (1848–1855), the centennial of which occurred in the

1950s. The romanticized image of a gold miner striking it rich, jumping in the air, and clicking his heels, as Walter Huston does in the film *The Treasure of the Sierra Madre* (1948) had little to do with the reality of a uranium miner. The larger mining companies that could afford sophisticated equipment found most of the uranium. Rarely did a solitary miner strike it rich.

"Uranium Miner's Boogie" by Riley Walker and His Rockin-R-Rangers (1954) is a cheerful country blues song about miners who rise at the crack of dawn to "dig the yellow stuff that makes the atom bomb." The specificity in the lyrics indicates how deeply Walker was invested in the culture of the miners. He was a miner himself. He prospected for the ore on his own and worked at large government mines in Colorado and Utah, driving dump trucks full of the "yellow stuff" from the mines to the processing mills.[23] The song mentions Grand County, San Juan County, and the region of Cottonwood Wash in southeast Utah, all hotbeds of uranium mining in the 1950s. The song also references the large US mining organizations VCA (Vanadium Corporation of America), USV (United States Vanadium Corporation), and the AEC (Atomic Energy Commission).[24] The physical appearance of the 45 single adds much to an appreciation of the song and shows that it is a product of the uranium-mining culture in Utah in the 1950s. Walker released the song through a company he and his friend Johnny Mabrito founded, and appropriately named, Atomic Records.[25] Peter Vogel writes that the color of the paper label on the 45 single "is a color that only a person familiar with the uranium mining and milling industry would recognize. It's the exact yellow that gives refined uranium ore its name: yellow cake."[26] Some of the 45s were pressed on blue vinyl, giving the record an eerie glow.[27] Although radioactive elements themselves do not actually glow in the dark, popular culture often depicts them as if they do.[28] So here we have a 45 single produced by Atomic Records with a yellow label to match the color of uranium ore and pressed on blue vinyl to make it appear radioactive. Later in this book, we will see many examples of how musicians used album packaging and sleeve design to enhance the meaning of their music, but it was rare to see such a clever design in a single in 1954, just five years after the first 45s made their appearance.

While Riley Walker wrote about workers in the large mining companies, the other three songs are about solitary uranium miners. "Uranium Blues" by Arizona songwriter Loy Clingman tells the typical tale of one such miner. He lives a simple, happy life with his wife until he starts mining uranium. A pastime turns into an obsession. He leaves his wife and home for the quest but finds "not a trace" of uranium. Even after his wife divorces him, he still cannot give up the hunt. At the end of the song, he prays others will not follow his "unhappy way."

The miner in Elton Britt's "Uranium Fever" is just as unsuccessful as Clingman's miner, but at least he can laugh at himself. He trades his Cadillac in for a

Jeep, and after he's "saddled" it, he heads out West. Perusing a map from the AEC showing where potential uranium deposits might be, he drives one hundred miles over bumpy roads and climbs up a steep mountain with his Geiger counter in hand. He hears some clicking but realizes it's not coming from the Geiger counter. It's the sound of "the bones in [his] back that had gone astray." He drives to another remote spot but discovers seventeen other miners have already arrived before him. A honky-tonk piano provides a light-hearted accompaniment and a staccato guitar ostinato musically represents a miner picking the ground with his pick. Elton Britt and his wife, Penny, who wrote the song together, made prospecting trips to Utah to find uranium. Their experiences inform the song and give it authenticity.

While Clingman's "Uranium Blues" is melancholy and Britt's "Uranium Fever" is humorous, Rudy Gaddis's "Uranium Fever" (1955) is haunting and evocative and hints at the frightening elemental power that the uranium miners are unearthing. The abundance of place names in the first verse situates the listener in the uranium-rich Colorado Plateau. The verse describes the long distances the miners travel and the toil they spend "turning every stone" in search of uranium. The miners' search is elevated to the level of a spiritual quest with the line "they trod across the desert as if guided by a star." The search is compared to the three wise men's journey to find the Christ child. The second verse offers more vivid imagery. Uranium prospecting is compared to a wild-animal hunt, with the miners tracking their prey—not with guns but with Geiger counters. The miners have no interest in finding silver or gold; uranium is the only prize for them.

The majority of the country songs in this chapter address the Cold War mostly through lyrics, but some use an artful combination of both music and lyrics. Gaddis's "Uranium Fever" is one such song. Although the accompaniment is sparse and its verse-chorus form is simple, the music creates a vivid and memorable setting for the lyrics. The melody of the verses consists almost entirely of the notes A and E, reflecting the obsessiveness of the miners and their fixation on the quest. Mournful passages on pedal steel guitar capture the landscape of the Southwest, summoning up barren deserts, mule trains, and lonesome miners. The chorus brings a swifter tempo, a bluegrass picking pattern, and a shift to E major, representing the hope the miners have of striking it rich. Along with the pedal steel guitar, the verses, especially the second, feature a simple, persistent drumbeat. The drum sounds much like a Native American drum, often called a "tom-tom." This drumbeat has frequently been used in popular music, cartoon music, and film soundtracks, especially Westerns, to signify or mimic Native Americans. Philip J. Deloria writes, "The Indian sound, as it crops up in the folklore of non-Indian Americans, has a melancholy, vaguely threatening, minor-key melody and a repetitive pounding drumbeat, accented in a 'tom-tom' fashion: 'DUM dum

dum dum DUM dum dum dum.'"[29] The "Indian sound" appears prominently in Hank Williams's "Kaw-Liga" (1953) about a wooden Indian statue who wants to express his love for a female Indian statue but cannot because his heart is made of "knotty pine." The form and musical accompaniment of Gaddis's "Uranium Fever" bear a striking resemblance to that of "Kaw-Liga," especially its "Indian sound." But why would a song about uranium miners have an Indian drumbeat?

From the late 1940s into the 1980s, thousands of Navajo men worked in uranium mines. The Navajo reservation at the Four Corners region, where Colorado, New Mexico, Arizona, and Utah meet, had hundreds of mines. Working with uranium ore is moderately dangerous in the open air, but underground mining is extremely dangerous because of exposure to concentrated amounts of radioactive radon gas. Navajo workers were the first to enter the mines after detonation and were paid less than White workers. Showers and change houses were not provided on site, so after work the miners walked into their homes or tents with their clothes, hair, and shoes covered with uranium dust. The mining companies and the AEC provided insufficient ventilation for the mines, offered little or no health insurance, denied compensation benefits to sick workers, and resisted compensation when thousands of Navajo—including women and children—were dying early from radiation-caused illnesses.[30] Even today, the US government has not cleaned up hundreds of abandoned uranium mines on the Navajo reservation. The soil, rivers, and wildlife of the area show obvious signs of radioactive contamination. In 2017, the US Department of Justice announced that the Environmental Protection Agency was given $600 million to clean up ninety-four abandoned uranium mines on Navajo land. Yet these ninety-four are only 20 percent of all the mines requiring remediation.[31]

No mention is made in "Uranium Fever" of Native Americans. Rudy Gaddis may have been completely unaware of how uranium mining was adversely affecting the lives of the Navajo. Gaddis may not even have intended the drumbeat to represent Native Americans. Perhaps he heard the drumbeat in "Kaw-Liga," one of Hank Williams's biggest hits, and liked how it sounded. Whether it was intentional or not, the drumbeat lends an ominous tone to the song and conjures up the "Indian sound." An understanding of the suffering of the Navajo people from uranium mining informs our hearing of the song in a way that was not possible when it was released in 1955.

ANTICOMMUNIST COUNTRY SONGS

As mentioned in the introduction to this chapter, country musicians held extreme hostility toward Soviet communism, more so than any other group of songwriters. They did not view communism as a nebulous threat that might slowly infiltrate America; they saw it as an immediate crisis, as if communism was at their doorstep, as if the soul of America was at stake. Communism in America, which had its origins in the labor movement and the 1917 Bolshevik Revolution, has had a long and complicated history. In the years between the two world wars, the Communist Party USA (CPUSA) and other left-wing, socialistic parties sought to address the ill effects of unregulated capitalism in the industrial sector—long hours, hazardous working conditions, low wages, inadequate health insurance—by encouraging workers to form unions. Unions grew strong in the northeastern states and began providing better working conditions, but many overstepped their bounds and resorted to threats, bribery, and violence to obtain their objectives. Unions were much less popular in the South for several reasons. One, Southerners saw unions as breeding grounds for communists; therefore they viewed unions as a threat to their way of life. Second, Jim Crow laws prevented the huge number of Southern Black laborers from forming or joining unions, partly causing the great migration to the northern industrial cities. Third, the South did not industrialize or urbanize as rapidly as the North and thus did not experience the ill effects of factory labor as keenly. Southern historian W. J. Cash, in his seminal book, *The Mind of the South*, summarizes the mindset against unions in this way, "Labor organizer equals Communist organizer."[32]

Country musicians combated communism with patriotic and nationalistic songs. Southerners viewed writing protest songs as un-American since many of them were union songs, and union songs were thought of as communist songs. While songwriters in other styles of popular music viewed the Cold War as a multifaceted conflict with military, economic, social, and political dimensions, most country musicians simply viewed it as an armed conflict, a war like any other war. The songs invoke America to rise up, march to battle, and defeat the foe. On the back cover of the 1966 compilation album *Country Music Goes to War*, the liner notes read, "It is significant that Country Music artists have never been identified with the so-called 'protest' songs or 'Peace Marches.' . . . Our country, may she always be right. But right or wrong, Country Music stands with our Country. When America goes to war—Country Music also Goes to War."[33] Melton A. McLaurin writes, "Patriotic country music is intense. The cold war . . . presented Americans with more complex realities, which elicited more complex responses. But country music, with its strong southern heritage, continued to view the cold war as it had more traditional conflicts—in terms of black and white rather than in shades of gray. Country music also frequently questioned the patriotism of those who saw the cold war in more ambiguous terms or questioned the appropriateness of government policies."[34]

Numerous songwriters in this book questioned the United States' actions during the Cold War and used popular music as a forum for public debate, but the country songwriters were unvarying in their support of America's policies and actions. They believed that the advance of socialism would bring about the downfall of America. By the early 1950s, anticommunism and antisocialism were common themes in country songs.

The anticommunist country songs, shown in table 3.2, came in two waves that corresponded to the Korean War and the Vietnam War. While the early to mid-1950s songs address the Korean War, they also address several interrelated aspects of the Soviet Union's influence on the United States. These aspects, which we will consider in this section, are the Soviet Union's spies in America, its militaristic and imperialistic intentions, its atheism, its threat to traditional American values, and its brainwashing of American prisoners of war. The Vietnam-era songs from 1966 to the early 1970s also address some of these subjects but focus mostly on the counterculture. Many Southerners thought that hippies and draft dodgers were "fellow travelers" in league with the Soviets to conquer America.

"Let's Keep the Communists Out," "The Fiery Bear," "The Red We Want Is the Red We Got," and "I'm No Communist" warn of the dangers of communism infiltrating America. During the period these songs were written (1950–1952), the HUAC, Senator Joseph McCarthy, and FBI director J. Edgar Hoover were busy accusing thousands of Americans—sometimes with substantial proof, more often without it—of having communist leanings or of being actual Soviet spies. "I'm No Communist," written by Scotty Wiseman, is the most incisive of the group. The song's title is mostly likely a reference to the title of an article that actor Humphrey Bogart penned in 1948 after he was accused by the HUAC of being in association with the "Hollywood Ten," a group of screenwriters and actors who were blacklisted for supposedly being communists.[35] In the first two verses, Wiseman points out the dangers of the communist threat and commends the activities of these government bodies for rooting out who is a patriotic American and who is a "low-down Red." In the third verse, Wiseman inveighs against those who plead the Fifth Amendment under questioning, who "shut up like a clam" when asked if they are communists. The song infers that those on trial who plead the Fifth, refusing to possibly incriminate themselves, must be communists since patriotic Americans would deny it instantly. This reflects the thinking of Joseph McCarthy, who once said, "A witness's refusal to answer whether or not he is a Communist on the ground that his answer would tend to incriminate him is the most positive proof obtainable that the witness is a Communist."[36] In case any listener should have a shred of doubt about his patriotism, Wiseman proudly proclaims in the title of the song and in the chorus that he is not a communist. He says he'll shout it so loud that Stalin himself can hear it. The song was first recorded by Scotty Wiseman and his wife, known as the duo Lulu Belle & Scotty; then by Grandpa Jones, who later achieved nationwide fame on the television show *Hee Haw*; and

Table 3.2 Country Songs Denouncing Communism

Song	Songwriter
"Let's Keep the Communists Out"	Ferlin "Terry Preston" Husky
"The Fiery Bear"	Shorty Thompson and Jim Lowe
"The Red We Want Is the Red We Got"	Jimmy Kennedy and Bickley Reichner
"When They Drop the Atomic Bomb"	Howard
"They Locked God Outside the Iron Curtain"	Brad Crandall and Elmo Ellis
"I'm No Communist"	Scotty Wiseman
"I Changed My Mind"	Joan Javits and Charles Randolph Grean
"The Red Deck of Cards"	Dave McEnery
"Ain't I Right"	Marty Robbins
"Hammers and Sickles"	H. Jackson Brown, Jr.
"The Commies Are Coming"	Tommy James
"Okie from Muskogee"	Merle Haggard and Roy Edward Burris
"The Fightin' Side of Me"	Merle Haggard

then by Carson Robison, whose version became the most popular. Reflecting the hysteria of McCarthyism and the fear of a Soviet-style government, the first three verses and chorus try to convince the listener that there is no room for silence, dissent, or even a politically moderate position. You either applaud America outright and out loud, or you are a communist.

In the chorus and second group of three verses, the song shifts from the HUAC hearings to the difference between the economic and political systems of the United States and the Soviet Union. The chorus praises private ownership while the remaining three verses admonish the US government for being too large, hiring too many dishonest public servants, increasing taxes, and losing control of the national debt. In other words, Wiseman is concerned that the US government and economy is turning into a Soviet government and economy. If this happens, he fears the communists will be able to take over America and "never fire a shot." Yet there is a fundamental contradiction in the song. The first half applauds a large-scale government program to police the actions of the public in order to expose communists, but the second half wants limited government intrusion into the lives of Americans.

Several of these songs address the imperialistic intentions of the Soviets, warning that they will soon attempt to conquer America. Stalin's brutal domination of Eastern Bloc countries, the Berlin Blockade (1948–1949), the detonation of the Soviet Union's first nuclear weapon (1949), and the spread of communism

Performer	**Year**
Ferlin "Terry Preston" Husky	1950
Jack Holden & Frances Kay	1950
Elton Britt	1950
Jackie Doll and His Pickled Peppers	1951
Jim Eanes, Little Jimmy Dickens, and Wesley Tuttle	1952
Lulu Belle & Scotty, Grandpa Jones, and Carson Robison	1952
Eddie Hill	1954
"Red River Dave" McEnery	1954
Marty Robbins	1966
The Charades	1966
Tommy James	1969
Merle Haggard	1969
Merle Haggard	1970

to China (1949) lent credence to this view. In 1947, the CIA was established to investigate and uncover the intentions of the Soviets. The Truman Doctrine, the Marshall Plan, and NATO were formed to prevent the spread of communism to other countries—often referred to as the policy of containment. The first countries to receive American aid were Greece and Turkey in 1946–1947. Truman provided financial assistance to help them become more stable and resist being folded into the Eastern Bloc. When North Korean forces invaded South Korea in 1950, aided by China and the Soviet Union, the US military became involved in the Cold War. The Korean War essentially established America as the world's policeman and first defense against communism. Even though Korea was a vast distance away, country songwriters felt that the Soviet Union was right next door. As more and more communist spies were uncovered in the US government, songwriters were convinced that the American mainland would soon be invaded by the Soviets. As James Perone writes, "The pro-government songwriters clearly placed great stock in the domino theory."[37]

In Shorty Thompson and Jim Lowe's "The Fiery Bear" (1950), the bear is, of course, Russia, which has been symbolized as such by Western Europe and America for hundreds of years. The first verse draws a parallel between the imperialism of the Axis powers during World War II and the Soviet Union. The chorus asks the bear, "Is there no stopping your prowl?," assuming that the Soviets will extend their reach as far as they can. The second verse enumerates the glories of

America (baseball, apple pie, the county fair, the American flag) and its Christian heritage, stressing that it is no place for a bear. The third verse implies America will use atomic weapons, if necessary, to stop the bear's prowl. This is precisely the suggestion given in "When They Drop the Atomic Bomb" (1951). This "finger on the button" song advocates for General Douglas MacArthur to the drop the atomic bomb on North Korea by saying it is the only thing that can stop Soviet aggression. Some songs simply ramp up American patriotism as a defense against Soviet expansion, such as "The Red We Want Is the Red We Got" (1950) by Jimmy Kennedy and Bickley Reichner. The compilers of the *Atomic Platters* box set characterize this song as a "straight-ahead patriotic chest thumper."[38] Like the others in this section, it paints the superpowers in black-and-white terms: the United States is good and the Soviet Union is bad. There may be red in both of their flags, but America has the "right red" instead of the "wrong red"; America's flag has a "brave red" rather than a "slave red."

Many of these songs criticize communism by emphasizing the atheism of the Soviet system or claiming it is a satanic cult. The best example is Brad Crandall and Elmo Ellis's "They Locked God Outside the Iron Curtain" (1952), whose chorus laments that the Soviets have "placed a kingly crown" on Satan. Claiming the Soviet Union is ruled by Satan is no surprise given the rhetoric coming from Christian pulpits in America, especially the South, in the early 1950s. Billy Graham, possibly the most recognized and revered preachers of the twentieth century, refers to communism as "demon-possessed" at the end of his sermon from 1951 titled "Christianism vs. Communism."[39] In a 1954 sermon titled "Satan's Religion," Graham says of communists, "The devil is their god; Marx, their prophet; Lenin, their saint; and Malenkov their high priest. Denying their faith in all ideologies except their religion of revolution, these diabolically inspired men seek in devious and various ways to convert a peaceful world to their doctrine of death and destruction."[40]

In a 1957 interview in *U.S. News and World Report,* Graham said, "My own theory about communism is that it is masterminded by Satan."[41] Working with Graham, President Eisenhower and Secretary of State John Foster Dulles shaped the early Cold War not just as a political, ideological, and military battle but as a spiritual one as well. Responding to the threat of communism's atheistic principles, Eisenhower and Dulles sought to "spiritualize" America in the mid- to late 1950s, which blurred the separation between church and state.[42] In June 1954, Eisenhower and Congress enacted a law to include the phrase "under God" in the Pledge of Allegiance and in 1956 made "In God We Trust" the national motto of the United States, replacing the unofficial motto "E Pluribus Unum." "In God We Trust" was also placed on paper currency beginning in 1957, although it had already been on coins since 1864. Thus, the spiritual dimensions of the Cold War that preachers and country songwriters were concentrating on in the early 1950s had reached the highest levels of US government by the mid- to late 1950s.[43]

During the Vietnam War, country songwriters were not as prowar as they were during the Korean War, but they were just as diligent against communist infiltration into America. With the rise of the counterculture in the mid-1960s, Southerners had a new enemy to confront: hippie protesters. James Perone writes, "The country songs relating to the Vietnam Conflict . . . frequently incorporate stereotypes of various types of characters, from patriotic, brave soldiers, to obedient, understanding spouses, to those in the anti-war movement, frequently characterized as cowardly, long-haired, poorly dressed, hip-talking students influenced by liberal, atheistic, Communist-leaning college professors."[44]

This dichotomy between Southerners and hippies comes out clearly in Marty Robbins's "Ain't I Right." The song presents a scenario where a communist comes to a town in the South to gain converts. The communist is regarded as an invader who brings only trouble and misery. His followers are a "bearded, bathless bunch," undoubtedly a reference to hippies. This alliterative appellation sets hippies apart from Southerners and also brings up associations with Karl Marx and Fidel Castro, who were notorious, not only for propagating communism but for sporting prominent beards. Merle Haggard and Roy Edward Burris's "Okie from Muskogee" from 1969 is another song that contrasts Southerners and hippies. Hippies are stereotyped as those who practice little to no hygiene, dress shabbily, live in ungoverned communes, and snub their noses at authority figures. Southerners, on the other hand, are portrayed like military personnel: clean-cut, clean-shaven, well governed, and patriotic. The song spent four weeks at number one on the US *Billboard* Hot Country Songs chart and became an anthem for Southern conservatives. Haggard said in interviews it started out as a joke and he had mixed feelings about its legacy as a Southern anthem.[45] Another practice associated with the counterculture, draft dodging, is addressed in at least four country songs: "Ain't I Right," "The Commies Are Coming," "Okie from Muskogee," and "The Fightin' Side of Me." These songs view any form of dissent as unpatriotic, a betrayal of America. Conscientious objection to military service is seen as disgraceful. Bill C. Malone writes, "Country singers and composers did not defend the Vietnam War so much as they protested against the protestors. Very few songs actually defended the war . . . Rather than defending American policy in Southeast Asia, the country songs defended what were perceived as 'traditional' values: service to one's country, deference to authority, unquestioning patriotism, or better yet, loyalty to a policy even if one questions it."[46]

These songs regard the hippie value system as unpatriotic, a betrayal of the troops, and a red-carpet invitation for communists.

Some songs use grotesque and monstrous terms to portray communists. In "When They Drop the Atomic Bomb," they are described as "no good," "dirty minded," "murdering thieves," and an "atrocious bunch." Some descriptions reach outrageous and ridiculous proportions. Apparently, communist countries forbid toys. "They Locked God Outside the Iron Curtain" begins by describing the Soviet Union as a place "where little children cannot play." In "Hammers and Sickles" children can play, but they won't have very much fun. If America succumbs to communism, kids will have to abandon their "crayons and building blocks" and play with "hammers and sickles." Even after the commie-baiting tactics of Joseph McCarthy and the HUAC had long been condemned; after the Cuban Missile Crisis in 1962, where Khrushchev and Castro backed down; and after the Soviets were willing to negotiate arms-reduction treaties in the mid- to late 1960s, some Southern songwriters continued to regard Soviets as almost subhuman.

ANTICOMMUNIST RECITATION SONGS

Reflecting the influence of preachers and preaching in Southern culture, several of these anticommunist songs are—either in full or in part—spoken recitations. They almost sound like anticommunist sermons. Although there are fewer in number in recent decades, "recitation songs" have had a strong presence throughout the history of country music, some notable examples being "Pictures from Life's Other Side" by Hank Williams (1951, as Luke the Drifter), "What Would You Do? (If Jesus Came to Your House)" by Porter Wagoner (1956), "A Boy Named Sue" by Johnny Cash (1969), and "The Devil Went Down to Georgia" by the Charlie Daniels Band (1979). They reflect not only the influence of preaching but also the traditions and practices of Appalachian folklore, cowboy poetry, ballads, talking blues, and Southern storytelling.

"Let's Keep the Communists Out" (1950) by Ferlin Husky, under the pseudonym Terry Preston, is the first example of this type of song. With "My Country, 'Tis of Thee" played on piano and pedal steel guitar in the background, Husky intones a solemn, meandering monologue in rhyming couplets. It is a plea for Americans to take pride in their country, preserve democracy, and be on guard against communists. It is heartfelt and earnest, but it does have its comical moments. One consequence of a communist takeover the song notes is that "our children would not have Santa Claus." The mention of an atomic bomb (and the sound of an explosion) interrupts the feeling of calm repose near the end but is restored by Husky's fervent vow that he would be "willing to die before [he sees] the communists come in."

Another spoken-word song is "The Red Deck of Cards" (1954) by "Red River Dave" McEnery. It reflects the belief that American prisoners of war were brainwashed, a term that became well-known in the American consciousness during the Korean War after journalist Edward Hunter published his influential 1951 book, *Brain-washing in Red China*.[47] "The Red Deck of Cards" is an adaptation of "Deck of Cards" (1948) by T. Texas Tyler. In Tyler's song, a soldier is caught playing with a deck of cards during a church service. He explains to his sergeant that the deck is his Bible and each card represents some element of Christian doctrine: the ace stands for one God, the two for the Old and New Testaments, the three for the trinity, the four for the gospel writers, and so on. McEnery's song follows a similar pattern but with a Cold War spin. A soldier just freed from a Korean prisoner of war camp tells his fellow soldiers he despises cards because communists used them to brainwash him and ridicule his Christian faith. They told him the ace stood for "one God, the state," the two for Lenin and Stalin, the three for Catholicism, Protestantism, and Judaism ("three religious superstitions that the Reds would soon destroy"), the four for the four corners of the earth, which the Soviet Union will command, etc. At the end of the song, the soldiers tear the cards to pieces and "with shining faces, walk toward a simple chapel in Korea." The song features an accompaniment by organist Eva Joe Allpress (indicated on the single's label) playing a gospel hymn. The presence of the organ in the background brings up resonances with a Baptist worship service, making the song sound almost like a sermon. The ending of the song (in which the soldiers walk to the chapel), the connection with Tyler's song (in which the deck of cards is like the Bible), and the organ accompaniment (in which a hymn is played) fill the song with Christian resonances in order to counter the atheism of communism. Did brainwashing actually occur during the Korean War? A Department of the Army study from 1956 determined that no American POWs were brainwashed during the war.[48] Nevertheless, soldiers, such as decorated US marine Frank Schwable, were subjected to intense interrogation, communist indoctrination, isolation, physical abuse, and other miseries.[49]

"The Commies Are Coming" (1969) by Tommy James has a recitation bookended by two sung sections. The recitation sounds much like a speech to soldiers before a momentous battle, like General George S. Patton's rousing speech to the Third Army on the day before D-Day. The recitation begins, "Fellow Americans, awaken, rise up, and be counted." It speaks to all Americans as if they are soldiers called to battle against communists, wherever they may be found within the United States or the Soviet Union. It shames protest marchers, draft dodgers, and those who "boo" America's leadership. The speech ends with the not-so-subtle directive to "rally forth, stand tall, and let's give the commies hell!" A pedal steel guitar softly playing "The Battle Hymn of the Republic" in the background augments the gravity of the speech. This hymn roused the Union soldiers to battle during the Civil War. Since the Reconstruction, it has been revered by both the North and the South because it symbolizes that God is on America's side. The hymn underscores the religious dimensions of the recitation, American Christianity versus Soviet atheism. During the Cold War, "The Battle Hymn of the Republic" was closely associated with Billy Graham, who used it at the beginning and end of his weekly *Hour of Decision* radio broadcast. Regarding this, John Stauffer and Benjamin Soskis write, "The 'Battle Hymn,' and Graham's crusades, thus inspired Americans in their apocalyptic battle against international communism."[50]

A final recitation song of interest, Charlie Daniels's "Uneasy Rider" (1973), is vastly different from the previous ones in this section. Although Charlie Daniels was a conservative, a Christian, and a patriotic Southerner, he was also a hippie, a member of the "bearded, bathless bunch" who were denounced in Marty Robbins's "Ain't I Right" and other songs. When Daniels wrote "Uneasy Rider," he was himself a "long haired country boy," the title of his 1975 hit. "Uneasy Rider" shows the identity struggles of Southern evangelicals regarding communism and the counterculture during the Vietnam War. This song is rich in detail and sets up distinct cultural, political, and religious differences between Southerners and hippies by making references to the Ku Klux Klan, conservative governor George Wallace, liberal senator George McGovern, homosexuals, Baptists, and the John Birch Society. Mark Kemp, a music journalist specializing in Southern rock, writes, "In the South, the battle between longhairs and rednecks was nearly as heated as the battle between the races. At that time [the early 1970s], having long hair in the South was only a notch above having black skin."[51] While many older Southerners regarded hippies as communists, many younger Southerners agreed with the counterculture—that the Vietnam War was a needless waste of human life.

"Uneasy Rider" is a musical reworking of the film *Easy Rider* (1969). In this iconic film, two hippie bikers make money on a drug deal and travel through the South on their way to Mardi Gras in New Orleans and then Florida. They are harassed by Southerners and are shockingly gunned down by two rednecks in a pickup truck. In "Uneasy Rider," Daniels plays on the Southern stereotype of hippies—they are communists and out of place in the South. The song's protagonist is driving west in his car through the South on his way to Los Angeles and stops into a bar called the Dew Drop Inn in Jackson, Mississippi. He notices it is a "redneck lookin' joint," so he stuffs his hair into his hat as he enters. Before having a chance to drink his beer, he decides to leave since someone has noticed a peace sticker on his car. As he walks out the door, "five big dudes" accost him and tell him to tip his hat to a lady with them. When he obliges, his long hair spills out. He realizes he is about to get attacked. Thinking quickly, he accuses one of his attackers of being a "friend of them long-haired, hippie-type, pinko fags," who even has a "commie flag" in his garage. This causes the other attackers to turn instantly on their friend and allows the protagonist to flee the scene. He escapes the fate of the bikers in *Easy Rider* by using the Southern stereotype on his attackers. Daniels said in an interview with Mark Kemp, "The whole point of 'Uneasy Rider' is that you don't have to take crap from people. Are you gonna let some guy come up and shoot you like they did in that movie?"[52] The song ends with the protagonist chasing the attackers around the parking lot with his car and then driving directly north to Omaha, Nebraska—in order to get out of the South as fast as possible—before going through the Midwest states to LA. This song shows the conflicted South of the Vietnam War era, one that is known for being conservative, Christian, and anticommunist but has to face liberal, non-Christian, and socialistic ideas. Like his fellows in Southern rock, the Allman Brothers Band and Lynyrd Skynyrd, Charlie Daniels amalgamated conservative and countercultural aspects of Southern identity during a time when they were viewed as utterly incompatible.

COLD WAR COUNTRY IN THE 1980S

After the Watergate scandal, the acrimonious end of the Vietnam War, the disappointment of Jimmy Carter's presidency (whom Southern musicians supported), an energy crisis, and a hostage crisis, Americans were ready for a new beginning in the 1980s. That new beginning was Ronald Reagan. Southerners embraced him and applauded his firm stance against the Soviet Union. Few anticommunist country songs were written in the 1980s since Reagan's muscular foreign policy pleased most Southerners. The perfect example of Southern Reaganism in country music is "In America" (1980) by none other than the Charlie Daniels Band. Daniels begins the first verse by summing up the 1970s as a period when America was floundering. The rest of the verse uses biblical imagery to describe the rebirth of America in the 1980s, a country putting itself back on the "paths of righteousness" (from the 23rd Psalm). Daniels doesn't pass up a chance to taunt the Russians, saying if they don't believe America is back on top of the world, "they can all go straight to hell." The second verse beckons all Americans to unite and stick together, specifically calling out to "cowboys" (Westerners), "hippies" (the counterculture), "rebels" (Southerners), and "yanks" (Northerners). The troubles between the rednecks and the hippies in "Uneasy Rider" have no place in this new America. Decades later, many Southerners still see Reaganism as the solution to Russian imperialism. When Russian President Vladimir Putin threatened to invade Ukraine in 2014, Charlie Daniels wrote on *Soapbox*, his online blog, "Ronald Reagan put the Soviet Pandora back in the box with an arms race and an iron will . . . I don't want to go to war with Russia and don't think it would be necessary. We can defeat Russia the same way we did before. Put missile defense systems in Eastern Europe [and] restore our military to Cold War levels . . . Diplomacy alone does not work with bullies."[53]

One of the few country songwriters strongly critical of Reagan's foreign policy was John Denver. "Let Us Begin (What Are We Making Weapons For?)" from his 1986 album, *One World,* asks the question, "Why keep on feeding the war machine?" It argues that money spent on nuclear weapons takes food from the "mouths of our babies" and money from the "hands of the poor." Although Denver transcended country music and became a hugely successful international entertainer, he situates this song in the South by singing from the perspective of an Oklahoma farmer about to lose his farm. As a teenager, Denver worked on his grandmother's small rural farm in Corn, Oklahoma. The song addresses the plight of family farms in the early 1980s threatened by foreclosure. Denver played at the first Farm Aid concert on September 22, 1985, which raised over $9 million for farmers, brought national awareness to the problem of farm foreclosures, and led to the Agricultural Credit Act of 1987, which helped to preserve and protect family farms. In "Let Us Begin," Denver directly links the financial distress of farmers with the billions of dollars the Reagan administration was spending on nuclear weapons.

In 1984, the Soviet Union of Composers personally invited Denver to play in the Soviet Union. He returned to the country to perform in 1985 and 1986. He also played "Let Us Begin" with Russian rock singer and songwriter Alexander Gradsky during the Earth '90: Children and the Environment concert in 1990. In *John Denver: The Complete Lyrics,* he explains that the song "was written after my first trip to what was then the Soviet Union, during which I had a whole list of unforgettable experiences. . . . On my return to the United States, the front page of *The New York Times* was about the plight of the small family farmer here in our country. . . . There are so many things I could tell you about how these two things connect for me. There is neither the time nor the space. Hopefully the song will suffice."[54]

Charlie Daniels and John Denver both desired a strong America but differed greatly on how they defined *strong.* The capitalist in Daniels said to spend money on weapons to make America's defense strong. The socialist in Denver said to spend money on infrastructure to decrease poverty and make America's struggling workers strong. Daniels viewed the Russians as a threat; Denver viewed them as neighbors in a global village. These two songs convey the powerful emotions stirred by the debate in the 1980s between national security and social security.

CONCLUSION

The overwhelming majority of these country songs defend all of America's actions during the Cold War. Time has proven the songs correct in their assessment of Soviet leaders and Soviet-style communism. Joseph Stalin and Mao Zedong rank with Adolf Hitler as the worst tyrants of the twentieth century. The scholars of *The Black Book of Communism* assert that almost one hundred million people perished as a direct result of communist dictators.[55] Nikita Khrushchev and Leonid Brezhnev renounced Stalin's brutality, but Russians still lived under a shroud of fear and subjugation for decades. Communist spies did infiltrate the US government, and the Soviet Union did spread their brand of oppressive communism to other countries. But was the cost to human life in the proxy wars, especially in Korea and Vietnam, worth it? Could communism have been contained without ruining the lives of so many Americans during the HUAC and McCarthy hearings? Could the Cold War have been won without spending billions of dollars on tens of thousands of nuclear weapons? Most Southern songwriters felt the means (the proxy wars, McCarthyism, suppression of dissent, the arms race, etc.) were justified as long as they brought about the desired end—the defeat of communism.

A fundamental issue these country songs highlight is the place and value of dissent in a democratic society during wartime. Country songwriters believed that dissent was unpatriotic, threatened the unity of the nation, made America more vulnerable, and weakened its position in the world. Dissent was a betrayal of the soldiers who were sacrificing their lives. Many of these songs show that country songwriters loathed war protesters almost as much as they loathed communists. Should freedom of speech be restrained in times of war in order to wholeheartedly support the troops abroad and present a strong, unified front at home against the foe? Country songwriters predominantly thought this was permissible and laudable, while songwriters in other styles such as folk—as seen in the first two chapters—did not.

NOTES

1. For more on "plain folk Americanism" in country music about the Cold War, see Kevin S. Fontenot, "'Dear Ivan': Country Music Perspectives on the Soviet Union and the Cold War," *Country Music Goes to War*, ed. Charles K. Wolfe and James E. Akenson (Lexington: University Press of Kentucky, 2005), 143–151.

2. Charles K. Wolfe, "'Jesus Hits Like an Atom Bomb': Nuclear Warfare in Country Music 1944–56," *Country Music Goes to War*, ed. Charles K. Wolfe and James E. Akenson (Lexington: University Press of Kentucky, 2005), 107, 111.

3. John Cline and Robert G. Weiner, "A Screaming Comes across the Dial: Country, Folk, and Atomic Protest Music," *Routledge History of Social Protest in Popular Music*, ed. Jonathan C. Friedman (New York: Routledge, 2013), 96.

4. Wolfe, "'Jesus Hits Like an Atom Bomb,'" 110–111.

5. Wilbur M. Smith, *This Atomic Age and the Word of God* (Boston: W. A. Wilde, 1948), 45–57.

6. Charles H. Lippy, *Bibliography of Religion in the South* (Macon, GA: Mercer, 1985), 436.

7. George M. Marsden, *Reforming Fundamentalism: Fuller Seminary and the New Evangelicalism* (Grand Rapids, MI: W. B. Eerdmans, 1987), 73.

8. Jens Lund, "Fundamentalism, Racism, and Political Reaction in Country Music," *The Sounds of Social Change: Studies in Popular Culture*, ed. R. Serge Denisoff and Richard A. Peterson (Chicago: Rand McNally, 1972), 79–82.

9. Charles P. Roland, *The Improbable Era: The South since World War II* (Lexington: University Press of Kentucky, 1975), 124.

10. Fontenot, "Dear Ivan," 146.

11. Charles K. Wolfe, *In Close Harmony: The Story of the Louvin Brothers* (Jackson: University Press of Mississippi, 1996), 28.

12. 2 Peter 3:10, *New American Standard Bible.*

13. Wayne Flynt, *Alabama Baptists: Southern Baptists in the Heart of Dixie* (Tuscaloosa: University of Alabama Press, 1998), 408.

14. 1 Thessalonians 4:16–17, *New American Standard Bible.*

15. This line is also in the Pilgrim Travelers' and the Soul Stirrers' gospel versions of "Jesus Hits Like an Atom Bomb."

16. Harry S. Truman, *Off the Record: The Private Papers of Harry S. Truman*, ed. Robert H. Ferrell (New York: Harper and Row, 1980), 55.

17. Harry S. Truman, "August 9, 1945: Radio Report to the American People on the Potsdam Conference," Presidential Speeches, Harry S. Truman, University of Virginia, Miller Center, https://millercenter.org/the-presidency/presidential-speeches/august-9-1945-radio-report-american-people-potsdam-conference.

18. *People Take Warning! Murder Ballads & Disaster Songs, 1913–1938* (Tompkins Square TSQ1875, 2007), three-CD set.

19. Tom Zoellner, *Uranium: War, Energy, and the Rock That Shaped the World* (New York: Viking, 2009), viii.

20. "How to Hunt for Uranium," *Popular Science*, February 1946, 121–123, 208.

21. *Prospecting for Uranium* (Washington, DC: United States Atomic Energy Commission and the United States Geological Survey, 1949). This publication is available for viewing on the HathiTrust Digital Library here: http://babel.hathitrust.org/cgi/pt?id=mdp.39015003999797#view=1up;seq=4.

22. Andreas Feininger, "History's Greatest Metal Hunt" *Life* 38, no. 21 (May 23, 1955): 25.

23. Peter Vogel, "Uranium Miners Have a Blast: Rockin-R-Rangers Lay Down a Boogie Beat," *New Mexico*, January 1989, 46.

24. Vanadium is an element often found with uranium.

25. Vogel, "Uranium Miners Have a Blast," 49. "Atomic Records" was a different label from "Atomic," which released one of the most famous early Cold War songs, "Atomic Cocktail" by Slim Gaillard and His Quartette.

26. Peter Vogel, "Uranium Miners Have a Blast," 49.

27. Kim Simpson, "Riley Walker, Uranium Minstrel (redux)," *Boneyard Media*, http://www.boneyardmedia.com/?p=1275.

28. For example, in the opening sequence of *The Simpsons*, Homer is shown working with a glowing green rod of uranium or plutonium at the Springfield Nuclear Power Plant.

29. Philip J. Deloria, *Indians in Unexpected Places* (Lawrence: University Press of Kansas, 2004), 183.

30. Two books that address these issues are Judy Pasternak, *Yellow Dirt: An American Story of a Poisoned Land and a People Betrayed* (New York: Free Press, 2010), and Doug Brugge, Timothy Benally, and Esther Yazzie-Lewis, eds., *The Navajo People and Uranium Mining* (Albuquerque: University of New Mexico Press, 2006).

31. "Justice Department, EPA and The Navajo Nation Announce Settlement for Cleanup of 94 Abandoned Uranium Mines on The Navajo Nation," United States Department of Justice, https://www.justice.gov/opa/pr/justice-department-epa-and-navajo-nation-announce-settlement-cleanup-94-abandoned-uranium.

32. W. J. Cash, *The Mind of the South* (New York: Knopf, 1941), 297.

33. *Country Music Goes to War* (Starday Records, SLP 374, 1966, LP).

34. Melton A. McLaurin, "Proud to be an American: Patriotism in Country Music," *America's Musical Pulse: Popular Music in Twentieth-Century Society*, ed. Kenneth J. Bindas (New York: Greenwood, 1992), 25–26.

35. Humphrey Bogart, "I'm No Communist," *Photoplay*, March 1948, 52–53, 86–87.

36. Joseph McCarthy, from a November 9, 1953, wire message to Harvard University president Dr. Nathan Pusey concerning communist professors at Harvard University, "Pusey vs. McCarthy," *Congressional Quarterly Almanac, 83rd Congress 1st Session-1953, Volume IX* (Washington, DC: Congressional Quarterly News Features, 1953), 348.

37. James E. Perone, *Songs of the Vietnam Conflict* (Westport, CT: Greenwood, 2001), 72.

38. Bill Geerhart and Ken Sitz's liner notes on the five-CD, one-DVD box set *Atomic Platters: Cold War Music from the Golden Age of Homeland Security* (Hambergen, Germany: Bear Family Records BCD 16065 FM, 2005).

39. Billy Graham, "Christianism vs. Communism" message from Minneapolis, MN, 1951, Billy Graham Evangelistic Association, http://billygraham.org/audio/christianism-vs-communism/.

40. Billy Graham, "Satan's Religion," *American Mercury*, August 1954, 42.

41. Billy Graham, "Does a Religious Crusade Do Any Good?" *U.S. News & World Report*, September 27, 1957, 78.

42. Jonathan P. Herzog, *The Spiritual-Industrial Complex: America's Religious Battle against Communism in the Early Cold War* (New York: Oxford University Press, 2011).

43. Lori Lyn Bogle, *The Pentagon's Battle for the American Mind: The Early Cold War* (College Station: Texas A&M University Press, 2004), 100–106.

44. James E. Perone, *Songs of the Vietnam Conflict*, 72.

45. Bryan Di Salvatore, "Profiles Ornery [Merle Haggard]" *New Yorker*, February 12, 1990, 39–77, http://www.newyorker.com/magazine/1990/02/12/ornery.

46. Bill C. Malone, *Don't Get above Your Raisin': Country Music and the Southern Working Class* (Urbana: University of Illinois Press, 2002), 240.

47. Edward Hunter, *Brain-washing in Red China: The Calculated Destruction of Men's Minds* (New York: Vanguard, 1951).

48. "The exhaustive efforts of several Government agencies failed to reveal even one conclusively documented case of the actual 'brainwashing' of an American prisoner of war in Korea." *Communist Interrogation, Indoctrination, and Exploitation of Prisoners of War.* Pamphlet no. 30–101 (Washington, DC: US Department of the Army, 1956), 19, 27, 51, https://www.academia.edu/16427644/DA_PAM_30-101_Communist_Interrogation_Indoctrination_and_Exploitation_of_Prisoners_of_War.

49. Raymond B. Lech, *Tortured into Fake Confession: The Dishonoring of Korean War Prisoner Col. Frank H. Schwable, USMC* (Jefferson, NC: McFarland, 2011).

50. John Stauffer and Benjamin Soskis, *The Battle Hymn of the Republic: A Biography of the Song That Marches On* (New York: Oxford University Press, 2013), 230.

51. Mark Kemp, *Dixie Lullaby: A Story of Music, Race, and New Beginnings in a New South* (Athens: University of Georgia Press, 2006), 100.

52. Kemp, *Dixie Lullaby*, 101.

53. Charlie Daniels, "Peace through Strength" from *Soapbox* section on the Charlie Daniels Band website, March 21, 2014, http://www.charliedaniels.com/soap-box?b_id=366&pg=31.

54. John Denver, *The Complete Lyrics* (New York: Cherry Lane Music, 2002), 149.

55. Mark Kramer, ed., *The Black Book of Communism: Crimes, Terror, Repression* (Cambridge, MA: Harvard University Press, 1999), 4.

FOUR

NOVELTY AND COMEDY SONGS

The Cold War as a Big Joke

IF PEZ, PEEPS, AND POP ROCKS are a sugar rush for the tongue, then novelty songs are a sugar rush for the ear. They may offer us nothing more than fun and frivolity, but they are hard to resist. The great number of novelty songs about the Cold War attests to the fact that people needed to defuse their fears of the Soviet Union, and the possibility of nuclear war, with humor and satire. But can anything substantial be expressed about an immense subject like the Cold War through the medium of a novelty or comedy song? Would not the weight of the subject matter make the form crumble, like a straw house against an atomic blast? Does not a grand subject require a grand scope and structure, such as an opera like John Adams's *Doctor Atomic*? We will explore these questions in this chapter.

Novelty songs in general can be traced back to the Tin Pan Alley songwriters, who dominated American popular music in the late nineteenth and early twentieth centuries. Novelty songs became a part of mainstream culture by the 1930s when humorous vaudeville and British music hall songs were published as sheet music, played on early radio, and released on early phonograph records. They have been with us ever since and thanks to artists such as "Weird Al" Yankovic are still popular.

Novelty songs are often considered to be a subgenre of comedy music, but there is much overlap between the two in that they both encompass popular music meant to be humorous. Novelty songs often have lyrics about taboo subject matter ("My Ding-a-Ling" by Chuck Berry), outrageous sound effects ("Der Fuehrer's Face" by Spike Jones and His City Slickers), high-pitched vocals (Tiny Tim's version of "Tiptoe through the Tulips"), inane rhyming ("The Name Game" by Shirley Ellis), relentless repetition ("Surfin' Bird" by the Trashmen), and tongue-twisting titles ("Supercalifragilisticexpialidocious" from *Mary Poppins*).

They tend to have a short life span on the charts and vanish quickly but suddenly reappear when the shifting sands of popular culture make them relevant again. They are notorious for reappearing during holidays, especially Christmas. What would Christmas be without "Grandma Got Run Over by a Reindeer" by Elmo & Patsy?

Novelty songs are to popular music what comic strips are to newspapers: they poke fun and entertain yet can reveal truths about an event in unusual ways. Most are harmless and amusing, while some contain persuasive and biting social commentary. Defending the genre, often maligned for being nothing more than musical flotsam and jetsam, Steve Otfinoski writes, "No apologies need be made for the novelty song itself. Although not always known for its taste and sophistication, the best of novelty has been literate, challenging, and wonderfully subversive."[1] Many Cold War novelty songs carry the weight of their subject matter and express substantial viewpoints. A great example would be any of Tom Lehrer's Cold War songs, such as "We Will All Go Together When We Go" (1958), covered in depth at the end of the chapter. At the other end of the spectrum, Doris Day's "Tic, Tic, Tic" (1949) compares the beating heart of someone in love to a Geiger counter. Here indeed is a song with no shame, possibly the most inane and annoying Cold War song ever written. Yet even a song such as this is worth discussing since it reveals common attitudes about Cold War issues as they were unfolding—in this case naivete about the dangers of radioactivity.

Because of their lyrical specificity and topical nature, novelty songs rarely have timelessness, a quality of being universally revered and forever relevant. Yet this lack can be seen as a gain that gives novelty songs an often overlooked virtue: timeliness. They are time capsules that, when opened, give insight into particular historical events. The Cold War novelty songs we will consider have this quality of timeliness, capturing and preserving specific historical moments. This chapter begins with one of the most well-known songs from the Cold War, the children's song "Bert the Turtle (The Duck and Cover Song)." Next, it explores the several Cold War–themed songs of Dickie Goodman, who along with "Weird Al" Yankovic, made a career out of recording comedic songs. Topical songs about Geiger counters, fallout shelters, and radioactivity are then analyzed. The chapter ends with a discussion on the dark humor in the greatest Cold War novelty song, "We Will All Go Together When We Go" by Tom Lehrer.

DUCK AND COVER

From the late 1940s to the early 1960s, Cold War anxiety was an inescapable part of everyday life. Atomic bombs and fear of the Soviets were not just the concern of adults but children as well. Kids had their own version of the Cold War. Children's toys of the 1940s through the 1960s were rife with Atomic Age themes. There were board games like Uranium Rush and Air Raid. Kids sucked on atomic fireball candies while reading atomic comics like *Atomic Man*, *Captain Atom*, and *Nukla*. For boys, there were atomic disintegrator pistols, kid Geiger counters, and O scale model train sets that transported nuclear weapons and waste. For girls, there was a fallout shelter paper doll cut out book. In 1951 during the Korean War, the Bowman Gum Company created a series of forty-eight "Red Menace" trading cards, some of which were titled "Fleeing the Reds," "Atomic Doom," and "War-Maker" (Mao Zedong's card).

One of the best-remembered relics of Cold War culture is "Bert the Turtle (The Duck and Cover Song)" written for the civil defense educational film *Duck and Cover* (1951). The team of Leo Carr, Leon Corday, and Leo Langlois, who wrote commercial jingles, composed the song. It exists in two versions. Jazz musician Dave Lambert arranged the first version, which is used in the film, and recorded it with an unknown vocal ensemble. Dick "Two Ton" Baker, a novelty song artist from Chicago who hosted several radio shows and children's television programs, recorded a 78 single in 1953. Like the Atomic Age toys, the *Duck and Cover* film and song attempted to render the Cold War in terms children could understand and be comfortable with.

The Federal Civil Defense Administration commissioned the nine minute, black-and-white film, produced by Archer Productions, and sent it to public schools all over America in 1952. The majority of schoolchildren in the United States watched it throughout the 1950s and early 1960s. The purpose of the film was to teach children to duck under furniture if they were at school or home (or find shelter if they were outside) and cover their heads when a nuclear attack was imminent. The film begins with Bert, an animated, anthropomorphized turtle, ducking into his shell to protect himself from a monkey wielding a stick of dynamite. While a nuclear bomb differs quite a bit from a stick of dynamite, the film tried to show the merits of ducking and covering. By the late 1960s and 1970s, the film was largely forgotten and its advice deemed unrealistic, even worthless, in the face of a twenty-megaton hydrogen bomb. Ducking and covering was regarded as nothing more than psychological solace and offered no actual physical protection. The song and film became emblems of Cold War kitsch when portions of them were included in the 1982 documentary film *The Atomic Café*.[2] Throughout the 1980s and 1990s, and into the present, *Duck and Cover* has been derided as propaganda, a vain attempt by the US government to justify its continual buildup of nuclear weapons by showing that children could be protected from a nuclear bomb by ducking under a school desk.

Nevertheless, in the last decade or so, a few scholars, such as Glenn Harlan Reynolds, have attempted to rescue the film and song from derision and show that ducking and covering was, and still is, a useful action to take in a nuclear attack.[3] The point of the cartoon was not to prove that ducking and covering will save your life but to show that doing something to protect yourself is better than doing nothing and giving in to despair. The reasoning behind duck and cover is based on the physics of a nuclear explosion. A flash, many times brighter than the sun to the naked eye, comes first and is followed by a blast wind that can exceed the speed of sound (approximately 760 mph). For someone within a mile of the explosion, these events will occur simultaneously, but at a greater distance, there will be a span of seconds in which one can seek protection. The time between the initial flash and the blast wind varies—depending on wind speed, terrain, weather, and one's distance from ground zero—and is somewhat analogous to the delay between a flash of lightning and the sound of thunder. The third result of an atomic explosion is radioactive fallout. One has from minutes to up to an hour to seek shelter, depending on the amount of fallout, distance from the explosion, and wind speed and direction. Most of the deaths from the Hiroshima and Nagasaki bombings were caused by people standing in the open, staring at the explosion, and being lacerated or crushed by flying debris caught up in the blast wind. Ducking and covering would have been somewhat beneficial by decreasing the chances of getting injured by debris and reducing the extent of radiation burns to the skin. The benefits of shielding oneself in a nuclear blast have been documented in scientific studies.[4] Yet the sheer magnitude of such explosions (hydrogen bombs can be up to one thousand times more powerful than the Hiroshima bomb) and their psychological effect made people skeptical of sheltering in the 1950s and make them even more skeptical today.

Thus, it is difficult to take "Bert the Turtle" seriously, not only because of its incredulous advice but because of its music and lyrics. It is an example of an "inadvertent novelty song," an earnest, educational song that has been branded a novelty by posterity. Although not intended to be a novelty or comedy song, "Bert the Turtle" has many traits in common with them. The first being the song's repetition of the phrase "duck and cover," which is pounded into the listeners' brain numerous times. Second, the tune has catchiness, the earworm quality all advertising jingles have. It's a song you cannot get out of your head. The simple, cheery, diatonic melody distracts the listener from confronting what the song is actually about: trying to survive a nuclear attack. Third, the conventional form of the song and its simple harmonic scheme project peace and calm. The scansion of the lyrics is orderly with plenty of rhymes to keep the song neat and tidy. In fact, the first three lines of the song contain six rhymes: "turtle" (twice), "Bert" (twice), "alert," and "hurt." These aspects of the music and lyrics give the impression that as long as one remains calm, follows the rules, and heeds civil-defense instructions, one will be safe even during a nuclear war.

Other musical elements contribute to the campiness of the song. The version from the film begins with a disarming ditty, "Dum-dum, deedle dum dum," which establishes a blithe and carefree ambiance before the narrator starts describing the horrors of nuclear explosions and firestorms. Dick "Two Ton" Baker's version has a slide whistle throughout to aurally illustrate Bert ducking inside his shell. Slide whistles have a long history of being used in comedy films and cartoons to illustrate comedic effects (pulling someone's pants down, slipping on a banana peel, etc.). The song's similarity to advertising jingles makes it suspicious to modern listeners, being more aware of the subliminal effects of advertising than those in the 1950s. They may feel they are being manipulated. These elements contribute to the "campiness factor" of the song and cause the viewer/listener to take it less seriously. The modern viewer of the cartoon cannot help but chuckle derisively, because the cultural aesthetics of the 1950s are so foreign. The viewer/listener focuses on the camp and the kitsch, missing the information actually being presented.

Can a deadly serious message about nuclear war be conveyed in a cartoon with a catchy song? The filmmakers and songwriters are not to blame for the geopolitical culture that made such a film and song necessary. They had the unenviable task of warning children about the dangers of nuclear weapons without causing panic. They had to simultaneously infuse and defuse fear. As Melvin E. Matthews, Jr. writes, "When it came to nuclear destruction, a generation of public school children were taught to regard it as nothing more than another problem of modern living."[5] We can only point the finger generally at twentieth century militarism, which created a reality in which children had to be taught to hide under desks from nuclear bombs that could explode anywhere, anytime, and without warning.

CUTTING IT UP WITH DICKIE GOODMAN

While the writers of "Bert the Turtle" unintentionally created a novelty song, American record producer Dickie Goodman turned the genre into an art form. In his thirty-year career from the mid-1950s to the 1980s, his songs poked fun at current events, politicians, dance crazes, films, and, especially, the Russians. He is best known for creating and popularizing the "break-in," a technique of inserting brief portions of popular songs into a ludicrous narrative to comically respond to and comment on current events. According to his son Jon, Dickie Goodman was "the first recording artist to successfully use mixing and sampling."[6] This practice began with his first recording, "The Flying Saucer," in 1956, which he produced with songwriter Bill Buchanan. Jon Goodman continues, "Splicing tape together to make their words, sound effects and the music fit smoothly, it took primitive technical wizardry to create such a finely tuned sound recording, to say none the least for coming up with a story that would make sense in the funniest way. No computer-controlled digital sound here, just white lab suits and razor blades."[7]

The song was a parody of Orson Welles's *The War of the Worlds* radio drama. Taking advantage of the spate of alleged UFO sightings in the 1950s, the song used current pop hits by the Platters, Little Richard, Fats Domino, Chuck Berry, Elvis Presley, and others to comment on an alien spacecraft landing on earth. The song sold over five hundred thousand copies nationwide and reached number three on the *Billboard* chart in August 1956, just behind "Hound Dog" by Elvis Presley and "My Prayer" by the Platters.

Like a magician's box with a false bottom, many Cold War songs conceal surprising things in their small packages. As noted previously, novelty songs can be much more discerning and revealing than they are given credit for. Take, for example, Goodman's 1959 instrumental song "Stroganoff Cha Cha."[8] It is an unlikely mishmash of Russian and Cuban music. This song shows that even a novelty song with no lyrics can be meaningful, even prophetic. This Russian/Cuban alliance in sound was released in late January 1959, not only before the Bay of Pigs invasion and the Cuban Missile Crisis but before Nikita Khrushchev had even met Fidel Castro. The song features the melody of the traditional Russian work song "Song of the Volga Boatmen" ("Ey, ukhnem!") played with a raunchy tone on saxophone combined with the Cuban cha-cha-chá rhythm. "Song of the Volga Boatmen" is one of the most well-known Russian folk songs in America and has come to symbolize the toil of Russian peasants under oppression.

Even the title of the song makes the Russian/Cuban connection explicit. Beef stroganoff—a dish consisting of beef chunks, sour cream, and noodles—originated in eighteenth-century Russia and became popular in America in the 1940s and 1950s. The cha-cha-chá, a dance of Cuban origin created in the late 1940s by composer, violinist, and bandleader Enrique Jorrín, has been an emblem in America of Cuban music and dance since the mid-1950s. The combination of a slow and heavy Russian work song with a light and frisky Cuban dance must have sounded odd in early 1959 since there was little connection at the time between the cultures of the two countries. A brief review of Soviet/Cuban relations will show how strangely prophetic the song was.

Fidel Castro came into power on January 1, 1959, by ousting president/dictator Fulgencio Batista. Soon he began to sever the capitalist connection between the United States and Cuba. Castro had been intrigued by Marxism since the late 1940s.[9] Yet, when the American Society of Newspaper Editors invited him to the United States in April 1959, he claimed he was not a communist.[10] The April 21, 1959, issue of the *New York Times* quotes Castro as saying, "Cuba has not received any offer of economic aid from the Soviet Union. . . . We are against all kinds of dictators . . . that is why we are against communism."[11] Disbelieving this, President Eisenhower refused to meet with him and went on a golfing trip to Augusta, Georgia. Khrushchev took little notice of Castro when he overthrew Batista and didn't even consider him as a possible ally, since the United States had such a strong hold in the Western Hemisphere.[12] When Khrushchev heard about Eisenhower's snub, he became interested in Castro. Soon Castro had Khrushchev in his good graces, and an alliance was made between them. Although CIA-backed Cuban exiles failed to oust Castro in the April 1961 Bay of Pigs invasion, this incident convinced the two leaders that Cuba needed to be armed against another US invasion. A year and a half later, in October 1962, American U-2 spy planes supplied photographic evidence of Soviet nuclear-missile bases in Cuba, ninety miles off the coast of Florida. Suddenly the Soviet Union, its nuclear weapons, and communism were at America's doorstep.

Although Castro was suspected of being a communist in the 1950s, Batista's alliance with the United States made most Americans unafraid of Cuba coming under the influence of the Soviet Union. Perhaps Goodman thought otherwise and imaging a Soviet/Cuban alliance created the song as soon as Castro came to power on January 1, 1959. Goodman could not have known how significant this Soviet/Cuban alliance would become or that it would result in a potential nuclear war with America. The song is uncannily prophetic. When it was released in late January 1959, Castro had been in power less than a month, and Khrushchev knew little about him. Since we live after the Cuban Missile Crisis and appreciate how dangerous the confrontation was, it is difficult not to "read" the event into the song. We assume a song about Russians and Cubans has something to do with Khrushchev, Castro, and the crisis, even though it doesn't. In 1963, a group called the Zanies released the novelty instrumental "Russian Roulette." It is clearly modeled on "Stroganoff Cha Cha"; a raunchy saxophone even plays "Song of the Volga Boatmen." Here the connection with the Cuban Missile Crisis is explicit and unmistakable since the song ends with the sound of a massive bomb exploding. What Goodman was trying to conjure up in January 1959 with his song remains a mystery. Perhaps it has nothing to do with Cold War politics. Perhaps Goodman just wanted to make a silly song about the Volga boatmen wishing they were on holiday in Havana, dancing the cha-cha-chá, and eating beef stroganoff.

The next two Goodman songs that deserve exploration give comically exaggerated impressions of Soviet media control. The first, "Russian Bandstand," is among the most sinister and tasteless of all Cold War songs. Released two months after "Stroganoff Cha Cha," it uses the instrumental track of that song as its foundation. A parody of *American Bandstand*, the song imagines what the show might be like if Nikita Khrushchev hosted instead of Dick Clark. It begins with the host, "Nikita Clarkchev," introducing himself in a mock Russian accent and observing that almost everyone in Russia watches the show. After the sound of machine-gun fire, he announces with a sneer "now everybody watches 'Russian Bandstand,'" implying he has just shot the last person in the country not watching it. He then announces the number one song in Russia (Chuck Berry's "Maybellene" played backward) and shoots anyone who says they don't like it. After another tape-reversed snippet (by "Nikita Presleychev") and another shooting, the song ends with the secret police shooting the host. Although the song is a hyperbolic parody of Soviet media control, it reflects real fears of 1950s and 1960s America about state-monopolized radio and television. While the technologies of radio and television were "born free" in America and England, Laura Roselle writes that "in the Soviet Union . . . the television system was centrally controlled and the leadership could and did manipulate the depiction and interpretation of many subjects. . . . A direct phone line from the desk of the Soviet leader to the head of *Gostelradio* suggests the degree to which Soviet leaders were involved in the state's use of media."[13]

In addition, the Soviet government attempted to prevent its citizens from picking up any foreign broadcasts by jamming radio stations such as Voice of America (VOA), the BBC World Service, and Radio Free Europe (RFE). "Russian Bandstand" takes two vital twentieth-century avenues of freedom of expression—radio and television—and strips them of their soul by stripping away their freedom.

Two years later in 1961, Goodman made his next Cold War song, "Berlin Top Ten," again a commentary on government-policed radio. The song begins with traditional Bavarian "oom-pah" music, which is interrupted by the sound of marching soldiers and a cold, shrill voice announcing, "Achtung! Achtung! Zis is radio-free East Berlin." The voice is disc jockey "Happy Hans Kaput," who proceeds to play a snippet of the supposed number one song in East Berlin, "Don't Fence Me In."[14] This is undoubtedly a sarcastic commentary on the Berlin Wall, which had just begun to "fence in" East Berlin when the song was released.[15] Happy Hans is then machine-gunned by the "secret police" and replaced by "Boris the Spinner, the people's disc jockey." After a few more news announcements and song snippets depicting everyday life in East Berlin—secret police knocking on doors, missile sabotage, threats about taking a trip to "beautiful" Siberia—the sounds of marching soldiers and machine guns are heard once again. It is Boris's turn to face the secret police, and he signs off with a snippet of "I'll Never Smile Again" by the Platters.

The "secret police" mentioned twice in the song is either the KGB, the Soviet intelligence agency / military police, or the Stasi, the East Berlin equivalent. Both are considered to be among the most repressive and invasive state agencies in modern history. The song comically portrays the extent to which East Berlin radio was controlled by these two organizations. Nicholas J. Schlosser's writes,

"The Stasi were able to employ informants in all areas of radio operations . . . thus insuring . . . the continued dominance of the party over radio stations."[16] Dickie Goodman grew up listening to American radio during its "Golden Age" (1920s to the 1950s), before the ascendancy of television. He knew and worked with many American disc jockeys and radio personalities and garnered airplay for his songs by hawking them around radio stations. Thus it is fitting he would create a song like "Berlin Top Ten," which, although comical, shows the plight of radio disc jockeys in countries where broadcast freedom is denied. As Jon Goodman says of his father's craft, "It was funny, and made fun of stuff, but there's social commentary hidden within it."[17]

While the song is notable for satirizing state-controlled radio in East Berlin, its pertinence to the construction of the Berlin Wall is truly remarkable. The border between West Berlin and East Berlin was closed on August 13, 1961, by means of a barbed wire fence. A few days later, cement blocks began to be put in place.[18] Goodman conceived the song, recorded it, and got it released a little over two months later on October 23, 1961.[19] At the time, Goodman could not have known the pervasive impact the Wall would have on world politics for almost thirty years, nor could he have known how prescient his song was. Although the song wasn't a hit, only reaching number 116 on the *Billboard* Hot 100 Singles chart, his use of "Don't Fence Me In" helped to establish that song as emblematic commentary on the Berlin Wall. The song became closely linked with the Wall in early 1962, when the East Berlin disc jockey "Barbara" used it as her theme song. Although it was East Berlin being cloistered to prevent its citizens from defecting, she used the tune as propaganda in an attempt to make American soldiers in West Berlin feel as if they were the ones trapped.[20]

Goodman took a break from satirizing the Cold War from the mid-1960s until the early 1980s. He then began addressing topics such as the Watergate scandal, movie crazes like *Jaws* and *Star Wars*, presidential elections, and the energy crisis. When he did come back to the Cold War with "Radio Russia" in 1983, the topic was the nuclear-arms race. The song uses snippets from early 1980s popular songs to depict a futile conversation between a pushy Ronald Reagan and a tight-lipped Yuri Andropov, the Soviet general secretary at the time, regarding a Soviet "secret weapon." The song begins with an instrumental snippet from the beginning of John Cougar Mellencamp's "Crumblin' Down," an ominous allusion to the walls that would crumble as a result of a nuclear explosion. The song ends with the sound of the secret weapon going out of control and a nuclear explosion. Displaying his usual prescience, Goodman's song about a communication breakdown between the superpowers was as relevant as the daily newspaper. In late November 1983, when the song was released, Andropov ordered his representatives to walk out of a Soviet/US intermediate-range nuclear-missile reduction meeting in Geneva. This broke off arms negotiations until after Mikhail Gorbachev came into power in March 1985. The communication failure in the song reflects the communication failure between the two countries, which marked November 1983 to early 1985 as a period of heightened fear of nuclear confrontation. Thankfully, the only nuclear explosions heard during this period were in remote underground test sites—or tacked on to the ends of novelty songs.

"YOU'LL TIC TIC ALL DAY LONG"

While Doris Day's 1956 hit "Que Sera, Sera (Whatever Will Be, Will Be)" is a bit maudlin, it continues to pull on heartstrings and has aged well. "Tic, Tic, Tic," her song from 1949 about a Geiger counter, has not. Yet this song is interesting and valuable in that it captures the ignorance of Americans in the late 1940s and 1950s regarding the dangers of radioactivity. Like fallout shelters and gas masks, Geiger counters were a Cold War consumer fad in the 1950s. They first appeared in the 1950 Sears, Roebuck & Co. catalog, one of the best indicators of consumer trends in the twentieth century.[21] Uranium mining was the main impetus for their sudden popularity. In addition, people bought Geiger counters to test the radiation levels in their homes since rumors were being spread of rising radioactivity in the air due to nuclear-bomb testing. Joanna Bourke writes, "Radioactivity was like a household germ that could be destroyed. The Geiger counter was marketed as just another household appliance."[22] Geiger counters were also bought to keep in fallout shelters to test radiation levels after a nuclear attack. In his memoir *Chronicles Volume One*, Bob Dylan recounts, "The general opinion was, in case of nuclear attack all you really needed was a surplus Geiger counter. It might become your most prized possession, would tell you what's safe to eat and what's dangerous. Geiger counters were easy to get. In fact, I even had one in my New York apartment."[23]

Doris Day's song, with lyrics by Ralph Blane and music by Harry Warren, is from the romantic comedy *My Dream Is Yours* (1949). In the film Day plays a single mother, Martha, who is trying to break into radio with the help of Doug (Jack Carson), a talent scout. She sings "Tic, Tic, Tic" during an audition for the radio show "Hour of Enchantment." She eventually wins the spot as a radio singer, replaces the current radio star Gary (Lee Bowman), and goes on to fame. Although she has an infatuation with Gary, she falls in love with the more down-to-earth Doug in the end. The lyrics compare the beating heart of someone falling in love to the ticking of a Geiger counter. The love interest in the song is described as radioactive, making the pursuer's heart tic, or beat, incessantly. The song has little to do with the plot of the film. It simply acts as a vehicle to show Day's infatuation with Gary.

"Tic, Tic, Tic" comes across less as a love song and more of an exercise in how many times one word can be repeated in a song—a hallmark of novelty tunes. In the course of its two-and-half minutes, Day manages to sing the word *tic* seventy-one times and rhyme it with ten other words (*click, trick, electric, realistic, hick, kick, stick, quick, candlestick,* and *politics*). Meanwhile, the pizzicato violins in the orchestral accompaniment drive the point home by "ticking" along with every *tic*; this practically gives the listener a nervous tic. The song works well as a showcase for Day's charm and talent, but in the context of the Cold War, it is a puzzler. Blane's lyrics show both the fascination and the naivete the American public had regarding radioactivity, which is explored in depth in the following section.

"GIMME SHELTER!"

Of the dozen or so songs we've found that are specifically about fallout shelters and avoiding radioactive fallout, most of them are comedy or novelty songs. Few Cold War topics were such fodder for parody, and a closer look at the US government's civil defense program in the 1950s and 1960s will explain why. In the late 1940s and early 1950s, the US government eagerly built up the nation's nuclear arsenal, especially after the Soviet Union joined the "nuclear club" in 1949 by successfully testing their first atomic bomb. Yet the US government was unwilling to invest in a shelter system for the American public. As the Soviet Union began to match the United States in nuclear technology, manufacturing its own hydrogen bombs and ICBMs in the mid- to late 1950s, this oversight became more glaring. Until the mid-1950s, the American public knew little about the actual destructive power of hydrogen bombs. By the late 1950s, the Soviet Union's ICBMs had advanced to a degree that they could launch from Russian soil and drop hydrogen bombs on US cities within thirty minutes. ICBMs brought the two distant countries closer, transforming the spatial dimensions of modern warfare. War was no longer localized; the "front lines" could be anywhere. As Kenneth Rose succinctly describes it, "The American home had been put on the front lines of the Cold War."[24] Civilians were now as much participants in warfare as soldiers were. The soldier's foxhole during World War II was now the family's fallout shelter during the Cold War with one major difference: the World War II soldier could jump out and attack the enemy. The Cold War family could not as the enemy was radioactive fallout. The disheartening aspect of civil defense was that it was only a defensive action. No offensive action can be taken by civilians in a nuclear war. Essentially civil defense showed people the best way to run and hide.

The task of the US government's Civil Defense Administration, established by President Truman in 1950, was to equip civilians to defend themselves during a nuclear attack. This was a daunting task since there had been a sharp divide between military and civilian life in America in the early decades of the twentieth century. In Europe, civilians were much closer to war. For example, air-raid sirens and communal sheltering in subway stations became a part of everyday civilian life in London and other cities during the German blitzkrieg of World War II. Americans were not used to having their homeland attacked. World War I, the Pearl Harbor attack during World War II, and the Korean War were all at least an ocean away from the American mainland. Americans depended on their military to fight and were ill prepared for a war that might come to their front door. By the late 1950s, the American public realized the government was harping on them to build shelters because nuclear weaponry had become such an integral part of the nation's defense policy. The fallout shelter and radiation novelty songs are a reaction against this civil-defense indoctrination.

The US government made a half-hearted attempt to stock food and supplies in the basements of designated buildings in large cities.[25] The rusty yellow-and-black "fallout shelter" signs, which still can be seen on certain buildings today, are evidence of this. Yet both the government and the populace looked at these communal shelters with skeptical eyes since they hinted at communism.[26] Home shelters, therefore, were promoted consistently, keeping in line with American's desire for individualism and private ownership. Home fallout shelters became a genuine consumer fad in the late 1950s. Melvin and Maria Mininson garnered national attention when they spent a fourteen-day honeymoon in a fallout shelter in July 1959.[27] By accomplishing this feat, sponsored by Bomb Shelters, Inc. of Miami, they earned a "real" honeymoon in Mexico. The fallout shelter became a hot topic in 1961 as a result of President Kennedy's televised July 25 speech in which he discussed the tensions between East and West Berlin—which would lead, a month later, to the building of the Berlin Wall—increases in military personnel and defense spending, and the importance of public and private fallout shelters.[28] Kennedy published a message to the American people about the importance of shelters in the September 15, 1961, issue of *Life* magazine, and *Newsweek* and *Time* magazines had major stories about them that year.[29] The *Life* magazine issue also had a twelve-page spread instructing the public how to build four different types of private bomb shelters. Reflecting this trend, all the fallout shelter and radiation novelty songs are about private shelters rather than communal ones, and all except for one are from the height of fallout paranoia, 1960–1964. Unsurprisingly, because of the privacy the shelters provided to young couples in love, all the songs have sexual overtones.

The first song, "Fallout Shelter," was recorded by two performers, one American and one British. Although the music and lyrics of both versions are—for the most part—the same, they reflect the different attitudes Americans and Britons had toward civil defense and fallout shelters. As Lawrence J. Vale writes, "At no point did Britain's political leadership rally behind civil defense as did the United States under Kennedy."[30] The American Peter Scott Peters wrote the song and released it on the Lute label in the fall of 1961. In the lyrics, Peters celebrates the coziness of his shelter because it has a stereo, lots of wine, plenty of food, and his girlfriend. Although the song is intended to be satirical, his serious, deadpan delivery—especially in the verses—downplays the comedy and projects genuine confidence in the protective ability of his shelter. The song almost sounds like an advertisement. The lyrics are below.

Lyrics to "Fallout Shelter." Words and music by Peter Scott Peters (1961).

Chorus 1: I'm not scared
I'm prepared
I'll be spared

Verse 1: I've got a fallout shelter, it's 9 by 9
A hi-fi set and a jug of wine
Let the missiles fly from nation to nation
It's party time in my radiation station

A 14 day supply of multi-purpose food
Water, medicine, be sure to include
Build your bomb bungalow, you needn't postpone
With no down payment and an FHA loan

Bridge 1: Let the tests go on in the atmosphere
In my fallout shelter, I'll have no fear
My baby and me, cozy we'll be
Away from radioactivity

Verse 2: Twenty megatons is the size of the boom
And if they let it go, I'll feel no doom
Let the cats run about helter-skelter
Gonna live, live, live in my fallout shelter

Chorus 2: I'm not scared
I'm prepared
I'll be spared

Bridge 2: Twenty megatons is the size of the boom
And if they let it go, I'll feel no doom
Let the cats run about helter-skelter
Gonna live, live, live in my fallout shelter

Verse 3: So if you want to be full of confidence
Get survival jazz and civil defense
You'll live like a king in your fallout pad
'Til the all clear sounds on CONELRAD
Dial six-four-o, twelve-four-o—CONELRAD.

The British brothers Mike and Bernie Winters, a popular television comedy team, released their version of the song on the Oriole label near the end of 1961. They play up the comedy in the lyrics, making their version more subversive, absurdist, and derisive of shelters. This derisive posture comes through most clearly in a small but significant alteration in the second chorus. While the chorus of the Peter Scott Peters version is, "I'm not scared / I'm prepared / I'll be spared," the Winters brothers change their second chorus to, "I'm not scared / I'm petrified / We'll be spared." The "I'm petrified" line undermines the confidence projected in the Peters version and exposes the real feelings of the British brothers about shelters. The line can also be heard as "I'm petrified we'll be spared," as if the brothers are more afraid of surviving a hydrogen bomb and living in a bleak postapocalyptic world than they are of dying. The endings of the two songs also show how the British were more jaded toward shelters than Americans. Peters's version ends by encouraging listeners to tune in to the CONELRAD frequencies (640 and 1240) on their AM radios for information on how to survive a nuclear attack. The British version ends with Bernie Winters sputtering out a dismissive, "So what!"

While both versions of "Fallout Shelter" have a man and a woman ensconced in the shelter, the next several novelty songs present scenarios where radiation harms women regardless of whether or not they are in shelters. Ironically, the men are never harmed. The songs are indicative of the trend of equating women with radioactivity in 1950s and 1960s popular culture, especially in horror films. The songs have an affinity with atomic horror films, such as *The Astounding She-Monster* (1957), where a radioactive female alien kills people with her touch; *Attack of the 50 Foot Woman* (1958), where a woman is exposed to radiation by an alien and grows to monstrous proportions; *Queen of Outer Space* (1958), where the queen of a female colony on Venus removes her mask to reveal radiation burns caused by "men and their wars"; and *Mothra* (1961), where we meet Godzilla's friend and sometime rival, a feminized, irradiated monster moth. This unsavory connection between women and radiation can be found not only in popular culture but in official US government literature. In 1972, an instructional booklet titled *Your Chance to Live* was produced by the Defense Civil Preparedness Agency, an agency reporting to the secretary of defense and later absorbed into FEMA

Table 4.1 Popular Songs Comparing Women to Radioactivity

Song	Songwriter	Performer	Year
"Crawl Out Through the Fallout"	Sheldon Allman	Sheldon Allman	1960
"Radioactive Mama"	Sheldon Allman	Sheldon Allman	1960
"Fallout Filly"	C. B. Cerf and L. M. Chazen	Chris Cerf	1961
"Fallout Shelter"	Frank D'Amico and Herb Alpert	Dore Alpert (Herb Alpert)	1962
"My Radiation Baby (My Teenage Fallout Queen)"	George McKelvey	George McKelvey	1964

(Federal Emergency Management Agency). The section "Nuclear Disaster" informs the public about the dangers of fallout and radiation poisoning. Accompanying the text is a crude illustration of three seductive, full-figured ladies in swimsuits with banners draped across their bodies reading, "Alpha," Beta," and "Gamma," as if they are the winners of a radioactive beauty contest.[31]

The alteration of women's bodies by radiation can be linked to other controversies over the alteration of women's bodies, such as the corset, the brassiere, foot-binding, female genital mutilation, dieting, and cosmetic surgery.[32] In these next songs, listed in table 4.1, radiation poisoning turns women into bombshells or monsters, or both at the same time. While films, television dramas, and novels from the 1950s and 1960s have their fair share of men plagued by radioactive fallout, the men in popular songs seem impervious to it. Women are more often the victims.

In 1960, actor, singer, and songwriter Sheldon Allman released a concept album of science fiction comedy songs entitled *Folk Songs for the 21st Century*. In "Crawl Out Through the Fallout," the male protagonist encourages his lady to break out of her shelter ("kick the wall out") and crawl to him through the radioactive rubble. Although she seems to be inside the shelter, somehow she is the one who has been burned by radioactive fallout. Through some miracle, radiation has apparently left the man unharmed even though he is outside the shelter. The man valiantly claims he can ease her suffering and kiss her burns away. In another song on the album, "Radioactive Mama," the irradiated woman's kiss shoots gamma rays through the man, which should actually kill him, but the extent of his injuries is the loss of his hair, including his eyebrows. His teeth shine in the dark as well. Chris Cerf, who wrote the music and lyrics for many *Sesame Street* songs, released "Fallout Filly" in 1961. In this song, a woman's exposure to radiation makes her a terror to the crowd since she shoots gamma rays out of her eyes and mushroom clouds out of her mouth. Yet her "atomic kiss" makes her a bombshell to her man. The story ends with the couple holing up "in a shelter of eternal bliss." In "Fallout Shelter" by Dore Alpert (1962), a man has been scorned by a woman.[33] He then regards her not only as cruel and heartless but also radioactive. Fearing she will break his heart—and contaminate him with radiation—he escapes by locking himself inside a shelter. In "My Radiation Baby (My Teenage Fallout Queen)" by George McKelvey (1964), two young lovers on a date see a bright flash in the sky. They flee for the fallout shelter, but the boy doesn't notice his girl has gone back to retrieve the class ring he gave her. While he makes it safely to the shelter, radiation exposure causes her to grow a third arm and has given her the ability to make objects glow in the dark. Her hair is also falling out. On the bright side, the radiation has cleared up her acne. A crude music video was made for this song. It includes a scene where McKelvey pulls the tube of a Geiger counter out from under his coat (an obvious phallic symbol) and holds it near the girl as he lip-synchs the line "my Geiger counter tells me that you're hot."

What are we to make of songs like these? Does their campiness and comedy lighten the dreadfulness of women subjected to radiation poisoning? Are they humorous or are they simply crass? These songs are the products of a society that never experienced the horrors of a nuclear attack firsthand, nor learned of the scale of human devastation in the Hiroshima and Nagasaki bombings. As Laura Hein and Mark Selden write, "Beginning in 1945, United States officials prevented wide distribution of most images of the bomb's destruction, particularly of the human havoc it wrought, and suppressed information about radiation, its most terrifying effect."[34] The only opportunity for most Americans to read about or see the actual effects of radiation on the human body were in John Hersey's 1946 book, *Hiroshima*, or photographs of Hiroshima and Nagasaki bomb victims published in the September 29, 1952, edition of *Life* magazine.[35] The US government censored the film footage taken by Japanese reporter Akira Iwasaki—which was shot in the days after the bombings and showed numerous men, women, and children scarred by radiation burns—for twenty-five years until 1970.[36] In November 1945, Brigadier General Leslie Groves, the director of the Manhattan Project, told a Senate committee this about dying from radiation sickness, "As I understand it from the doctors, it is a very pleasant way to die."[37]

Furthermore, publications and educational films by the Atomic Energy Commission (AEC) and the Office of Civil Defense (OCD) until the early to mid-1960s were vague and circumspect about the effects of radiation exposure on the human body. In the 1950 US-government pamphlet *Survival under Atomic Attack*, radiation exposure is compared to sunburn and its effects are described as mostly vomiting and hair loss. The pamphlet claims that victims would have a "better than an even chance of making a complete recovery."[38] In the 1955 pamphlet

Facts about Fallout, the most citizens are told about radiation is that "it will hurt you! It may even kill you!"[39] The 1961 publication *Fallout Protection: What to Know and Do about Nuclear Attack* goes into more detail, describing the effects of mild, moderate, and severe radiation sickness.[40] In these three widely distributed publications and others of their kind, little information is given about death from radiation exposure, and little is mentioned about hemorrhaging, damage to internal organs, infections, cancer, cell mutation, birth defects, sterility, or shell shock (now called post-traumatic stress disorder). While little was known about some of these effects in the 1940s, by the late 1950s, scientific and medical knowledge had progressed far beyond what was divulged to the public. Yet public outcry in response to knowing the full effects of radiation might have hindered the government's plans for future nuclear-weapon development. It might also have called into question the widely held belief that the Japan bombings were a necessity since they saved American and Japanese lives by bringing World War II to a swift end and kept the Allied forces from having to invade Japan. While some discretion about the effects of radiation was necessary to prevent widespread alarm among the American populace, many Cold War historians believe the degree of discretion was outright deception.[41] Thus, for many years Americans knew little about what actually happened to the victims in Hiroshima and Nagasaki or the true effects of radiation poisoning, so they wrote songs about sexy women with three arms, gamma rays shooting out of their eyes, and mushroom clouds exploding from their mouths.

NUCLEAR DARK HUMOR

The last novelty song to consider is "We Will All Go Together When We Go" by Tom Lehrer. While several songs in this chapter employ dark humor, this is the most crafty and clever. Dark humor treats grim topics, such as war, disease, and death, with comedy in order to make a social critique. As Patrick O'Neill writes, it "allows us to envisage the facelessness of the void and yet be able to laugh rather than despair."[42]

Considered to be among to the greatest musical satirists in the twentieth century, Tom Lehrer began writing his unique songs while a student at Harvard University. He earned an MA in mathematics there and was accepted into their doctoral program. He never completed his degree. He had a multifaceted career, serving in the US Army, composing for television shows, recording albums, performing as a solo artist, and teaching mathematics, political science, and musical theater at various universities. In his songs, he addressed many taboo subjects in the 1950s and 1960s (some of which are still taboo today), such as pornography, masochism, drug dealers, venereal disease, the Oedipus complex, and racism.

Many of his songs use major keys, pleasant melodies, and engaging rhythms juxtaposed with macabre lyrics like "Poisoning Pigeons in the Park." He composed several songs about the Cold War. "The Wild West Is Where I Want to Be" (1953) pairs cowboy music with lyrics about the continual nuclear bomb tests conducted in the Western deserts. "MLF Lullaby" (1964) considers the implications of including Germany in the Multi-Lateral Force, a coalition of NATO countries, which sought to collectively arm warships and submarines with nuclear weapons in the late 1950s and early 1960s. The music of a soft, peaceful lullaby couches the disconcerting lyrics. This juxtaposition highlights the conundrum of using nuclear weapons to maintain peace and international security. "Wernher von Braun" (1965) questions the Nazi rocket scientist's motives in helping the United States build ballistic missiles. "So Long, Mom (A Song for World War III)" (1965) is about a bomber pilot who encourages his mother to tune in to the evening news to see him drop a nuclear bomb during World War III. He promises to sift through the debris and look for her when the war has ended "an hour and a half from now," implying he will not be detained by the war for long, since nuclear weapons cause devastation so quickly. "Who's Next?" (1965) considers the various nations that own nuclear weapons, or greatly desire them, and who they want to bomb. As each stanza goes by, enumerating all the countries interested in nuclear weapons, the music continually modulates up a half step (D minor, E-flat minor, E minor, F minor, F-sharp minor, G major, G minor). This creates increasing tension and musically depicts the escalation of the arms race.

But Lehrer's greatest Cold War song is "We Will All Go Together When We Go" (1958), a sardonic celebration of international unity, a unity achieved through global extinction by hydrogen bomb warfare. First released on his live album *An Evening Wasted with Tom Lehrer* (1959), the song's form consists of a recitative-like prelude, three verses, a bridge, three more verses, a second bridge, and a final verse. The form shifts between three different sections and styles: the mock funereal prelude, the bright, marchlike verses, and the melodramatic bridges. The song keeps the listener on his or her toes, not knowing what to expect next, like a practical joke, or a nuclear war. The lyrics are below.

Lyrics to "We Will All Go Together When We Go."
Words and music by Tom Lehrer (1958).

Prelude: When you attend a funeral
It is sad to think that sooner or
Later those you love will do the same for you
And you may have thought it tragic
Not to mention other adjec-
tives to think of all the weeping they will do
(But don't you worry.)

No more ashes, no more sackcloth
And an arm band made of black cloth
Will someday nevermore adorn a sleeve
For if the bomb that drops on you
Gets your friends and neighbors too
There'll be nobody left behind to grieve

Verse 1: And we will all go together when we go
What a comforting fact that is to know
Universal bereavement
An inspiring achievement
Yes we all will go together when we go

Verse 2: We will all go together when we go
All suffused with an incandescent glow
No one will have the endurance
To collect on his insurance
Lloyd's of London will be loaded when they go

Verse 3: Oh we will all fry together when we fry
We'll be French fried potatoes by and by
There will be no more misery
When the world is our rotisserie
Yes we all will fry together when we fry

Bridge 1: Down by the old maelstrom
There'll be a storm before the calm

Verse 4: And we will all bake together when we bake
There'll be nobody present at the wake
With complete participation
In that grand incineration
Nearly three billion hunks of well-done steak

Verse 5: Oh we will all char together when we char
And let there be no moaning of the bar
Just sing out a Te Deum
When you see that I.C.B.M.
And the party will be come-as-you-are

Verse 6: Oh we will all burn together when we burn
There'll be no need to stand and wait your turn
When it's time for the fallout
And Saint Peter calls us all out
We'll just drop our agendas and adjourn

Bridge 2: You will all go directly to your respective Valhallas
Go directly, do not pass Go, do not collect two hundred dollas

Verse 7: And we will all go together when we go
Every Hottentot and every Eskimo
When the air becomes uranious
We will all go simultaneous
Yes we all will go together
When we all go together
Yes we all will go together when we go.

Used with the kind permission of Tom Lehrer.

Lehrer sings/speaks the prelude in the style of a recitative, in F minor, with a mournful vocal delivery and solemn chords. The lyrics express the sadness of funerals and the grief felt for the deceased by those left behind. The song then shifts to F major just before the first mention of the bomb. The rest of the song, a bouncy march in F major, "cheers" the listener by pointing out that if humanity is destroyed in a nuclear war, no one will have to grieve, because no one will be left behind. Lehrer begins the first and second verses with the title of the song, "we will all go together when we go," describing universal death by nuclear holocaust with the somewhat innocuous and indirect word *go*. He makes the verbs increasingly more grotesque with each succeeding verse, piling on more and more dark humor: "fry," "bake," "char," and "burn." Allusions to human bodies as cooked food abound: "French fried potatoes," "rotisserie," and "well-done steak." Each of the seven verses has the rhyme scheme AABBA, which is found in limericks, a form known for its risqué humor.

Two melodramatic bridges alter the marchlike rhythm of the song. The first is a parody of "Down by the Old Mill Stream," one of the most popular American songs from the early twentieth century. Lehrer adopts the three-quarter meter of "Old Mill Stream," imitates its melody, and plays rapidly arpeggiated chords to simulate old-time piano. He changes, "Down by the old mill stream where I first met you" to "down by the old maelstrom, they'll be a storm before the calm," referring to the nuclear explosion's blast wind. The second bridge harkens back to the solemn minor chords of the prelude. Yet by this time in the song, Lehrer has laid enough of an absurd foundation that he can describe nuclear annihilation using arcane references to Norse mythology (Odin's hall Valhalla) and the board game Monopoly. The song ends triumphantly with a sense of joyful madness. The dark humor of the song is even apparent in the score, which Lehrer prepared with the help of arranger Frank Metis. The five-measure introduction to the song, for piano alone, has the expressive marking, "eschatologically."[43] *Eschatology* is a theological term for the study of the destiny of humankind and end of the world.

One more detail in this song is worthy of note. Lehrer quotes a snippet of the bugle call "Retreat" on piano just after he sings the first line of the first, fourth, and final verses.[44] This seemingly insignificant musical quotation is quite meaningful. The bugle call and the marchlike accompaniment of the song give it a martial bearing. Lehrer served in the US Army from 1955 to 1957 as an enlisted man and would have become familiar with various bugle calls.[45] "Retreat" is played on military bases just before sunset when the US flag is lowered. In the context of the song, the quotation could be interpreted as the lowering of the flag at sunset on the final day of the human race. This musical "lowering of the flag" signals the end of the United States and by implication the end of all nations. The name of the bugle call, "Retreat," could also be taken literally. A global nuclear war would cause the whole human race to retreat from the face of the earth. Since nuclear weapons put civilians on the front lines, all of earth's citizens are soldiers in the Cold War and could potentially die together in battle. Lehrer packs many of his songs with quotations and allusions such as these. On the crafty content of his songs, he says, "I actually laugh out loud at Monty Python and some of these other things, because they're so carefully crafted. They're not just, 'Here's a joke. Here's something funny.' Once you've heard the joke, it's not funny anymore, but it's the way it's told. And I think that's the same with the music: The reason some of my songs have lasted longer is there's a lot of stuff packed in there."[46]

Lehrer proves well that a novelty song can contain astute and valuable social criticism, especially about nuclear warfare.

CONCLUSION

The steady stream of novelty and comedy songs about the Cold War died down in the mid-1960s. This coincides with the coming of the détente period after the Cuban Missile Crisis, when tension began to subside with the superpowers pursuing nuclear-arms-reduction treaties. Few humorous songs about the Vietnam War existed since they could not adequately express the vehement emotions the war generated. For example, Country Joe and the Fish's "I-Feel-Like-I'm-Fixin'-to-Die Rag" (1967) has some elements in common with novelty and comedy songs (a catchy, sing-along chorus, sound effects, lots of repetition, and dark humor), yet the anger expressed in the song overshadows its humorous elements. The 1980s Cold War songs were, for the most part, more serious than those written during the 1950s and 1960s. The last hurrah for the Cold War novelty song would have to be "Weird Al" Yankovic's "Christmas at Ground Zero" (1986), in which nuclear war interrupts Christmas celebrations.[47] The lyrics are full of dark humor, such as the line "I'll duck and cover with my Yuletide lover underneath the 'missile'-toe." The music video, directed by Yankovic himself, is clever and adds much to the song since it uses civil-defense films from the 1950s, including *Duck and Cover,* and stock footage of life in the 1950s. The video also includes a black-and-white clip of Ronald Reagan (presumably from when he was host of *General Electric Theater* from 1954 to 1962) addressing his television audience in front of a Christmas tree, "Well, the big day is only a few hours away now. I'm sure you're all looking forward to it as much as we are." Although Reagan, who was president when Yankovic made the video, was speaking of Christmas day, the context of the video makes Reagan appear to be saying the "big day" is the nuclear apocalypse.

How effective are novelty and comedy songs in expressing opinions about serious matters such as nuclear weapons, fallout shelters, and radiation poisoning? Do they achieve the objective of the best satire by revealing truths that cannot be expressed through more direct means? Does comedy blunt a message or make it more incisive? In some of these songs, Cold War events are simply used as vehicles for mindless amusement, such as the songs about radioactivity. In others, such as Tom Lehrer's songs, humor is employed to make an erudite social critique. Regardless of their intentions, they are spoonfuls of sugar that helped the medicine go down and made the Cold War a bit easier—or perhaps harder—to swallow.

For most listeners, our first reaction to these songs—especially the inane ones about the atom bomb—is usually a laugh or a snicker. We enjoy satire, camp, and comedy, and nothing fits the bill like a song from the 1950s about the bomb. Yet, a second reaction always follows: the sinking realization a single nuclear weapon can kill more than a million people in a minute. We should be grateful for both reactions. The first brings us relief that all-out nuclear war has thus far been avoided. We can joke about it. The second never lets us underestimate the effects such weapons would have on humans and the planet.

NOTES

1. Steven Otfinoski, *The Golden Age of Novelty Songs* (New York: Billboard, 2000), 7.

2. *The Atomic Café,* 20th anniversary edition, produced and directed by Kevin Rafferty, Jayne Loader, Pierce Rafferty (New Video Group NVG-9496, 2002, DVD).

3. Glenn Harlan Reynolds, "The Unexpected Return of 'Duck and Cover,'" *Atlantic,* January 4, 2011, http://www.theatlantic.com/national/archive/2011/01/the-unexpected-return-of-duck-and-cover/68776/.

4. Mardelle L. Reynolds and Francis X. Lynch, "Atomic Bomb Injuries among Survivors in Hiroshima," *Public Health Reports* 70, no. 3 (March 1955): 261–270; *The Impact of the A-Bomb, Hiroshima and Nagasaki, 1945–85,* Committee for the Compilation of Materials on Damage Caused by the Atomic Bombs in Hiroshima and Nagasaki, trans. Eisei Ishikawa and David L. Swain (Tokyo: Iwanami Shoten, 1985).

5. Melvin E. Matthews, Jr., *Duck and Cover: Civil Defense Images in Film and Television from the Cold War to 9/11* (Jefferson, NC: McFarland, 2012), 25.

6. Jon Goodman, *The King of Novelty, Dickie Goodman* (Bloomington, IN: Xlibris, 2000), 15.

7. Goodman, *King of Novelty,* 24.

8. Goodman created "Stroganoff Cha Cha" with the help of his close friend Mickey Shorr, a Detroit disc jockey. They worked under the pseudonym "Spencer and Spencer," whom the record is credited to on the label.

9. Fidel Castro and Ignacio Ramonet, *Fidel Castro: My Life; A Spoken Autobiography,* trans. Andrew Hurley (New York: Scribner, 2008), 99–100.

10. Peter Shearman, *The Soviet Union and Cuba* (London: Routledge and Kegan Paul, 1987), 6.

11. Dana Adams Schmidt, "Castro Stresses Land Reform Aid," *New York Times,* April 21, 1959, 1.

12. Sergei Khrushchev, *Khrushchev in Power: Unfinished Reforms, 1961–1964,* trans. George Shriver (Boulder, CO: Lynne Rienner, 2014), 160.

13. Laura Roselle, *Media and the Politics of Failure: Great Powers, Communication Strategies, and Military Defeats* (New York: Palgrave Macmillan, 2006), 15.

14. "Don't Fence Me In" was written by Cole Porter and Robert Fletcher in 1934. The version heard in "Berlin Top Ten" was recorded by Bing Crosby and the Andrews Sisters in 1944.

15. The Berlin Wall actually surrounded West Berlin, which was located in East Germany, rather than East Berlin. West Berliners were free to move in and out, but East Berliners were prevented from accessing West Berlin, West Germany, and the rest of Western Europe.

16. Nicholas J. Schlosser, "The Berlin Radio War: Broadcasting in Cold War Berlin and the Shaping of Political Culture in Divided Germany 1945–1961" (PhD diss., University of Maryland, College Park, 2008), 179–180.

17. Jon Goodman interview by Dave Lefkowitz on the radio show "Dave's Gone By," December 8, 2012, 8:48–8:52, http://www.youtube.com/watch?v=RkMBeqRppJs.

18. Alexandra Hildebrandt, *The Wall: Figures, Facts* (Berlin: Haus am Checkpoint Charlie, 2002), 124–126.

19. Goodman, *King of Novelty,* 200.

20. "Barbara Is Moscow Molly to U.S. Soldiers in Berlin," *Reading Eagle,* January 11, 1962, 4, http://news.google.com/newspapers?nid=1955&dat=19620111&id=wBIrAAAAIBAJ&sjid=oZsFAAAAIBAJ&pg=5712,3789556.

21. "National Radiation Instrument Catalog, 1920–1960," http://national-radiation-instrument-catalog.com/new_page_34.htm.

22. Joanna Bourke, *Fear: A Cultural History* (Emeryville, CA: Shoemaker and Hoard, 2006), 284.

23. Bob Dylan, *Chronicles: Volume One* (New York: Simon and Schuster, 2004), 271–272.

24. Kenneth D. Rose, *One Nation Underground: The Fallout Shelter in American Culture* (New York: New York University Press, 2001), 4.

25. Nathan Tempey, "Helter Shelter: NYC's Fallout Shelters Basically Don't Exist Anymore," *Gothamist*, March 9, 2017, http://gothamist.com/2017/03/09/fallout_shelters_nyc.php.

26. Laura McEnaney, *Civil Defense Begins at Home: Militarization Meets Everyday Life in the Fifties* (Princeton, NJ: Princeton University Press, 2000), 40–67; David Monteyne, *Fallout Shelter: Designing for Civil Defense in the Cold War* (Minneapolis: University of Minnesota Press, 2011), 13.

27. "Atomic Honeymooners: 'Well-Sheltered Love May Last a Lifetime,'" *CONELRAD*, http://www.conelrad.com/atomic_honeymooners.html.

28. John F. Kennedy, "Radio and Television Report to the American People on the Berlin Crisis, July 25, 1961," John F. Kennedy Presidential Library and Museum, https://www.jfklibrary.org/archives/other-resources/john-f-kennedy-speeches/berlin-crisis-19610725.

29. John F. Kennedy, "A Message to You from the President," *Life*, September 15, 1961, 95; "Shelter Boom," *Newsweek*, September 18, 1961, 31; "Civil Defense: The Sheltered Life," *Time*, October 20, 1961, 21–25.

30. Lawrence J. Vale, *The Limits of Civil Defence in the USA, Switzerland, Britain, and the Soviet Union: The Evolution of Policies Since 1945* (New York: St. Martin's, 1987), 123.

31. Tamara C. Lowery, ed., *Your Chance to Live* (San Francisco: Far West Laboratory for Educational Research and Development; Washington, DC: Department of Defense, Defense Civil Preparedness Agency, 1972), 79.

32. Susan Bordo, *Unbearable Weight: Feminism, Western Culture, and the Body*, 10th anniversary ed. (Berkeley: University of California Press, 2003); Nancy L. Etcoff, *Survival of the Prettiest: The Science of Beauty* (New York: Doubleday, 1999).

33. Dore Alpert is actually a pseudonym for Herb Alpert, the trumpet player, songwriter, and record executive most known for his group Tijuana Brass.

34. Laura Hein and Mark Selden, "Commemoration and Silence: Fifty Years of Remembering the Bomb in American and Japan," in *Living with the Bomb: American and Japanese Cultural Conflicts in the Nuclear Age*, ed. Laura Hein and Mark Selden (Armonk, NY: M. E. Sharpe, 1997), 4.

35. John Hersey, *Hiroshima* (New York: Knopf, 1946). The entire book was first published in the *New Yorker* magazine. John Hersey, "A Reporter at Large, Hiroshima," *New Yorker*, August 31, 1946, 15–68; "When Atom Bomb Struck—Uncensored," *Life* 33, no. 13 (September 29, 1952): 19–25.

36. Historian and documentarian Erik Barnouw acquired access to Iwasaki's footage and edited it into a sixteen-minute documentary titled *Hiroshima Nagasaki, August 1945*, released in 1970. For more information, see Philip L. Simpson's entry "Hiroshima-Nagasaki, August 1945" in *Concise Routledge Encyclopedia of the Documentary Film*, ed. Ian Aitken (New York: Routledge, 2013), 367–369. The film is available on YouTube here: https://www.youtube.com/watch?v=qh41SVycYBQ.

37. Leslie Groves, US Congress, Senate, Special Committee on Atomic Energy, 79th Congress, 1945–1946, *Hearings* (Washington, DC, 1946), 37. Quoted in Sean L.

Malloy, "A Very Pleasant Way to Die: Radiation Effects and the Decision to Use the Atomic Bomb against Japan," *Diplomatic History* 36, no. 3 (June 2012): 518.

38. *Survival under Atomic Attack* (Washington, DC: Civil Defense Office, 1950), 12, http://www.orau.org/ptp/Library/cdv/Survival%20Under%20Atomic%20Attack.pdf.

39. *Facts about Fallout* (Washington, DC: Federal Civil Defense Administration, 1955), 3, http://research.archives.gov/description/306714.

40. *Fallout Protection: What to Know and Do about Nuclear Attack* (Washington, DC: Office of Civil Defense, 1961), 34, http://www.dahp.wa.gov/sites/default/files/Fallout%20Protection%20What%20to%20Know%20and%20Do.pdf.

41. Two of several books written on the subject are Barton C. Hacker, *Elements of Controversy: The Atomic Energy Commission and Radiation Safety in Nuclear Weapons Testing, 1947–1974* (Berkeley, CA: University of California Press, 1994) and Robert A. Jacobs, *The Dragon's Tail: Americans Face the Atomic Age* (Amherst, MA: University of Massachusetts Press, 2010).

42. Patrick O'Neill, "The Comedy of Entropy: The Contexts of Black Humour," *Canadian Review of Comparative Literature* 10, no. 2 (June 1983): 165.

43. Tom Lehrer, *Too Many Songs,* piano arrangements by Tom Lehrer and Frank Metis (New York: Pantheon Books, 1981), 81. Another Cold War song "Who's Next?," about the nuclear-arms race, begins with the expressive marking "Disarmingly" on p. 120.

44. US War Department, *Cavalry Drill Regulations, United States Army* (Washington, DC: Government Printing Office, 1918), 406–407.

45. Lehrer also quotes the bugle call "Reveille" on piano in "It Makes a Fellow Proud to Be a Soldier" (1958).

46. Tom Lehrer, "Tom Lehrer," interview by Stephen Thompson, *A.V. Club,* May 24, 2000, http://www.avclub.com/article/tom-lehrer-13660.

47. Although many American radio stations play a glut of Christmas novelty songs during December, this song has received little airplay since 2001 because the "Ground Zero" in its title brings up mistaken associations with the 2001 attack on the World Trade Center. The original meaning of ground zero was the point at which a bomb explosion, earthquake, or other disaster originates.

FIVE

EARLY ROCK AND OTHER STYLES

Rocking the Bomb

ALTHOUGH DATA FROM NUCLEAR SCIENTISTS never surfaced to substantiate the claim, atomic energy apparently fueled Elvis Presley and his hips. For his concert on April 23, 1956, the Frontier Hotel in Las Vegas billed Elvis as the "atomic powered singer."[1] For those staying at the hotel, mushroom clouds from bomb tests seventy-five miles away at the Nevada Test Site could be seen by the naked eye. The phrase "the nation's only atomic powered singer" was actually placed directly under his name on his 1956–1958 concert appearance contracts.[2] According to a *Variety* magazine writer, he was an "atomic-age phenomenon."[3] In a *Time* magazine article, he was described dangerously as "hotter than a radioactive yam."[4] When rock and roll blasted into American culture in the mid- to late 1950s, only atomic adjectives could sufficiently capture its impact. Rock and roll and the Atomic Age developed simultaneously.

This chapter explores songs from several styles of popular music from the 1940s to the 1960s not covered in the first four chapters: early rock, rockabilly, doo-wop, calypso, musicals, blues, and spirituals. Some of these styles were considered to be suitable vehicles to voice serious concerns about Cold War matters, while others were not. Many early rock and rockabilly songs were written about the Cold War, but few have anything substantial to say about the conflict. The lyrics to songs such as "Atom Bomb Baby," and "Rock H-Bomb Rock" go no deeper than their titles suggest. Tom Waldman writes,

> In the 1950s, rock and roll stars didn't tell their fans how to vote or what causes to embrace. They didn't offer opinions on the Issues of the Day, nor were they asked. . . . There were many issues in the 1950s that would have been perfect candidates for the rock and roll treatment: a Ban the Bomb concert, a new pro-Civil Rights song, a benefit for peace. But the high school

> kids that comprised the vast majority of the audience just wanted to dance, and the performers gave them exactly what they wanted—they left politics to the politicians.[5]

This remained the case until rock music came under the spell of folk musicians like Bob Dylan in the mid-1960s. Until Dylan came along, few musicians viewed rock music as a proper medium to seriously express political opinions about the Cold War. Dylan blurred the lines between folk and rock when he "went electric" in 1965 with his albums *Bringing It All Back Home* and *Highway 61 Revisited*. Following his lead, an increasing number of rock musicians invested more time in their lyrics and used their songs to vent opinions on contemporary matters. The Cold War–themed rock music of the 1950s and 1960s vividly shows this shift from being a music for fun and dancing to a music that tackled serious subjects. The Cuban Missile Crisis and the Vietnam War produced a sharp increase in the number of rock songs with political themes from the mid-1960s on.

Although the early rockers wrote few serious songs about the Cold War, musicians in other styles, such as doo-wop, calypso, musicals, blues, and spirituals, wrote several. These songs show the perspective of minority groups, specifically Latin Americans and African Americans, concerning issues like US imperialism in the Caribbean, the lack of adequate fallout protection for those in urban areas, and the Berlin Wall in Selma, Alabama. But before we get to the serious songs, let's follow the advice of the early rockers and bop to the bomb.

BOPPING TO THE BOMB

The rock and roll revolution in the mid-1950s also brought about a dance revolution. The first decade of rock music intertwined closely with numerous dance crazes of the period: the bop, the hand jive, the jerk, the swim, the monkey, the mashed potato, the Watusi, and the twist. Lisa Jo Sagolla writes, "None of the early rock 'n' roll performers simply stood still and sang. They all moved, usually with furious abandon and often quite provocatively."[6] Chubby Checker's "The Twist" hit number one in 1960 and then again in 1962—the only song to reach the top of the *Billboard* chart in two separate chart runs. Checker didn't miss the year in between either. "Let's Twist Again" went to number eight in 1961. Some songs, like "Land of 1000 Dances" by Wilson Pickett and "Do You Love Me" by the Contours, enumerated how many different dances were around. Teens learned new dances not only on the dance floor or at concerts but in the movie theaters (*Rock around the Clock, The Girl Can't Help It*) and in their living rooms (*American Bandstand*). Throw the atomic bomb and the space race into the mix, and you get some of the weirdest dance songs of the 1950s.

Teens who wanted to dance to the beat of the bomb had "Rock H-Bomb Rock" (1952) by Robert "H-Bomb" Ferguson. Ferguson was a jump-blues singer from Cincinnati whose powerful voice earned him his explosive moniker. While dancing to the "Atomic Bounce" (1955), Johnny LaTorre sings that he will flip his lid and blow his top. In "A Bomb Bop" by Mike Fern (1959), the singer suggests that when the "missile whistle" is heard, the best thing to do is not look for the nearest shelter but simply start dancing to "that wonderful A-bomb beat." Bill Haley and His Comets agree. In Haley's song "Thirteen Women" (1954), the protagonist dreams that only he and thirteen women have survived an H-bomb explosion. There's not much to do after a nuclear attack, so the women start doing the mambo and Ballin' the Jack. In 1962, Ann-Margaret turned the tables with her version of the song, "Thirteen Men." Russell Reising quips that this song is "surely one of the most sensuous accounts of the destruction of the human race."[7] Dancing was also something you could do on satellites, on guided missiles, around the moon, or whizzing through outer space at the speed of light, as in "Satellite Baby" by Skip Stanley (1956), "Sputnik (Satellite Girl)" by Jerry Engler and the Four Ekkos (1957), and "Satellite No. 2" by Carl Mann (1958).

Even subatomic particles got into the act and hit the dance floor. In "Rock and Roll Atom" (1959), Red McCoy gives the listener a simple lesson in nuclear physics to the beat of early rock. The electrons are "swingin'" around the nucleus, while inside the protons are dancing with the neutrons. McCoy then anthropomorphizes the particles, making himself out to be a proton and his girl an electron. They are attracted to each other because he is positively charged and she is negatively charged. (Sadly, the neutron is left alone on the dance floor because it has no charge.) In the last stanza, Cupid lays down his dart (i.e., arrow) and instead shoots a "rock and roll atom right through your heart."

MISSILES AND BOMBSHELLS

With their provocative dancing, hip gyrations, and outrageous antics, some early rock musicians, such as Elvis Presley, Little Richard, and Jerry Lee Lewis, were criticized for being obscene and overtly sexual. Many parents judged their lyrics to be offensive. Frank Sinatra despised the early rockers for their "sly, lewd, in plain fact, dirty lyrics."[8] American journalist Abel Green referred to rock lyrics as "leer-ics" in a 1955 *Variety* article.[9] Songs about bombs and rockets were even more unsubtle, given their phallic shape. In 1958, Jimmie Logsdon (under his pseudonym Jimmy Lloyd) released his rockabilly classic, "I Got a Rocket in My Pocket." His manager, Vic McAlpin, came up with the title, and they both wrote the lyrics. While the recorded song is not overtly sexual, the first draft was. Lloyd said in an interview, "We had to tone it down a little. Too risqué."[10] "Atomic Love" (1953) by Little Caesar with the Red Callender Sextette leaves little to the imagination with its first line, "Boom, something exploded down inside." In his "biography" *The Bomb: A Life*, Gerard J. DeGroot quips that "as a sexual metaphor, the Bomb was particularly well-endowed."[11]

One can also find this unsubtle connection between bombs and sex in Stanley Kubrick's film *Dr. Strangelove or: How I Learned to Stop Worrying and Love the Bomb* (1964). Near the end of the film, the crew aboard a B-52 bomber faces a predicament: they cannot drop their hydrogen bomb on the "Russkies," because the bay doors won't open. The ever-resourceful Major Kong climbs down to the bomb bay and, straddling the bomb, manages to open the doors. Waving his cowboy hat, hooting and hollering, he descends to earth with an H-bomb between his legs.

One would expect to find this type of lewd, rude, and crude behavior in the world of popular entertainment. But in a tale of truth being stranger than fiction, the phallic imagery used by some nuclear scientists and Pentagon officials makes these songs sound tame in comparison. During the Cold War, military power was often equated with phallic power. The shape of rockets, missiles, and bombs; the pillar of a mushroom cloud; and the magnitude of atomic detonations were all fodder for phallic allusion. Physicist and science professor Brian Easlea, who studied under the Manhattan Project physicist Niels Bohr, noted the explicit language employed by nuclear scientists.[12] Of the Manhattan Project scientists, Easlea writes, "In what one might take to be the austerely asexual world of theoretical and experimental physics practiced at Los Alamos, it is surely remarkable how both sexual and birth metaphors frequently make an appearance in the writings, memoirs and reminiscences of participants."[13] Carol Cohn, a scholar who has written extensively on war and gender, recounted her experiences in 1984 and 1985 when she worked at a certain university's center for defense technology and arms control. In "White Men in Ties Discussing Missile Size," a section of her article, she writes she heard nuclear weapons routinely described in terms of erections, penetrations, and ejaculations.[14] Throughout history, victory in battle and sexual potency have often been considered the ultimate test of masculinity and manliness, and nuclear weapons took this correlation to frightening new levels.

As if this were not disturbing enough, songs correlated female sexuality to the bomb far more often than to male sexuality. We've found at least seven that in some way liken women to bombs. See table 5.1. In "Atom Bomb Baby," recorded by Dude Martin and His Roundup Gang in 1948, a red-haired woman is "block bustin'," "jet propelled," and "supercharged." Ironically, a woman—Ann Jones, who led one of the first all-female country and western groups, the Western Sweethearts—wrote this song. Another song named "Atom Bomb Baby" from 1957 (recorded by the Five Stars and written by J. F. Young) expresses similar sentiments. The woman here has "nuclear fission in her soul," which makes her a

Table 5.1 Popular Songs Comparing Women to Bombs

Song	Songwriter
"Atom Bomb Baby"	Ann Jones
"Atomic Baby"	F. Hayward and M. Tucker
"Your Atom Bomb Heart"	Howard Vokes and Hank King, arranged by Chaw Mank
"B. Bomb Baby"	Johnny Torrence
"Satellite Baby"	Skip Stanley
"Fujiyama Mama"	Earl Burrows
"Atom Bomb Baby"	J. F. Young

"million times hotter than TNT." In "Atomic Baby," written by F. Hayward and M. Tucker (1950), the protagonist calls his woman "U92," the symbol and atomic number for uranium. He has to "handle her with care" because she, like uranium, is an unstable element liable to explode at any moment.

The strangest and most disturbing of this type of song is "Fujiyama Mama," recorded by blues singer Annisteen Allen, nightclub singer Eileen Barton (both in 1955), and rockabilly singer Wanda Jackson (1957). Written by Earl Burrows—otherwise known as Jack Hammer, who cowrote Jerry Lee Lewis's hit "Great Balls of Fire"—the lyrics have a female protagonist explain she gets her explosive sexual power by drinking sake, smoking dynamite, chewing tobacco, and drinking nitroglycerine. She compares herself not only to Mount Fuji, the massive volcano outside Tokyo, but to the atom bombs dropped on Hiroshima and Nagasaki. She sings, "The things I did to them baby, I can do to you!" As Bill Geerhart and Ken Sitz write, "Earl Burrows' lyrics demonstrate that the bombings in Japan a decade earlier were still viewed as being an impressive display of American might without any consideration given to the moral implications of the wholesale destruction unleashed on the enemy."[15] Despite the song's projection of female power, Leah Branstetter sees the song as an example of the American feminization of Japan, which "helped Americans transition from viewing the Japanese as enemies to viewing them as an ally merely in need of a masculine rescuer."[16] The song was not a hit in the United States, but unbelievably, Wanda Jackson's version was in Japan. Jackson toured Japan in February and March 1959 and was a sensation. Izumi Yukimura and Tamaki Sawa, two female Japanese singers, even did their own versions of the song and included the line about being as explosive as the bombs dropped on Hiroshima and Nagasaki. Perhaps the Japanese wanted so eagerly to embrace American rock and roll in the late 1950s that they disregarded, or perhaps misunderstood, the lyrics.

Performer	Year
Dude Martin and His Roundup Gang	1948
Amos Milburn and Linda Hayes with the Red Callender Sextette	1950, 1953
Hank King with Bud Williams and His Smilin' Buddies	1955
The Jewels	1956
Skip Stanley	1956
Annisteen Allen, Eileen Barton, and Wanda Jackson	1955, 1957
The Five Stars	1957

These songs reflect the distasteful connection between women and bombs in the 1940s and 1950s in American culture. "Bombshell" was a common name for a sexually alluring female. Actress Linda Christian was nicknamed "the Anatomic Bomb" in a 1945 *Life* magazine feature. The 1955 film *Kiss Me Deadly* explicitly links female sexuality with a deadly nuclear explosion. The bikini swimsuit, designed by French engineer Louis Réard, was named after the Bikini Atoll, where the fourth atomic bomb was detonated on July 1, 1946. The US military also got into the act. At the same test, the Able of Operation Crossroads at Bikini Atoll, a pinup of Rita Hayworth from her 1946 film, *Gilda*, was plastered onto the bomb.[17] Perhaps the strangest manifestation of this phenomenon was the numerous atomic beauty queen contests. In 1950's Nevada, several pageants were held to entertain military personnel on nuclear-testing sites, promote Las Vegas as a vacation hot spot, and make nuclear testing seem fun and harmless to the general public.[18] In 1955, the winner of the "Miss Atomic Energy" pageant in Grand Junction, Colorado, was awarded a truckload of uranium ore.[19] Models, dancers, actresses, and showgirls were variously named "Miss Atomic Bomb," "Miss Atomic Blast," "Miss Uranium," and "Miss Cue" (named for the Operation Cue test in 1955). Most of the women wore mock mushroom clouds over their swimsuits. "Miss Cue" wore a mushroom cloud–shaped crown on her head. In a 1953 parade in St. George, Utah, a preteen girl was perched atop a mock mushroom cloud on a float. She was named "Our Little A-Bomb" and won first place in the parade.[20]

What was the cause of all this? What social factors contributed to such a crass and insulting comparison? The unease American men in the 1950s had toward strong, independent women played a major societal factor. Before the equal rights era, most of the male population expected women to be coy, quiet, subservient, and homebound. Bombshells were dangerous, possibly uncontrollable. As Kristina Zarlengo summarizes, "In general, atomic age female types took the form of either the good housewife and mother . . . or the dangerously powerful temptress."[21] Elaine Tyler May writes that independent women in the 1950s were often thought of as "subversives at home, Communist aggressors abroad, atomic energy, sexuality, the bomb, and 'bombshell' [who] all had to be 'harnessed for peace.'"[22] These songs also reflect the desire of nuclear scientists to harness the atom, to tame the elemental energy of Mother Nature. In the song "Atom Bomb Baby," by Dude Martin and His Roundup Gang, the male needs a "secret weapon," or Superman, to "harness her energy." Just as these songs viewed women as elemental forces of nature, nuclear scientists saw the earth as a female they could tame, probe, and harness with science. Before the environmental movement in the 1960s and 1970s, scientists had fewer qualms about exploiting Mother Nature's resources for economic, political, and military gain.

These songs also show among the American public an acceptance of, and an acclimation toward, nuclear weapons. In her discussion of "the mushroom cloud as political kitsch," A. Costandina Titus writes, "The government—with the help of the media—successfully diverted the public's attention from asking substantive questions about possible negative consequences and costs. Dazzled by atomic eye candy, citizens were virtually hypnotized into acceptance. . . . The mushroom cloud ingrained itself in the American psyche."[23]

Yet not all songs about nuclear weapons were crass and unsavory. The next sections explore songs mostly by Latin American and African American songwriters in the styles of doo-wop, calypso, musicals, blues, and spirituals that ask substantive questions about the bomb and other Cold War issues.

DOO-WOP: "SH-BOOM" GOES THE BOMB

With its nonsense syllables, bright vocal harmonies, and lyrics about teenagers in love, doo-wop is a music steeped in dreamy 1950s nostalgia. The Chords, a vocal quintet from the Bronx, were one of the groups that fashioned the template for doo-wop. Their one hit, the classic "Sh-Boom" from 1954, is a unique song for several reasons. It was one of the first records to introduce White audiences to Black R&B music.[24] It was among several songs musicologists and critics believe to be the first doo-wop record, maybe even the first rock and roll record.[25] For decades it has embodied the spirit of the Fabulous Fifties through its use in TV shows, like *Happy Days* (1974–1984), and films, such as Pixar's *Cars* (2006). Lastly it captures, in its onomatopoeic title, the presence of the bomb in 1950s popular culture. On March 1, 1954, the United States detonated its largest hydrogen bomb, a fifteen megaton monster codenamed "Castle Bravo," on Bikini Atoll. Two weeks later, on March 15, the Chords recorded "Sh-Boom."[26] What does this song have to do with the bomb? Early-rock historian Marv Goldberg interviewed the Chords' first tenor, Jimmy Keyes, who told him, "'Boom' was the slang word. If you was standing in this block [in the Bronx] for five minutes, you'd hear that slang word fifteen times or more. . . . We thought we would take the 'boom' and make it sound like a bomb: 'shhhhhh-BOOM.'"[27] In 1954, the fireballs in the Pacific Ocean were making front-page headlines, generating street slang, and inspiring the titles of chart-topping songs.

In 1956, the Cuff Links recorded "Guided Missiles" a doo-wop song written by Alfred Gaitwood. In the lyrics, a woman's scorn is compared to missiles aimed at the protagonist's heart. He warns her that in the end he will retaliate in like manner. Thus a failed relationship is described in terms of nuclear warfare. Although this song has a dark subject matter, it still sounds romantic and pleasing to the ear because the elements of doo-wop music are prominent: bright vocal harmonies, smooth delivery, and an easygoing 12/8 meter. The background vocals also lighten the dark lyrics. Nonsense syllables like "doo-wop," "shoobie-doo," "dip-da-dip," "shang-a-lang," and "sh-boom" pack most doo-wop songs. In "Guided Missiles," the singers mimic the speed of missiles by singing "zoom" all the way through the song.

There are many melancholy doo-wop songs, but is it possible to write a truly dark and depressing one? "A Mushroom Cloud," sung by Sammy Salvo and released in 1961, is just that. Written by Boudleaux Bryant—a songwriter most famous for penning (with his wife, Felice) the Everly Brothers' three biggest hits, "Bye Bye Love," "Wake Up Little Susie," and "All I Have to Do is Dream"—the song stands apart in this chapter because its gloomy lyrics are matched with equally gloomy music. The first chord in E-flat minor sets the mood.[28] It moves to G-flat in the bridge, the relative major, but a few major chords cannot dissipate the gloom. The meter is 12/8, like "Guided Missiles" and many other doo-wop songs, yet the drummer plays the beat with great rigidity and stiffness, creating a tense atmosphere. The smooth, leisurely pace of the meter has been replaced with a staccato attack. The electric guitar (in the left channel) has a tremolo effect, producing a nervous timbre, an appropriate sound for projecting the fear of living in a world with hydrogen bombs. The heavily plucked bass guitar and overarticulated "ba-ba-ba-wop" vocal accompaniment (both in the right channel) also contribute to the unease of the song. The recording has thick reverb on all the instruments and vocals. This studio effect provided 1950s recordings with spaciousness and presence but sounds menacing here. "A Mushroom Cloud" distorts the musical elements of doo-wop and turns the song into an angst-filled lament.

The protagonist of the song, a despondent teenager, expresses a fervent wish for a peaceful life, yet the specter of a mushroom cloud continually haunts his dreams. He seems doubtful he and his girlfriend will live to see adulthood. In the lyrics of the bridge, he moves rapidly from praying, to partying, to laughing, and back to praying. He feels trapped in an endless cycle of hope, blissful ignorance, and despair. In the last verse, he concedes that the Latin motto *carpe diem* ("seize the day") may be the only solution: "tomorrow looks black so we live for the day." Salvo's teenager wants to live the dream of the Fabulous Fifties as portrayed in *American Graffiti*, *Happy Days*, and "Sh-Boom," but his reality is closer to Allen Ginsberg's "Howl" (1955) or "America" (1956). The three doo-wop songs in this section display the fractured reality of growing up in the Atomic Age. As Paul Boyer writes, "Along with the shock waves of fear, one also finds exalted prophecies of the bright promise of atomic energy. . . . These two responses that seem so contradictory—the terror of atomic war and the vision of an atomic Utopia—were in fact complexly interwoven."[29] Teens felt at one moment that "life could be a dream," but the next moment they conceded that "tomorrow looks black."

CRITIQUES IN CALYPSO

Outside of the folk songs covered in the first two chapters and a few comedy songs covered in chapter 4, only a handful of outright antibomb popular songs emerged from the 1940s and 1950s. The majority of the protest songs came after the Cuban Missile Crisis in 1962. The main reason is that most Americans felt Japanese aggression at Pearl Harbor and throughout the rest of World War II justified the dropping of the bombs on Hiroshima and Nagasaki. The bomb genuinely frightened Americans, but the fact it was in America's hands eased their fears. In addition, the US government shielded the public from the true magnitude of the bomb's destructive potential, as discussed in chapter 4.

Yet for Latin Americans, the fear was greater. Although they were in "America's backyard" and enjoyed the benefits of tourism, commerce, and technology from the most robust economy in the world, they paid a price: the presence of the US military, capitalist exploitation of natural resources, and right-wing dictators planted by the US government.[30] As the number of US military bases grew in the Caribbean in the 1950s, Latin Americans felt their islands were becoming greater targets for atomic bombs. Rather than feeling protected, they felt imperiled and colonized. Thus, we find antibomb protest songs from Latin American songwriters or in Latin American musical styles.

It may come as a surprise to many readers that three of these antibomb songs are in the calypso style. Calypso is often thought of as music one listens to while soaking up the sun, sipping a piña colada, and reclining in a beach chair on the deck of a Caribbean cruise ship. With its syncopated Latin rhythms and instrumentation of steel drums, maracas, and brass ensembles, calypso music sounds like leisure and pleasure. Yet, this style has often been used as protest music to inveigh against American colonialism in the Caribbean Islands.[31] The origins of calypso go back to the early twentieth century on the islands of Trinidad and Tobago, just northeast of Venezuela's coast. Harry Belafonte popularized calypso in the United States with his 1956 song "Day-O (The Banana Boat Song)" about poor Black laborers working all night ("on a drop of rum") hauling bananas in Jamaica.

Sir Lancelot's "Atomic Energy" from 1947 is among the first antibomb protest songs. Lancelot, whose real name was Lancelot Victor Edward Pinard, was a calypso singer and songwriter from Trinidad, who greatly influenced Belafonte. Lancelot wrote the music while Ray Glaser wrote the lyrics. Both were members of the proleft organization People's Songs, discussed in chapter 1. "Atomic Energy" reflects the view of some of the general populace, and two of the most famous scientists J. Robert Oppenheimer and Albert Einstein, that the production of ever more powerful nuclear bombs should not simply go on indefinitely.[32] Oppenheimer was the most well-known Manhattan Project nuclear scientist, yet his reservations about developing the hydrogen bomb resulted in a four-week hearing in which the Atomic Energy Commission questioned his loyalty to the United States. Albert Einstein had similar qualms. In 1946, he cofounded the Emergency Committee of Atomic Scientists, whose aim was to educate the public about how destructive nuclear bombs were and how much more powerful they would become. The lyrics of "Atomic Energy" closely echo the goal of this committee, as stated in the June 1947 issue of *Bulletin of the Atomic Scientists*, "To ensure that atomic energy will be used for the benefit of mankind and not for humanity's destruction."[33] Sir Lancelot's chorus encourages people "to crusade to see that no more bombs are made" and says that atomic energy should be used only for "peace and democracy."

This fleeting hope was brought to an unambiguous end by two developments in 1949 and 1950. First, the Soviet Union successfully tested its first atomic bomb on August 29, 1949, making the nuclear-arms race inevitable. Second, in January 1950, President Truman announced that America would go forward with the development of the hydrogen bomb. Thus, "Atomic Energy" captures that unique era in the history of atomic science between 1945 and 1949. During this time several leading scientists tried to walk the tightrope between promoting further research into atomic energy and arguing against the development of the hydrogen bomb.

The second antibomb calypso song is "Atomic Nightmare" by the Talbot Brothers of Bermuda. This calypso band of five brothers and a cousin achieved acclaim in America and appeared on *The Ed Sullivan Show*. Released ten years after Sir Lancelot's "Atomic Energy," "Atomic Nightmare" from 1957 shows how frightening nuclear bombs had become, just as Oppenheimer and Einstein predicted. Unlike Sir Lancelot, the protagonist in this song has no interest in the debate about the pros and cons of atomic weapons. He is not going to be brave and heroic and "stand still like a soldier." He is convinced that the best course of action in the event of a nuclear attack is to simply "run, run, run like a son of a gun." David Janssen and Edward Whitelock write that "the Talbots had no time for the 'duck and cover' platitudes of the Federal Defense Administration" and expressed "a very real distrust in the calm assurances that the American government offered regarding the survivability of nuclear blast or radioactive fallout."[34] The relentless strumming pattern on the ukulele depicts the protagonist's skedaddling feet.

The third calypso song to address the bomb is "Leave de Atom Alone," sung by Broadway singer Josephine Premice. The team of composer Harold Arlen and lyricist E. Y. "Yip" Harburg, who wrote "Over the Rainbow" from *The Wizard of Oz* and other classics from the mid-twentieth century, wrote the song. "Leave de Atom Alone" is from the 1957 musical *Jamaica,* which was nominated for a Tony award in 1958. The musical was conceived with Harry Belafonte in mind, following on the coattails of his successful 1956 album, *Calypso,* although he didn't appear in the production. On the surface, the musical parodies the commercialization of calypso in America, often called the "fad from Trinidad," while simultaneously participating in the commercialization. But at its heart, it critiques American imperialism in the Caribbean Islands.

Jamaica is about a young girl, Savannah (played by Lena Horne), who wants to escape Pigeon Island, a fictional island off the coast of Jamaica. Savannah wants to live a life of ease in New York City. Koli, a local fisherman, is in love with her but cannot fulfill her dream of a wedding in the big city. She sees her opportunity to escape when New York businessman Joe Nashua visits the island to exploit its rich pearl oyster harvest. Savannah considers leaving with Joe for Manhattan, but her island appears to be hit by a nuclear bomb—although it is in fact a hurricane. As Shane Vogel writes, "It may be the only Broadway musical to stage, just before intermission, a mushroom cloud."[35] This sets the scene for "Leave de Atom Alone," the first song in Act II. The song is lighthearted and comedic, but its placement in the musical gives it great weight. It comes just after a mushroom cloud, which leads the audience to believe during the intermission that the beautiful island and its inhabitants have been destroyed by a hydrogen bomb. In the end, Savannah forsakes Joe and the glamour of living in New York, realizes the value of her simple life on Pigeon Island, and falls in love with Koli.

Sung from the point of view of Savannah's friend Ginger, played by Josephine Premice, the lyrics pose a series of wry questions to Americans in general and to the US nuclear-defense industry in particular. If you want to keep riding in your Cadillacs, smoking your cigars, watching Wall Street prosper—in essence enjoying your American way of life—then do not delve too deeply into the science of nuclear weapons. If you go too far, we may all become "fissionable material." Like many of Arlen's songs from the musical, "Leave de Atom Alone" is overloaded with so much Broadway schmaltz that very little actual calypso comes through. The lyrics by Harburg are another matter though. As Vogel writes, "The political poetry of Harburg's lyrics bears a closer resemblance to a Trinidadian tradition of coded protest, topical commentary, and cutting mockery."[36]

Harold Arlen and Yip Harburg had a fascinating relationship since they were on opposite sides of the fence politically. Arlen biographer Edward Jablonski recounts their collaboration on "Leave de Atom Alone" in this way,

> Like Arlen, [Harburg] was an enthusiastic walker, and they often engaged in ambulatory discussions. During one such walk the subject of the atom bomb arose. Harburg maintained that the root of the problem behind the stockpiling of atomic bombs was the American capitalist economy that thrived on it. Arlen contended that a solution might be a better understanding between the peoples of the Soviet Union and the United States. Harburg disagreed, apparently laying most of the blame on the American economy and its dependence on continuing the Cold War. Arlen returned home in an agitated state, swearing that he would never discuss politics with Harburg again—only art and songs. Yet before too long they would collaborate on a song entitled "Leave de Atom Alone." Arlen did not disagree with Harburg's views in that song.[37]

Harburg was a democratic socialist, so his identification with Caribbean protest against American capitalism, consumerism, and colonialism should come as no surprise. Like Vern Partlow's "Old Man Atom" analyzed in chapter 1, "Leave de Atom Alone" presents a viewpoint that, during the red scare of the 1950s, would get a lyricist blacklisted. A cautionary tale about nuclear weapons would be interpreted as subversive communist propaganda that sought to undermine the security of the United States. The House Un-American Activities Committee (HUAC) indeed blacklisted Harburg throughout the 1950s.[38] Like other left-wing songwriters and composers, such as Pete Seeger, Earl Robinson, and Leonard Bernstein, he also found his name listed in *Red Channels*.[39] Harburg's troubles with the HUAC began when he became president of the Hollywood Democratic Committee, which promoted the principles of President Roosevelt's New Deal. In December 1950, Metro-Goldwyn-Mayer attorney J. Robert Rubin questioned Harburg at length about his political beliefs. In a letter to Rubin on Christmas Day, 1950, Harburg responded,

> None of the organizations to which I have belonged have ever, so far as I know, advocated or promulgated anything but democratic principles. If at any time it is ever proven to me that any organization to which I belong is in reality subversive of the best interests of this country or owes allegiance to a foreign power which threatens this country, I would of course, sever

> connections forthwith. . . . It is cruel and unfair to label communist all those who wish to help bring about healthy needed change. Our constitution provides for the possibility of change. The machinery is there. As long as we have ballots, it would be criminal to join groups who would use bullets.[40]

Because of the blacklist, Harburg was prevented from writing for film, television, and radio. The only creative avenue available to him was writing for musicals—and even there he was harassed and his work manipulated.

While some writers in the performing arts produced facile material in order to avoid getting into trouble with the HUAC, others like Harburg resisted. He believed the theater was not a "platform that must be for sheer entertainment, with no thought, with no controversy, with nothing to think about, with nothing that will stir your juices to say right or wrong. . . . I don't work that way."[41] The lyrics of "Leave de Atom Alone" echo the tradition of free expression, wry humor, and protest that calypso musicians practiced in opposing American colonialism and militarism in the Caribbean. The presence of the American military in Latin American countries became a more prominent subject in 1980s popular music, explored in the sections on U2 and Sting in the next chapter.

NOWHERE TO HIDE BLUES

The purpose of this book is to show how popular songs inform our understanding of the social history of the Cold War. In this section, we have a case where a lack of songs informs our understanding. In the previous chapter on comedy songs, we explored several about fallout shelters, all of them by White songwriters. We have found no songs about fallout shelters by Black songwriters. The most likely reason for this is that African Americans had fewer opportunities to build, or even gain access to, fallout shelters during the early years of the Cold War. In 1963, Nathan Hare wrote, "The general notion seems to be that—in event of a nuclear war—all Americans face a similar fate, but the fact is that the Negro's probability of being decimated is much higher than that of whites. . . . Negroes in our big cities now live in bull's-eyes enclosed by white satellite suburban rings."[42]

This has much to do with housing segregation, which dates back to the era of slavery. After the Civil War, Jim Crow laws perpetuated injustice, and few African Americans had the opportunities to purchase homes. This resulted in the containment of Blacks and other minorities in tenement housing in the inner cities, where the bombs were likely to be dropped. The US government never embarked on a wide-scale enterprise to build underground communal shelters to protect people in large cities. Many buildings had the yellow-and-black "Fallout Shelter" signs placed on them in the early 1960s, but these would have provided protection to just a small percentage of the population. In addition, many of these buildings were inadequately stocked with food and supplies. As Dean Brelis writes, "The sad fact is that there isn't much that can be done for the vulnerable central cores of our cities . . . no civilian-defense plan could hope to provide adequate protection for people in the great target areas—the big industrial cities."[43]

African Americans were also concerned about the prospect of shelter segregation.[44] In 1950, President Truman appointed Florida governor Millard Caldwell as head of the Federal Civil Defense Administration (FCDA). Caldwell openly advocated segregation.[45] During the 1950 Senate session in which Caldwell was nominated for the FCDA position, Clarence Mitchell, director of the NAACP Washington Bureau, imagined a plausible scenario with Caldwell in charge of civil defense: "If a bomb drops we do not want regulations that require citizens to run 10 blocks to a separate racial shelter when one marked for 'white only' is just around the corner."[46] Thus, Blacks, and minorities in general, had nowhere to hide. As David Monteyne summarizes, "A white citizenry would survive on the fringes of the city where the effects of atomic bombs would be attenuated by distance from ground zero. Meanwhile, inner cities were places projected for the containment of nonwhite residents and other 'sitting ducks' whose existence challenged the myth of a unified American identity in the 1950s. The unified America, the one to be preserved by civil defense preparations, was clearly imagined as a nonurban place."[47]

If a nuclear attack was imminent, middle- and upper-class citizens had two options: flee to the countryside in their cars or hunker down in either their basements or fallout shelters. Minorities and lower-class Whites in the inner cities had fewer desirable options: protect themselves as best they could in their tenements, flee on foot, or dig a hole. Let's take a look at three songs by African American musicians that reflect this reality. In two of the songs, the best option is to simply pray. All three were written in 1951 during the Korean War.

Along with Robert Johnson, Muddy Waters, John Lee Hooker, and B. B. King, Sam "Lightnin'" Hopkins (1912–1982) was one of the great African American blues guitarists and singers. In the first verse of his "War News Blues," he hears warnings and sad news on his radio about the war. The second verse addresses the experience of civilians in a nuclear war. Children are running and crying and ask their mother what to do. The mother has to admit she doesn't have an answer, since she is in the same predicament as her children. All that can be done is pray. In the third verse, Hopkins sings, "I'm gonna dig me a hole this morning." Hopefully, the bomb will explode far enough away that he will just hear the echo.

Another blues musician, Arthur "Big Boy" Crudup, got busy digging. In his "I'm Gonna Dig Myself a Hole," he says he'll be down there with his woman, his "class card" for identification, and a canary.[48] In the refrain of each verse, he sings that when he comes out of his hole "there won't be no wars around." This could mean that he is confident humans will have learned their lesson about the destructiveness of nuclear war and will never start another one; it could also mean war has killed everyone except him, and he is unlikely to start a war with himself.

A third song from 1951 is "I'd Rather Be Like a Hermit" by Frankie Ervin with Austin McCoy and His Combo. Ervin dispenses with the "dig" option and, like the Talbot Brothers in "Atomic Nightmare" covered earlier, decides to "run like a son of a gun." Ervin tells all the "jive cats" standing on the street corner exactly where to run: straight to the forest to live like hermits. Ervin concludes the song by saying even the forest may not provide enough protection. The best thing to do is "ask the Lord up above for shelter." Such a belief echoes what Martin Luther King, Jr. wrote in his 1963 book of sermons, *Strength to Love*, "We need not join the mad rush to purchase an earthly fallout shelter. God is our eternal fallout shelter."[49]

THE BERLIN WALL IN SELMA, ALABAMA

In 1961, the Berlin Wall went up. Four years later, a Berlin Wall of another sort went up in Selma, Alabama. It was not made of brick or concrete but of rope and inspired a song about the civil rights movement. In March 1965, a group of African Americans were gathering regularly in front of Brown Chapel AME Church on Sylvan Street in Selma. They were planning a march to Montgomery, the capital of Alabama, to demand the right to register to vote without interference or harassment. Although the Civil Rights Act of 1964 outlawed racial segregation and discrimination, it did not eliminate restrictions that systemically prevented African Americans from voting. In Selma, a city of thirty thousand with slightly more Blacks than Whites, only 2 percent of Blacks (between three hundred and four hundred people) were registered.[50]

Nonviolent demonstrations had begun to receive national attention in January 1965 when Martin Luther King Jr. and other prominent civil rights leaders came to join the protest. A march to Montgomery began on March 7, but the marchers never got out of the city. The day came to be known as "Bloody Sunday." Between five hundred and six hundred people were beaten and teargassed on the Edmund Pettus Bridge by the Selma police. On Tuesday, March 9, King led the marchers to the bridge for a second attempt but turned them back to Selma. He did not want to violate an injunction stating that marches could not advance outside the city limits. He also wanted protection from the National Guard to prevent any more beatings. While the marchers waited several more days, the police took opportunities to prevent marches even within the city. On Wednesday, March 10, in front of Brown Chapel, the Selma police formed a line along Sylvan Street to prevent a march. Public safety director Wilson Baker also had a wooden barricade put up.

On the morning of March 11, the protestors saw that the police had put a rope, or clothesline, across Sylvan Street. The marchers called it both the "Berlin Wall" and the "Selma Wall."[51] The Friday, March 12, 1965, issue of the *Selma Times-Journal* reported on the front page that "civil rights demonstrators continued standing behind a single strand of rope on Sylvan Street throughout the rainy morning and vowed to continue their march attempt at least until Saturday."[52] The front page also had a photograph of the marchers standing behind the rope. The caption reads, "The white rope in the foreground marks the boundary line for the demonstrators who have orders to remain behind what they have termed 'The Berlin Wall.'"[53] By 1965, the wall in Berlin had become an iconic image of oppression and division to Americans. Brian C. Etheridge writes, "Because so many stories about the Berlin Wall involved the forced separation of peoples, the wall became a particularly powerful symbol for highlighting segregation in the American South."[54]

Shortly after the rope went up, the protestors started singing a song called "Berlin Wall," adapted from the African American spiritual "Joshua Fit the Battle of Jericho."[55] Carl Benkert was at the scene with his reel-to-reel tape recorder hidden under his jacket. Benkert, an interior decorator from Detroit, had traveled to Selma to participate in the march. His recording of the protestors singing "Berlin Wall" was included on the 1965 LP *Freedom Songs* released by Folkways Records.[56] It was recorded on the same day, Monday, March 15, that President Johnson invoked the spiritual "We Shall Overcome" in his televised address to Congress and the American people about African American voting rights.[57]

"Joshua Fit the Battle of Jericho" dates back to the Civil War and was inspired by the story of how Joshua and the Israelites captured the city of Jericho in Joshua 6:1–27. In the biblical account, the Lord instructs Joshua to have seven priests blow seven trumpets for seven days while marching with the Israelite army around Jericho. On the seventh day, the "walls came tumblin' down," as the spiritual recounts. The Selma marchers used the spiritual to equate the rope across Sylvan Street to the walls of Jericho. The lyrics equate the rope to the Berlin Wall: "We've got a rope that's a Berlin Wall in Selma, Alabama." In a broader context, the music equates the struggle of African Americans from slavery to full citizenship with the Israelites' flight from slavery in Egypt to the Promised Land, Canaan. The lyrics equate African Americans barricaded from the voting booths with the East Berliners barricaded from West Berlin and West Germany. Paul M. Farber sums up this musical and lyrical synthesis by saying, "The gathered protesters [merged] Jericho, Berlin, and Selma into a shared frame."[58] On the borrowing and adapting of spirituals, Bernice Johnson Reagon writes, "The core song repertoire of the civil rights movement was formed from the reservoir of Afro-American traditional song, performed in the older style of singing. . . . It was sung unrehearsed in the tradition of the Afro-American folk church.... From this reservoir, activist songleaders made a new music for a changed time. Lyrics were transformed, traditional melodies were adapted, and procedures associated with old forms were blended with new forms to create freedom songs capable of expressing the force and intent of the movement."[59]

Benkert's recording of the spiritual is incomplete on *Freedom Songs*. This is indicated on the lyric page included with the LP. It shows the first verse as, "We're gonna break this Berlin Wall in Selma, Alabama" and enclosed in parentheses, implying Benkert pressed the record button shortly after the song began. A more complete version of the song is on another 1965 Folkways recording about the Selma marches, *Songs of the Selma-Montgomery March*.[60] Here, folk singers Pete Seeger and Len Chandler, who were in Selma for the marches, recreate the songs in a recording studio along with a group called the Freedom Voices. They also tell stories about how the songs were composed on the spot and used in the marches.

The most complete version of the song is in the sheet music collection *Sing for Freedom* published in 1990.[61] The first verse states plainly, "We've got a rope that's a Berlin Wall." In the rest of the verses, the protestors sing that they will break the wall, will stay until the wall falls, hate is what built it, love will make it fall, and they will stand there until it does. The first verse then repeats at the end. There is also a verse referring to George Wallace, which says that he helped to build the wall. Wallace, the governor of Alabama at the time, had declared, "Segregation now . . . segregation tomorrow . . . segregation forever," in his 1963 inaugural address.

While they were waiting for the injunction to be lifted and National Guard protection to be secured, the protestors stood behind the rope for several days and continuously sang "Berlin Wall" and other songs. Public safety director Wilson Baker eventually removed the rope. He was heard to say that he was "tired of hearing them sing about the damned thing."[62] Just as Berliners would chip off pieces of their wall with hammers twenty-four years later in 1989, the Selma protestors cut up theirs with scissors and kept pieces of the rope as souvenirs. After, they made up a humorous new verse, "The invisible wall is a Berlin Wall, in Selma, Alabama."[63] It didn't remain invisible for long though. Baker put a line of police cars where the rope was. Naturally, this inspired yet another verse about the troopers' cars being a Berlin Wall. On Sunday, March 21, the injunction was finally lifted, and the wall of policemen, police cars, wooden barricades, and rope was removed. Protected by the federalized Alabama National Guardsmen, the marchers commenced their fifty-four-mile trek to Montgomery. After four days, they arrived in the state capital on March 25, and King gave one of his greatest speeches, commonly referred to as "How Long Not Long." In the speech he invoked the spiritual sung at the Selma Wall, "The Bible tells us that the mighty men of Joshua merely walked about the walled city of Jericho and the barriers to freedom came tumbling down. I like that old Negro spiritual, 'Joshua Fit the Battle of Jericho.' In its simple, yet colorful, depiction of that great moment in biblical history, it tells us that 'Joshua fit the battle of Jericho, Joshua fit the battle of Jericho, and the walls come tumbling down.'"[64]

Four-and-a-half months later, on August 6, 1965, the Voter Rights Act was passed. The Berlin Wall that kept African Americans from the voting booths came down. Meanwhile over in Berlin, East Berliners were still stuck behind their wall and would be for another twenty-four years.

In the first five chapters, we have seen how most of the Cold War songs from the Atomic Age had comical elements. Folk and country musicians wrote serious songs, but they were in the minority. As we move into the Vietnam War era, and especially the 1980s, we will see that the number of serious songs becomes much greater than the number of comical songs. The deeper the superpowers dug their heels into Cold War politics, the darker the songwriting became. We will also see a shift in geography. Americans wrote most of the Cold War songs from the Atomic Age. In the 1980s, the number of these songs written by British songwriters becomes greater.

NOTES

1. Przybys, John. "50 Years Ago, the King Came Back." *Las Vegas Review-Journal*, July 22, 2019. https://www.reviewjournal.com/entertainment/shows/elvis-came-to-las-vegas-50-years-ago-and-history-was-made-1807088/.

2. Lee Cotten, *The Elvis Catalog: Memorabilia, Icons, and Collectibles Celebrating the King of Rock 'n' Roll* (Garden City, NY: Doubleday and Company, 1987), 16.

3. Mike Kaplan, "Mdse. Swells Record Take," *Variety*, October 24, 1956, 1.

4. "Impresarios: The Man Who Sold Parsley," *Time*, May 16, 1960, 62.

5. Tom Waldman, *We All Want to Change the World: Rock and Politics from Elvis to Eminem* (Lanham, MD: Taylor Trade, 2003), 58.

6. Lisa Jo Sagolla, *Rock 'n' Roll Dances of the 1950s* (Santa Barbara, CA: Greenwood, 2011), 17.

7. Russell Reising, "Iron Curtains and Satin Sheets: 'Strange Loves' in Cold War Popular Music," *Cultural Logic* 10 (2003): 9. https://ojs.library.ubc.ca/index.php/clogic/article/view/191911/188872.

8. Gertrude Samuel, "Why They Rock 'n' Roll—And Should They?" *New York Times Magazine*, January 12, 1958, 19.

9. Abel Green, "A Warning to the Music Business," *Variety*, February 23, 1955, 2.

10. Jimmie Logsdon interviewed by Randy McNutt, *Rockabilly: The Twang Heard 'round the World: The Illustrated History*, ed. Michael Dregni (Minneapolis: Voyageur, 2011), 118.

11. Gerard J. DeGroot, *The Bomb: A Life* (Cambridge, MA: Harvard University Press, 2005), 274.

12. Brian Easlea, "Patriarchy, Scientists, and Nuclear Warriors," in *Beyond Patriarchy: Essays by Men on Pleasure, Power, and Change*, ed. Michael Kaufman (New York: Oxford University Press, 1987), 195–215.

13. Brian Easlea, *Fathering the Unthinkable: Masculinity, Scientists and the Nuclear Arms Race* (Suffolk: Pluto, 1983), 92.

14. Carol Cohn, "Sex and Death in the Rational World of Defense Intellectuals," in *Exposing Nuclear Phallacies*, ed. Diana E. H. Russell (New York: Pergamon, 1989), 133–136; "Within and Without: Women, Gender, and Theory," *Signs* 12, no. 4 (Summer 1987): 687–718, http://genderandsecurity.org/sites/default/files/carol_cohn_sex_and_death_in_the_world_of_rational_defense_intellectuals.pdf.

15. Bill Geerhart and Ken Sitz's liner notes for the five-CD, one-DVD box set *Atomic Platters: Cold War Music from the Golden Age of Homeland Security* (Hambergen, Germany: Bear Family Records BCD 16065 FM, 2005), 40.

16. Leah Branstetter, "Wanda Jackson Goes to Japan: The Hidden Histories of 'Fujiyama Mama,'" paper presented at the EMP Pop Conference, Seattle, WA, April 24–27, 2014.

17. Bill Geerhart, "Atomic Goddess Revisited: Rita Hayworth's Bomb Image Found!" *CONELRAD*, blog post, August 19, 2013, http://conelrad.blogspot.com/2013/08/atomic-goddess-revisited-rita-hayworths.html.

18. Masako Nakamura, "'Miss Atom Bomb' Contests in Nagasaki and Nevada: The Politics of Beauty, Memory, and the Cold War," *U.S.-Japan Women's Journal* 37 (2009): 132–136.

19. Michael A. Amundson, *Yellowcake Towns: Uranium Mining Communities in the American West* (Boulder: University Press of Colorado, 2002), 84.

20. A. Costandina Titus, *Bombs in the Backyard: Atomic Testing and American Politics*, 2nd ed. (Reno: University of Nevada Press, 2001), 114K.

21. Kristina Zarlengo, "Civilian Threat, the Suburban Citadel, and Atomic Age American Women," *Signs* 24, no. 4 (Summer 1999): 950.

22. Elaine Tyler May, *Homeward Bound: American Families in the Cold War Era*, 20th anniversary edition (New York: Basic, 2008), 108.

23. A. Costandina Titus, "The Mushroom Cloud as Kitsch," in *Atomic Culture: How We Learned to Stop Worrying and Love the Bomb*, ed. Scott C. Zeman and Michael A. Amundson (Boulder: University Press of Colorado, 2004), 105, 107, 109.

24. Kevin Phinney, *Souled America: How Black Music Transformed White Culture* (New York: Billboard, 2005), 158–159.

25. Jim Dawson and Steve Propes, *What Was the First Rock 'n' Roll Record?* (Boston: Faber and Faber, 1992), 137–141; Carl Belz, *The Story of Rock* (New York: Oxford University Press, 1969), 25–26.

26. Marv Goldberg, *Marv Goldberg's R&B Notebook*, "The Chords," http://www.uncamarvy.com/Chords/chords.html.

27. Jimmy Keyes in "How Sh Boom Originated," (0:06–0:30), http://www.youtube.com/watch?v=3dUK9j5X7Zw. See also Jimmy Keyes interviewed for *Marv Goldberg's R&B Notebook*, "The Chords," http://www.uncamarvy.com/Chords/chords.html.

28. Bryant originally wrote the song in D minor, but Salvo and his band play it in E-flat minor.

29. Paul Boyer, *By the Bomb's Early Light: American Thought and Culture at the Dawn of the Atomic Age* (Chapel Hill: University of North Carolina Press, 1994), 109.

30. For more on this, see Michael Grow, *U.S. Presidents and Latin American Interventions: Pursuing Regime Change in the Cold War* (Lawrence: University Press of Kansas, 2008); Robert Freeman Smith, *The Caribbean World and the United States: Mixing Rum and Coca-Cola* (New York: Twayne, 1994).

31. Louis Regis, *The Political Calypso: True Opposition in Trinidad and Tobago, 1962–1987* (Barbados: Press University of the West Indies, 1999).

32. As discussed in chapter 1 with Vern Partlow's song "Old Man Atom," Oppenheimer and Einstein contributed to the 1946 publication *One Word or None*, which was designed to educate the public about the dangers of atomic weapons. *One World or None*, ed. Dexter Masters and Katharine Way (New York: McGraw-Hill, 1946).

33. Albert Einstein, chairman, "A Statement: Emergency Committee of Atomic Scientists," *Bulletin of the Atomic Scientists* 3, no. 6 (June 1947): 136.

34. David Janssen and Edward Whitelock, *Apocalypse Jukebox: The End of the World in American Popular Music* (Brooklyn: Soft Skull, 2009), 46–47.

35. Shane Vogel, "*Jamaica* on Broadway: The Popular Caribbean and Mock Transnational Performance," *Theatre Journal* 62, no. 1 (March 2010): 1.

36. Vogel, "*Jamaica* on Broadway," 10.

37. Edward Jablonski, *Harold Arlen: Rhythm, Rainbows, and Blues* (Boston: Northeastern University Press, 1996), 263–264.

38. Harriet Hyman Alonso, *Yip Harburg: Legendary Lyricist and Human Rights Activist* (Middletown, CT: Wesleyan University Press, 2012), 189–218.

39. American Business Consultants, *Red Channels: The Report of Communist Influence in Radio and Television* (New York: American Business Consultants, 1950), 72–74.

40. E. Y. Harburg to J. Robert Rubin, December 25, 1950, Series II, folder 23/196, MSS83 in the E. Y. Harburg Collection in the Irving S. Gilmore Music Library of Yale University, quoted in Alonso, *Yip Harburg*, 194.

41. Alonso, *Yip Harburg*, 212.

42. Nathan Hare, "Can Negroes Survive a Nuclear War? *Negro Digest* 12, no. 7 (May 1963): 26, 28.

43. Dean Brelis, *Run, Dig or Stay? A Search for an Answer to the Shelter Question* (Boston: Beacon, 1962), 110, 168.

44 Rufus Wells, "What Would Happen If the Bomb Falls?" *Sepia*, January 1962, 9–11.

45. Andrew D. Grossman, *Neither Dead nor Red: Civilian Defense and American Political Development during the Early Cold War* (New York: Routledge, 2001), 91–101.

46. Clarence Mitchell in the United States Congress, Senate, Subcommittee of the Committee on Armed Services, "Nomination of Millard Frank Caldwell, Jr. to be Federal Civil Defense Administrator," Eighty-second Congress, first session, January 15, 1951 (Washington, DC: United States Government Printing Office, 1951), 6.

47. David Monteyne, *Fallout Shelter: Designing for Civil Defense in the Cold War* (Minneapolis: University of Minnesota Press, 2011), 12.

48. Caged canaries were sometimes kept in coal mines. If the canary died, it was an indication that noxious gases were present in the mine.

49. Martin Luther King, Jr., *The Papers of Martin Luther King, Jr. Volume VI: Advocate of the Social Gospel, September 1948–March 1963* (Berkeley: University of California Press, 1992), 543.

50. *Selma 1965: The Photographs of Spider Martin* (Austin: University of Texas Press, 2015), 2.

51. Two of the best eyewitness accounts of the Selma wall are in Rich Wallace and Sandra Neil Wallace, *Blood Brother: Jonathan Daniels and His Sacrifice for Civil Rights* (Honesdale, PA: Calkins Creek, 2016), 104–114, and Richard D. Leonard, *Call to Selma: Eighteen Days of Witness* (Boston: Skinner House Books, 2002), 26–32, 52–54.

52. "Mayor Rejects Request from Civil Rightists," *Selma Times-Journal*, March 12, 1965, 1.

53. Ibid.

54. Brian C. Etheridge, *Enemies to Allies: Cold War Germany and American Memory* (Lexington: University Press of Kentucky, 2016), 252.

55. The word *fit* is a southern Appalachian English dialect word for "fought."

56. *Freedom Songs: Selma, Alabama: A Documentary Recording by Carl Benkert* (Folkways Records FH 5594, 1965, LP; Smithsonian Folkways Recordings, 2006, CD).

57. For a transcript and video of this speech, see "President Johnson's Special Message to the Congress: The American Promise" on the Lyndon Baines Johnson Library and Museum website, http://www.lbjlibrary.org/lyndon-baines-johnson/speeches-films/president-johnsons-special-message-to-the-congress-the-american-promise/.

58. Paul M. Farber, "Boundaries of Freedom: An American History of the Berlin Wall" (PhD diss., University of Michigan, 2013), 5.

59. Bernice Johnson Reagon, "Let the Church Sing 'Freedom,'" *Black Music Research Journal* 7 (1987): 106.

60. *Songs of the Selma-Montgomery March* (Folkways Records FH 5595, 1965, LP; Smithsonian Folkways Recordings, 2007, CD).

61. *Sing for Freedom: The Story of the Civil Rights Movement through Its Songs*, edited by Guy and Candie Carawan (Bethlehem, PA: Sing Out, 1990), 254.

62. Sheyann Webb and Rachel West Nelson, *Selma, Lord, Selma: Girlhood Memories of the Civil-Rights Days as Told to Frank Sikora* (Tuscaloosa: University of Alabama Press, 1980), 121.

63. Robert F. Darden, "The Other Berlin Wall—And What It Can Teach Us Today," *Huffington Post*, November 5, 2014, updated January 5, 2015, http://www.huffingtonpost.com/robert-f-darden/the-other-berlin-walland-_b_6102746.html.

64. Martin Luther King, Jr., "Address at the Conclusion of the Selma to Montgomery March," March 25, 1965, Martin Luther King, Jr. Research and Education Institute, Stanford University, https://kinginstitute.stanford.edu/king-papers/documents/address-conclusion-selma-montgomery-march.

SIX

MAINSTREAM ROCK

Bowie, U2, Sting, Billy Joel, and Springsteen

IN MATTERS OF INTERNATIONAL POLITICS, the opinions of rock stars are typically not held in high regard. For example, when an assessment of the fall of communism comes out of the mouth of someone like Steven Tyler of Aerosmith, it makes for great comedy. Consider the following exchange from "Wayne's World" in the February 17, 1990, broadcast of *Saturday Night Live*.[1]

> WAYNE: "With the recent developments in Eastern Europe, do you think that communism is on the decline, or is this just a temporary setback?"
>
> STEVEN TYLER, SINGER OF AEROSMITH: "Wow, man, that's a hard question. But I would have to respond with a qualified yes. Although it seems that socialism is in repose, until you remove the Stalinist era party *apparatchiks*, there will be no real change in the Soviet Union."
>
> TOM HAMILTON, BASS PLAYER OF AEROSMITH: "No, I disagree, man. There's never been a blueprint for the dictatorship of the proletariat, so there's bound to be mistakes. However, if you study history, you'll see that since the rise of the nation-state, socialism has been an historical inevitability, dude."
>
> GARTH: "Excellent! Excellent!"
>
> WAYNE: "Fascinating!"[2]

Do rock stars have anything valuable to add to world politics? Can rock music, much of which is about sex, drugs, and having a good time, even be considered a suitable medium for espousing a cogent political argument? Regardless of what one thinks of rock music, it has had a massive impact on global culture simply by what it represents: freedom of expression, individuality, and a voice against oppression. Sometimes it doesn't even matter what the singers are singing about. All that matters is that they have a microphone or guitar in their hands and their amplifiers are turned up to eleven. Jeff "Skunk" Baxter of Steely Dan and the Doobie

Brothers describes the electric guitar as "a symbol of freedom. [It represents] a whole generation of a country that allowed people to have free thought. It's an incredible instrument. It's an incredible symbol."[3] Not only can rock music reflect cultural change, it can instigate cultural change. It stirs the cauldron, bringing whatever is sitting on the bottom up to the surface.

This chapter is about how five rock superstars, David Bowie, Bono of U2, Sting, Billy Joel, and Bruce Springsteen, stirred the cauldron. They became concerned about and involved in Cold War politics to a degree few other popular musicians did. A primary reason for this was travel. David Bowie traveled to West Berlin to record in a studio near the wall. Bono and Sting traveled to Nicaragua, El Salvador, Chile, and Argentina in the 1980s and wrote songs about how Cold War politics were affecting Latin Americans. Billy Joel became the first Western rock musician to stage full rock concerts in the Soviet Union. Bruce Springsteen played to approximately three hundred thousand people in communist East Berlin, a year before the wall came down. Like Joan Baez living through the US bombing of Hanoi, North Vietnam, in December 1972 (recounted in chap. 2), these musicians found themselves in places where the Cold War happened. As a result of their stardom, they brought international attention to the conflict in ways they could not have imagined.

Because of rock music's pervasive presence in global culture in the past several decades, its connections to the Cold War can be explored in myriad ways, much more than simply interpreting lyrics or analyzing music. This chapter explores some songs in depth but is focused more on how musicians expressed opinions about the Cold War in other ways: stagecraft during concerts, places where they traveled and performed, what they said in interviews, and organizations they supported and partnered with, such as Amnesty International.

DAVID BOWIE IN WEST BERLIN

David Bowie holds the distinction of being the first major American or British popular musician to record an album in a Cold War hot spot. At Hansa Tonstudio, five hundred yards away from the Berlin Wall, he completed the mixing and overdubs for *Low* and recorded the entirety of *"Heroes,"* both of which he released in 1977. The mood of West Berlin itself, a free city surrounded on all sides by communist East Germany, is palpable in several tracks from *Low*. "Weeping Wall" evokes the misery caused by the wall with quivering synthesizer lines, distorted guitar riffs, wordless wailing, and an insistent polyrhythmic ostinato. Bowie plays synthesizer, guitar, vibraphone, and xylophone on the song and sings the wordless chorus. The slow and ponderous "Subterraneans" portrays life in East Berlin and ends with Bowie playing saxophone. According to Bowie, the song represented people who "got caught in East Berlin after the separation—hence the faint jazz saxophones representing the memory of what it was."[4] The inconclusive, fragmentary character of these songs reflects the tone of the fragmented city. Bowie said these mostly instrumental tracks were "more an observation in musical terms: my reaction to seeing the East Bloc, how West Berlin survives in the midst of it, which was something I couldn't express in words. Rather it required textures."[5] Before *Low* and *"Heroes,"* Bowie was known mostly as a vocalist and songwriter. With the help of producers Tony Visconti and Brian Eno, these two albums brought him respect as a synthesizer player and composer of instrumental sound collages. Living in Cold War Berlin opened a radical new dimension in his songwriting.

Since the fall of communism, the song "Heroes" has become something of an anthem to the Berlin Wall. The lyrics describe the experience of two lovers meeting and kissing at the wall, in spite of the danger posed by armed guards positioned there. The song was specifically about a tryst between record producer Tony Visconti and German vocalist Antonia Maaß, whom Visconti met while working with Bowie on the album.[6] The refrain, "We can be heroes, just for one day," encourages ordinary Berliners to rise above the repressive atmosphere of their divided city. On June 6, 1987, during his Glass Spider tour, Bowie played "Heroes" and many other songs live in West Berlin. The concert stage was in front of the Reichstag, Berlin's historic parliament building, next to the Berlin Wall. The concert's promotor and producer, Peter Schwenkow, said that at least a quarter of the amplifiers were pointed toward the Berlin Wall in an obvious attempt to allow the East Berliners to hear the concert.[7] Approximately three thousand East Berliners massed on the other side to hear Bowie. This concert became a highlight of his career. Bowie recounts,

> I'll never forget that. It was one of the most emotional performances I've ever done. I was in tears. They'd backed up the stage to the wall itself so that the wall was acting as our backdrop. We kind of heard that a few of the East Berliners might actually get the chance to hear the thing, but we didn't realize in what numbers they would. And there were thousands on the other side that had come close to the wall. So it was like a double concert where the wall was the division. And we would hear them cheering and singing along from the other side. God, even now I get choked up. It was breaking my heart. I'd never done anything like that in my life, and I guess I never will again. When we did "Heroes" it really felt anthemic, almost like a prayer.[8]

At the end of the song "Time Will Crawl," Bowie introduced his bandmates and then said in English and German, "This is, as you know, a special evening for us. Wir schicken unsere besten Wünsche zu alle unseren Freunden, die auf der anderen Seite der Mauer sind. [We send our best wishes to all our friends who are on the other side of the Wall.]" Six days after the concert, at the Brandenburg Gate near the Reichstag, President Reagan gave his famous "Mr. Gorbachev, open this gate! Mr. Gorbachev, tear down this Wall!" speech. Two-and-a-half years later, the wall came down. The next time Bowie played a concert in Berlin, on April 8, 1990, the city and the country were one again. When Bowie died on January 10, 2016, the German Foreign Office posted this tweet as a tribute to him, "Good-bye David Bowie. You are now among Heroes. Thank you for helping to bring down the wall."[9]

Bowie's concert in 1987 was one of several iconic rock concerts at, or near, the Berlin Wall. Bruce Springsteen, Crosby, Stills & Nash, Roger Waters from Pink Floyd, and even actor David Hasselhoff would perform there in the late 1980s and early 1990s. These performances helped ensure the demise of this Cold War icon would have a rousing soundtrack (see chap. 10). Much has already been written about Bowie's Berlin period. For a closer look at his time there, see authors David Buckley, Tobias Rüther, Thomas Jerome Seabrook, Hugo Wilcken, and the documentary *David Bowie: The Berlin Trilogy.*[10] In addition, an eleven-CD box set released in 2017 chronicles this period in his career.[11]

U2: BONO IN CENTRAL AMERICA

Few musical acts engaged in Cold War issues as often, or in so many varied ways, as U2. The band's album covers, concerts, music videos, travels, activism, and interviews are awash in Cold War significance and symbolism. U2 addressed the Cold War in their lyrics, but their concerts, interviews, and Bono's philanthropic efforts more articulately expressed the band's views about the conflict.

While the band addressed nuclear weapons in songs from the early 1980s such as "A Celebration" and "Seconds," their focus shifted in the mid-1980s to the proxy wars, the heavy-handed influence of the United States on civilians in Latin America to stop the spread of socialist revolutions. Two songs that speak to this issue are "Bullet the Blue Sky" and "Mothers of the Disappeared" from *The Joshua Tree* (1987). These reflect U2's participation in Amnesty International's A Conspiracy of Hope tour in June 1986 and Bono's trip to Nicaragua and El Salvador in July 1986.[12] Bono and his wife, Alison, traveled to Central America with the Sanctuary Movement, an interdenominational Christian organization established to aid Central American refugees, and the human rights group Central American Mission Partners (CAMP). Here they witnessed the effects of the American military presence firsthand. Summing up the band's love/hate relationship with America at the time, Bono said, "We love America. We love to be here. And yet we struggle with it sometimes, cause it's worth struggling over. It's worth arguing about. It's worth criticizing. Though we feel really close to America as Irish people, at the same time, we react and pull back when we see, for instance, what America is doing to a tiny little country like Nicaragua. Because as people coming from a tiny little country, called Ireland, we feel very close to Nicaragua. We remember what it was like when we had the British Empire breathing down our necks."[13]

Instead of *The Joshua Tree*, U2 briefly considered titling the album *The Two Americas*, reflecting their mixed feelings about American foreign policy in the 1980s.[14]

When Bono took his trip in 1986, the Sandinista National Liberation Front, a socialist party that took over the government in 1979 from the US-backed dictator, Anastasio Somoza Debayle, ruled Nicaragua. Jimmy Carter and Ronald Reagan, especially, reviled the Sandinistas since they received military training in Cuba and weapons from both Cuba and the Soviet Union. As Kenneth Branagh narrates in the episode "Backyard" of CNN's documentary *Cold War*, "To the United States, Castro's nationalism and left-wing policies were a Trojan horse for Soviet communism."[15] The US government, fearing that Nicaragua would be the next Latin American domino to fall to communism, provided military aid to a group of indigenous militias called the Contras beginning in 1982 in order to bring down the Sandinista regime. Reagan also enacted a trade embargo on Nicaragua in 1985. Unfortunately, this caused more suffering for the civilian population than it did for the Sandinistas.[16] Bono said of this embargo, "Wandering around Nicaragua, seeing their supermarkets empty—nothing on the shelves—seeing their people starving because of the blockade the United States had put on it. . . . I could see the cost. This was the other side of America as far as I was concerned at that time: America, the neighborhood bully."[17]

While the Sandinistas committed numerous atrocities against civilians, including false imprisonment, rape, torture, mutilation, and murder, evidence shows the Contras were even more brutal.[18] The US government's commitment to the Contras became especially odious in light of the Iran-Contra affair, in which antitank missiles were sold secretly and illegally to Iran to fund the Contras. Although Reagan was never conclusively linked to this scandal, fourteen high-ranking government officials were, including Secretary of Defense Caspar Weinberger.

Reagan was afraid that the next country to succumb to communism after Cuba and Nicaragua would be El Salvador. In a speech on March 10, 1983, Reagan said, "The nations of Central America are among our nearest neighbors. El Salvador, for example, is nearer to Texas than Texas is to Massachusetts. Central America is simply too close, and the strategic stakes are too high, for us to ignore the danger of governments seizing power there with ideological and military ties to the Soviet Union."[19]

Although Castro supplied Soviet weapons to the FMLN (Farabundo Martí National Liberation Front), the left-wing socialist party seeking to overthrow the

US-backed Salvadoran government, the Soviet Union itself had little interest in the country.[20] During the Salvadoran Civil War (1979–1992), which resulted in over seventy-five thousand total deaths, the US-backed government was responsible for the majority of the fifty to sixty thousand civilian deaths.[21] One of the several US-trained death squads, the Atlacatl Battalion "remains perhaps the most appalling violator of human rights in El Salvador," according to the human rights organization Americas Watch.[22] The involvement of the US military to roll back the influence of communism in Central America simply made a bad situation worse for civilians.

Although Bono was against Reagan's heavy-handed methods, he knew well the track record of communism in the twentieth century, saying, "Communism did not produce freedom or prosperity for anybody. It has produced a hundred years of some of the most heinous crimes ever committed by human beings on one another. So I can understand now why America had such a fear of it in Central America."[23] Nevertheless, he viewed the human rights violations and civilian deaths caused by US-backed forces as a greater immediate crisis than stopping the spread of communism and focused on this in his lyrics to "Bullet the Blue Sky" and "Mothers of the Disappeared." Bono realized that distilling his thoughts about these events into concrete polemics would be difficult, so he used poetic imagery to express the suffering of the civilian population and depended on his bandmates to complete the picture. Regarding Edge's playing in "Bullet the Blue Sky," Bono said,

> Edge can say more about the struggle in El Salvador with his guitar than I can with words.[24] I described what I had been through, what I had seen, some of the stories of people I had met, and I said to Edge: "Could you put that through your amplifier?" I even got pictures and stuck them on the wall. I brought in film of the horrors and put it on a video and said: "Now, do it!" . . . I wanted it to feel like hell on earth. . . . All these images of fire-bombing. . . . And outside it's America.[25]

U2 released *The Joshua Tree* on March 9, 1987, and began their tour for the album on April 2. The band's performance of "Bullet the Blue Sky" highlighted the tour and can be seen in the *Rattle and Hum* documentary (1988). In the film, the song is prefaced by Adam Clayton being interviewed in a pub saying, "There are people would say that you shouldn't mix music and politics, or sport and politics, or whatever. But I think that's kind of bullshit."[26] This is followed by footage of the band playing "Bullet the Blue Sky" at Sun Devil Stadium in Tempe, Arizona, on December 20, 1987. But before they start the song, Jimi Hendrix's rendition of "The Star-Spangled Banner" from Woodstock is played through the stadium's PA system while an LED display of the American flag appears from the top of the stadium. The lights slowly flicker out, making the flag look like it is disintegrating.[27] The band begins playing "Bullet the Blue Sky" as the flag slowly disappears. Later in the song, while Edge is playing his slide guitar solo, which portrays the suffering of Central American civilians, Bono shines a handheld spotlight on Edge's guitar. This image was used for the front cover of *Rattle and Hum* and on promotional materials for the album and film. Bono then repeatedly moves the spotlight from the guitar to the audience.[28] It's as if he is using the spotlight to project the sound of the guitar, the horrors of the Salvadoran Civil War, into the audience so they can see *and* hear the battle for themselves. Bono acts as a war correspondent using the sound of Edge's guitar as combat film footage. During the final monologue that ends the song, Bono adds a reference to San Salvador, the capital of El Salvador, which is not on the studio version: "And I feel a long way from the hills of San Salvador, where the sky is ripped open, and the rain pours through a gaping wound, pelting the women and children, pelting the women and children, who run, who run, into the arms of America."[29] Is Bono speaking of real rain here or a rain of bullets? "Arms" could also mean weapons. "Into the arms of America" may look comforting and maternal on the page and may resonate with the Statue of Liberty and Emma Lazarus's poem "The New Colossus" ("Give me your tired, your poor, your huddled masses"), but the dark music and the violent verb *pelting* (*howling* on the studio version) makes the point clear. The song is about Central American civilians whose countries are invaded, terrorized, and forced to assimilate into America and the geopolitics of the 1980s. Before he says, "Of America," Bono, wearing a cowboy hat, holds the spotlight to his side and then "draws" it, much like a cowboy would draw his pistol from his holster in a Western film. Bono wants to hit the audience with, and shine a light on, something he witnessed firsthand, something that Americans may not be aware of, something not covered on nightly news programs as much as it should have been: the high price in civilian lives America made Central America pay to impede the spread of communism.

Even without the obvious reference to Jimi Hendrix's rendition of "The Star-Spangled Banner" at the beginning of "Bullet the Blue Sky," Edge's slide guitar solo can easily be linked with Hendrix. Hendrix used distortion, feedback, vibrato bar dive bombs, and tritones to musically depict falling and exploding bombs and the cries of civilians in Southeast Asia during the Vietnam War. (See the Jimi Hendrix section in chap. 7.) Likewise, Edge used distortion, feedback, vibrato bar dive bombs, and his slide to depict the armed conflicts and civilian cries in the Salvadoran Civil War.

Like "Bullet the Blue Sky," "Mothers of the Disappeared" (the final song on *The Joshua Tree*) is a response to the Salvadoran Civil War in particular and the US military presence in Latin America in general. At the first concert of the 1986 Conspiracy of Hope tour in San Francisco, Bono met René Castro, a Chilean mural artist who was freed by Amnesty International. He had been imprisoned and tortured for two years because his artwork criticized Augusto Pinochet. Pinochet, a militant anticommunist, ousted the democratically elected, socialist, Chilean president Salvador Allende in a 1973 coup. Through René Castro and Amnesty International, Bono learned of the *desaparecidos* (the disappeared ones) in Chile, El Salvador, and other Latin American countries. "Disappearing" people became a systematic method the Salvadoran government used to suppress dissent.[30] "Enforced disappearance of persons" is the "arrest, detention or abduction of persons by . . . a State or political organization, followed by a refusal to acknowledge that depravation of freedom or to give information on the fate or whereabouts of those persons, with the intention of removing them from the protection of the law for a prolonged period of time."[31] Often this implies murder.[32]

While Bono was in El Salvador, he met with a group of women called COMADRES (Committee of the Mothers Monsignor Romero) commonly known as the "Mothers of the Disappeared." The COMADRES were founded in 1977 with the help of Archbishop Óscar Romero to shed light on the increasing number of people disappearing during the Salvadoran Civil War. "Armed with a short list of missing relatives," Lynn Stephen writes, "they demanded to know who was in the jails, forced the evacuation of clandestine cemeteries, and made the repression tactics of the [El Salvadoran] government known to an international audience."[33] The number of persons who were disappeared during the Salvadoran Civil War is unknown. Estimates range from four thousand to eight thousand or higher, but since these persons were never found, they unfortunately must be counted among the seventy-five thousand total deaths.[34]

US military personnel and the CIA trained many of the death squads responsible for disappearing people during the Salvadoran Civil War.[35] The United States maintained a heavy military presence and intelligence operation in Honduras, which borders El Salvador, throughout the 1980s to assist and arm Salvadoran government death squads.[36] Learning of this during his trip to El Salvador, Bono recounted, "There is no question in my mind that the people of America through their taxes are paying for the equipment that is used to torture people in El Salvador. In my trip to Salvador, I met with mothers of children who had disappeared. There's no question in my mind of the Reagan administration's involvement in backing the regime that is committing these atrocities. I doubt if the people of America are even aware of this."[37]

Bono's lyrics focus on the anguish the mothers feel over their lost loved ones. The mothers hear the beating of their hearts and see their tears in the rain. Adam Clayton said of the background track to the song, "The sound, which was the sound that [producer] Brian [Eno] came up with for that drum loop that starts off 'Mothers,' was very, very evocative of that sinister, death squad darkness."[38]

Colm O'Hare writes, "The key sonic element of the recording is the drone-like texture running through it, evoking an abstract sense of evil and dread."[39] Bono intones the lyrics in a near whisper at the beginning, adopts a desolate falsetto in the middle, and then sings in full voice. Over the drum loop, Edge plays a gentle, mournful theme. Near the end, Brain Eno adds sustained chords on synthesizer that sound eerily like women wailing.

These two U2 songs raise questions about the presence of US military in Central American countries during the Cold War, which started in 1954 with the Guatemalan coup d'état and reached a peak during the 1980s. While Reagan correctly foresaw that the Soviet Union would applaud any socialist uprising in Latin America, the Soviets knew not to risk a nuclear response from the United States. Neither superpower wanted a nuclear war. Yet, Soviet weapons had been in the hands of Castro, who was more than happy to pass them along to other socialist revolutionaries. Reagan wanted to remove as much Soviet influence in Central America, South America, and the Caribbean as he could, even if that meant supporting corrupt anticommunist regimes. Was Reagan right in providing military weapons to the Contras in Nicaragua and the Salvadoran government, two heinous perpetrators of human rights abuses on civilians? Did anticommunism make life in Latin America any better than communism did? What do death squads and disappearing people have to do with spreading democracy? Bono, who saw the situation firsthand, believed the cost in civilian lives was too high. He said, "And whilst communism turns out to be one of the worst ideas the world ever came up with, idealism turned in on itself; to support everything that's anti-communist was a really bad idea."[40] This parallels the thoughts of Michael Parenti, who wrote, "Our fear that communism might someday take over most of the world blinds us to the fact that anti-communism already has. Hundreds of billions of dollars have been expended, and hundreds of thousands of lives have been sacrificed on its behalf. . . . American anti-communists find license to commit any number of heinous actions in order to counter the 'menace'; thereby they perpetrate greater human miseries and dangers than the ones they allegedly seek to eradicate and they become the very evil they profess to combat."[41]

Bono's assessment of Reagan's foreign policy in Central America could be summarized in a phrase from "Peace on Earth," from U2's 2001 album, *All That You Can't Leave Behind,* "You become a monster so the monster will not break you."

STING: COLD WAR POLITICS IN "RUSSIANS"

In 1982, French street artist Thierry Noir moved to West Berlin. The city attracted him simply because David Bowie and Iggy Pop had recorded there. He lived in a small bedsit overlooking the Berlin Wall in the Kreuzberg district. The wall's gloomy presence, stark whiteness, and sheer drabness soon became an annoyance to him. In April 1984 he decided to start painting murals on it, a risky and dangerous affair. East Berlin guards armed with machine guns often chased him away. Other artists were also painting on the wall, and by the mid-1980s, colorful, riotous graffiti filled large sections of the West Berlin side. Some artists added to, or simply painted over, other artists' work, creating an ever-evolving commentary on the wall and its meaning. The graffiti chipped away at the austerity and authority of the wall and played a part in undermining those who constructed it. Most of Noir's murals consisted of cartoonlike heads in profile, and were distinctive for their bright colors, large lips, noses for foreheads, and resemblance to the Easter Island statues. Sometime in 1985 or 1986, not far from Checkpoint Charlie, an unknown artist painted the words "IF YOU LOVE SOMEBODY SET THEM FREE" along the rounded top ridge of the wall.[42] Noir chose this location to paint a mural of six heads. The 1986 German experimental film *Berliner Blau,* directed by Hartmut Jahn, shows him painting the mural. The film explores the effect the wall had on the psyche of Berliners. It could be considered a protest film against the wall. Noir told us in an interview,

> The title "If You Love Somebody Set Them Free" was already written on the top of the Berlin Wall, so I chose this place to paint the mural. It was perfect for me as a title. I chose to paint the Wall because it was a nonviolent action. It was a political act to paint the wall. The wall was built 5 meters [16 feet] beyond the official border, so the East German soldiers were allowed to arrest any person standing near the wall. Because of this, to paint the wall was absolutely forbidden and dangerous. The painters had to be quick, always painting with one eye, the other watching for soldiers.[43]

The mural is shown in figure 6.1, in a photograph taken by Saba Laudanna on June 18, 1986. The titles of other Western rock songs were painted on the Berlin Wall in the mid- to late 1980s before it was dismantled, such as "Another Brick in the Wall" by Pink Floyd.[44] The person who painted the title of Sting's hit song seems to have been using it to sum up his feelings on East Germans: set them free. The wish came true when the words and the mural disappeared into rubble at the hands, and chisels, of wall peckers (*Mauerspechte*) in 1990. Thus a popular song became a Cold War political statement, even without its music or lyrics present—or the songwriter's intent or involvement—simply by its title being painted on the Berlin Wall.[45]

Although "If You Love Somebody Set Them Free" became a commentary on the Berlin Wall without Sting's involvement, the Cold War looms large in his songs with the Police and as a solo artist. Sting, Andy Summers, and Stewart Copeland

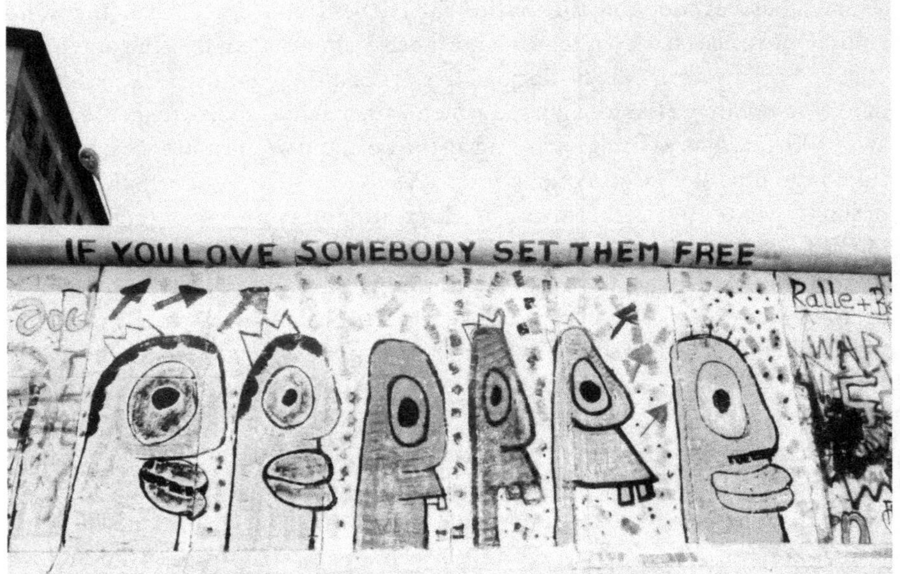

FIG. 6.1 Photograph taken by Saba Laudanna on June 18, 1986, of the Berlin Wall mural painted by Thierry Noir. *Reprinted by permission of Saba Laudanna.*

first played together in 1977 in a band called Strontium 90. Strontium-90 is the deadly component in radioactive fallout. "Fall Out," written by Copeland, was the first single of The Police. "Bring on the Night" from *Reggatta de Blanc* (1979) and "When the World Is Running Down, You Make the Best of What's Still Around" from *Zenyatta Mondatta* (1980) portray life after a nuclear holocaust. Sting said the two songs "share a chord sequence and a post-apocalyptic vision . . . such vanity as to imagine one's self as the sole survivor of a holocaust with all one's favourite things still intact!"[46] "Walking in Your Footsteps" from *Synchronicity* (1983) suggests atomic warfare will make us go the way of the dinosaur. "Every Breath You Take," Sting's most well-known song, also has Cold War overtones. When it came out in 1983, many regarded it as a love song and played it at wedding ceremonies. Sting said of this, "People think it's a very lovely song that's a symbol of their relationship. 'We got married to "Every Breath You Take,"' I hear people say. Good luck!"[47] In more recent years, thanks to Sting's explanation, it has been rightly understood as a song about stalking, obsession, control, and fear. He also sees it as a song about Cold War espionage and surveillance. He recounts, "I didn't realize at the time how sinister it is. I think I was thinking of Big Brother, surveillance, and control. These were the Reagan, Star Wars [SDI—Strategic Defense Initiative] years."[48] This section takes a close look at Sting's most iconic song about the Cold War, "Russians" (1985).

Along with Nena's "99 Luftballons," "Russians" is probably the most well-known song about the Cold War from the 1980s. Released as a single from his first solo album, *The Dream of the Blue Turtles*, it reached number twelve on the UK singles chart and number sixteen on the US *Billboard* singles chart. The music of "Russians" is based on the main theme of the "Romance" movement of Sergei Prokofiev's suite for symphony orchestra *Lieutenant Kijé* from 1934, which the composer adapted from the score he composed for the Russian film of the same name. Taking place in the late eighteenth century during the reign of Tsar Paul I, *Lieutenant Kijé* is a satirical film on government bureaucracy. In the tale, a hapless clerk compiles a list of the tsar's military personnel and bungles a phrase while taking dictation, mistaking the Russian phrase "parootchiki, zheh" ("the lieutenants, however . . .") for "Parootchik Kizheh ("Lieutenant Kijé"). The tsar reads the document and thinks there is a Lieutenant Kijé among his guards. The tsar's aides and military officers create an elaborate career for Kijé rather than admit to the pedantic and temperamental tsar that a clerical error has been made. Although Kijé does not exist, he manages to do quite well for himself; he receives a promotion, falls in love, and gets married. When he is commanded to appear before the tsar, the aides fabricate Kijé's death, and he is buried with military honors.

The five movements of the suite depict episodes in Kijé's "career." The "Romance" movement represents Kijé's amorous exploits. It is the slow and subdued exception to an otherwise brisk and humorous score. Prokofiev's main theme, played in turn by double bass, tenor saxophone, celeste, and harp, sounds languid and sensuous. The theme as it appears in Sting's "Russians"—played by Kenny Kirkland on synthesizers—sounds stiff, mechanical, and threatening to match the dark tone of the lyrics.[49] Sting seems to have chosen the theme more for its slow tempo and stately bearing rather than for what it represents in the Prokofiev suite. "Russians" is in C minor with brief modulations to the relative major of E-flat. While Prokofiev's "Romance" is also in minor keys—G minor, B-flat minor, and E-flat minor—its theme comes across more as sensual and sad rather than dark and menacing. Sting takes a melancholy love theme and uses it in a song about fear between the superpowers and possible nuclear devastation. "Russians" sounds "Russian" because it fits the common clichés Westerners have about Russian classical music and opera: it is serious, weighty, and mighty. The end of "Russians," with its bells tolling, tam-tam resounding, and Prokofiev's theme blasting out like trumpets, almost has the grandeur and gravity of the coronation scene from Modest Mussorgsky's opera *Boris Godunov.* Sting forthrightly included a transcription of the theme on the back cover of *The Dream of the Blue Turtles* with the note "I borrowed this theme from Sergei Prokofiev for the Russians."[50] The theme's note values are twice that of Prokofiev's theme (half notes for quarter notes, etc.). The tempo is roughly the same.[51]

"Russians" begins with the sound of ticking, an ominous allusion to the Doomsday Clock, a symbolic depiction of how close the world is to a global catastrophe, whether it be by nuclear conflict, climate change, or some other cause.[52] A low G pedal point on synthesizer joins the ticking along with recordings of news reporters speaking in Russian. The ticking actually counts out four measures of sixteenth notes, establishing the tempo. It functions simultaneously as a metronome and as a metonym of the Doomsday Clock. "Russians" has an uncomplicated strophic form of three eight-line verses, concluding with the final four lines of the second verse slightly altered. The Prokofiev theme appears twice after the second verse, once after the third verse, and then takes center stage at the end. Before the song fades out, the ticking returns.

The lyrics as a whole place blame on both the United States and the Soviet Union for the Cold War, as in the line, "There is no monopoly of common sense on either side of the political fence." Yet the final line of each verse calls into question the humanity of the Soviets. In verses one and four, Sting sings that the world will be saved "*if* the Russians love their children too" (emphasis added). In the second and third verses, the line is "*I hope* the Russians love their children too" (emphasis added). It appears Sting is saying the world will be saved from nuclear holocaust only if the Russians love their own children like those in the West love theirs. This implies the Soviets are so bent on winning the arms race they appear unconcerned about preserving a future for their posterity. Russian journalist Vladimir Pozner took Sting to task about this line in a 2010 interview. Voicing the opinion of his fellow Russians regarding the lyrics, Pozner said, "Did [you] actually believe that we don't love our children? . . . [Do you] not think we're human beings?"[53] Sting tempered the tone of the lyrics by telling Pozner that what he meant was the world can be saved "*because* the Russians love their children too" (emphasis added).[54] During his Symphonicities tour in 2010 and 2011, which can be seen on the concert film *Sting: Live in Berlin* (2010), he sings in the last line, "*That* the Russians love their children too" (emphasis added), portraying the Soviets in a positive light. The line also appears this way on the lyric sheet that came with the original LP recording. But on the original recording, he clearly sang, "*If* the Russians love their children too" (emphasis added), which can be read as questioning the humanity of the Soviets.

Yet Sting did not need to be dodgy in the interview with Pozner. Unfortunately, many Americans and Europeans in the early to mid-1980s felt exactly the same way and regarded the Russian people simply as monsters. Many Russians also regarded Americans as monsters.[55] Sting acknowledged this mindset when he said to Pozner, "I was born and brought up in the West and we were educated and conditioned to look at the Soviet Union as an ideological fortress. Because they were our ideological enemies, perhaps we would fight a war one day. It's easier to fight a war against people who, perhaps, aren't quite human. I was aware that was happening to me, in the media, in education generally. I wrote the song in the early eighties. It was another one of those frigid times in the Cold War."[56]

The song honestly portrays Western attitudes toward the Soviets in the early 1980s. The lyrics appear below, as sung by Sting on the single.

Lyrics to "Russians" by Sting (1985)

Verse 1:
In Europe and America
There's a growing feeling of hysteria
Conditioned to respond to all the threats
In the rhetorical speeches of the Soviets

Mister Khrushchev said, "We will bury you"
I don't subscribe to this point of view
It'd be such an ignorant thing to do
If the Russians love their children too

Verse 2:
How can I save my little boy
From Oppenheimer's deadly toy?
There is no monopoly of common sense
On either side of the political fence

We share the same biology
Regardless of ideology
Believe me when I say to you
I hope the Russians love their children too

Verse 3:
There is no historical precedent
To put words in the mouth of the president
There's no such thing as a winnable war
It's a lie we don't believe anymore

Mister Reagan says "We will protect you"
I don't subscribe to this point of view
Believe me when I say to you
I hope the Russians love their children too

Verse 4: We share the same biology
Regardless of ideology
What might save us, me and you
Is if the Russians love their children too

In the concert film *Sting: Live in Berlin,* Sting explains the genesis of "Russians." In the 1980s he knew a research scientist at Columbia University who had a device that could steal the signal from a Russian satellite. This enabled them to watch Russian TV, but as Sting recounts,

> It was late Saturday night in New York City so it was early Sunday morning in Moscow and we were forced to watch Russian children's programs, Russian cartoons, and a Russian version of *Sesame Street.* As I was watching these programs, it struck me how well they were made, how much care, attention, and clearly love had gone into making these programs. And a very obvious thought struck me. Well, of course the Russians love their children the same way we love ours. And this, of course, was the basis of détente. The reason we didn't blow each other up was because all of us had a stake in the future which was our children.[57]

In one line in the song, Sting wonders if he can save his son from "Oppenheimer's deadly toy," nuclear weapons. Footage of Sting's wife Trudie Styler giving birth to their son Jake is shown in a moving section in the film *Bring on the Night.* "Russians" plays in the background during the birth scene.[58] The line also contains a surreptitious reference to a "little boy" other than Jake. "Little Boy" was the codename of the first atomic bomb dropped on Hiroshima on August 6, 1945. Acknowledging the madness of the arms race in the early 1980s and the failure of politicians to curb its escalation, Sting hopes with "Russians" that an appeal to the lives of children will turn the tide.

Although space does not allow us to treat the subject adequately, Sting continued to engage in Cold War issues throughout the rest of the 1980s and into the early 1990s. "They Dance Alone" from his second solo album, . . . *Nothing Like the Sun* (1987), brought attention to the Chilean mothers of the disappeared (as U2 did the same year) and directly confronted the atrocities of US-backed dictator Augusto Pinochet. During the Amnesty International–sponsored *Human Rights Now!* tour (1988), Sting performed "They Dance Alone." Sting wanted the tour to go to Chile, but of course, Pinochet did not allow it. Nevertheless, neighboring Argentina held concerts. On October 14–15 in Mendoza and Buenos Aires, Sting invited the Mothers of the Plaza de Mayo and the Chilean mothers onstage during his performance of "They Dance Alone." He sang the song in Spanish with Peter Gabriel.[59] A year and a half later on March 11, 1990, the election of Patricio Aylwin ended Pinochet's reign in Chile.[60] Amnesty International organized two benefit concerts called "*Desde Chile . . . un abrazo a la esperanza*" ("From Chile . . . A Hug and a Hope") to celebrate the beginning of a new democratic era in Chile. The concerts were known as "An Embrace of Hope" and were held on October 12–13, 1990, at the National Stadium in Santiago, Chile, the site Pinochet used as a prison camp following his 1973 coup. The place where thousands had been tortured became a place where thousands celebrated the end of the tortures. Sting again sang the song in Spanish, and more than twenty Chilean women joined him onstage, holding photographs of loved ones who had been disappeared.[61]

BILLY JOEL: THE PIANO MAN IN MOSCOW AND LENINGRAD

While David Bowie, U2, and Sting witnessed the Cold War in Berlin and Latin America, Billy Joel walked straight into the mouth of the dragon. In the summer of 1987, he and his band pumped thousands of watts of glasnost out of their amplifiers and into Soviet audiences. Bridging the cultural divide with his openness and charisma, he connected with the Soviets to a degree few Westerners had done before.

Billy Joel's seven concert tour of the Soviet Union in July and August 1987 was a massive undertaking. No rock show of this scale had ever been attempted in the Soviet Union. Joel flew into Moscow with his eight-member band, over 130 crew members and assistants, his wife Christie Brinkley, and one-year-old daughter, Alexa. In addition, a caravan of six tractor trailers full of instruments, sound equipment, and lighting rigs made the journey from England to Moscow. Joel gave one solo performance in Tbilisi, Georgia, and three full-scale concerts in both Moscow and Leningrad (now called Saint Petersburg).

Although Joel conceded that his trip was heavy-laden with American-Soviet politics, he did not want to speak about politics in interviews or during the concerts. His reason was shaped by his experience at the Havana Jam in Cuba in March 1979. He found that political speeches during that festival turned people off because they wanted to hear the music and have a good time. Joel simply played and united the Cuban crowd in song. He said, "If I can get that kind of response in Havana, maybe we can get that kind of response in Moscow, and we can make some kind of contact here. . . . In a situation like this, to spout a lot of politics would be counterproductive. They've heard it, we've heard it. What they haven't heard is the music and what our people haven't seen is their reaction to the music."[62] Joel wanted to connect with the Soviets on a personal, not a political, level.

Joel sung entirely in English during the concerts but had Oleg Smirnoff—a freelance interpreter chosen by Joel himself—translate his song introductions. Joel also connected with the audiences in many nonverbal ways. This helped overcome the language barrier. He slapped hands with people in the front row. He ran down the aisles with a wireless microphone to sing with fans in the back row. He brought people onto the stage with him. He fell backward into the audience and crowd-surfed. He had security guards smiling, jumping on empty chairs, singing, and dancing, before they were scolded by their superiors. Audience members sang, screamed, and wept. Such freedom of expression was rarely encountered during concerts before Mikhail Gorbachev took office in 1985. Joel credited the Russian leader by saying, "Gorbachev opened the doors. If it hadn't been for him, we wouldn't have been able to go."[63]

For a rock star, Joel turned out to be an excellent cultural ambassador, both inside and outside the concert hall. He appeared live on the Russian TV variety show *The Ring*. He sang medieval chants with a Georgian men's choir in a mountaintop monastery in Tbilisi and then taught them some classic American doo-wop hits like the Marvelows's "I Do." He met the mother of famous poet, actor, and musician Vladimir Vysotsky.[64] He talked with young Russian metal fans and told them that he, like them, was looked on with scorn as a teenager for having long hair. He gave two million dollars of his own money to finance the trip since the Soviets couldn't pay him much, and he couldn't get American corporate sponsorship. In addition, he did not allow legal issues or contractual stipulations to get in the way. Tour manager, Rick London, said, "The contract we signed is two pages. In the States when we go and perform, it's about 50 pages. . . . [This Soviet tour is] basically a matter of trust."[65] "A Matter of Trust," both the phrase and the song, became the theme of the trip. While rock stars rarely bring their families on the road, especially to a place such as the Soviet Union, Joel brought his wife Christie Brinkley and their one-year-old daughter, Alexa. He said, "I wanted to show the Russian people I trusted them enough to bring my own child with me. . . . I want you to see my family and I want my family to see you. It turned out to be a very important part of our trip. . . . We made friends by having our family with us."[66]

The second Leningrad concert was the first rock concert to be broadcast on state radio in the Soviet Union. Europe and the United States also simulcast it. The satellites that the superpowers were using to spy on each other now linked up to broadcast music. Joel said, "That was one of the emotional high points, to know that kids in the States were listening to kids here in the Soviet Union, cheering."[67] Putting the whole trip in perspective, he recounts, "Once the genie is out of the bottle, you can't put it back in. I think [the tour] had a lot to do with how things changed over there, because not too long after that, the Wall did come down and the communist party was kicked out. . . . There were a number of dynamics going on at that time. We were just one of them, but it was an important one."[68]

Joel's 1987 trip was the inspiration for "Leningrad," from his 1989 album, *Storm Front*. The song is based on Viktor, a man Joel met during the Moscow leg of the tour. Viktor worked as a clown at the Gorky Park Circus and got to meet Billy when he and Christie took Alexa there to see the animals. Confirming how well Joel connected with the Russian audience despite the language barrier, Viktor told him he could be a bridge between the two countries.[69] Viktor also traveled to Leningrad to see all three of Joel's concerts. At the foot of stage, he was the most expressive audience member, repeatedly gesturing with his arms and hands that his heart was exploding or that he was giving his heart to the band.[70] He and Joel developed a close friendship, which inspired the song.

"Leningrad" contrasts the lives of Billy and Viktor. Joel fictionalizes certain aspects of Viktor's early life to create the backstory of a typical Russian boy growing up in 1950's Leningrad. The lyrics speak of Viktor being born in 1944, losing his father in the Siege of Leningrad near the end of World War II, growing up in oppressive state schools, serving his time as a civil servant, and drowning his sadness, hate, and misery with vodka. Joel then describes his own childhood, growing up in Levittown, New York, during McCarthyism and the Korean War, doing duck-and-cover drills in elementary school, and fearing the communists. Viktor became a clown, turning his misery into children's laughter, while Joel lived through the Cuban Missile Crisis in 1962 and watched his friends go off to Vietnam in the late 1960s. Viktor, as a typical Russian, is not tyrannical and warlike but is someone struggling through poverty and oppression. He wants to find joy in life. Joel, as a typical American, is surprised that Viktor is so kind and open since he was taught that Russians were the opposite. The last line is "we never knew what friends we had until we came to Leningrad." The intent of the song is to dispel the common American stereotype of the Cold War: all Russians are mini-Stalins bent on spreading revolution and communism to every corner of the globe. Joel said of "Leningrad," "In a way that song kind of encapsulates how that trip changed me. . . . I met these people and they weren't the enemy."[71] The song is in AABABA form (extended AABA form) and the lyrics are below.

Lyrics to "Leningrad" by Billy Joel (1989)

A: Viktor was born in the spring of '44
And never saw his father anymore
A child of sacrifice, a child of war
Another son who never had
A father after Leningrad

A: Went off to school and learned to serve the state
Followed the rules and drank his vodka straight
The only way to live was drown the hate
A Russian life was very sad
And such was life in Leningrad

B: I was born in '49
A cold war kid in McCarthy time
Stop 'em at the 38th Parallel
Blast those yellow reds to hell
And cold war kids were hard to kill
Under their desks in an air raid drill
Haven't they heard we won the war
What do they keep on fighting for?

A: Viktor was sent to some Red Army town
Served out his time, became a circus clown
The greatest happiness he'd ever found
Was making Russian children glad
And children lived in Leningrad

B: But children lived in Levittown
And hid in the shelters underground
Until the Soviets turned their ships around
And tore the Cuban missiles down
And in that bright October sun
We knew our childhood days were done
And I watched my friends go off to war
What do they keep on fighting for?

A: And so my child and I came to this place
To meet him eye to eye and face to face
He made my daughter laugh, then we embraced
We never knew what friends we had
Until we came to Leningrad

Joel imbues the song with the grandeur of late romantic Russian symphonic music (Tchaikovsky, the Mighty Five, Rachmaninoff), although he doesn't quote any work specifically, like Sting does in "Russians." The clue to the song's "Russianness" is Joel's practice of writing music without lyrics in the vein of classical composers.[72] Joel told interviewer Robert L. Doerschuk, "The music was conceived, before the lyrics, as a classical piece, way before I went to Russia. Sometimes I just write classical pieces for my own enjoyment. . . . I rarely show this stuff to people, but once in a while it does surface in a song. I'll bet you I've used them [classical composers] without even knowing it. That's where 'Leningrad' came from."[73]

When Doerschuk asked him if the music of Sergei Rachmaninoff influenced the song, Joel said, "Actually, Tchaikovsky, with the suspensions and the descending bass line."[74] Because "Leningrad" begins with an introduction on solo piano and ends with symphonic accompaniment, it has both the intimacy of solo piano music and the weight of symphonic music. Two pieces by Tchaikovsky, for each of these mediums, have similarities to the song.[75] "March of the Wooden Soldiers" from *Children's Album*, op. 39 has a dotted eighth note rhythm and a melodic contour similar to the theme in "Leningrad." The main theme from the first movement of Tchaikovsky's Violin Concerto in D major, op. 35 (stated by the solo violin about one minute in and then the whole string section at six and nine minutes in) is marked by a turn-like phrase over a descending bass line. Trade in the turn for dotted eighth notes and the theme would sound very much like "Leningrad." Both of these pieces and "Leningrad" are in D major. Thus Joel gives the song a generalized Russian character by incorporating melodic and rhythmic features he intuitively picked up from Russian composers like Tchaikovsky.

Contrasting Sting's "Russians" (1985) with Billy Joel's "Leningrad" (1989) shows how rapidly Gorbachev and glasnost changed Western perceptions of the Soviets from the mid-1980s to the late 1980s. "Russians" depicts Soviets as a massive, singular, unfeeling entity. "Leningrad" is about one Soviet person, Viktor, who worked as a circus clown. "Russians" portrays the Soviets from afar with fear and uncertainty. "Leningrad" portrays Viktor from personal experience, a face-to-face meeting and a friendship. "Russians" is about fear between enemies, while "Leningrad" is about discovering an enemy is a friend.

BRUCE SPRINGSTEEN IN EAST BERLIN

As recounted at the beginning of this chapter, in June 1987 David Bowie played a concert in West Berlin at the wall. To the annoyance of East German government officials, the concrete edifice could not prevent the sound from drifting into the ears of East Berliners on the other side. In 1988, East Berlin officials realized it was impossible to stem the tide of Western culture and decided they needed to do something to appear magnanimous and respectable to the youth. For the first time, they allowed Western rock musicians to play on their side. Bob Dylan, with Tom Petty and the Heartbreakers as opening act, played in 1987. In 1988, Depeche Mode, Joe Cocker, Bryan Adams, and James Brown played. But no one was prepared for the Boss. On July 19, 1988, Bruce Springsteen and the E Street Band came to East Berlin, and the floodgates opened. Approximately one hundred and sixty thousand tickets were sold, but estimates of the crowd size were between two hundred thousand and half a million, nearly the size of Woodstock. Rock music had made its way over the Berlin Wall.

This was not Springsteen's first trip to East Berlin. In April 1981, the E Street Band played in West Berlin during the tour for *The River*. Springsteen and guitarist Steven Van Zandt passed through Checkpoint Charlie to spend an afternoon in East Berlin. Springsteen recounts, "It was a different society; you could feel the boot, the Stasis in the streets, and you knew the oppression was real. It changed Steve permanently. After our European trip, the man who had preached that rock 'n' roll and politics should never mix became an activist, his own music turning defiantly political. The power of the wall that split the world in two, its blunt, ugly, mesmerizing realness, couldn't be underestimated. It was an offense to humanity; there was something pornographic about it, and once viewed, it held a scent you couldn't quite get off of you."[76]

In fact, Van Zandt wrote a song about the experience called "Checkpoint Charlie" on his 1984 album, *Voice of America*. The song laments the division the wall has caused between family members and within the nation itself. Unfortunately, Van Zandt didn't play at the 1988 East Berlin concert, having left the E Street Band in 1984 to pursuit his solo career.

The concert was held at the Radrennbahn Weissensee, a cycling track a few miles from the Berlin Wall. Free German Youth, the East German socialist youth movement organized it. When Springsteen arrived in East Berlin, he found out the organizers were trying to put a communist spin on the concert by displaying posters and banners that called it a benefit for Nicaragua.[77] As recounted in the section on U2 in this chapter, the US government at the time was backing the Contras in their fight against the socialist Sandinista government in Nicaragua. When Springsteen found out about the spin, he threatened to back out, refusing to have his words and persona reduced to political propaganda. The signage was diligently removed, but the ticket stubs still had "Konzert für Nikaragua" ["Concert for Nicaragua"] on them.[78] He was quite frustrated because it was not the first time his music had been politically appropriated. Without consulting him, Ronald Reagan's campaign had coopted "Born in the U.S.A." to bolster his re-election in 1984.[79]

Although Springsteen did not want the concert to be a political event, he did not shy away from the obvious political ramifications of a Western rock star playing in a communist country. Immediately before the concert, he wrote a short speech and enlisted the help of West German interpreter and chauffer Georg Kerwinski to translate it into German.[80] Before playing Bob Dylan's 1964 song "Chimes of Freedom," Springsteen read his speech: "Es ist schön in Ost-Berlin zu sein. Ich möchte euch sagen ich bin nicht hier für oder gegen eine Regierung. Ich bin gekommen um rock'n'roll zu spielen für Ost-Berlinern in der Hoffnung dass eines Tages alle Barrieren abgerissen werden." ["It's nice to be in East Berlin. I want to tell you that I'm not here for or against any government. I have come to play rock 'n' roll for East-Berliners in the hope that one day all barriers will be torn down."] As Erik Kirschbaum notes in his book *Rocking the Wall,* Springsteen originally intended to say, "Alle Mauern abgerissen werden" ["all walls will be torn down"] but was advised by Kerwinski and manager Jon Landau just before the speech that such a statement would be too inflammatory and provocative. To directly encourage protest within the city of East Berlin could lead to disastrous consequences, as Kerwinski realized more clearly than Springsteen. Landau said, "We weren't there in East Berlin to take an openly confrontational approach. We weren't there to protest to the government of East Germany. We were there to do a concert for those 160,000 people or 300,000 people or however many there were in East Berlin. I agreed to the word change because, in the big scheme of things, I was sure the audience would understand Bruce's deeper meaning."[81]

The crowd seemed to get the deeper meaning. Audience member Jörge Beneke said, "Everyone knew exactly what he was talking about—tearing down the Wall. We had never heard anything like that from anyone in East Germany. That was a moment some of had been waiting a lifetime to hear. It was just incredible. We all felt locked up, and if we could have gotten over the Wall, many of us would have. Springsteen won everyone's heart over with that."[82]

The speech also resonated with the call to freedom from repression explicit within the lyrics of Dylan's "Chimes of Freedom." The song was a perfect match for the speech and even provided the controversial word deleted from the speech, "In the city's melted furnace, unexpectedly we watched / with faces hidden while the walls were tightening." "Chimes of Freedom" displays some of Dylan's most complex and literary songwriting. As Joanna Smolko summarized, "The first half of each verse sets a metaphorical scene; the narrator and a companion watch a storm. In a synesthetic moment, chimes flash and lightning tolls. The melody drops, resolving to a full cadence on the tonic. The second half of the verses names those whom the lightning bells are honoring and illuminating—refugees, rebels, poets, painters, prisoners, the disabled and the disenfranchised—hauntingly enumerating those who are misunderstood and downtrodden."[83]

Early in his career, Springsteen was promoted as "the new Dylan." Though he admired Dylan greatly, he distanced himself from Dylan's musical style and made his own path as a songwriter. Springsteen said in a 1999 interview that in his early twenties, he shied away from using loosely strung together images, characteristic of Dylan's lyrics.[84] Yet from the late 1970s to the present, Springsteen has covered many of Dylan's songs. Springsteen first performed "Chimes of Freedom" in 1978 on his tour for *Darkness on the Edge of Town*. During the Detroit concert, he said it was one of his favorite songs when he was in high school.[85] He scaled the song back from Dylan's six verses to three (1, 5, and 6). Springsteen did not perform the song again until 1988, when he sang it on his *Tunnel of Love Express* tour, which included the East Berlin concert. Performing in Copenhagen a week after the East Berlin concert, he introduced "Chimes of Freedom" by saying, "This is one of the greatest songs about human freedom ever written."[86] He recognized the song's ability to express universal human suffering and used it as a call for social change. His 1988 version begins with a chime-like setting on the keyboard, played by Danny Federici, and slowly accumulates other instruments, including backup vocals. Springsteen also added verse two, whose imagery of walls tightening certainly resonated with those in East Berlin. The song was central to Springsteen's political awakening in the latter half of the 1980s. He continued to use the song in September and October 1988 during Amnesty International's *Human Rights Now!* tour as a plea for basic human rights and social justice. On that tour, he sang it with Sting, Peter Gabriel, Tracy Chapman, Youssou N'Dour, and others.

Springsteen's concert in East Berlin lasted almost four hours. In his autobiography, *Born to Run*, Springsteen wrote,

> There in an open field stood the largest single crowd I'd ever seen or played to, and from center stage, I couldn't see its end. Home-stitched American flags flew in the East German wind. . . . I went from being a complete nobody sashaying unmolested down the streets of East Berlin, on the day *before* our show, to a national superstar in twenty-four hours. . . . We partied at the East German consulate and then headed back to West Berlin and a show for seventeen thousand that, despite our good West German fans, felt a lot less dramatic than what we'd just experienced.[87]

The concert was later broadcast on state television (without the speech before "Chimes of Freedom"). This allowed the whole country to witness the event. One year and four months after the concert, the wall came down. Erik Kirschbaum puts the impact of Springsteen, as well as others such as David Bowie and Billy Joel, in perspective when he writes,

> It's hard to pinpoint a direct cause-and-effect with the Springsteen concert and the Berlin Wall falling. And obviously there were a lot of other things going on in that era before the concert with Gorbachev in the Soviet Union, Solidarnosc in Poland, and then later the opening of Hungary's border to Austria in early 1989, the mass exodus of East Germans in the summer and fall of 1989 and the Monday rallies in Leizpig and elsewhere. That said, I think it is clear that the concert was an important spark and had a major effect. . . . rather than appeasing East Germans, it only made them even hungrier for the freedom and fun times that Springsteen seemed to embody up there on stage.[88]

Springsteen tapped into rock music's powerful force as a conductor of change. Tolling out the chimes of freedom, he reflected and amplified the longing already present in the hearts of the East Berlin people.

CONCLUSION

This chapter has shown what happened when rock musicians came in close contact with the Cold War. David Bowie gave Britons and Americans an impression of what life divided by the wall was like in 1970s Berlin. U2 and Sting exposed human rights abuses in Latin America caused by US-backed death squads and right-wing dictators. Billy Joel and Bruce Springsteen showed Westerners how young people in the Eastern Bloc craved the freedom of expression they found in American and British rock music. Popular musicians such as these played a part in ending the Cold War simply by being where it happened. They stirred the cauldron.

NOTES

1. In this recurring sketch on *Saturday Night Live,* and in two films, Mike Myers played Wayne Campbell and Dana Carvey played Garth Algar, two hard rock fans who broadcasted their own public access TV show from their basement.

2. "Wayne's World" sketch, *Saturday Night Live,* February 17, 1990, *Saturday Night Live* Transcripts, http://snltranscripts.jt.org/89/89mwaynesworld.phtml.

3. Jeff "Skunk" Baxter, from episode "Guitar Heroes," *The History of Rock 'n' Roll,* created and produced by Jeffrey Peisch (Time-Life Video & Television, Warner Home Video 34991, c1995, 2004, DVD 4), 44:28–44:40.

4. David Bowie, "The Thin White Duke Has Gone. Here's the New David Bowie," interview with Tim Lott, *Record Mirror,* September 24, 1977, https://timlottwriter.wordpress.com/2016/01/11/my-interview-with-bowie-1977/.

5. David Bowie, "Who Was that (Un)masked Man?" interview with Charles Shaar Murray, *New Musical Express,* November 12, 1977.

6. Nicholas Pegg, *The Complete David Bowie,* 6th ed. (London: Titan Books, 2011), 100.

7. Jennifer Chase, "'87 Concert Was a Genesis of East German Rebellion," *Deutsche Welle,* July 4, 2007, http://www.dw.com/en/87-concert-was-a-genesis-of-east-german-rebellion/a-2663850.

8. Bill DeMain, "The Sound and Vision of David Bowie," *Performing Songwriter* 11, no. 72 (September–October 2003): 47.

9. Krishnadev Calamur, "'Heroes' at the Wall," *Atlantic,* January 11, 2016, http://www.theatlantic.com/notes/2016/01/bowie-berlin-1987/423564/.

10. David Buckley, "Revisiting Bowie's Berlin," in *David Bowie: Critical Perspectives,* ed. Eoin Devereux, Aileen Dillane, and Martin J. Power (New York: Routledge, 2015), 215–229; Tobias Rüther, *Heroes: David Bowie and Berlin,* trans. Anthony Matthews (London: Reaktion, 2014); Thomas Jerome Seabrook, *Bowie in Berlin: A New Career in a New Town* (London: Jawbone, 2008); Hugo Wilcken, *David Bowie's Low* (London: Continuum, 2005); *David Bowie: Under Review 1976–1979: The Berlin Trilogy* (Films Media Group 49263, 2006, DVD).

11. David Bowie, *A New Career in a New Town [1977–1982]* (Parlophone Records, 2017), eleven-CD set.

12. McGee, *U2: A Diary,* 97–98; *A Conspiracy of Hope* was a series of six benefit concerts held in US cities to raise awareness of human rights violations around the world and to celebrate the twenty-fifth anniversary of Amnesty International. Musicians included U2, Sting (solo and with the Police), Peter Gabriel, Lou Reed, Joan Baez, Bryan Adams, and the Neville Brothers.

13. Bono, "Interview with U2, 1987, Part 4/6" interview by NBC music correspondent Rona Elliot on September 11, 1987 (4:14–4:52), https://www.youtube.com/watch?v=nNmROSiqb7U.

14. Bono, *U2 by U2,* 177.

15. "Backyard" episode from *Cold War: The Complete Series,* Jeremy Isaacs Production for Turner Original Productions, narrated by Kenneth Branagh (Warner Home Video 3000042713, 2012, six-DVD set), 0:53–1:02.

16. Edward A. Lynch, *The Cold War's Last Battlefield: Reagan, the Soviets, and Central America* (Albany: State University of New York Press, 2011), 175.

17. Bono, *Bono: In Conversation with Michka Assayas* (New York: Riverhead, 2005), 179.

18. Americas Watch, *Violations of the Laws of War by Both Sides in Nicaragua, 1981–1985* (New York: Americas Watch Committee, 1985); Americas Watch, *Human Rights in Nicaragua: Reagan, Rhetoric, and Reality* (New York: Americas Watch Com-

mittee, 1985); Amnesty International, *Nicaragua: The Human Rights Record* (London: Amnesty International, 1986).

19. Ronald Reagan, "Remarks on Central America and El Salvador at the Annual Meeting of the National Association of Manufacturers," March 10, 1983, Ronald Reagan Presidential Library and Museum, https://www.reaganlibrary.gov/research/speeches/31083a.

20. David Arbel and Ran Edelist, *Western Intelligence and the Collapse of the Soviet Union, 1980–1990: Ten Years That Did Not Shake the World* (Portland, OR: Frank Cass, 2003), 97–99.

21. Mitchell A. Seligson and Vincent McElhinny, "Low-Intensity Warfare, High-Intensity Death: The Demographic Impact of the Wars in El Salvador and Nicaragua," *Canadian Journal of Latin American and Caribbean Studies* 21, no. 42 (1996): 223–224.

22. Americas Watch, *El Salvador's Decade of Terror: Human Rights since the Assassination of Archbishop Romero* (New Haven, CT: Yale University Press, 1991), 20.

23. Bono, *Bono: In Conversation with Michka Assayas*, 185.

24. Mick Wall, *Bono: In the Name of Love* (New York: Thunder's Mouth, 2005), 182.

25. Bono, *U2 by U2*, 179.

26. Adam Clayton in *U2: Rattle and Hum (1988)* (Paramount Home Video 32228, 1999, DVD), 1:09:24–1:09:39.

27. *U2: Rattle and Hum*, "Bullet the Blue Sky," 1:09:39–1:10:11.

28. Ibid., 1:13:04–1:14:00.

29. Ibid., 1:14:47–1:15:17.

30. Amnesty International, *El Salvador: "Death Squads": A Government Strategy* (London: Amnesty International, 1988).

31. From Article 7(2)(i) of the Rome Statute of the International Criminal Court, quoted in Walter Kälin and Jörg Künzli's *The Law of International Human Rights Protection* (New York: Oxford University Press, 2009), 339.

32. Leslie Alan Horvitz and Christopher Catherwood, *Encyclopedia of War Crimes and Genocide* (New York: Facts on File, 2006), 124.

33. Lynn Stephen, *Women and Social Movements in Latin America: Power from Below* (Austin: University of Texas Press, 1997), 38.

34. Aldo A. Lauria-Santiago, "The Culture and Politics of State Terror and Repression in El Salvador," in *When States Kill: Latin America, the U.S., and Technologies of Terror*, ed. Cecilia Menjívar and Néstor Rodríguez (Austin: University of Texas Press, 2005), 96; Paul R. Bartrop, *A Biographical Encyclopedia of Contemporary Genocide: Portraits of Evil and Good* (Santa Barbara, CA: ABC-CLIO, 2012), 68.

35. Cynthia J. Arnson, "Window on the Past: A Declassified History of Death Squads in El Salvador," in *Death Squads in Global Perspective: Murder with Deniability*, ed. Bruce B. Campbell and Arthur D. Brenner (New York: St. Martin's, 2000), 85–124; Thomas Sheehan, "Friendly Fascism: Business as Usual in America's Backyard,"

in *Fascism's Return: Scandal, Revision, and Ideology since 1980*, ed. Richard J. Golsan (Lincoln: University of Nebraska Press, 1998), 260–300.

36. Joan Kruckewitt, "U.S. Militarization of Honduras in the 1980s and the Creation of CIA-based Death Squads," in *When States Kill: Latin America, the U.S., and Technologies of Terror*, ed. Cecilia Menjívar and Néstor Rodríguez (Austin: University of Texas Press, 2005), 170–197.

37. Bono, "The Enduring Chill: Bono and the Two Americas" in *U2: The Best of Propaganda: 20 Years of the Official U2 Magazine* (New York: Thunder's Mouth, 2003), 63–64.

38. Adam Clayton, *U2: The Joshua Tree* (Eagle Rock Entertainment ID9074ERDVD, 1999, DVD), 22:20–22:36.

39. Colm O'Hare, "The Secret History of 'The Joshua Tree' (Part 2)," *Hot Press*, November 21, 2007, http://www.atu2.com/news/the-secret-history-of-the-joshua-tree-part-2.html.

40. Bono, *U2 by U2*, 179.

41. Michael Parenti, *The Anti-Communist Impulse* (New York: Random House, 1969), 4, 9.

42. The words and mural were near the corner of Wilhelmstraße and Niederkirchnerstraße.

43. Thierry Noir from email interview with Tim and Joanna Smolko on August 28, 2016.

44. On another part of the wall, someone painted the marching hammers that appear on the inside gatefold of the album cover of Pink Floyd's *The Wall*. The marching hammers also appear in the film of *The Wall*. For more information on this, see the section on *The Wall* in chapter 10.

45. Although Sting himself had nothing to do with his song title being painted on the wall, he was aware of it and included it in a video montage at the beginning of his concert film *Sting: Live in Berlin* (Deutsche Grammophon BOO14981–59, 2010, Blu-Ray), 0:00:17–0:00:23.

46. Chris Welch, *The Complete Guide to the Music of the Police & Sting* (New York: Omnibus, 1996), 66.

47. "Sting–Behind the Music (September 26, 1999)." Uploaded December 6, 2019, YouTube. https://www.youtube.com/watch?v=xAcxTOfD3RE.

48. Sting, "Sting: How We Mock Our Most Serious Star, Our National Friend of the Earth. Shouldn't He Be a Protected Species? Or at Least a Respected One?," interview by Hunter Davies and Giles Smith, *Independent*, May 1, 1993, http://www.independent.co.uk/life-style/interview--sting-how-we-mock-our-most-serious-star-our-national-friend-of-the-earth-shouldnt-he-be-a-protected-species-or-at-least-a-respected-one-2320343.html.

49. Sting (on an Oberheim OB-8) and Kenny Kirkland (on a Yamaha DX7) can be seen rehearsing the theme in the documentary/concert film *Sting! Bring on the Night*, directed by Michael Apted (A&M Records 9880428, 2005, DVD), 1:17:26–1:17:52.

50. From back album cover of Sting's *The Dream of the Blue Turtles* (A&M Records SP-3750, 1985, LP).

51. Sergei Prokofieff, *Lieutenant Kijé, Suite Symphonique, op. 60* (Boca Raton, FL: Kalmus, 1980), 14.

52. For a fuller explanation of the Doomsday Clock, see the section on Iron Maiden's song "2 Minutes to Midnight" in chapter 7.

53. Sting, interview by Vladimir Pozner, *Pozner*, Channel One Russia, December 26, 2010, 31:00–31:25, http://www.youtube.com/watch?v=GHcsGZzJWds.

54. Sting, interview by Vladimir Pozner, 31:25–31:27.

55. Robert English and Jonathan J. Halperin, *The Other Side: How Soviets and Americans Perceive Each Other* (New Brunswick: Transaction, 1987); Eugene Anschel, ed., *American Appraisals of Soviet Russia, 1917–1977* (Metuchen, NJ: Scarecrow, 1978).

56. Sting, interview by Vladimir Pozner, 31:27–32:09.

57. *Sting: Live in Berlin* (Deutsche Grammophon BOO14981–59, 2010, Blu-Ray), 26:18–26:56.

58. *Sting! Bring on the Night*, 1:17:53–1:22:02.

59. *Released! The Human Rights Concerts, 1986–1998* (Shout! Factory, Amnesty International 82666313562, 2013, six-DVD set, Human Rights Now! concert), 1:41:10–1:51:48, https://www.youtube.com/watch?v=-P9m-3mrflo.

60. Although he was voted out of office, Pinochet still wielded considerable power as commander-in-chief of the army. His self-appointed status of "senator-for-life" granted him immunity. He was never convicted in court for his human rights violations.

61. *Released!: The Human Rights Concerts 1986–1998*, An Embrace of Hope concert, 58:06–1:09:06, https://www.youtube.com/watch?v=10aDCbNRkAs.

62. Billy Joel, "Billy Joel '87 intvw ussr part 1," interview by Rona Elliot, *Today Show*, 2:12–2:18, 5:33–5:45, https://www.youtube.com/watch?v=YIVrrof6ODA.

63. Billy Joel, "A Documentary Film," in *A Matter of Trust: The Bridge to Russia* (Columbia 88883759762, 2014, DVD), 46:31–46:35.

64. Vysotsky has often been compared to Bob Dylan and John Lennon, yet he created his own uniquely Russian style of folk/protest music.

65. Rick London, "Billy Joel '87 intvw ussr part 1," interview by Rona Elliot, 4:42–5:02.

66. Billy Joel, "A Documentary Film," 24:21–25:04.

67. Billy Joel, "Billy Joel '87 intv ussr part 2," interview by Rona Elliot, *Today Show*, 5:43–5:52, https://www.youtube.com/watch?v=tDLSWR4akB4.

68. Billy Joel, "A Documentary Film," 1:04:31–1:04:34, 1:05:20–1:05:35.

69. Ibid., 26:50–27:34.

70. Drummer Liberty Devitto, Christie Brinkley, Billy Joel, and others speak of Viktor's hand gesture in "A Documentary Film," 22:09–22:29, 49:12–50:06.

71. Ibid., 1:09:33–1:09:39, 1:11:51–1:11:55.

72. In 2001, Joel released an album of his solo piano compositions, *Fantasies & Delusions*, which reflected his love of classical music literature.

73. Billy Joel, "Billy Joel: The Piano Man Rocks On," interview by Robert L. Doerschuk, in *Keyboard Presents Classic Rock*, ed. Ernie Rideout (New York: Backbeat, 2010), 73.

74. Ibid.

75. Thanks to Josh Bedford for pointing out these similarities.

76. Bruce Springsteen, *Born to Run* (New York: Simon and Schuster, 2016), 288.

77. Erik Kirschbaum, *Rocking the Wall: Bruce Springsteen: The Berlin Concert That Changed the World* (New York: Berlinica, 2013), 68–71.

78. Kirschbaum, *Rocking the Wall*, 12, 94.

79. Joanna Smolko, "Politics and Protest in Springsteen's 'Born in the U.S.A.,'" *Avid Listener*, last modified September 19, 2016, http://www.theavidlistener.com/2016/09/politics-and-protest-in-springsteens-born-in-the-usa.html.

80. Kirschbaum, *Rocking the Wall*, 93–94.

81. Ibid., 98.

82. Ibid., *Rocking the Wall*, 100.

83. Joanna Smolko, "Springsteen and Human Rights: 'Chimes of Freedom,'" *Avid Listener*, last modified November 14, 2016, http://www.theavidlistener.com/2016/11/springsteen-and-human-rights-chimes-of-freedom-embed-video-httpswww youtubecomwatchvg3onnjubs18-caption-b.html.

84. Bruce Springsteen, "Interview," interview by Mark Hagen, *Mojo*, January 1999, in *Talk about a Dream: The Essential Interviews of Bruce Springsteen*, ed. Christopher Phillips and Louis P. Masur (New York: Bloomsbury, 2013), 251.

85. "Bruce Springsteen—Chimes Of Freedom (Detroit, September 1, 1978) [audio]," https://www.youtube.com/watch?v=ybFC3lhn9QU.

86. "Bruce Springsteen—Chimes of Freedom," live in Copenhagen, July 25, 1988, https://www.youtube.com/watch?v=G3onnJuBS18.

87. Springsteen, *Born to Run*, 352–353.

88. David Crossland, "Chimes of Freedom: How Springsteen Helped Tear Down the Wall," *Spiegel Online*, June 19, 2013, http://www.spiegel.de/international/germany/book-says-springsteen-concert-helped-bring-down-berlin-wall-a-906236-2.html.

SEVEN

HARD ROCK AND HEAVY METAL

The Electric Guitar as the Bomb

URANIUM AND PLUTONIUM ARE OFTEN referred to as heavy metals. Thus it is fitting that some of the most intense songs about their destructive effects would come from heavy metal bands. Because it is such an intense style of music, heavy metal is an ideal medium to convey the existential angst of living in a world under the threat of nuclear warfare. The predominant themes in heavy metal lyrics—war, masculinity, madness, death, and the end of the world—overlap with many Cold War issues.

While the Cold War–themed lyrics of heavy metal songs merit close inspection, it is the music—the actual sounds created by the musicians—that makes the songs in this chapter remarkable. In heavy metal music, elements such as timbre, volume, harmony, and rhythm are just as important as the lyrics in projecting a song's meaning.[1] This book thus far has explored Cold War songs primarily through lyrics rather than music, largely because the lyrics carry the greater weight of meaning. The early Cold War songs were set in a specific style, country, folk, gospel, etc., and the music was for the most part indistinguishable from other songs in those various styles. The music was not specifically tailored to characterize the Cold War. Sometimes instrumental effects were added, such as the pedal steel guitar depicting a descending bomb, like in Fred Kirby's "When That Hell Bomb Falls" (1950). Occasionally, stock sound effects were overdubbed onto recordings, like the exploding bombs in "Love That Bomb" by Dr. Strangelove and the Fallouts (1964). Yet the lyrics primarily marked these early songs as Cold War songs. In some styles—such as country and novelty explored in chapters 3 and 4—dark lyrics were paired with spirited singing and jaunty rhythms, creating an odd clash between word and music. It wasn't until the hard rock musicians of the late 1960s came along that both music and lyrics could equally be about the

Cold War. The actual sounds generated by the musicians allow listeners to "feel" the tumult of warfare and contemplate the consequences of a nuclear apocalypse in a way that earlier styles of music could not. In this chapter, songs by Jimi Hendrix, Black Sabbath, Ozzy Osbourne, Rush, Iron Maiden, and Metallica will be explored in detail.

WARFARE IN MUSIC

The sounds of war have been depicted musically for hundreds of years. Beethoven's "Wellington's Victory" (1813) and Tchaikovsky's "1812 Overture" (1882) are well-known examples. But in the late 1960s, hard rock musicians found new ways to replicate the sounds of war with their instruments, due in large part to advancements in instrument and studio technology. Electric guitarists used high-output amplifiers, distortion, the vibrato bar (also called tremolo bar or whammy bar), feedback, and effects pedals (such as wah, flange, and chorus) to broaden the tonal palette of the instrument. Unsurprisingly, the electric guitar, which has defined rock music since its origins, became the primary instrument used to create aural depictions of war.[2]

This new interest in depicting war using instrument technology coincided with the heavy coverage of the Vietnam War through another burgeoning technology, television. Although the threat of nuclear war had waned slightly in the mid-1960s, after the scare of the 1962 Cuban Missile Crisis, the Cold War still raged in the form of the Vietnam War. Color footage of injured and dead American soldiers and South Asian civilians was new to television and brought an alarming immediacy to warfare. Journalists and reporters were given more access to the fighting on the front lines and the military did not censor film footage. Television news reports showed bombs exploding, machine gun exchanges, and the burning of South Asian villages.

Responding to this, rock musicians of the 1960s counterculture translated the new immediacy television brought to warfare not only into lyrics but into sounds. This use of sound itself to portray military and civilian fatalities is a unique characteristic of Cold War music that came from the hard rock and heavy metal bands. Electricity became the crucial factor. An acoustic guitar cannot realistically conjure up the noise of modern mechanized warfare. A telling example of the power of electricity is a comparison between Bob Dylan's "All Along the Watchtower" from his *John Wesley Harding* album (released in December 1967) and the Jimi Hendrix Experience's cover version. The ambiguous lyrics of the Dylan song have just a vague intimation of war. They suggest a mythical or medieval setting by mentioning a "joker," "princes," "barefoot servants," and "riders." Some music critics have found biblical allusions to the book of Isaiah.[3] The lyrics have little to connect explicitly to then-current events, such as the Vietnam War or the Cold War. Dylan's original has a humdrum three-chord progression and a sparse acoustic guitar, harmonica, bass, and drum accompaniment. The song was released as a single but did not chart. Yet Jimi Hendrix's version, released as a single in September 1968 and included on *Electric Ladyland,* was a hit. It was his highest charting single on *Billboard,* reaching number twenty, and one of his most well-known songs. It has been interpreted as a Vietnam War anthem since its release. Russell Reising writes that it "seemed to become part of the soundtrack to the Vietnam War."[4] Since the lyrics are the same as the Dylan original, the music must give the song its atmosphere of war. Hendrix's dramatic vocal delivery makes the lyrics seem more apocalyptic than they really are, but his guitar playing mostly gives the song its warlike impression. Two months after the single was released, Tony Palmer wrote in the *New Musical Express,* "It is an assault . . . which must be like the roaring one hears moments before being disintegrated by an exploding hydrogen bomb."[5] Michael J. Kramer effusively describes it this way: "A song such as 'All Along the Watchtower' could communicate the terror *and* the attractive beauty of warlike sounds and feelings all at once.[6] Dylan's lyrics hint at impending violence and disaster, but only when Hendrix's electric-guitar solo swoops in does the song's full power erupt. His guitar becomes a helicopter gunship, its rotor blades spinning, its nose dipping and soaring, its automatic weaponry blazing. The electric bass, played by Hendrix himself on the recording, drops bombs that seem to leave huge craters in the hypnotic major-minor harmonic progression."[7]

The level of specificity in these descriptions demonstrates the evocative nature of Hendrix's playing.

THE NOISES OF WAR: HOW THE ELECTRIC GUITAR BECAME THE BOMB

The road to Hendrix's explosive sound is marked with remarkable discoveries, some intentional and some serendipitous. The electric guitar developed into the ultimate instrument of rock music during the same period the bomb developed into the ultimate instrument of warfare, the 1940s to the 1960s. Electric guitarists began experimenting with volume, distortion, and feedback in the 1940s, but the exploration of "noise as music" in a more general sense can be traced back to the Italian Futurism movement of the 1910s. Founded by Italian poet Filippo Tommaso Marinetti in 1909, Futurism's objective was to move the arts beyond their current modes of expression and embrace a new aesthetic based on technology, machines, speed, and war. In essence, the Futurists wanted to bring the achievements of the Industrial Revolution into art. Luigi Russolo, an Italian composer, applied the ideals of Futurism to music. He sought to move music beyond the "anemic sounds" in concert halls and incorporate the noises of machinery.[8] He states in his 1913 manifesto, *The Art of Noises*, "From the beginning, musical art sought out and obtained purity and sweetness of sound. Afterwards, it brought together different sounds, still preoccupying itself with caressing the ear with suave harmonies. As it grows ever more complicated today, musical art seeks out combinations more dissonant, stranger, and harsher for the ear. Thus, it comes ever closer to the *noise-sound*."[9]

Russolo also adds this interesting tidbit: "Nor should the newest noises of modern war be forgotten."[10] He built a variety of experimental instruments (*intonarumori*) to make up a "futurist orchestra" and defined six families of "noise-sounds." The first family generated noises associated with warfare: roars, thunderings, explosions, hissing roars, bangs, and booms.[11] A year after he wrote his book, World War I commenced with its all-too-real explosions, bangs, and booms.

While Russolo most likely did not directly influence rock musicians, they were on the exact same wavelength. Brain Eno sounds like a card-carrying member of the Futurists when he writes, "One history of music would chart the evolution and triumph of noise over purity in music. . . . Rock music is built on distortion: on the idea that things are enriched, not degraded, by noise."[12] Guitarists from the early 1940s to the present day have been caught up in the pleasures and possibilities of noise. Jazz guitarist Charlie Christian turned up the gain on his amplifier to slightly distort the tone of his Gibson ES-150, hollow-body electric guitar.[13] In this period Les Paul perfected the solid-body electric guitar, a landmark in instrument technology. Les Paul's desire was to produce a pure tone free from any of the extraneous noise that plagued hollow-body guitars with electric pickups.[14] Ironically, his innovations opened the door to the expressive possibilities of distortion and feedback. In 1951 Jackie Brenston and His Delta Cats released "Rocket 88," written by Ike Turner.[15] It is famous for being among the first records with a distorted guitar sound, caused by a mishap with an amplifier. Guitarist Willie Kizart, the band, and producer Sam Phillips of Sun Studio, where the song was recorded, loved the distorted sound. The song was a hit on the R&B charts and has gone down in history as one of the first rock records, largely because of its distorted guitar. "Rumble" by Link Wray, recorded in 1954, also highlights the ability of the electric guitar to produce "noise-sounds."

While guitarists such as Charlie Christian, Les Paul, and Willie Kizart incorporated their new sounds into existing styles—jazz, swing, and rhythm and blues—blues guitarists, such as Muddy Waters, Elmore James, and Buddy Guy took distortion further, laying the sonic foundation for rock and roll. These innovations made their way across the Atlantic and then exploded among a young generation of guitarists in England. Dave Davies of the Kinks, wanting a grittier sound from his guitar, slashed the cone of his amplifier to get the heavy distortion on "You Really Got Me," recorded July 1964.[16] The Beatles were the first to intentionally include feedback on a recording. When Paul McCartney played a low A on his Hofner bass, John Lennon's electrified acoustic guitar produced feedback.[17] George Martin had captured this on tape, so they tacked it onto the beginning of "I Feel Fine," recorded October 1964. Along with distortion and feedback, the sheer decibel level at which guitarists of the mid- to late 1960s played shocked audiences. Eric Clapton, Pete Townshend, and others used Marshall amplifiers primarily because they were the loudest available at the time. Jimi Hendrix would develop and amalgamate all of these sounds and techniques—and invent many of his own—to produce a spacious tonal palette, essentially turning his electric guitar into a synthesizer.

JIMI HENDRIX

The connections between Hendrix, his music, and the Vietnam War (hence the Cold War) are filled with ambiguities, and these ambiguities find their nexus in his rendition of "The Star-Spangled Banner." Although he played his most well-known rendition of the national anthem at Woodstock on August 18, 1969, he performed it at least sixty-one times in concerts between August 1968 and August 1970.[18] His rendition encapsulates the Vietnam War like no other piece of music from the period. Hendrix has been viewed for decades as a major figure in the counterculture's protest against the war, yet he served in the military as a paratrooper. He enlisted in the army in May 1961 in order to avoid a prison sentence for two charges of joyriding in stolen cars.[19] After basic training he was assigned to the most famous paratrooper division, the 101st Airborne, which during World War II fought in the D-Day invasion, Operation Market Garden, and the Battle of the Bulge. He was thrilled to receive a "Screaming Eagles" patch on his shoulder and loved jumping out of planes. He disliked other aspects of military life however. He was incompetent with weapons and fell asleep while on command watch. Officers reprimanded him more than once for tardiness and for focusing on his guitar rather than his duties.[20] He was given an honorable discharge in June/July 1962 after serving a little over a year of a three-year enlistment. He admired the men he trained with and understood the importance of national defense, yet he found he was ill-equipped to be a soldier. Thus, because of the circumstances of his enlistment and poor performance, not to mention his race, he was both an insider and an outsider to the military.

Another ambiguity is Hendrix's relationship with the counterculture and his view of the Vietnam War. Few musicians are so closely aligned with Vietnam War protest music as Hendrix. Lauren Onkey writes, "The image of Hendrix playing the national anthem has become symbolic of the counterculture."[21] Yet, in some interviews he expressed strong prowar, right-wing opinions about the Vietnam War and the threat of communism. In a January 1967 interview with *Melody Maker*, he said, "After China takes over the whole world, then the whole world will know why America's trying so hard in Vietnam."[22] In late February he told the Dutch magazine *Kink*, "The Americans are fighting in Vietnam for a completely free world. As soon as they move out, they [the Vietnamese] will be at the mercy of the communists. For that matter the yellow danger [China] should not be underestimated. Of course, war is horrible, but at present it's still the only guarantee of peace."[23]

Despite this, Hendrix often aligned himself with the political views of the counterculture. Prior to Woodstock in August 1969, Hendrix provided politically oriented commentary before and during his renditions of "The Star-Spangled Banner." At his concert at the Los Angeles Forum on April 26, 1969, he introduced the anthem by saying, "Here's a song we were all brainwashed with," and punctuated some phrases of the anthem with sarcastic comments, such as "yeah right" and "bullshit."[24] He was aware the majority of the Woodstock audience would be counterculture hippies, the political stance of the event was antiwar, and his musical interpretation of the words of the anthem would create some controversy in the mainstream press.

Although Hendrix's performance at Woodstock is purely instrumental, the words themselves play a large factor since Hendrix interprets the various phrases in different ways. He performs the first two phrases ("O say can you see" and "whose broad stripes") with embellishments, such as trills and bends, but does not veer far from the melody. The next line in the song presents a new melody and the dramatic leap of a major tenth, from the E on the last syllable of "were so gallantly streaming" to the G-sharp at the onset of "and the rockets' red glare." Hendrix takes full advantage of this leap, the widest in John Stafford Smith's original melody, and gives this section a new intensity. After the line "and the rockets' red glare," he creates an extended barrage of noise—using varying combinations of distortion, feedback, string bends, vibrato bar, his Uni-Vibe phasing pedal, and his Vox wah pedal—to depict the cataclysm of war. After playing the line "the bombs bursting in air," Hendrix hammers on the tritone B-flat and E, suggesting the sound of an ambulance siren, or an air-raid siren. He then uses the vibrato bar to create the sounds of bombs descending and exploding—this technique came to be known as the "dive bomb"—mixed with upper register string bends that sounded very much like people screaming in pain. He stops the noises of war and calmly plays the melody of the line "gave proof through the night that our flag was still there." He then interjects, with little use of effects, a moving version of "Taps," the bugle call played in commemoration of fallen military servicemen or great statesmen. This straightforward rendition of "Taps," a paean for the dead, is the only section not drenched in heavy distortion or feedback. Hendrix plays the last lines of the anthem with some alterations to the melody and again employs feedback, wah pedal, and vibrato bar.[25]

Hendrix's rendition of the national anthem has elicited a wealth of commentary over the years. Since Hendrix himself gave no definite interpretation, pinning any specific meaning onto this piece is extremely difficult. It produces numerous ambiguous and contradictory meanings in listeners who are amazed by Hendrix's mastery of the instrument yet appalled at what the sounds described. On the one hand, it has widely been interpreted as a protest against the Vietnam War. Jason Zapator, who attended the Woodstock Festival recounts,

> Hendrix was using sound effects through the guitar to complement the lyrics. I mean, you definitely *heard* the bombs bursting in air, you definitely *heard* the rockets going off when he played. At the time, of course, if you were thinking of war, you were thinking of Vietnam, so Hendrix was calling up revolutionary feelings in us. His playing was reminding everyone that "the rockets' red glare" and "the bombs bursting in air" was really the napalming of the villages. Like this was the supreme irony that the lyrics and the song were supposed to be about the defense of freedom.[26]

However, seeing both sides of the political fence, Eric F. Clarke writes, "The performer is playing *with* the anthem rather than playing it. . . . Nationalism and its counterculture are simultaneously and antagonistically specified in the sounds of the performance."[27] Charles Cross plays down the piece's political significance in his Hendrix biography, *Room Full of Mirrors*, "For Jimi, it was a musical exercise, not a manifesto. If he had any intention of making a political statement with 'The Star-Spangled Banner,' he didn't speak of it to his bandmates, friends, or even later to reporters."[28] What did Hendrix himself say of his rendition? At a press conference two weeks after Woodstock, on September 3, 1969, he said, "Nowadays when we play it, we don't play it to take away all this greatness that America is supposed to have. We play it the way the air is in America today. The air is slightly static, isn't it."[29] Hendrix seems to be referring to the static or white noise from a badly tuned radio or the "snow" on an analog television set with a shoddy antenna. In other words, he is saying that the air is crackling with conflicting opinions about the war and Americans are having trouble tuning in to one specific frequency. As Eric F. Clarke noted above, Hendrix's intention seems to be to complicate the nationalistic pride inherent in the anthem with the noises of war (bombs descending and exploding) and its effects (civilians and soldiers dying). Thus, the Hendrix rendition expresses both patriotism and protest, reflecting the ambiguities of the war itself.

BLACK SABBATH

While Hendrix was most likely depicting napalm bombs dropped on Southeast Asian civilians in "The Star-Spangled Banner," rather than conjuring up total nuclear war, he showed the expressive possibilities the electric guitar had to aurally depict modern warfare. Black Sabbath, whom we turn to next, took Hendrix's innovations to the apocalyptic extreme. With their heavily distorted guitars, plodding tempos, tritone intervals, and doleful vocal delivery, no band could dish out doom—apocalyptic doom—like Black Sabbath. They are widely considered to be the band that laid the blueprint for the style we know today as heavy metal. The musicians grew up in the Aston area of Birmingham, England in the 1950s and 1960s, an environment with bombed-out buildings, hazy, polluted skies, and the noise of metal pounding against metal rumbling out of the factories and steel mills.

Bass guitarist Geezer Butler, born on July 17, 1949, wrote most of the lyrics for the band, including their atomic-themed songs. The images of wartime devastation he created in songs like "Electric Funeral" and "War Pigs" came right out of where he lived. During World War II, Birmingham sustained heavy aerial bombing by the German *Luftwaffe* since the city was a major war-manufacturing center. Ozzy Osbourne recounts in his autobiography, *I Am Ozzy*, "Aston had taken a pounding during the Blitz. On every other street corner when I was a kid there were 'bomb building sites'—houses that had been flattened by the Germans when they were trying to hit the Castle Bromwich Spitfire factory. For years I thought that's what playgrounds were called."[30]

The Birmingham Blitz, which lasted for almost three years from the summer of 1940 to the spring of 1943, killed over two thousand people, injured over six thousand more, and destroyed or damaged several thousand houses and buildings. In his autobiography, *Iron Man*, guitarist Tony Iommi describes the view from the shop his parents owned when he was a young boy in the 1950s, "Our shop looked out on three or four 'terraced houses'—which means they were all stuck together—across the road, but next to those was a big space full of nothing but rubble. Whether it was a Second World War bomb that had caused that I don't know; it might just have been a house that had been knocked down, but we called it the 'bombed buildings.'"[31]

Growing up in this environment undoubtedly influenced Butler's lyrical depictions of scorched landscapes, Osbourne's doomsday vocal delivery, Bill Ward's thunderous drumming, and Iommi's down-tuned, heavily distorted guitar timbre.[32] Butler said, "War was the main theme [of our songs]. My brothers were all in the army and I thought I'd have to go and fight in Vietnam. Then there was the atomic bomb and the feeling that we were all going to get blown up."[33]

While nuclear war became a common topic in heavy metal lyrics in the 1980s, one of the few metal bands to address it often in the early 1970s was Black Sabbath. Three songs on their second album, *Paranoid* (1970), have Cold War themes. "War Pigs" begins by denouncing generals who treat soldiers and civilians like pawns on a chessboard and ends with the generals begging for mercy on judgment day. Andrew Cope writes of "War Pigs," "The sirens and long sustained power-chords . . . combined with the slow, spacious and measured back-beat of the percussion part create a feeling of eerie space, as if surveying a landscape of devastation."[34] The lyrics of "Hand of Doom" describe the descent of a Vietnam veteran into drug abuse: "First it was the bomb, Vietnam napalm / Disillusioning, you push the needle in." His drug use is a direct result of experiencing the horrors of war. Geezer Butler said,

> I always remember we did [gigs at] these two American Army bases. It was where all the guys, once they had finished the tour of Vietnam, instead of going straight back to America, they'd have [to go to] a halfway house. There was one in Germany and one in England. We got to talking to the soldiers and everything, and they were in a terrible state, a lot of them doing heroin. [There was] nothing on the news about this. There was no programs telling you that the U.S. troops in Vietnam, to get through that horrible war, were fixing up and all this kinda thing. It just stuck in me head and when we did "Hand of Doom," that's what I wrote it about.[35]

The third song with a Cold War theme is "Electric Funeral," which describes living through a nuclear attack in gruesome detail.

Butler was not the first lyricist to depict the gruesomeness of nuclear devastation. Tom Lehrer describes irradiated humans as "French fried potatoes" and "well-done steak" in his "We Will All Go Together When We Go" (1958), but the humor and absurdity of the song slightly tempered these descriptions. Nothing shields the impact of Butler's grotesque lyrics in "Electric Funeral," which has lines such as, "Eyes melt into blood." While Lehrer's wry and comic vocal delivery diffuses the horror in his lyrics, Osbourne's doom-laden vocals heighten the horror in Butler's depiction. Yet the lyrics do not primarily make the song as dark as it is; it's the music.

The plodding tempo and wah-drenched guitars of "Electric Funeral" portray the scorched landscape of earth despoiled by nuclear war. Tony Iommi masterfully creates guitar riffs that paint vivid pictures in the mind of the listener. When one hears the well-known riff from "Iron Man," one easily visualizes a monstrous, plodding, hulking figure made of metal. Similarly, when one hears the two primary riffs of "Electric Funeral," one easily conjures up a mental image of a scorched landscape, even without knowing what the lyrics are about. What is it about the song, besides the lyrics, that conveys this sense of dread?

First and foremost, it is the barbaric timbre of Iommi's guitar. The heavily distorted riffs, with their low tessitura and descending contours, give the impression of earth defiled beyond recognition. The wah effect on the guitar also gives the impression of human voices that have been ravaged and are groaning in pain, voices that are unable to articulate words. The "wah-wah" sound can be traced back to the 1920s in jazz bands, where trumpet and trombone players would create the sound by slightly covering and uncovering the bell of their instruments with a cone or plunger mute. This distinctive effect exemplified Duke Ellington's orchestra during his tenure in the late 1920s at the Cotton Club in Harlem. The invention of the wah pedal—the most popular being the Thomas Organ / Vox Cry Baby wah-wah, which manipulates the spectral glide of the guitar's tone — brought this sound into rock music. The spectral glide, according to musicologist Robert Erickson, describes the "modification of the vowel quality of a tone."[36] In the hands, and feet, of musicians like Jimi Hendrix in "Voodoo Child (Slight Return)" and Eric Clapton (with Cream) "White Room," the wah pedal gave the electric guitar a vocal quality not heard before. While most guitarists use the pedal to produce ecstatic utterances, Tony Iommi uses it in "Electric Funeral" to convey mutilated human voices, voices unable to express in words the horrors they are experiencing. In this interpretation, the wah pedal performs the same function as the extended bowing techniques and microtonal tone clusters in Krzysztof Penderecki's *Threnody to the Victims of Hiroshima* (1960). The groaning in "Electric Funeral" is akin to the screaming in Penderecki's *Threnody.*

The second factor conveying nuclear dread in the music is its melody, especially its descent marked by a tritone. The second riff in "Electric Funeral," which Ozzy's vocal line mirrors, seems to be an extension of the riff from "Black Sabbath," the first song on their first album, which was also called *Black Sabbath* (1970). The "Black Sabbath" riff with its octave leap from G1 to G2 and lingering trill on C-sharp, creating a tritone, became an essential building block in the harmonic vocabulary not only of Black Sabbath but of heavy metal music in general. This interval has been referred to as *diabolus in musica* ("the devil in music") since it is the most dissonant interval. This quality has made it resonate with heavy metal musicians from Black Sabbath to the present day.[37] In a documentary on the album *Paranoid,* Geezer Butler recounts how the English composer Gustav Holst and his orchestral suite *The Planets* (1914–1916) inspired the band's interest in the tritone, "The first song we wrote was actually 'Wicked World' and then the second song was 'Black Sabbath.' . . . I was a medium-sized fan of Holst's *The Planets* suite, particularly 'Mars.' One of the days we were rehearsing, I was going [plays G, D, C-sharp] trying to play 'Mars' and then the next day Tony . . . went [plays G, G, C-sharp] and that's how 'Black Sabbath' came about."[38]

While Butler says the riff of "Black Sabbath" grew from the opening theme in Holst's "Mars," the second riff in "Electric Funeral" is even closer. This riff, just like the Holst theme, features a rising fifth followed by a half-step descent [E, B, B-flat] creating a tritone. The connection becomes tighter when one realizes Holst was not simply depicting the planet Mars but the Roman god the planet is named after, the "bringer of war." Butler links the concept of war with the tritone interval as Holst did before him.

The third musical factor conveying dread in the song is the vocal line, which exactly follows the second riff. In most rock music, the vocal line provides some degree of contrast from the accompaniment. That is not the case here. In mirroring the guitar riff, the vocal line articulates the suffering the electric guitar, representing mutilated voices, cannot. The repetitiveness of the vocal line and riff is also a factor. The first riff is repeated four times each time it appears, and the second riff, which accompanies the vocals, is repeated eight times. Their stark and unvarying nature portrays a stark and unvarying landscape of ash and dust. The fixation of the vocal line, the electric guitar, and bass guitar on a single melody creates an ominous feeling of entrapment. The only section of the song that provides any musical variety is the bridge, yet this section only intensifies the feeling of dread because of its faster tempo and Ozzy's frenzied vocals. Here is a dark song indeed, possibly the darkest song even written about nuclear war. If the band intended to torment listeners with visions of nuclear catastrophe, they surely succeeded. Although the remainder of Black Sabbath's albums would have few Cold War songs, Ozzy Osbourne would address the subject in several songs during his solo career beginning in 1980.

OZZY OSBOURNE

In September 1980, Ozzy released his first solo album, *Blizzard of Ozz*. The single, "Crazy Train," helped make the album a hit and has come to symbolize Osbourne's entire solo career. While Randy Rhoads wrote the guitar riff and Ozzy sketched out the melodies, bass player Bob Daisley maintains that he wrote the bulk of the song, including the lyrics.[39] The song is a plea for peace in the midst of a world gone mad. The third verse of the song refers to the 1980s generation as "heirs of the Cold War." Daisley says of growing up in the 1950s, "As a child, I remember the feeling of fear. I knew Ozzy would like that [concept] because he felt like that, too, having been through it himself. He was kind of frightened about the threat of World War III and how we, as young people, had inherited these troubles, influenced by the threat of nuclear holocaust throughout our lives."[40] The lyrics to "Crazy Train" were used to embody the general attitude of teenagers about nuclear war at an academic conference in British Columbia in 1984 called "Nuclear War: The Search for Solutions." In her paper titled "Living in the Shadow: The Effects of Continual Fear," Joanna Santa Barbara states that "teenagers feel rather powerless to change the worrying state of the world. Around two-thirds of Southern Ontario teenagers feel there is nothing they or their parents can do to prevent nuclear war."[41] American and British teenagers at the time felt the same as their Canadian peers, that the world was "going off the rails on a crazy train."

Ozzy continued to address nuclear war on his fourth solo album, *The Ultimate Sin* (1986). The cover shows a woman and a demon (with Ozzy's face) gazing at the viewer while a nuclear explosion in the distance billows into a mushroom cloud. The landscape portrayed on the cover appears to be hell come to earth in the form of nuclear war. Although the lyrics to the title track are vague, Osbourne told Mary Turner on her "Off the Record" radio program, "To me the ultimate sin is nuclear weapons. This is the ultimate sin. I don't know about Ozzy Osbourne being crazy. Don't you think these lunatics are crazier, building these bombs to blow us all [up]?"[42] Two songs on the album specifically address nuclear war, "Thank God for the Bomb" and "Killer of Giants." Bob Daisley wrote the lyrics of both.[43] The two songs taken together crystalize the opposing viewpoints on the nuclear-arms race in the 1980s. While most popular songs present only the left-wing perspective on political issues, these two songs considered together provide a rare example of both right-wing and left-wing viewpoints being equally voiced. Let the debate begin.

The first song, "Thank God for the Bomb," takes the right-wing stance and agrees with Ronald Reagan's "Peace through Strength" doctrine, which says nuclear war can be prevented if America has an equal or greater stockpile of nuclear weapons than the Soviets. Proponents of this theory, known as deterrence theory, see nuclear weapons as the greatest instrument of peace in the modern era. They reason that although World War II escalated to the use of nuclear weapons, all subsequent wars have not. The Korean War and the Vietnam War, bloody as they were, were mitigated precisely because of the nuclear threat. As the lyrics say, "Make a threat of their annihilation and nobody wants to play." In the early 1980s, Reagan based his reasoning for the massive increase in military spending on his view that the nuclear balance had shifted greatly to the Soviet Unions' favor. In a nationally televised speech on November 22, 1982, Reagan stated, "Today, in virtually every measure of military power, the Soviet Union enjoys a decided advantage. . . . If my defense proposals are passed, it will still take five years before we come close to the Soviet level. Yet the modernization of our strategic and conventional forces will assure that deterrence works and peace prevails."[44]

Describing this strategy in his autobiography, Reagan said, "I wanted to go to the negotiating table and end the madness of the MAD [mutual assured destruction] policy, but to do that, I knew America first had to upgrade its military capabilities so that we would be able to negotiate with the Soviets from a position of *strength*, not weakness."[45] The lyrics to "Thank God for the Bomb" conclude that since humankind is inherently aggressive, all we can hope for is balanced nuclear arsenals. Fifteen years earlier, in a song with a similar title, "Thank Christ for the Bomb," the British rock band the Groundhogs expressed the same sentiment. The song ends with the line "for peace we can thank the bomb."

The other Cold War song on *The Ultimate Sin*, "Killer of Giants," takes the left-wing position. It begins with the elephant in the room: if no one wants nuclear war, why do we have so many nuclear weapons? How can more nuclear weapons (referred to as "mountains of madness") actually make the world a safer place? It inveighs against the right-wing belief that increasing the stockpile of nuclear weapons can preserve peace and sums up the left-wing criticism of Reagan's "Peace through Strength" policy. In June 1982, Senator Edward Kennedy said, "The Reagan approach is nothing more nor less than voodoo arms control, which says that you must have more in order to have less." Kennedy compared Reagan to a "diet doctor advising you to eat more today so that you can take more off tomorrow."[46] Secretary of Defense Caspar Weinberger sought to alleviate concerns about a possible nuclear war by saying, "We are not going to launch a protracted nuclear war. We don't believe a nuclear war can be won."[47] This statement caused the opposite reaction. Reagan's policy of making more nuclear weapons and then supposedly decreasing them at the bargaining table with the Soviets was viewed as dubious by the general public, and virtually insane by left-wing, antinuke organizations. Sidney Lens, a major figure in the peace movement from the 1960s to the 1980s, wrote that Reagan and his administration "insist against all logic that they require more nuclear weapons so they can fight an *unwinnable* war."[48] The lyrics to "Killer of Giants" refer to Reagan and his nuclear policy advisors as "sleeping giants, winning wars within their dreams." In the end, Reagan got to have his cake and eat it too. In his first term, the United States became the dominant player in the arms race. In his second term, he met several times with Mikhail Gorbachev, and together they signed the 1987 Intermediate-Range Nuclear Forces Treaty, which reduced the number of nuclear weapons in the world and set a precedent for further nonproliferation treaties with Russia.

In the early 1980s, Osbourne cemented his reputation as a madman. Among his outrageous antics were biting the head off a live dove at a CBS Records executive meeting; biting the head off a dead bat that a fan threw on the stage during a concert, which he thought was a toy rubber bat; and publicly urinating on a monument in San Antonio, which unfortunately was the Alamo Cenotaph, while wearing his future wife Sharon's evening gown. While Ozzy surely wasn't any type of role model, he and several other metal musicians were castigated throughout the 1980s as great menaces to society.[49] He used his reputation as a madman to make a point about the arms race. In 1982, on the popular television program *Entertainment Tonight,* he questioned this backlash against himself by saying, "Who's got the right to say who's mad and who's not? What's more insane: building a bomb to blow us all to bits or me getting on the stage in my crazy way entertaining people? Who's the crazy one?"[50] His point was America regarded metal musicians as threatening when they should have been regarding Pentagon officials increasing the stockpile of nuclear weapons as much more threatening. Ozzy was saying that the heavy metal (uranium and plutonium) in nuclear weapons was a much greater menace to society than the heavy metal in concert halls and record stores.

Since Black Sabbath and Ozzy Osbourne created the blueprint for heavy metal and influenced many musicians after them, later bands emulated their interest in the Cold War. The rest of this chapter will explore Cold War songs by Rush, Iron Maiden, and Metallica. The important role the Scorpions played—their participation in the Moscow Music Peace Festival, their iconic song "Wind of Change," and their meeting with Mikhail Gorbachev—will be covered in chapter 10.

RUSH AND THE RUSSIANS

Few lyricists in the broad genre of popular music have addressed Cold War topics as often, or with such intelligence, as Neil Peart of the Canadian progressive hard rock band Rush. Peart referred to the Cold War as "the all-pervasive background to my childhood."[51] Peart was the band's drummer and lyricist beginning with their second album, *Fly by Night* (1975). He created a distinctive style of lyric writing marked by conciseness, precision, and depth of thought. His lyrics had numerous allusions to literary classics and philosophy. Early in his career, Peart was influenced by Russian American novelist and philosopher Ayn Rand.[52] The first song the band created after Peart joined the group (and the opener of *Fly by Night*) was "Anthem," titled after the 1938 Rand novella of the same name.[53] This anticommunist/proindividualist song can be seen as a seed that blossomed and branched out into other areas. Chris McDonald sees the twenty-minute song suite "2112" (1976) as having palpable Cold War overtones when he writes, "Just as *Anthem* reflects its 1930s red scare context, '2112' updates the anxiety about communism for the late Cold War period by merging political collectivism with an ominous, threatening technology."[54] This futuristic, dystopian story is about an individual whose musical originality gets stamped out by an arrogant assembly of priests, the overseers of a collectivist state called the Solar Federation. While much has been written on the individualist v. collectivist ideas in Peart's lyrics from the 1970s ("Anthem," "2112," "The Trees"), less has been written on his 1980s and 1990s lyrics. As the Cold War intensified in the 1980s, it rose in importance in his lyrics. Over a dozen Rush songs from 1981 to 1991 address the subject. We will briefly survey the content of five of these songs in this section.

Three songs from *Grace Under Pressure* (1984) have explicit Cold War themes ("Distant Early Warning," "Red Lenses," and "Between the Wheels") and the album as a whole projects a feeling of impending catastrophe. In "Distant Early Warning," this feeling of impending doom is expressed using varied allusions to environmental pollution, the sinking of the Titanic, radar surveillance, and the search for absolute truth in a world of moral relativism. The title itself conveys imminent danger since it refers to the Distant Early Warning Line (or DEW Line), a series of radar installations that projected a continuous three-thousand-mile radar across the northern Canadian artic regions, including Alaska and Baffin Island. Constructed between 1954 and 1957 by scientists and engineers from both Canada and the United States, the DEW Line's purpose was to provide ample time for evacuation of target cities if approaching Soviet bombers were detected. It failed to live up to expectations. As Tarah Brookfield writes, "It was believed that, once complete, the DEW Line would provide Canadians with a three-hour warning before planes leaving the Soviet Union entered Canadian airspace. Yet evacuation drills . . . proved that three hours was too short to evacuate the entirety of most target cities."[55]

In addition, the DEW Line could not detect ICBMs or submarine-launched missiles, which the Soviets had armed themselves with by the early 1960s. Thus, Peart's allusion to the sinking of the Titanic in the chorus ("I see the tip of the iceberg") is quite perceptive. Just as Frederick Fleet and Reginald Lee in the crow's nest of the Titanic did not have enough time to warn the captain to steer clear of the iceberg, the DEW Line in the "crow's nest" of Canada would not provide enough time for North Americans to take evasive action in the event of a nuclear attack. The music video for the song features a young boy taking a joy ride on a ballistic missile that is reminiscent, as Durrell Bowman points out, of Major Kong's bomb ride in Stanley Kubrick's *Dr. Strangelove or: How I Learned to Stop Worrying and Love the Bomb* (1964).[56] Both the music video and the film highlight the fallibility of humans as they wrangle with military technology, both offensive and defensive, that is beyond their control.

"Red Lenses" is an amalgamation of human responses to, and interpretations of, the color red. Guitarist Alex Lifeson's shimmering C-sharp minor seventh chords provide an aural representation, while Peart's lyrics relate the color to a headache, a heartbeat, a sunrise, war, bright clothes, the planet Mars, the film *The Red Shoes*, acid rain, rising temperatures, and rising tempers. Peart doesn't miss the opportunity to jab at the Soviets either. He first refers to them as "the blues" and then describes them as monsters under the bed with the line "the reds, under your bed." Although the music has a serious tone, the lyrics have some humorous moments that provide a slight respite from the dark, brooding atmosphere of the album. But it doesn't last long. The next song, "Between the Wheels," which ends the album, is one of Rush's darkest songs. Neil A. Florek describes it as expressing "the nebulous alienation and malaise of a mechanical, post-industrial culture."[57] Few popular or rock songs encapsulate the feeling of nuclear anxiety in the 1980s like this one. The song has a rudimentary musical foundation, considering the complex arrangements and virtuosity for which the band is usually known. Rush songs from the 1980s commonly featured Geddy Lee playing intricate bass lines, which often constituted the main riffs of the song; guitarist Alex Lifeson overlaying ringing, sustained seventh chords; and Peart playing complex groove patterns on his drum kit, usually incorporating his battery of acoustic and electronic percussion instruments. In this song, especially the verses, the music is reduced to just the repetition of two chords (a D minor seventh chord with an added sixth on top and an A minor chord over a D pedal point) played on the offbeat. Although the song contains more up-tempo sections and an intense guitar solo by Lifeson, the funereal mood of the two chords, played by Lee on a Roland Jupiter-8 synthesizer, defines the song. The slow and steady tempo portrays an inexorable march toward destruction. The chorus ends with a plea: humanity cannot afford "another war, another wasteland, and another lost generation." Geddy Lee said that the music inspired the lyrics to this song. Peart more often wrote the lyrics first, and then Lee and Lifeson created music to fit them. Lee says, "In that case, the chords that I stumbled onto, and the jamming that followed, were so emotive that they inspired Neil to write the words."[58] In his essay "Pressure Release" in the *Grace under Pressure* tour book, Peart recounts his impression of the year 1983: "Yes, it was a year of crisis and tragedy—both globally and on the home front. . . . This was the time of the Korean 747 murders, the on-going cruise missile controversies, acid rain (one of my pet protests) was large in the Canadian news, wars raged everywhere . . . Songs like 'Distant Early Warning,' 'Red Lenses,' and 'Between the Wheels' were definitely interwoven with these thoughts and feelings."[59]

While "Between the Wheels" speaks of nuclear anxiety in broad terms, "Manhattan Project" from *Power Windows* (1985) focuses on the conception and consequences of the first atomic bomb dropped on Hiroshima forty years earlier on August 6, 1945. Before writing the song, Peart read a "pile of books" to get the historical facts straight and observed that "it wasn't easy to 'sell' the notion of a historical rock song, even to my bandmates."[60] Each stanza in the verses begins with the word *imagine* and centers on a specific aspect of the event. Of this structure for the song, Peart said, "We were trying to find a way to translate the dry historical facts to a lyrical format, and Geddy suggested we begin with the line 'Imagine a time . . .' That was a line he provided for me, and it really made it come alive. Then I began each of the three verses in that style, with 'Imagine a time . . . ,' 'Imagine a place . . . ,' 'Imagine a man. . . . .' It was exactly the piece I needed, it was a useful construct."[61]

The first stanza of verse one begins with "imagine a time," setting the scene during World War II when the United States, Germany, and Russia were vying to be the first country to develop an atomic bomb. The second stanza of verse one begins with "imagine a man," drawing a brief sketch of the physicists involved in the design and construction of the bomb. Since these first two stanzas do not mention the Manhattan Project, they convey to the listener that America was not the only country working on an atomic bomb. In the second verse ("imagine a place"), the song becomes more specifically about the Manhattan Project since it mentions a desert setting.[62] This setting refers either to Los Alamos, New Mexico, where the bomb was designed and constructed, or the Trinity site near Alamogordo, New Mexico, where the bomb was tested. The third verse begins again with "imagine a man," describing Paul Tibbets, the pilot of the B-29 bomber *Enola Gay*, which dropped the bomb on Hiroshima.

The sketchy details and use of the word *imagine* give the verses a mythical, almost fictitious atmosphere and serve the same function that "once upon a time" does in fairy tales. Yet the chorus presents the event as undeniably real and historical and considers the unforeseeable consequences such a weapon brings to humanity. Peart begins the chorus by referring to the Hiroshima bombing as the "big bang," linking it to the theory of the origin of the universe and intimating that the bomb has brought about some type of new beginning. Peart works a double meaning into the next line of the chorus, "Shot down the rising sun." It could refer to the intense brightness of the blast, which survivors said was much brighter than the sun, which was rising when the bomb went off at 8:15 a.m. Hiroshima time. At the Trinity test, J. Robert Oppenheimer supposedly adapted a verse from the *Bhagavad Gita* to describe the blast as "brighter than a thousand suns."[63] Secondly, the line could refer to the shooting down (or defeat) of Japan itself since the country is often called the "land of the rising sun" by those in the western hemisphere.

The final Rush song we will explore is "Heresy" from *Roll the Bones* (1991), written after the fall of the Berlin Wall on November 9, 1989. The first verse of the song contains Peart's reflections on life in Eastern Europe as it began to shed its communist past and reshape itself into a capitalist society. He describes the economic and societal transformation in this succinct phrase: "the counter-revolution at the counter of a store." In the days after the fall of the Berlin Wall, American news reporters honed in on the communist-to-capitalist shift by writing articles about East Berliners on shopping sprees in the fashionable shops of West Berlin. Two days after the East/West border opened, an article appeared in the *New York Times* with the headline, "A Day of Celebrations and a Bit of Shopping."[64] When Peart was traveling with Rush through Eastern Europe for the R30 tour in 2004, fifteen years after the fall of the Berlin Wall, he was disappointed to see touristy trinkets glutting not only the stores in the cities but in small, quaint villages. In his travelogue of that concert tour, *Roadshow* (2006), he describes a certain village in the Czech Republic near the German border as a "welter of desperate capitalism."[65] He questions the benefits of trading communism for capitalism. He describes capitalism with the same phrase he uses to describe communism, a "dull grey world." "Heresy" is as much a critique of vacuous Western consumerism as it is a lament for the years lost by Eastern Europeans under the oppression of communism.

In the second verse, Peart, who was born in 1952, reflects on growing up during the Atomic Age. The lyrics decry all the money spent on nuclear weapons and fallout shelters and all the fear and suffering it caused. In *Roadshow*, he describes the impact of the Cold War on his childhood in St. Catharines, Ontario: "The song expressed my angry disbelief over the effect on my own life: ten years old and hearing about atomic bombs that the Russians might drop on nearby Niagara Falls."[66] Canadians feared the Soviets would strike the falls since it provided power to the then-largest hydroelectric power plant in the Western world, which in turn provided electricity to a large portion of the eastern United States and Canada. In another of his books, *Traveling Music*, Peart writes again of being ten years old in 1962 during the Cuban Missile Crisis, "I watched my father making preparations that now seem so touchingly futile: filling a corner of the basement in our split-level house with sleeping bags, canned foods, water, flashlights, batteries, and radio, as he tried to make preparations for his family to survive a nuclear bomb exploding 30 miles away."[67]

It is no wonder that the Cold War looms so large in Peart's lyrics; he was confronted with its perils at a young, impressionable age. The lyrics are below.

Lyrics to "Heresy" by Rush (1991)

Verse 1: All around that dull grey world
From Moscow to Berlin
People storm the barricades
Walls go tumbling in
The counter-revolution
People smiling through their tears
Who can give them back their lives
And all those wasted years?

All those precious wasted years—
Who will pay?

All around that dull grey world
Of ideology
People storm the marketplace
And buy up fantasy
The counter-revolution
At the counter of a store
People buy the things they want
And borrow for a little more
All those wasted years
All those precious wasted years
Who will pay?

Chorus 1: Do we have to be forgiving at last?
What else can we do?
Do we have to say goodbye to the past?
Yes, I guess we do

Verse 2: All around this great big world
All the crap we had to take
Bombs and basement fallout shelters
All our lives at stake
The bloody revolution
All the warheads in its wake
All the fear and suffering—
All a big mistake
All those wasted years
All those precious wasted years
Who will pay?

Chorus 2: Do we have to be forgiving at last?
What else can we do?
Do we have to say goodbye to the past?
Yes, I guess we do

Fadeout: All those precious wasted years

Who will pay?

HERESY
Words by NEIL PEART
Music by GEDDY LEE and ALEX LIFESON

IRON MAIDEN

Like Neil Peart, the members of the British heavy metal band Iron Maiden are history buffs. They've written songs about humans' first attempts at controlling fire in the Paleolithic era ("Quest for Fire"), the ancient Egyptians ("Powerslave"), the ancient Greeks ("Alexander the Great"), the Vikings ("Invaders"), the Crimean War ("The Trooper"), both World Wars (several songs), and of course, the Cold War. Written by lead singer Bruce Dickinson and guitarist Adrian Smith, "2 Minutes to Midnight" (1984) uses grotesque imagery to present a blistering critique of the Cold War. The lyrics place an emphasis on the toll war takes on civilians. The last verse makes the point that the destitute ("starving millions") suffer not only from the threat of nuclear war but from the scarcity of economic resources offered to them since so much money is being spent on manufacturing nuclear weapons. The lyrics also focus on children, placing the horror of nuclear war in perspective by highlighting its possible effects on those who are the most vulnerable. The last phrase of the chorus "to kill the unborn in the womb" is puzzling. It seems to compare a nuclear war to an abortion, intimating a nuclear apocalypse prematurely terminates the human race. It could also mean no one is safe in a nuclear war, not even a baby in the womb, a universal symbol of security and protection. Nuclear conflict moves the theater of warfare well beyond the armed forces; it affects civilian life worldwide—even in the womb. This theme of children suffering and dying was also present in other hard rock / heavy metal songs from the period, such as in Gillan's "Mutually Assured Destruction (M.A.D.)" (1981) and Gary Moore's "Hiroshima" (1984). Punk rock bands addressed this theme in more depth and will be covered in the next chapter.

The title of "2 Minutes to Midnight" refers to the Doomsday Clock, a symbolic and theoretical depiction of how close the world is to a nuclear conflict or environmental catastrophe. "The hands that threaten doom," a line in the chorus, are the hands on the clock inching toward midnight, a symbol of the end of the world. The closer the minute hand is to midnight, the greater the threat. The Doomsday Clock was the brainchild of the board of directors of the *Bulletin of the Atomic Scientists*, a group of Manhattan Project physicists who formed after the atomic bombings of Hiroshima and Nagasaki. The clock face, and its current "time," is featured on each cover of the *Bulletin*, a scientific magazine that "informs the public about threats to the survival and development of humanity from nuclear weapons, climate change, and emerging technologies in the life sciences."[68] A brief review of the clock's history gives a summation of the nuclear-arms race. When the clock was created in 1947, it was set at seven minutes to midnight. In 1953 it was pushed forward to two minutes to midnight. This was due to the first hydrogen bomb tests performed by the United States (Ivy Mike in November 1952) and the Soviet Union (Joe 4 in August 1953).[69] Tensions eased slightly in the late fifties with the IGY (International Geophysical Year) and Nikita Khrushchev's visit to the United States but gradually intensified in the early 1960s. Although the Cuban Missile Crisis was the closest the world came to a nuclear conflict during the Cold War, it happened so quickly the clock could not account for it. The crisis planted a seed of caution and resulted in the Partial Nuclear Test Ban Treaty in 1963, which permitted only underground bomb tests. This treaty and other factors turned the clock back to twelve minutes. Several events in the mid- to late 1960s, including China joining the nuclear club and the intensification of the Vietnam War, pushed the clock forward to seven minutes. Nuclear anxiety eased again with the détente period in the 1970s, where it was set back again to twelve minutes. The tension reached a new peak in the early 1980s when the Soviet Union invaded Afghanistan and Ronald Reagan advocated for a massive nuclear-arms buildup. This prompted the Soviets to increase their nuclear weapons budget, and the arms race began again in full swing. In 1981, the clock was pushed to four minutes. By 1984, the year of the Iron Maiden song, the clock was at three minutes to midnight. During this period, the number of nuclear weapons in the world had reached seventy-thousand. As a result of Reagan and Gorbachev's arms-reduction talks, the fall of the Berlin Wall, and the end of the Cold War, the minute hand was set back in 1991 to a comfortable seventeen. Since then, the minute hand has been slowly creeping ever closer to midnight. In January 2018, it was set again at an unnerving two minutes to midnight, the title of the song. In January 2020, due to climate change and the breakdown in nuclear-disarmament negotiations, especially between the United States, Russia, Iran, and North Korea, the clock breached the two-minute barrier and was set at 100 seconds. It is unlikely that the clock will be set back any time soon.

The cover sleeve of the "2 Minutes to Midnight" single is as meaningful as the song. It shows Eddie, the band's mascot, sitting amid rubble with a machine gun in hand. A mushroom cloud billows in the background. A row of nine multinational flags is shown, bringing to mind the row of multinational flags at the UN headquarters in New York City. The flags represent countries engaged in war in the early 1980s or have a close connection with nuclear weapons. They are, from left to right, the Soviet Union, Afghanistan, Iraq, Iran, England, Argentina, the United States, Israel, and Cuba. All the flags are flying at half-mast, or half-staff, a universal symbol of mourning or distress. Eddie, created and painted by British graphic artist Derek Riggs, is pointing his finger directly at the viewer. This is reminiscent of British army-recruitment posters from World War I, which show

Lord Kitchener, England's secretary of state for war, pointing his finger at the viewer and saying, "YOUR COUNTRY NEEDS YOU." This in turn inspired James Montgomery Flagg's iconic depiction of the US army's mascot, "Uncle Sam," in recruiting posters from World War I and II ("I WANT YOU FOR U.S. ARMY"). Like Lord Kitchener and Uncle Sam recruiting young men for a stint in the army, Eddie is sardonically recruiting belligerent countries for a nuclear apocalypse.

METALLICA

Jimi Hendrix used his vibrato bar to emulate bombs descending and exploding. Tony Iommi of Black Sabbath used his wah pedal to portray the scorched landscape of a postnuclear earth. Metallica used their fast and ferocious riffs to depict the tumult of nuclear war. In "Fight Fire with Fire," the first song on Metallica's second album, *Ride the Lightning* (1984), the electric guitar is used as much as the lyrics to paint an aural picture of nuclear warfare. But the song begins not with a bomb exploding, which comes at the end, but with a calm and restrained instrumental prelude. It evokes a regal and stately atmosphere with its Renaissance/Baroque–sounding theme. The prelude's stepwise ascending motive, ornamentation, and pavane-like pulse give it a refined, courtly bearing. The instrumentation—James Hetfield playing a twelve-string acoustic guitar and Kirk Hammett playing electric guitar with no distortion—contributes to its archaic sound, redolent of lute music. In fact, Wolf Marshall describes the prelude as a "mutated Renaissance lute consort."[70] What this music has to do with the incendiary title of the song is soon evident when the stately music gives way to heavily distorted electric guitars playing a tumultuous barrage of notes. This musical contrast can be interpreted as the transition in warfare from conventional weapons to nuclear weapons. Conventional warfare, with its rules of engagement, chivalry, and ordered ranks of soldiers has been relegated to the past. It has been replaced by nuclear warfare, whose potential for chaos and destruction is beyond human comprehension. While conventional warfare in World War II (the bombing raids on Dresden, Coventry, and Tokyo) was just as deadly as Hiroshima and Nagasaki, nuclear warfare brought a qualitative new order of destructive capability. Glenn T. Pillsbury writes that the prelude "function[s] primarily as contrast . . . with the elements of orchestration and counterpoint standing out against the aggressive thrash metal."[71] The prelude gives the impression of control and restraint, with its measured tempo, its discernible melodies, and its harkening back to the past. The rest of song gives the impression of chaos, total destruction, and an unknowable future. In fact, the song could symbolize civilized culture (the prelude) being destroyed by nuclear war (the rest of the song).

The opening line of the lyrics is as arresting as the music. The song begins with "do unto others as they've done to you," which at first glance appears to be the Golden Rule. Yet it actually flips the Golden Rule ("treat people the same way you want them to treat you") on its head by using its construction to express retribution and revenge, the "eye for an eye, tooth for a tooth" mentality. The lyrics assume the worst about human nature concerning warfare; when one country launches a nuclear weapon, the targeted country will do the same with either equal or greater force, fighting fire with fire. The lyrics address the possible failure of the strategies that thus far have deterred nuclear war, such as "second strike capability," which deters a nuclear-armed state from attacking another nuclear-armed state for fear of reprisal, and "mutual assured destruction, or MAD," which deters a nuclear launch for fear it would escalate into a confrontation that would render earth uninhabitable. The ending of the song has Hetfield singing, "Fight fire with fire," in rapid succession, as if each repetition of the phrase is a warhead launched in retaliation to the previous one. The song ends, unsurprisingly yet convincingly, with the sound of a massive nuclear explosion after Kirk Hammett "dive-bombs" with his vibrato bar.

"Blackened," the first song on Metallica's fourth album, *. . . And Justice for All* (1988), takes the premise of "Fight Fire with Fire" to its logical conclusion: the destruction of earth. The nuclear confrontation unleashed in "Fight Fire with Fire" results in a blackened earth of dust and ash. The primary riff in "Blackened," with its 7/4 meter and frantic mishmash of octaves, minor seconds, and tritones, gives the impression of disorder, upheaval, and general mayhem. Unlike the obvious contrast between controlled music and chaotic music in "Fight Fire with Fire," "Blackened" has little musical contrast within, suggesting an unchanging, permanent state of devastation. Hetfield describes the permanence of a blackened earth in the lines "never a rebirth" and "never will it mend." While not as extreme as Iron Maiden's "2 Minutes to Midnight," the lyrics to "Blackened" use grotesque imagery to present an unflinching examination of a scorched earth.

CONCLUSION

Although heavy metal bands often expressed concerns about the dangers of technology, especially nuclear war, the power of technology still drew them in, be it electric guitars or hydrogen bombs. They rarely abandoned their guitars or amplifiers to take an antitechnology stance. While antinuclear country and folk singers from the 1950s and 1960s used acoustic instruments and emphasized lyrics over music, metal bands always put the music first. As Glenn T. Pillsbury writes, "Overwhelming whatever political viewpoints might surface within song lyrics was the importance of maintaining music as the primary purpose of metal."[72]

Thus, the "noise as music" explored in this chapter proved to be an apt medium to express conflicting emotions toward technology and its effects on humans.

Like the parents of teenagers in the 1980s, many people today wonder why heavy metal has to be so dark and gloomy. Why would so many metal musicians write such dreadful songs about human annihilation in a nuclear war? How has this music reached such a global audience when it is so disquieting? Perhaps the answer lies in why Halloween, horror films, and murder mysteries are as popular as ever. Joanne Cantor says, "One reason often advanced for the attraction of scary media is that people expose themselves to frightening entertainment to help them cope with their apprehensions and fears about real threats in their own lives."[73] Psychologists call this "exposure therapy," actively confronting the things you fear in order to manage their effects on you. The sound of Tony Iommi's heavily distorted, down-tuned, and wah-drenched guitar in "Electric Funeral" is literally a "toxic wasteland in your ear canal," reflecting the line in Styx's 1983 song "Heavy Metal Poisoning." Heavy metal songs about nuclear annihilation sound poisonous and toxic in order to make the listener comprehend and confront what they describe. Metal bands embodied nuclear terror in several ways. First, bands adopted nuclear themes in their names, such as Megadeth, Nuclear Assault, and Atomkraft. Second, their music created aural depictions of falling bombs, explosions, a devastated earth, and human cries of agony. Third, their lyrics and album covers used grotesque imagery to portray nuclear holocaust. Lastly, onstage pyrotechnics, with their ear-splitting explosions and fireballs, brought miniaturized versions of nuclear explosions into concert halls.

In his autobiography, Ozzy Osbourne recounts that Black Sabbath rehearsed near a cinema, and they would see people lined up around the corner when it showed a horror film. Osbourne writes that Tony Iommi told him, "Isn't it strange how people will pay money to frighten themselves? Maybe we should stop doing blues and write *scary* music instead."[74] Heavy metal bands have been frightening themselves, their fans, and the general public with their tales of nuclear doom ever since.

NOTES

1. Robert Walser, *Running with the Devil: Power, Gender, and Madness in Heavy Metal Music* (Hanover, NH: Wesleyan University Press, 1993), 41–51.

2. Electric guitars have even been used visually to depict nuclear war. Gibson guitars created an advertising poster in the 1980s or 1990s that showed side-by-side the fiery-red mushroom cloud from a nuclear bomb explosion and a Gibson Les Paul with a sunburst finish. The caption read "Welcome to ground zero."

3. Seth Rogovoy, *Bob Dylan: Prophet, Mystic, Poet* (New York: Scribner, 2009), 122–123.

4. Russell Reising, "Covering and Un(covering) the Truth with 'All Along the Watchtower': From Dylan to Hendrix and Beyond," in *Play It Again: Cover Songs in Popular Music*, ed. George Plasketes (Farnham: Ashgate, 2010), 161.

5. Tony Palmer, from the November 23, 1968, issue of *New Musical Express*, quoted in Steven Roby, *Black Gold: The Lost Archives of Jimi Hendrix* (New York: Billboard, 2002), 95–96.

6. Michael J. Kramer, "The Multitrack Model: Cultural History and the Interdisciplinary Study of Popular Music," in *Music and History: Bridging the Disciplines*, ed. Jeffrey H. Jackson and Stanley C. Pelkey (Jackson: University Press of Mississippi, 2005), 244.

7. Michael J. Kramer, *The Republic of Rock: Music and Citizenship in the Sixties Counterculture* (New York: Oxford University Press, 2013), 145.

8. Luigi Russolo, *The Art of Noises*, trans. Barclay Brown (New York: Pendragon, 1986), 25.

9. Ibid., 24.

10. Ibid., 26.

11. Ibid., 28.

12. Brian Eno, *A Year with Swollen Appendices* (London: Faber and Faber, 1996), 195.

13. Jay Hodgson, *Understanding Records: A Field Guide to Recording Practice* (New York: Continuum, 2010), 100.

14. Steve Waksman, *Instruments of Desire: The Electric Guitar and the Shaping of Musical Experience* (Cambridge, MA: Harvard University Press, 1999), 7–8, 45, 49–51.

15. The group was essentially Ike Turner's backing band, the Kings of Rhythm. They changed their name for this recording only.

16. Dave Davies, *Kink: An Autobiography* (New York: Hyperion, 1996), 1–3.

17. Geoff Emerick, interview by Andy Babiuk in his *Beatles Gear*, foreword by Mark Lewisohn, edited by Tony Bacon (San Francisco: Backbeat, 2001), 146. McCartney remembers the event differently, saying that the feedback occurred when Lennon simply leaned his guitar against his amp. Barry Miles, *Paul McCartney: Many Years from Now* (New York: Holt, 1997), 172.

18. Mark Clague, "'This Is America': Jimi Hendrix's Star Spangled Banner Journey as Psychedelic Citizenship," *Journal of the Society for American Music* 8, no. 4 (November 2014): 436, 471–475.

19. Charles R. Cross, *Room Full of Mirrors: A Biography of Jimi Hendrix* (New York: Hyperion, 2005), 80–84.

20. Steven Roby and Brad Schreiber, *Becoming Jimi Hendrix: From Southern Crossroads to Psychedelic London, the Untold Story of a Musical Genius* (Philadelphia: Da Capo, 2010), 18–19, 24–26.

21. Onkey, Laura. "Voodoo Child: Jimi Hendrix and the Politics of Race in the Sixties," in *Imagine Nation: The American Counterculture of the 1960s and '70s*, ed. Peter Braunstein and Michael William Doyle (New York: Routledge, 2002), 190.

22. Jimi Hendrix, from an interview in *Melody Maker*, January 28, 1967, Harry Shapiro and Caesar Glebbeek, *Jimi Hendrix: Electric Gypsy* (New York: St. Martin's, 1991), 387.

23. Jimi Hendrix, from an interview in *Kink*, February 25, 1967, Shapiro and Glebbeek, *Jimi Hendrix*, 387.

24. Waksman, *Instruments of Desire*, 171; Clague, "This Is America," 455–457.

25. Hendrix's performance of "The Star-Spangled Banner" at Woodstock is on *Woodstock: 3 Days of Peace and Music*, director's cut, two-disc 40th anniversary edition (Warner Bros. Pictures 2000007993-2000007994, 2009, two-DVD set) and *Jimi Hendrix. Live at Woodstock* (Experience Hendrix B0005283-09, 2005, two-DVD set). It is also available on YouTube here: https://www.youtube.com/watch?v=vgyGJl_xm6o.

26. Joan Morrison and Robert K. Morrison, *From Camelot to Kent State: The Sixties Experience in the Words of Those Who Lived It* (Oxford: Oxford University Press, 2001), 200.

27. Eric F. Clarke, *Ways of Listening: An Ecological Approach to the Perception of Musical Meaning* (Oxford: Oxford University Press, 2005), 54, 59.

28. Cross, *Room Full of Mirrors*, 271.

29. "Jimi Hendrix Press Conference," *Jimi Hendrix: Live at Woodstock* (Experience Hendrix B0005283-09, 2005, two-DVD set), 3:57–4:07.

30. Ozzy Osbourne with Chris Ayres, *I Am Ozzy* (New York: Grand Central, 2010), 5.

31. Tony Iommi with T. J. Lammers, *Iron Man: My Journey through Heaven and Hell with Black Sabbath* (Cambridge, MA: Da Capo, 2011), 10–11.

32. Andrew Cope explains the intricacies of Iommi's down tuning in *Black Sabbath and the Rise of Heavy Metal Music* (Burlington, VT: Ashgate, 2010), 31–32, 46–50.

33. Geezer Butler, "Black Sabbath: 'We Used to Have Cocaine Flown in by Private Plane,'" interview by Paul Lester, *Guardian*, June 6, 2013, http://www.guardian.co.uk/music/2013/jun/06/black-sabbath-cocaine-private-plane.

34. Cope, *Black Sabbath*, 29.

35. Geezer Butler, from an interview on *Black Sabbath: Paranoid* (Classic Albums, New York: Eagle Vision EV302959, 2010, DVD), 37:25–38:05.

36. Robert Erickson, *Sound Structure in Music* (Berkeley: University of California Press, 1975), 72.

37. Andrew Cope discusses the influence of the tritone in Black Sabbath and heavy metal in his *Black Sabbath and the Rise of Heavy Metal Music*, 51–57.

38. Butler, from an interview on *Black Sabbath: Paranoid*, 4:20–5:15.

39. For an account of the long battle Bob Daisley has had with the Osbournes over songwriting credits, see Daisley's book *For Facts Sake* (Moonee Ponds, Victoria, Australia: Thompson Music, 2013) and "Bob Daisley's History with the Osbournes" on his website, http://www.bobdaisley.com/interview/website.

40. Jackie Kajzer and Roger Lotring, *Full Metal Jackie Certified: The 50 Most Influential Heavy Metal Songs of the '80s and the True Stories behind their Lyrics* (Boston: Course Technology, 2010), 40.

41. Joanna Santa Barbara, "Living in the Shadow: The Effects of Continual Fear," in *Nuclear War: The Search for Solutions: Proceedings of a Conference Held at the Uni-*

versity of British Columbia, October 19–21, 1984, with special essays by Major-General Leonard V. Johnson, and Dr. Helen Caldicott, preface by the Hon. Walter L. Gordon, ed. Thomas L. Perry and Dianne DeMille (Vancouver, BC: Physicians for Social Responsibility, 1985), 96.

42. Ozzy Osbourne, "Off the Record with Mary Turner," Westwood One Radio, Part 4, 1985, 5:51–6:01.

43. Daisley says he was not given credit for the lyrics on the first five hundred thousand pressings of the album due to conflicts with Ozzy. For more information, see Daisley's book *For Facts Sake* and "Bob Daisley's History with the Osbournes," http://www.bobdaisley.com/interview/website.

44. Ronald Reagan, *Greatest Speeches of Ronald Reagan* (West Palm Beach, FL: NewsMax, 2002), 130, 132, http://www.youtube.com/watch?v=giLNQpwhWbU.

45. Ronald Reagan, *An American Life* (New York: Simon and Schuster, 1990), 13–14.

46. "Kennedy Denounces Reagan for 'Voodoo Arms Control,'" *New York Times,* June 22, 1982, http://www.nytimes.com/1982/06/22/world/kennedy-denouces-regan-for-voodoo-arms-control.html.

47. Quoted in Richard Halloran, "Weinberger Denies U.S. Plans for a 'Protracted' War," *New York Times,* June 21, 1982, http://www.nytimes.com/1982/06/21/world/weinberger-denies-us-plans-for-protracted-war.html.

48. Sidney Lens, "Revive the Ban-the-Bomb Movement," in *The Apocalyptic Premise: Nuclear Arms Debated: Thirty-One Essays by Statesmen, Scholars, Religious Leaders, and Journalists,* ed. Ernest W. Lefever and E. Stephen Hunt (Washington, DC: Ethics and Public Policy Center, 1982), 101.

49. In 1985, several heavy metal songs were included in the "Filthy Fifteen," a list of songs deemed offensive to adults and dangerous to children by the Parents Music Resource Center. Tipper Gore, the wife of Senator Al Gore (later vice president under Bill Clinton), headed the PMRC.

50. Ozzy Osbourne, "Ozzy Osbourne Interview 1982." Uploaded May 12, 2007, YouTube. https://www.youtube.com/watch?v=Vpvo-FppQ-8.

51. Neil Peart, "Shunpikers in the Shadowlands," from Neil Peart website, June 2013, http://www.neilpeart.net/index.php/space-for-news-items/june-2013-shunpikers-shadowlands1/.

52. For more on the connection between Peart and Rand, see Deena Weinstein and Michael A. Weinstein, "Neil Peart versus Ayn Rand" in *Rush and Philosophy: Heart and Mind United,* ed. Jim Berti and Durrell Bowman (Chicago: Open Court, 2011), 273–285.

53. Chris McDonald, *Rush, Rock Music and the Middle Class: Dreaming in Middletown* (Bloomington: Indiana University Press, 2009), 62.

54. McDonald, *Rush, Rock Music and the Middle Class,* 91.

55. Tarah Brookfield, *Cold War Comforts: Canadian Women, Child Safety, and Global Insecurity, 1945–1975* (Waterloo, Ontario: Wilfrid Laurier University Press, 2012), 52.

56. Durrell Bowman, "More Than They Bargained For," in *Rush and Philosophy: Heart and Mind United*, ed. Jim Berti and Durrell Bowman (Chicago: Open Court, 2011), 176.

57. Neil A. Florek, "Free Wills and Sweet Miracles," in *Rush and Philosophy: Heart and Mind United*, ed. Jim Berti and Durrell Bowman (Chicago: Open Court, 2011), 146.

58. Geddy Lee, "Geddy Lee of Rush," interview by Gary Armbruster, *Keyboard* 10, no. 9 (September 1984): 63.

59. Neil Peart, "Pressure Release," *Grace Under Pressure* tour book, 1984, 2.

60. Neil Peart, *Far and Away: A Prize Every Time* (Toronto: ECW, 2011), 182–183.

61. Neil Peart, quoted in Jeff Miers, "The Road Less Traveled: A Conversation with Neil Peart of Rush," *Metro Weekend*, October 17–23, 1996, http://www.2112.net/powerwindows/transcripts/19961017metroweekend.htm.

62. The project was called the Manhattan Project because plans for the atomic bomb were first conceived in a building at 270 Broadway in New York's Manhattan district.

63. Robert Jungk, *Brighter Than a Thousand Suns: A Personal History of the Atomic Scientists*, trans. James Cleugh (New York: Harcourt Brace, 1958), 201. "Brighter Than a Thousand Suns" is also the title of an Iron Maiden song from 2006 about the Hiroshima bombing.

64. Ferdinand Protzman, "A Day of Celebrations and a Bit of Shopping," *New York Times*, November 11, 1989, 6.

65. Neil Peart, *Roadshow: Landscape with Drums: A Concert Tour by Motorcycle* (Cambridge, MA: Rounder, 2006), 374.

66. Peart, *Roadshow*, 373.

67. Neil Peart, *Traveling Music: The Soundtrack to My Life and Times* (Toronto: ECW, 2004), 63.

68. Bulletin of the Atomic Scientist, "Purpose," https://thebulletin.org/purpose/.

69. "Joe 4" was the American nickname for the Soviet bomb.

70. Wolf Marshall, "Introduction," in *Metallica, Ride the Lightning* (Port Chester, NY: Cherry Lane Music, 1990), 3.

71. Glenn T. Pillsbury, *Damage Incorporated: Metallica and the Production of Musical Identity* (New York: Routledge, 2006), 38.

72. Pillsbury, *Damage Incorporated*, 84.

73. Joanne Cantor, "Fear Reactions and the Mass Media," in *The Routledge Handbook of Emotions and Mass Media*, ed. Katrin Döveling, Christian von Scheve, and Elly A. Konijn (New York: Routledge, 2011), 151.

74. Osbourne, *I Am Ozzy*, 82.

EIGHT

PUNK ROCK

Three Chords and the Apocalypse

OF ALL THE POPULAR MUSICIANS in the 1970s and 1980s, punks delivered their message most directly. They were in a hurry and had little time to waste. One can see this in the first issue of the fanzine *Sideburns* in January 1977, created by fans of the British punk band the Stranglers. The issue contains Tony Moon's now famous illustration, which neatly sums up the ethos of punk rock. It shows diagrams for three chords, A, E, and G, with the accompanying handwritten text: "This is a chord . . . this is another . . . this is a third . . . now form a band."[1] Punks did not detain their listeners for long. Their songs often lasted just a minute or two, disposing with introductions, guitar solos, fade-outs, or any extraneous exposition. They often wrote songs in a matter of minutes and recorded them in a few takes with no overdubs or studio gimmickry. Punks took great pains to make sure their recordings were as inexpensive as possible so anyone could afford to buy them. They relied on word of mouth, fanzines, T-shirts, posters, and constant gigging to generate publicity. Rather than hiring professional painters or graphic artists to create their album covers—as so many 1970s rock bands did—punks often found pre-existing images, warped them in some fashion, and combined them into ragged black-and-white collages. Lastly, they played at breakneck tempos, as if they were caught in an avalanche tumbling down a mountainside.

The punks who wrote songs specifically about nuclear war hurried even faster. They felt the world could end at any second. They had no time to waste by learning a fourth chord; three would do. Their guitars didn't need to be exactly in tune; distortion and feedback don't need to be. Punk singers didn't need to take voice lessons; shouting and screaming worked just fine. The tempos of their songs were so fast, it's as if they were using a rapidly ticking Geiger counter for a metronome. They felt the threat of the bomb looming over them, and they got busy.

This chapter begins with the Ramones and how World War II and the Cold War shaped their lives and their music. It then explains how and why the lyrics of punk songs about nuclear war were more explicit and disturbing than other styles—even more so than the heavy metal lyrics discussed in the previous chapter. The rest of the chapter explores Cold War songs by Crass, Discharge, and Scars. Major topics addressed in the songs are the legacy of Hiroshima and Nagasaki and the bombing of civilians. The conclusion questions the impact punk bands made on mainstream culture and why their message never reached the mass audiences other popular musicians did.

RAMONES: THE COLD WAR WITHIN A PUNK BAND

The Ramones were together from 1974 to 1996 and, like most bands with long careers, experienced some personnel changes. In their twenty-two years, they had two bass players, Dee Dee, who was a founding member and main songwriter, and C. J., who replaced Dee Dee in 1988. Their drummers were Tommy (founding member and songwriter), Marky (the drummer with the longest tenure), Richie (who could sing and play drums at the same time), and Elvis (Blondie's drummer, Clem Burke, who was "Ramoned" for two concerts). You would think the two permanent members, Joey and Johnny, who went to the same high school, Forest Hills High School in Queens, saw each other every day for over two decades, and played on every Ramones album and tour would develop a sense of camaraderie and friendship. They never did. One of the reasons was that they espoused extremely different political viewpoints.

Johnny (born John William Cummings in 1948) was a right-wing conservative of Irish descent. He was the son of a construction worker. Johnny greatly admired his father, who served in the military. Many people involved with the Ramones thought Johnny ran the band like a drill sergeant. He revered Ronald Reagan and George Bush and considered himself to be a conservative Republican from the time he was ten years old. "I was a Nixon man in 1960," he said in an interview from the documentary *End of the Century*.[2] He would have been twelve at the time of the 1960 election, in which John F. Kennedy defeated Nixon. Marky Ramone recounts a time, shortly after he joined the band in 1978, when he had to listen to Johnny rant that the media had framed Nixon during the Watergate scandal. Marky remembers, "It was surprising to see a rock musician, or any musician, for that matter, defend Richard Nixon."[3] In his autobiography, Johnny listed his top-ten favorite Republicans. Ronald Reagan and Richard Nixon were the top two. Charlton Heston, Arnold Schwarzenegger, Ted Nugent, and Rush Limbaugh also made the list.[4] When the Ramones were inducted into the Rock and Roll Hall of Fame in 2002, Johnny ended his speech by saying, "God bless President Bush and God bless America."[5] This was such an unconventional thing for a "punk" to express it was almost shocking: simple gratitude and pride for your president and your country. While punks shocked the world with their defiance, anarchy, and liberalism, Johnny shocked the punk world with his conservatism. He said, "When I was in the Ramones, I never wanted it to be about politics."[6] He also said, "Contemporary political issues were something that should be dealt with by hippies."[7] These are odd things for a punk rocker to say. Even among outsiders, Johnny was an outsider. Yet, he would say things just to get a reaction out of people, like this quip: "If I end up with no money, I'm gonna be a communist. If I end up rich, I'm gonna be a capitalist."[8]

Joey (born Jeffrey Ross Hyman in 1951) was a left-wing Jewish liberal. He was a hippie in his teens. Mickey Leigh, Joey's brother, described their teen years as "psychedelicized. . . . There was nothing stopping Jeff and me from happily succumbing to the ways of the 'counterculture.' . . . We were on our way to hippie freakdom."[9] Mickey told Legs McNeil, coauthor of the definitive oral history of punk, *Please Kill Me*, "My brother was a real hippie in those days. He used to walk around with no shoes on, and he went to San Francisco, and he hung out with real hippies. That's why John wasn't interested in knowing my brother at all. Joey was just a weirdo hippie. And John *hated* hippies."[10] In the 1980s, Joey emerged from being just a singer in a punk band to being a musician with a political stance. He participated in the 1985 song "Sun City," which openly criticized Reagan's soft position on apartheid in South Africa.[11] The song was written by "Little Steven" Van Zandt and performed by over forty popular music stars. Joey sings the line "constructive engagement is Ronald Reagan's plan."[12] Joey became even more politically active in the 1990s. He was instrumental in the Ramones's participation in the Rock the Vote campaign, an effort by MTV to get young voters registered.[13] Of the political differences between Johnny and Joey, bass player C. J. Ramone (Chris Ward) said, "It was so weird because Johnny is ultra-conservative and Joey is ultra-liberal."[14]

The tension between Joey and Johnny was a struggle, but other volatile political dynamics played within the band. Drummer Tommy (Erdélyi Tamás also known as Thomas Erdelyi) was born in Budapest, Hungary, in 1949. His parents were Holocaust survivors. He and his family were among the two hundred thousand Hungarians who fled the country when the Soviets sent tanks into Budapest to squelch the Hungarian Revolution of 1956, a democratic uprising.[15] Thus, his family suffered both Nazi and Soviet persecution in the span of a little over a decade. Tommy and his family arrived in New York City when he was seven. Bassist Dee Dee (born Douglas Colvin in 1951) grew up mostly in Berlin. He was the son of an American soldier, who fought in the Battle of the Bulge in World War II and in the Korean War, and a German mother, who survived the Allied saturation bombing of Berlin as a teenager near the end of World War II.[16] As a youngster Dee Dee made collecting Nazi paraphernalia scattered in the rubble of Berlin one of his hobbies.[17] He lived in the city before, during, and after the Wall was constructed.[18] He and his mother moved to New York City in 1956. The Nazi references in Dee Dee's lyrics, like in "Blitzkrieg Bop" and "Today Your Love, Tomorrow the World," never seemed to bother Joey and Tommy, of Jewish descent, since they were intended as dark humor. This meant Joey was a left-winger; Johnny was a right-winger; and Tommy and Dee Dee were somewhere in the middle. The families of the four original Ramones emerged from the chaos of World War II, and that legacy shaped the viewpoints of the band members as they lived through and wrote songs about the Cold War.

How did all these crazy political dynamics work themselves out in their music? As would be expected, they are all over the map. Some songs employ Nazi symbols, while others employ Jewish ones. Some songs express conservative opinions, while others express liberal ones. World War II and the Cold War are conflated into one continuous, overlapping, military maelstrom. Although most of their songs address themes such as mental disorders, drug use, relationship problems, and rebellious fun, several of their songs confront Cold War topics. "Havana Affair" (1976) is about a CIA spy in Cuba. Nicholas Rombes suggests the "Spy vs Spy" cartoon in *Mad* magazine, of which the Ramones were big fans, inspired the song.[19] It pokes fun at the CIA, implying the agency is so fearful of communist Cuba that it will make spies out of anyone, even banana pickers, and plant them in the most ludicrous of places, like a talent show. "Commando" (1977) is a prosoldier song about commandos doing their duty in Cold War hotspots like East Berlin and Hanoi, North Vietnam. They follow the orders of their superiors, fighting the good fight against communism and placing themselves in great danger to complete their missions. Yet these commandos are no ordinary commandos; they are Jewish commandos (eating "kosher salamis") stationed in communist East Berlin. Another soldier song is "Let's Go" (1980), which Johnny said is "about the Vietnam War. I enjoyed handling that subject in a heroic way, rather than a protest way."[20] "I'm Not Afraid of Life" and "Planet Earth 1988" from *Too Tough to Die* (1984) address the reality that, in the mid-1980s, the threat of nuclear war was a part of everyday life.

The Ramones most interesting political song is "My Brain Is Hanging Upside Down (Bonzo Goes to Bitburg)" about Ronald Reagan's May 1985 trip to Bitburg, Germany. Chancellor Helmut Kohl invited Reagan to visit West Germany to celebrate the fortieth anniversary of the end of World War II. Reagan wanted to oblige him, especially since West Germany was housing over one hundred American Pershing II nuclear missiles to keep the pressure on the Soviets.[21]

Reagan and Kohl were to meet at the German cemetery *Kolmeshöhe* in Bitburg, where World War I and World II soldiers were buried. Controversy arose when the media found out forty-nine members of the Third Reich's *Waffen-SS,* the combat branch of Hitler's *Schutzstaffel* (SS), were also buried there.[22] Many congressmen, both Republican and Democrat, felt this would be insensitive to Jews and Holocaust survivors and urged Reagan not to go. Before he visited the cemetery, Reagan calmed the controversy by visiting and giving a speech at the site of the Bergen-Belsen concentration camp. Yet some people still thought it was unwise. Joey said, "Reagan's thing was like forgive and forget. How can you forget six million people being gassed and roasted?"[23] The Ramone's song, written by Dee Dee, Joey, and Jean Beauvoir, includes the overblown and acerbic line "you're a politician, don't become one of Hitler's children." The Ramones released the song as a single in 1985 with the title "Bonzo Goes to Bitburg." The title of the song is a play on two comedy movies, *Bedtime for Bonzo* (1951), which starred Ronald Reagan, and its sequel *Bonzo Goes to College* (1952), in which Reagan did not appear. Bonzo is the name of the monkey in the movie. However, when the song was to be released on the album *Animal Boy* (1986), Johnny insisted the song be called "My Brain Is Hanging Upside Down," making the "Bonzo" phrase the subtitle.[24] He supposedly said, "You can't call my president a monkey!"[25] This song encapsulates the political paradoxes of the Ramones. It confronts Jewishness and Nazism. It mashes together World War II history with Cold War history. Even its title is a battle between Joey's anti-Reagan stance and Johnny's pro-Reagan stance.

Perhaps the best commentary the Ramones made about the Cold War is not in one of their songs but on one of their album covers, *Rocket to Russia* (1977). The back cover has an illustration of a punk riding a massive nuclear missile on its way to Russia. The origin of this illustration can be found on the back of their previous album *Leave Home* (1977), where one finds a parody of the Seal of the President of the United States by graphic designer Arturo Vega. This design became the Ramones's ubiquitous logo seen at concerts, on album covers, on t-shirts, and on tour programs. Instead of the words "Seal of the President of the United States" in a circle around the eagle, the logo has the names of the band members: "Johnny * Joey * Dee Dee * Tommy." In one talon, the eagle grasps an apple tree branch instead of the olive branch of peace on the official seal "since the Ramones were American as apple pie," as Vega said.[26] The arrows in the other talon of the eagle have been replaced with a baseball bat since, Vega says, "Johnny was such a baseball fanatic."[27] Yet the arrows are still present above the eagle. So instead of one symbol each of power and peace, the arrows and the olive branch, there are two symbols of power, the arrows and the baseball bat, to one of, well, apples. In addition, the banner in the eagle's beak does not read "E Pluribus Unum," as on the Great Seal. It reads, "LOOK OUT BELOW." Thus by removing the symbol of peace, the seal represents raw power, presumably the raw power of the Ramones's music—about to drop on the audience like a bomb.

The back cover of *Rocket to Russia* takes the symbolism to the next level. Here the Ramones's eagle with its baseball bat, arrows, and "LOOK OUT BELOW" banner is emblazoned on the side of a rocket that, unsurprisingly, is on its way to Russia. The back cover is a comic book illustration by John Holmstrom, who, like Legs McNeil, is a seminal figure in the history of punk. He also created the magazine *Punk* and drew illustrations for the Ramones. Riding the rocket is a punk rocker. But this is more than just a conventional rendering of a punk. It is Simon Metz, known as "Schlitzie," who appeared in the 1932 cult film about circus entertainers called *Freaks*. The Ramones saw *Freaks* in a Cleveland movie theater when a concert had been canceled.[28] They identified with Schlitzie, who was born with microcephaly, a disorder that left him with an unusually small brain and skull. The Ramones made him their mascot and wrote a song, "Pinhead" from *Leave Home*, about him. So we have the pinhead Schlitzie, a symbol of the punk rock outsider, riding a rocket to Russia. Instead of punks and freaks being the outcasts of society, they are combined into one image and perched on top of the most powerful weapon in the world.

The back cover of *Rocket to Russia* is meant to be cheeky satire rather than political commentary. We asked John Holmstrom about the origins of the cover and he replied,

> My memory is that Johnny, who made most decisions for the Ramones, approached me about the inner sleeve illustrations. Then when I turned those in, he liked them and asked me to draw the back cover. He gave me a crazy, short deadline that I somehow made. Johnny described it in such detail that I could visualize it as he spoke. He talked about ideas for the world map, explained the record's title *Rocket to Russia*, and went into detail about the map's cartoon images. I always considered this as collaboration between the two of us. It was meant to be fun, humorous and ridiculous, but with a sly message behind it all.[29]

Johnny Ramone had the same recollection in his autobiography, *Commando*, saying "I loved the back cover. John Holmstrom did the artwork and I worked with him on some of the ideas, doing the drawing with a military theme and playing into my strong anti-communist stance in a cartoonish manner. . . . I asked for a pinhead riding a rocket over a cartoon map of the world."[30]

Anyone familiar with the 1964 Stanley Kubrick film *Dr. Strangelove* will recognize the back cover's homage to the film.

PUNK PIONEERS ON THE COLD WAR

Besides the Ramones, other seminal punk groups wrote songs about the Cold War, or used Cold War imagery in concerts. Along with the Velvet Underground, the Stooges, and MC5, the hard rock/glam rock New York Dolls are widely considered to be among the bands that paved the way for punk. They recorded two influential albums, *New York Dolls* (1973) and *Too Much Too Soon* (1974), but poor sales and chart performance put them in danger of being dropped by Mercury, their record label. In late 1974, British impresario, visual artist, and clothes designer Malcolm McLaren left his native London with his girlfriend and fellow clothes designer, Vivienne Westwood, to help the Dolls rejuvenate their floundering career. Lead singer David Johansen, McLaren, and Westwood came up with the idea to turn communist and deck the band out in "Red Patent Leather," the title of one of their songs.[31] Cyrinda Foxe, who married Johansen and later married Aerosmith's Steven Tyler, hand-sewed a hammer and sickle image on a red banner to create a backdrop.[32] McLaren said, "I found a venue, hung a lipstick logo'd flag outside, and designed a backdrop—a banner with a hammer and sickle. . . . The Dolls came on stage soaked in a ray of red light. David [Johansen] waved Chairman Mao's *Little Red Book*. Everyone drank red-coloured cocktails and sat on red upholstered chairs."[33]

American audiences saw the ploy not as political, nor humorous or ironic, just juvenile and offensive. The Dolls' career continued to flounder, and their label dropped them in 1975. McLaren returned to England and was soon managing the Sex Pistols.

The bomb, the Berlin Wall, and communists appear again and again as metaphors for both power and paranoia in the songs of the early punk bands. In the Stooges' "Search and Destroy" (1973), Iggy Pop describes himself as "a runaway son of the nuclear A-bomb." In the Sex Pistols' "God Save the Queen" (1977), John Lydon ("Johnny Rotten") calls Queen Elizabeth II a "potential H-bomb," a pleasant appellation just in time for her silver jubilee. After a trip to Berlin in March 1977, the band wrote "Holidays in the Sun" about taking a vacation in a place of misery and seeing some Cold War history. In the lyrics, Lydon places himself at the Berlin Wall and desires to get over to the east. While most people were trying to reach the west, Lydon wants to go in the opposite direction. Perhaps he wishes to escape the capitalist West, where he finds "no future," the concluding refrain from "God Save the Queen." Yet communist East Berlin doesn't sound very appealing either, since it is referred to as the "new Belsen."[34] With no apparent solution, all he can say is, "I don't understand this thing at all." The Clash wrote several songs confronting Cold War matters. "London Calling" (1979) contains a reference to the accident ("meltdown," "a nuclear error") in March 1979 at the

Three Mile Island nuclear facility in Pennsylvania. "Stop the World" (1980) is a surreal journey through a postnuclear wasteland, a "burning junk heap for twenty square miles." "Ivan Meets G.I. Joe" (1980) reimagines the Cold War as a disco contest with the Soviet Union, United States, and China boogieing down at Studio 54, the nightclub that was to disco what CBGB was to punk. "Washington Bullets" (1980) is about American, Soviet, Chinese, and British weapons in the hands of militias in war-torn countries. The Clash's fourth album, *Sandinista!* (1980), was named after the Sandinista National Liberation Front, the socialist government in Nicaragua in the 1980s—who in turn took its name from Augusto César Sandino, who fought for Nicaragua against US occupation in the 1930s. Clash biographer, Pat Gilbert, notes that Joe Strummer's interest in global politics stemmed in part from his father's career traveling the world as a clerical officer in the British Foreign Office.[35]

While these seminal punk groups wrote about a variety of political issues other than the Cold War, dozens of punk groups from both sides of the Atlantic focused on one issue, the nuclear arms race. But before exploring these bands, it is imperative to probe the nature of their lyrics and why they were so explicit and graphic.

EXPLICIT PUNK LYRICS AND MILITARY EUPHEMISMS

Punk bands made their lyrics about nuclear warfare as repulsive and nauseating as they possibly could. No doubt they did this simply to shock and offend the older generation, as young people are wont to do. They also did it to intentionally break through the coded and indirect language created by military officials and military media personnel about nuclear weapons. George Orwell addressed this practice of "doublethink," "doublespeak," and "newspeak" in his novel *Nineteen Eighty-Four* (1948). In his 1946 essay, "Politics and the English Language," Orwell wrote, "Defenceless villages are bombarded from the air, the inhabitants driven out into the countryside, the cattle machine-gunned, the huts set on fire with incendiary bullets: this is called *pacification*. Such phraseology is needed if one wants to name things without calling up mental pictures of them."[36]

The language used by presidents, congress members, and military personnel throughout the Cold War (and today) abounds in euphemism.[37] President Truman referred to the Korean War, which claimed well over one million lives, as a "police action."[38] Bombs and bombing are referred to in innocuous, meaningless, or deceptive terms such as "clean bombs," "smart bombs," "servicing the target," "carpet bombing," and "ordnance delivery." Terms like "surgical strikes," "needle strikes," and "precision bombing" create the illusion warfare can be meticulously contained and controlled, like a surgeon performing a routine procedure. Accidents involving nuclear weapons are referred to as "broken arrows," "bent spears," or "empty quivers." War euphemisms often dehumanize humans. Civilians killed in war are referred to as "collateral damage." Soldiers killed in war are called "casualties." Soldiers accidentally killed by fellow soldiers are victims of "friendly fire." Not only do war euphemisms dehumanize people, they humanize weapons. Nuclear bombs are given cute names like "the gadget," "the gimmick," "Little Boy," "Fat Man," "Iron Mike," and "Joe 4." Nuclear missiles are given heroic names like "Patriot," "Peacekeeper," and "Tomahawk."

In recounting how he wrote his song "Tomahawk Cruise," released in November 1980, T. V. Smith of the British bands the Adverts and the Explorers says, "The politicians were all for [the missiles], but the public was proving harder to convince. At the time I was thinking, just the name of the missile—Tomahawk Cruise—was part of the attempt to persuade us. Has there even been a sexier, more stirring name for something designed for mass slaughter? How could we resist something so evocatively titled that it almost seemed to have its own personality."[39]

Reflecting this in the lyrics, Smith anthropomorphizes the weapon, giving it an authoritarian persona. The missile itself orders citizens to "choose between living and Tomahawk Cruise," giving them a choice between acceptance of the weapon or death.

One never sees such euphemisms in punk songs, unless the intention is to ridicule the deceptive language itself. For example, the Crass song "Yes Sir, I Will" (1983) has an entire verse about euphemisms created by military media personnel. Referring to the Thatcher administration's use of terms like "limited tactical response" and "collateral damage," one line of the song states plainly that "these terms are borrowed from their American counterparts and are designed to mask the ugly reality that they describe."

In punk lyrics about nuclear warfare, the perspective is not from behind the control panel in an underground bunker but at ground zero at the time of detonation. The songwriters wanted listeners to vividly imagine what it might be like to live through, or die in, a nuclear attack. Earth is described as hell, a burning pit of smoke and ash with suffocating heat, poisoned water, black rain, decimated animal and plant life, and unbreathable air permeated with the stench of death. Men, women, and children either scream in agony from radiation burns or die in silence. Yet the truly disturbing aspect of these lyrics is they are not gruesome enough to match the reality of what Japanese bomb victims experienced in August 1945. Reading the memoirs of actual Hiroshima and Nagasaki survivors and the eyewitness accounts on the "Voice of Hibakusha" webpage gives one an idea of what nuclear warfare actually does to humans.[40] People are described with their eyeballs melted into their sockets, blistering flesh dripping off their bones, and maggots festering in open wounds. As Nagasaki survivor Takashi Nagai

Table 8.1 British Punk Songs about Nuclear Weapons

Song	Songwriter
"Tomahawk Cruise"	T. V. Smith
"Warhead"	Charlie Harper and Paul Slack
"Nagasaki Nightmare"	Crass
"Seven Minutes to Midnight . . . (To Be Continued)"	Pete Wylie
"Your Attention Please"	Scars, Peter Porter
"Wrap Up the Rockets"	Chris Sievey
"Human Error"	Subhumans
All songs	This Heat
"Bomb Scare," "Another Hiroshima," and "Fighting for Reality"	Matt Dagnut, Ian Fisher, and John Igoe
All songs	Discharge
"Sadist Dream" and "Nuclear Disaster"	No Choice
"Massacred Millions, "Thatcher's Fortress," "Will They Never Learn?," and "The Bomb Blast"	The Varukers

writes, "The experts have shown cities demolished and fields laid waste. But very little has been said about *people* in an atomic war, *as people*."[41] Punk lyrics portray people in nuclear war as people. The songs in table 8.1, like the survivors' accounts, humanize nuclear war by putting the focus not on the supremacy of the victors but on the suffering of the victims.

BRITISH ANTINUKE PUNK

While many American punks wrote songs about the Cold War, the British were much more prolific.[42] The songs in table 8.1 are just a small sample of over one hundred songs written about nuclear weapons by British punks in the early 1980s. Increased tension in the Cold War in the late 1970s and early 1980s precipitated this passionate interest. Also influential were two decisions the British government made in 1980 under Prime Minister Margaret Thatcher that would greatly increase the number of nuclear weapons in England in the following years. In July 1980, the government announced it would be purchasing the United States' Trident I (C4) MIRV submarine-launched missile program for five billion pounds in order to replace its outdated Polaris missiles.[43] Two years later, the British government decided to purchase the more powerful and modern Trident II (D5) missiles for seven-and-a-half billion pounds since the Trident I missiles were going out of service.[44] Throughout the 1980s and 1990s, the British built four nuclear submarines (*Vanguard, Victorious, Vigilant,* and *Vengeance*) each of which could

Performer	Album/Single	Year
T. V. Smith's Explorers	single	1980
U.K. Subs	*Brand New Age*	1980
Crass	single	1980
Wah! Heat	single	1980
Scars	*Author! Author!*	1981
The Freshies	single	1981
Subhumans	*Demolition War* (EP)	1981
This Heat	*Deceit*	1981
Dead Man's Shadow	*Bomb Scare* (EP)	1982
Discharge	*Hear Nothing See Nothing Say Nothing*	1982
No Choice	*Sadist Dream* (EP)	1983
The Varukers	*Massacred Millions* (EP)	1984

carry sixteen of the US Trident II missiles. Each of these sixteen missiles could house up to twelve MIRVs. MIRVs (multiple independently targetable reentry vehicles) are smaller guided nuclear missiles that the Trident II could direct at various targets from the sky while maneuvering in suborbital free flight. Thus, the Trident is a missile that launches missiles. Each individual MIRV was armed with a warhead that could generate an explosion of between one hundred and three hundred kilotons. By way of comparison, the yield of the Hiroshima explosion was fifteen kilotons. If fully armed, each submarine could carry and launch 192 hydrogen bombs (sixteen missiles with twelve MIRVs each). Since 1998, arms-reduction treaties have greatly reduced the number of warheads each submarine can carry to forty, still an unimaginable amount of destructive capability for one submarine.[45]

The second decision the British government made in 1980 was to place 160 American BGM-109 class "Tomahawk" ground-based cruise missiles at the RAF Greenham Common and RAF Molesworth military bases by 1983.[46] While some Britons felt these missiles gave England a greater position in the nuclear club and served as a deterrent, others thought they made the country a greater target and put civilians in danger if an attack or accident occurred. Both of these military bases were just fifty to sixty miles from London. By way of contrast, America has vast stretches of desert land in the Southwest, like the Nevada Test Site, where many of its weapons were stored and tested. The United Kingdom, which is a fortieth the size of the United States, does not have this luxury. Texas alone is roughly three times larger than the land mass of England, Scotland, Wales, and Northern Ireland combined. An attack or accident at Greenham Common or Molesworth would have obliterated nearby towns, and the fallout would easily have reached the densely populated London, causing deaths that could possibly reach into the millions.

When news of these events hit the presses, punk bands across England got busy putting pen to paper and pick to string. They thought the weapons posed a threat to the British public and, rather than serving as a deterrent, increased the possibility of England becoming a Soviet target. In this section, we will focus on Crass' single "Nagasaki Nightmare," Discharge's album *Hear Nothing See Nothing Say Nothing*, and Scars' single "Your Attention Please."

Most of the songs in table 8.1 are by hardcore punk bands and anarcho-punk bands. These two styles deserve brief descriptions. British hardcore bands took elements from the punk pioneers, like Ramones, Sex Pistols, the Clash, and hard rock/heavy metal bands, like Black Sabbath and Motörhead, and created a wall of distorted sound over which vocalists would shout lyrics. These bands made the consequences of nuclear war shockingly vivid through their blunt, grotesque lyrics, screaming guitars, and shocking visual imagery on their album covers, EPs, and singles. Discharge was one of the most influential of these bands, and those who adopted their style were sometimes referred to as "D-beat" bands. Garry Maloney (drummer of the Varukers and Discharge) and Brian Roe (drummer of the Varukers) created a drumming pattern known as "D-beat," which formed the backbone of the style and influenced many other UK hardcore punk bands.[47] With cymbal strikes on every beat, snare drum beats on two and four, and a syncopated bass drum rhythm, hardcore drummers created a relentless, galloping groove that made the listener feel as if he or she were being pursued by a runaway freight train.

Anarcho-punk is more difficult to define than hardcore punk. As Ian Glasper writes, "By even trying to label anarcho punk as 'anarcho punk,' you seek to leech away much of its power, by stuffing it into a neat pigeonhole, where, once classified, it can be more easily controlled."[48] Many anarcho-punk bands were also hardcore bands, but some were not. Because anarcho-punks did not confine themselves to a galloping beat or heavily distorted guitars, their music was more diverse and experimental and incorporated other musical styles and instrumentation. For anarcho-punk bands, the ideology behind the songs and the messages communicated were often more important than the music. As Glasper summarizes, "Anarcho bands were bound together more by their ethics than any unwritten musical doctrine."[49]

Anarchism is even more difficult to define than anarcho-punk since it manifests itself in broad and diverse ways. Basically, it is an antigovernment, proindividualist ideology, an extreme form of libertarianism. Anarcho-punk bands espoused anarchism generally as a political philosophy but had no interest in being philosophers, economists, or political commentators. They took only those pieces from anarchism that interested them, which Jim Donaghey summarized neatly into five interrelated elements—shock tactics ("rhetorical posturing"), hippie hangover ("a continuation of the 1960s counterculture and the anarchistic threads therein"), reactive anarchism ("opposition to hierarchical, state, and societal repression"), practical necessity ("the DIY organizing principle"), and intuitive anarchistic politics ("the rejection of political parties").[50] Although most people are highly skeptical of anarchism as a viable political option, anarcho-punk bands justified their beliefs by pointing out the governmental structures of the twentieth century produced two world wars and have brought about a condition whereby humankind could possibly annihilate itself in nuclear war. For them, that was reason enough to be anarchist and reject all current political structures. The most influential anarcho-punk band was Crass, and the band's rhythm guitarist, Andy Palmer, describes how they came to fashion their own brand of anarchism: "There were both left wing and right wing influences who were trying to co-opt what we were saying, which was largely why we adopted the anarchy symbol. Then we came up against the established anarchists [who thought that] putting anarchy and peace together was a complete contradiction to the idea of what anarchy was. So we put up the peace banner together with the anarchy banner."[51]

CRASS

Crass put their ideology into practice in several ways. They were inspired by the proindividualist, antigovernment stance of the Sex Pistol's "Anarchy in the U.K.," yet they felt the Pistols abandoned the DIY ethic of punk when they signed contracts in 1976 and 1977 with major record labels, EMI, A&M, and Virgin. So Crass refused to align themselves with major record labels. They preferred working with small, independent labels or producing and distributing their music themselves. Fusing their anarchy with pacifism and nonviolent protest, they aligned themselves with the Campaign for Nuclear Disarmament (CND) in their efforts to eliminate nuclear weapons. They made their concerts about much more than just music and created a space where people could exchange ideas, pass out pamphlets, and learn about and get involved in social causes. Vocalist Steve Ignorant said, "We always saw ourselves as an information bureau, so by giving out the CND stuff, these kids of 14, 15, 16 . . . got interested, then it all built up. You can't hear the lyrics because I'm screaming . . . but maybe you'll understand the imagery . . . or the written word."[52] Drummer and main lyricist, Penny Rimbaud, recounts,

"We were responsible for introducing [CND] to thousands of people who would later become the backbone of its revival."[53]

Crass wrote many songs about the Cold War, and they are distinctive for several reasons. They combine male voices (Steve Ignorant and Penny Rimbaud) with female voices (Eve Libertine, Joy de Vivre, and Gee Vaucher). Their lyrics are more often spoken than sung, making them sound like editorials, rants, or cultural critiques. Their musical accompaniment often verges on noise and at times has no discernable melody, harmony, or rhythm, which aurally represents the destruction and chaos war creates. The packaging of their singles, EPs, and LPs are crammed with illustrations, maps, collages, and text with word counts in the thousands. Often their record packaging expresses as much—or more—than their music or lyrics do. One example of this is "Nagasaki Nightmare" from 1980.

"Nagasaki Nightmare," about the atomic bombing of Nagasaki on August 9, 1945, is an avant-garde piece in which the common musical elements of punk rock are almost completely absent. The eight-minute song falls into five sections. The first (0:00–1:36) begins with Penny Rimbaud beating slowly and softly on a saucepan, which sounds like a death knell, while Gee Vaucher plays mournful passages on flute. Over this, the voice of Aki Hayashi is heard speaking in Japanese of the Hiroshima and Nagasaki bombings, the death toll, and the long-term effect of radiation poisoning. Eve Libertine reads an English translation. A cymbal or gong swells and crescendos, drowning out the voices. The second section (1:36–4:28) has Phil Free and Andy Palmer playing staccato notes on electric guitars approximating a koto, a traditional Japanese plucked instrument developed in the sixteenth century, while bassist Pete Wright plays an ascending scale. Over this, Eve Libertine sings three verses in a high register with Steve Ignorant chanting, "Nagasaki Nightmare," after each line. The lyrics describe the suffering of Japanese civilians in the bombing. The third section (4:28–6:14) begins with Libertine singing wordless, inarticulate exclamations accompanied by guitar feedback and freeform playing by the band. Libertine begins chanting, "Rain," referring to the black rain of radioactive fallout, and the band slowly congeals around her. In the fourth section (6:14–7:50), the band establishes a steady rock beat with Libertine as she sings the remaining three verses in a more traditional rock style. The lyrics describe the "deadly rain" of radioactive fallout. The music slowly fades, and the last section (7:50–8:23) again features the slow beating of the death knell.

The single was packaged in a foldout, double-sided poster.[54] Both sides of the poster are packed with text, photographs, illustrations, slogans, and collages. One side has wording that fills up the left and right edges and consists of over fifty paragraphs grouped under twenty headings. It reads like a Campaign for Nuclear Disarmament (CND) pamphlet. As Matthew Worley writes, "Record sleeves doubled as detailed dossiers of data and intelligence."[55] The text is well-written, powerful, and persuasive but at times bombastic and sensationalistic, succumbing to the pitfalls of yellow journalism. Nevertheless, it contains enough veracity and serious food for thought to keep the reader up at night. The first four paragraphs alone raise alarming questions about nuclear weapons. The first paragraph begins, "H-bombs are mind-control. They kill people a little bit every day." The second and third paragraphs assert that life is being devalued by nuclear weapons by making people more likely to despair about the future and less likely to make long-term plans or care about their work. As a result, "short-life shoddiness is everywhere." The fourth paragraph claims the pursuit of nuclear power for "peaceful purposes" and to generate electricity can also be used as a mask to pursue nuclear weapons. The proliferation of nuclear power plants will result inevitably in greater access to fissionable material to make bombs. "Every time you turn on a light there's a Bomb behind the switch."

Issues addressed in the rest of the text include: the value of individual and collaborative nonviolent protest, the uselessness of public and private fallout shelters against hydrogen bombs, the uselessness of the *Protect and Survive* pamphlet, the well-built and elaborate shelters for government officials and military personnel, the higher death rate in a nuclear attack for poor people in urban areas, the lower death rate for rich people in suburbs and countryside estates, the government's attempt to normalize nuclear war by convincing citizens they have a good chance of surviving, the government's use of civil defense to control citizens and their conduct rather than protect them, and the danger of storing American cruise missiles at the Greenham Common and Molesworth RAF bases, which made Britain a greater target for the Soviet Union. The other side of the poster contains information about the Nagasaki bombing, eyewitness accounts by survivors, the process of uranium mining, the difference between uranium and plutonium, the current state of the arms race, and the problems involved with transporting and storing nuclear waste. By simply reading this record sleeve, one can become well informed of the tenor of the Cold War in the early 1980s. It is an extraordinary document in and of itself.

But the text is only half of the story. Just as thrashing, chaotic music accompanies Crass' spoken-word lyrics, shocking and disturbing images depicting the suffering of civilians, mostly women and children, accompanies the text on the packaging. The cover of the record sleeve has a photograph of a teenage boy carrying his scarred younger brother on his back, taken on the day after the Nagasaki bombing (August 10, 1945) by Japanese photographer Yosuke Yamahata.[56] The bulk of the space on the first side of the poster is taken up with a map of Great Britain, adapted from a map created by the Bristol Anti-Nuclear Group, showing the locations of the country's nuclear power plants, nuclear weapon manufacturing facilities, cruise missile sites, bomber bases, submarine bases, and nuclear waste dumps. Other images assault the eye and are impossible to unsee. At the bottom right corner of the poster is a US nuclear missile merged with the head of an erect penis. Above the map is a panel of three images. The first is a photograph of Queen Elizabeth II from her silver jubilee in 1977. In the second panel, the Queen's face has been cut out, exposing the lacerated and burned face of a baby underneath. Yet the Queen's hair and tiara from the first photograph remain. The third panel shows the complete photograph of the baby, again taken by Yosuke Yamahata on the day after the Nagasaki bombing.[57] Queen Elizabeth II had nothing to do with the bombs dropped on Japan by America. Yet her image is used as an emblem of nuclear-armed powers that exploit their status to mask the effects of dropping atomic bombs on civilians. The other side of the poster contains photographs (most by Yamahata) of Japanese women and children scarred black by radiation burns and a collage of world leaders (Margaret Thatcher, Ronald Reagan, Leonid Brezhnev, Mao Zedong, and Fidel Castro) standing in a wasted landscape. A mushroom cloud looms in the background while dead Japanese women and children are in the foreground. These images stir strong emotions in the viewer but cross the line into gratuitousness and crassness. Yet punk is a music of extremes, and few bands were as crass as Crass, so these images exemplify the punk aesthetic.

Crass and other punk bands used images such as these to bring attention to the issue of aerial bombardment of civilians in modern warfare.[58] Civilian immunity has been a central tenet of just war theory (*jus in bello* or "right conduct in war") for centuries, dating back to the ancient Indian epic *Mahabharata*, the Bible, the writings of St. Augustine in the fifth century, and the writings of Thomas Aquinas in the thirteenth century. The Second Hague Conventions of 1907, which America, Germany, Japan, and England ratified, prohibited civilian bombing.[59] Yet it was practiced in World War I and became widespread in World War II, setting a frightening precedent for its use during the rest of the twentieth century and into the present day. The occurrence that gained international attention was the bombing of Guernica by Germany in 1937 during the Spanish Civil War. Japan began bombing Chinese civilians in cities such as Shanghai, Beijing, and Chongqing in the late 1930s. On September 1, 1939, the same day Germany invaded Poland at the start of World War II, President Roosevelt sent an appeal to Germany, Italy, France, England, and Poland imploring that they "shall in no event, and under no circumstances, undertake the bombardment from the air of civilian populations or of unfortified cities."[60] Ignoring this, Germany bombed Warsaw throughout September 1939 and then bombed London, Coventry, Manchester, Birmingham, Belfast, and other cities in the early 1940s. The Allies had little alternative but to answer in like manner and themselves disregarded just war theory, the Hague

Conventions, and Roosevelt's own appeal. The British bombed Hamburg, Dresden, Cologne, Berlin, and many other German cities. America bombed Tokyo, Hiroshima, Nagasaki, and over sixty other Japanese cities. As a result, civilian deaths greatly outnumbered military deaths in World War II. Many people in the West were, and still are, unaware that the great majority of those who died in Hiroshima and Nagasaki were civilians. In his first official announcement about the bombing, President Truman stated that Hiroshima was simply "an important Japanese Army base," which was grossly misleading.[61] The Japanese Second Army was based in a district of Hiroshima, but the bomb was dropped in the center of the city of 350,000 people. Approximately twenty thousand military personnel were killed, but the rest of the sixty to eighty thousand victims were civilians. Nagasaki was a major port city and had military and shipbuilding factories but no substantial military base. The estimates of the number of deaths in the Nagasaki bombing are between thirty-five and seventy thousand. Fewer than one thousand of these were military personnel. Thus, at least 80 percent of the deaths in the two bombings were civilian.[62] These were just the deaths on the days (August 6 and 9, 1945) of the bombings. Tens of thousands more died in the following weeks, months, and years as a direct result of radiation poisoning and other injuries. As shown in chapter 4 on novelty songs about radiation, most photographs of, and information on, civilian deaths were censored from the public throughout World War II and the Cold War. Students rarely read of the horrific extent of all these bombings in American or British history books. Oddly enough, one could learn the truth from obscure, obnoxious punk records.

DISCHARGE

Another punk band that had much to say about the atomic bombing of civilians was Discharge. They hailed from Stoke-on-Trent, midway between the two industrial centers of Manchester and Birmingham. The band's lineup in the 1980s consisted of Kelvin "Cal" Morris (vocals), Anthony "Bones" Roberts (electric guitar), Royston "Rainy" Wainwright (bass), and Garry Maloney (drums). Some of their early albums and EPs, like *Never Again* (1981), *Why* (1981), and *Hear Nothing See Nothing Say Nothing* (1982), were almost exclusively about nuclear war. As with Crass, the specters of Hiroshima and Nagasaki loom large in their music, lyrics, and record packaging. Yet their lyrics are the polar opposite of Crass' in terms of form and expression. Crass is verbose, but Discharge is succinct. Whether intentional or not, the lyrics of Discharge bear a striking resemblance to haiku and tanka poetry written by Japanese poets about the atomic bombings. Artist and curator Mark Vallen also noted this connection, writing of this album on his website *Art for a Change*, "The band's brilliance lay in its sparse use of lyrics . . .

the songs were almost like Japanese haiku poetry."[63] To appreciate the lyrics, it would be helpful to briefly describe haiku and tanka and how these forms came to be a way for the Japanese to describe the horrible reality of experiencing a nuclear attack.

Haiku usually consist of seventeen *on*, divided into three groups of five, seven, and five *on* each. The Japanese use the *on* as their unit of phonetic sound, which is similar but not equivalent to a syllable. Many haiku, especially by the greatest master of the form, Matsuo Bashō (1644–1694), do not fit the pattern, having slightly more or less *on*. Traditional Japanese haiku are most often objective descriptions of nature or the seasons in the present tense. Haiku are usually written in a single vertical line—although they are also written as two or three lines. English translations of Japanese haiku, or haiku written in English, are typically rendered in three horizontal lines of five, seven, and five syllables.

Tanka poetry is older than haiku and dates back to the seventh century. Tanka consist of thirty-one *on*, divided into groups of five, seven, five, seven, and seven *on* each. In contrast to haiku, which capture nature objectively and descriptively in the present tense, tanka are often subjective, emotional, and incorporate the passage of time. According to the Japanese poet Sakutarō Hagiwara (1886–1942), "The difference between tanka and haiku can be compared to the contrast between the Dionysian and the Apollonian in poetry. . . . Tanka is sentimental and passionate and makes one feel a flaming fire, [whereas] haiku has observant, wisdom-filled eyes that gaze at its subject calmly."[64]

Haiku and tanka became popular ways for bomb survivors to write about their experiences, not only because of the forms' place of prominence in Japanese poetry but because of the ban the American military placed on writing about the bomb. After Japan surrendered in August 1945, the Allies established the Civil Censorship Detachment (CCD), which prevented Japanese writers from publishing materials describing the effects of the atomic bombings.[65] Instead of writing prose descriptions of their experiences, which would not have been published in mainstream newspapers or magazines anyway, they wrote more personal, and uniquely Japanese, haiku and tanka. They "published locally or in ways that escaped the eyes of the censor," as Ann Sherif writes.[66] She goes further to say, "In Hiroshima and Nagasaki, it was poets who first searched for an appropriate idiom to capture the disaster, at first gravitating toward pre-existing genres such as haiku and tanka. Many found these genres effective in evoking the survivor's experiences: the bodily sensations of extreme thirst; the agony and regret over the loss of loved ones; and the moments of horror at the death and pain surrounding them."[67]

Haiku and tanka about the bombings can be found in books by Kurihara Sadako, Yamaguchi Tsutomu, Atsuyuki Matsuo, and in the anthology *Outcry from the Inferno*.[68]

Although it is unlikely that the members of Discharge were well-versed in Japanese poetry, the lyrics of many of their early 1980s songs closely resemble haiku and tanka written about the bombings by Japanese poets. The lyrics do not fit precisely into the five-seven-five form of the haiku, nor the five-seven-five-seven-seven form of the tanka, but their phrases of five to fifteen syllables have the "feel" of both. The lyrics lack the depth, subtly, and craft of the Japanese poets, yet the aesthetics are the same: they attempt to capture a horror beyond words in as few words as possible. Westerners often have trouble understanding the nature of short poetic forms such as haiku and tanka. As William Howard Cohen writes, "To the Western reader, accustomed to a more wordy, rhetorical, philosophical type of poem, the haiku often seems fragmentary and incomplete."[69] Yet this misunderstanding of the forms makes them all the more fitting to describe the fractured reality of experiencing nuclear war. Using complete sentences with correct grammar and punctuation would be too cumbersome, too pedantic, and too proper. The lack of punctuation, especially commas, makes the words rush at the reader like an atomic flash, without pause and without filters. Like tanka, raw, gut-wrenching emotions fill Discharge's lyrics. Like haiku, they describe the effects of nuclear war in a cold, factual manner. The lyrics uncannily fuse the characteristics of tanka and haiku.

Their most acclaimed recording, *Hear Nothing See Nothing Say Nothing*, is a concept album about nuclear war. On closer inspection, the lyrics of the fourteen songs confront four interrelated themes. The first theme is the suffering of the victims in a nuclear attack, especially children, described in gory detail in "The Nightmare Continues," "A Hell on Earth," "Cries of Help," and "Q: And Children? A: And Children." Secondly, the songs "Hear Nothing See Nothing Say Nothing," "Protest and Survive," "I Won't Subscribe," and "Free Speech for the Dumb" stress the importance of speaking out against governments that deceive and coerce citizens—or leave them ignorant. The third theme is the power that the military establishment wields over the populace, addressed in "Drunk with Power," "Meanwhile," and "The Blood Runs Red." The last theme is the possibility of a global catastrophe brought about by nuclear war, heard in "The Final Bloodbath," The Possibility of Life's Destruction," and "The End."

All fourteen songs have similar tempos, rhythms, instrumentation, and chord progressions, making the album sound like one continuous barrage of noise and mayhem. The music is rudimentary, almost barbaric, reflecting the ethos that you don't need to be a virtuoso to play punk rock. The raging tempos and sheer intensity of the playing, however, demonstrate the band had a high level of musicianship. All the songs have two riffs (except "The Final Bloodbath" and "Free Speech for the Dumb," which have just one) made up of one to four power chords. The verses, which consist of one or two short phrases, are shouted over the first riff while the choruses, usually the titles of the songs, are shouted over the second riff. Wainwright (bass) and Roberts (guitar) play the same riffs, and Maloney's drumming locks in tightly, creating a relentless onslaught of sound. The tempos of some of the songs ("Drunk with Power," "Cries of Help," "The Possibility of Life's Destruction," "The Blood Runs Red") are so fast Maloney occasionally gets out of phase with the rest of band. His snare drum can be heard falling on beats one and three instead of the usual two and four, the backbeat. The chord progressions contain many half steps and augmented intervals that generate a pervasive mood of gloom, doom, and destruction. Despite the gloom and doom, the music is exhilarating to listen to. Its fervent empathy for the bombing victims is stimulating.

Some of the songs on the album incorporate, or make allusion to, Cold War literature (a civil defense pamphlet), film (a banned BBC drama about nuclear war), graphic art (an anti-Vietnam War poster), and music (a Black Sabbath song). "Protest and Survive" plays on the title of the British government's *Protect and Survive* pamphlet published in 1980.[70] Because of its trite instructions and limited scope, the British public widely ridiculed the pamphlet. *Protest and Survive* is also the title of a 1980 book written by E. P. Thompson, a leading figure of the Campaign for Nuclear Disarmament (CND) in the 1970s and 1980s.[71] The *Protest and Survive* book responds to the increasing number of American nuclear missiles on British soil and refutes the method of civil defense presented in the *Protect and Survive* pamphlet.

"Cries of Help" is interrupted by an audio excerpt from the 1965 BBC television drama *The War Game*. The fifty-five-minute film, directed by Peter Watkins, fictionally depicts what might occur in a Soviet nuclear attack on England. The film was deemed too disturbing to be shown on national television in 1965. The BBC finally broadcast it on July 31, 1985, commemorating the fortieth anniversary of the Hiroshima and Nagasaki bombings. The use of the excerpt in the song is very effective in giving the listener a palpable sense of the chaos created by a nuclear attack. The excerpt is from a segment depicting how a family experiences the attack—with the sound of the detonation followed by sirens wailing, babies crying, and people screaming. It ends with a voice-over comparing a thermonuclear explosion to the slamming of a door in hell. This line is then sung at the beginning of the next song, "The Possibility of Life's Destruction."

The song "Q: And Children? A: And Children" alludes to a poster titled *And Babies*, which was created in 1969 during the Vietnam War by the Poster Committee of the Art Workers' Coalition.[72] The poster is a color photograph of over twenty women and children lying dead on a dirt road. Across the top in large, blood-red letters is "Q. And babies?" Along the bottom is "A. And babies." US Army photographer Ronald Haeberle took the photograph during the My Lai Massacre, which occurred on March 16, 1968, and resulted in the death of between 347 and 504 Vietnamese civilians.[73] At one point during the massacre, Second

Lieutenant William Calley told soldiers to machine-gun a group of women and children. The words on the poster were taken from an interview Mike Wallace conducted with one of the soldiers, Paul Meadlo, on a national broadcast of the CBS news program *60 Minutes*. At one point in the interview, Wallace asked Meadlo, who was married and had a one-year-old boy at the time of the massacre, how many civilians he had shot. Meadlo answered, "Ten or fifteen." Wallace then asked: "Men, women, and children?" Meadlo: "Men, women, and children." Wallace: "And babies?" Meadlo: "And babies."[74] The message of the poster, and Discharge's song, is simple and direct: modern warfare, whether waged with machine guns or atomic bombs, often results in the death of children.

The lyrics of two songs make allusions to "War Pigs" by Black Sabbath, from their second album *Paranoid* (1970). "The End" borrows the first line of the last stanza: "Now in darkness, world stops turning." "Drunk with Power" likens modern warfare to a chess match, with generals and politicians using civilians as "disposable pieces." In the same way, "War Pigs" compares people to "pawns in chess," which generals and politicians manipulate. The influence of Black Sabbath's music and lyrics, analyzed in chapter 7, can be heard in many of Discharge's songs, especially on *Hear Nothing See Nothing Say Nothing*. These allusions show how fully engaged the band was in both Cold War history and in literature, film, art, and music written in reaction to the war.

The two British punk bands that addressed nuclear war most insightfully in the early 1980s, Discharge and Crass, used utterly different lyrical styles to express their views. Discharge used as few words as possible, while Crass used as many words as possible. The former is like the succinct Emily Dickinson and the latter like the verbose Walt Whitman. The former is so outraged they are almost speechless; the latter is so outraged all they can do is speak. The next song we consider, "Your Attention Please" by Scars, uses the words of an actual poem by the Australian/British writer Peter Porter.

SCARS

Peter Porter (1929–2010) was an Australian poet who worked for most of his life in London. He received many awards for his writing, including the Queen's Gold Medal for Poetry in 2002. His poem "Your Attention Please" was written in 1961 and first published in 1962, the year of the Cuban Missile Crisis.[75] The poem's form is an emergency news broadcast informing the public they are under nuclear attack and instructing them to proceed immediately to the nearest bomb shelter. BBC radio had to issue a public apology after a reading of the poem in October 1961 caused alarm from listeners who thought the poem was an actual warning of a nuclear attack.[76] Just as Orson Welles and H. G. Wells caused alarm with the realism of a martian attack in *The War of the Worlds*, Peter Porter caused alarm with the realism of a nuclear attack in "Your Attention Please." By mimicking the calm and pedantic tone of civil defense announcements of the early Cold War years, the poem accentuates the absurdity and impossibility of following such detailed instructions in the midst of a massive nuclear attack. The most shocking aspect of the poem is how the announcement calmly instructs people to confront horrible predicaments, like leaving pets and elderly people outside to die, sealing the shelter so no one else can enter, and giving suicide pills to family members. Porter can be seen reciting the poem as a civil defense announcement at the beginning of the thirty-minute documentary *Peter Porter: What I Have Written* from 1985.[77] He says in the documentary, "That poem seemed very relevant to the time of the Cuba crisis which happened, I think, about the year after I wrote that poem, yet here we are twenty odd years on and the world is in an even more fraught, terrible state."[78] When Porter wrote the poem in 1961 there were approximately twenty-seven thousand nuclear weapons in the world. At the time of the documentary in 1985, that number had increased to approximately sixty-five thousand.[79]

Scars was a postpunk band from Edinburgh, Scotland.[80] They formed in 1977 and wrote "Your Attention Please," based on Porter's poem, in 1978 or 1979. A live version of the song from a spring 1980 concert was released free as a gold flexi disc single with the first issue of the British fashion and youth culture magazine *i-D*. It was then included on their first and only album, *Author! Author!* (1981). The band consisted of Robert King (vocals), Paul Research (lead guitar), John Mackie (bass guitar), Calumn Mackay (drums until 1980), and Steve McLaughlin (drums from 1980 on). The following comparison shows the text of the original Porter poem alongside the lyrics of the studio version of the song from *Author! Author!* The passages in bold represent additions and alterations the band made to the poem. Some portions of the poem were left out of the lyrics.

"Your Attention Please"

Peter Porter (1961)	Scars (1981)
	Your attention please
The Polar DEW has just warned that	The Polar DEW has just warned that
A nuclear rocket strike of	**A nuclear strike of**
At least one thousand megatons	At least one thousand megatons
Has been launched by the enemy	Has been launched by the enemy
Directly at our major cities.	Directly at our major cities.
This announcement will take	**Immediately after this announcement ends**
Two and a quarter minutes to make,	**You have approximately three, repeat,**
You therefore have a further	**Three minutes**
Eight and a quarter minutes	

To comply with the shelter
Requirements published in the Civil
Defence Code—section Atomic Attack.

A specially shortened Mass
Will be broadcast at the end
Of this announcement—
Protestant and Jewish services
Will begin simultaneously—
Select your wavelength immediately
According to instructions
In the Defence Code. Do not
Take well-loved pets (including birds)
Into your shelter—they will consume
Fresh air. Leave the old and bed-
ridden, you can do nothing for them.

Remember to press the sealing
Switch when everyone is in
The shelter. Set the radiation
Aerial, turn on the geiger barometer.
Turn off your television now.
Turn off your radio immediately
The Services end. At the same time
Secure explosion plugs in the ears
Of each member of your family. Take
Down your plasma flasks. Give your
Children the pills marked one and two
In the C.D. green container, then put

Them to bed. Do not break
The inside airlock seals until
The radiation All Clear shows
(Watch for the cuckoo in your
perspex panel), or your District
Touring Doctor rings your bell.
If before this, your air becomes
Exhausted or if any of your family
Is critically injured, administer
The capsules marked "Valley Forge"
(Red pocket in No. 1 Survival Kit)
For painless death. (Catholics

To comply with the shelter
Requirements published in the Civil
Defence **Book**—section Atomic Attack,
Page 23a. Anyone found in the streets
Two minutes after curfew will be shot.

Do not, **repeat, do not**
Take well-loved pets (including birds)
Into your shelter—they will consume
Valuable fresh air. Leave the old and bed-
ridden, you can do nothing, **repeat, Nothing** for
them. **A special genocide squad**
Shall dispose of them humanely.
Remember to press the sealing
Switch when everyone is in
Your shelter. Set the radiation
Aerial, turn on the geiger barometer.
Turn off your television now.
Turn off your radio immediately,
This broadcast ends. At the same time
Secure **all** explosion **ear** plugs.

Take down your plasma flasks. Give your
Children the **pink** pills
In the C.D. green container,
Marked three and nine, and then put
Them to bed. Do not, **repeat, do not** break
The inside airlock seals until
The radiation All Clear shows
Or your District Touring Doctor
Rings your bell. (Watch for the cuckoo
In your perspex panel)
If before this your air becomes
Exhausted or any of your family
Is critically injured, administer
The **pills** marked "Valley Forge"
(**Black** pocket No 1 Survival Kit)
For painless death.

Will have been instructed by their priests
What to do in this eventuality.)
This announcement is ending.
Our President has already given orders for
Massive retaliation—it will be
Decisive. Some of us may die.
Remember, statistically
It is not likely to be you.
All flags are flying fully dressed on
Government buildings—the sun is shining.
Death is the least we have to fear.
We are all in the hands of God,
Whatever happens happens by His Will.
Now go quickly to your shelters.

This announcement is ended.
Our President has already given orders for
Massive retaliation—it will be
Decisive. Some of us may die.
But, statistically
It is not likely to be you.
All flags are flying fully dressed on
Government buildings—the sun is shining.
Death is the least we have to fear.
We are all in the hands of God,
Whatever happens happens by His Will.
Yea, though I walk through the valley of death
I shall fear no evil. For thine is the power
And the glory for ever and ever. Amen.

The band alters the ominous poem in several ways to create an even more ominous song. The word *immediately* is added to line six. The word *repeat* is added in four places to emphasize certain portions of the instructions. In the poem, the public has eight and a quarter minutes to get into a bomb shelter before the explosion. In the lyrics, they have just three. A portentous line was added to the lyrics, "anyone found in the streets two minutes after curfew will be shot," suggesting that it is better to die from a bullet wound than from the force of a nuclear shockwave. In the early 1960s when the poem was first published, the general public had begun to lose interest in bomb shelters. The realization of the magnitude and devastating effects of a hydrogen bomb explosion had set in, and many people believed in the futility of going underground. Yet, the poem still retains a degree of hope and optimism: "Some of us may die. Remember, statistically it is not likely to be you."

The band also conveys this mixture of dread and hope with its use of the opening motive of Beethoven's Fifth Symphony, played on electric guitar by Paul Research. This four-chord phrase is often referred to in Beethoven lore as the "Fate Motive."[81] It has been interpreted as a portent of doom ever since Anton Schindler, Beethoven's assistant and among his first biographers, wrote in his

1840 biography, "Beethoven expressed himself in something like vehement animation, when describing to me his idea: "It is thus that Fate knocks at the door."[82] Schindler has earned a negative reputation in Beethoven scholarship for his inaccuracies and falsifications, so this story has no basis in fact. Nevertheless, the use of Beethoven's motive creates a menacing opening for the song. But besides "fate knocking at the door," the motive has also come to symbolize hope, at least since World War II. Its note values (three eighth notes and a half note with a fermata) are akin to the Morse code (dot-dot-dot-dash) for the letter *v*. "V for victory" was an encouraging slogan and hand gesture used by the Allies to raise morale during World War II, and BBC newsreel reports about the war used the Beethoven phrase at the beginning.[83] Winston Churchill was often photographed in the early 1940s with his two-fingered victory sign.

Like Sting's "Russians," the studio version of "Your Attention Please" begins with the barely audible ticking of a watch, an allusion to the Doomsday Clock.[84] Suddenly guitarist Paul Research plays the riff that alludes to the Beethoven motive. Just as the BBC used the motive to announce news about World War II, the band uses the guitar riff to announce news about the Cold War—a nuclear attack is underway. The riff is played repeatedly at regular intervals throughout the song over a descending bass line in 12/8 meter. Like Peter Porter, Robert King recites the lyrics as if they are an emergency broadcast, reflecting the form of the poem itself. The band's playing and King's vocal delivery begin calmly but become progressively more intense as the song continues. The singing and playing reach a climax with, "This announcement has ended," where King's voice is treated with echo and reverb. The song ends with King screaming passages from the 23rd Psalm and the final lines of the Lord's Prayer, both additions to the poem. The comforting nature of biblical passages ("Yea, though I walk through the valley of death, I shall fear no evil") combined with the maniacal screaming communicate hope and terror simultaneously. Yet the intensity of the music and singing overwhelms the words, and the listener is left with a feeling of terror rather than hope. The song ends with a descending bass line yet it is cut off just before resolving to the tonic. The ticking returns for a few seconds until it too descends in pitch and is cut off.

Like the songs by Crass and Discharge, "Your Attention Please" is chilling because its realism and specificity place the listener in the moment. These songs by British punks are valuable because they provide a perspective on nuclear war that is underrepresented in the West: the view of nuclear war from the ground at the time of detonation. They also bring up the thorny issue of whether or not the bombing of civilians is a morally justifiable act in warfare. Most Cold War historians, and even some Hiroshima and Nagasaki bomb survivors, concur that the decision to drop the atomic bombs on Japan was the correct one, the lesser of two evils, in that it brought about a swift end to World War II and prevented further death on both sides from an Allied ground invasion of the Japanese mainland. Yet others point out that the lesser of two evils must still be acknowledged as a great evil. Nuclear bombs are not precision bombs; they cannot simply be targeted at military installations. They can cause total destruction to areas over fifteen miles in diameter, and deadly fallout can travel hundreds of miles. By nature, they kill civilians, and most often women, children, and the elderly suffer the worst. These punk songs vividly argue that intentionally bombing civilians is terrorism and genocide and therefore difficult to defend by any moral standard.[85]

CONCLUSION

Hardcore punk made the most forceful and direct critique of the nuclear-arms race by focusing on the physical effects of civilian bomb victims. Like heavy metal bands, with their distorted guitars, tumultuous drumming, and screamed vocals, punk bands conjured up the feeling of what living through a nuclear attack might be like. Yet their medium was not congenial to the tastes of the mainstream public. As a result, little of this music reached mass audiences. The cursing alone turned off most listeners. Bands' names, like Dead Kennedys, were intentionally offensive and provocative. Violent behavior at some concerts frightened people into thinking punks were nothing more than riotous hooligans. The average listener could not understand much of the lyrics, since they were screamed or shouted over a barrage of guitars and drums at breakneck speed. Singles, EPs, and LPs often provided the lyrics, but only punks would have sought these out. The sleeve artwork and photography often communicated valuable information, but the grotesque images may have been too much for the average person to stomach. They may have even been dismissed as having nothing more than shock value.

For example, the Campaign for Nuclear Disarmament looked at Crass suspiciously, even though they openly supported the organization, raised money for it, and passed out antinuke pamphlets during concerts. The annual Glastonbury Festival was organized in conjunction with the CND in the early 1980s and was known as the "CND Festival." Twenty to forty thousand people attended each year. It became the most popular concert festival in England in that period. It attracted big name performers, like Peter Gabriel, Jackson Browne, Van Morrison, Joan Baez, Elvis Costello, and Joe Cocker, but few hardcore or anarcho-punk bands were invited to play. Crass never played there, even though they did the most of any musical group to raise support and awareness for the CND. Crass drummer and lyricist, Penny Rimbaud, said, "A new and hitherto uninformed sector of society was being exposed to a form of radical thought that culminated in the great rallies of the early eighties, rallies that CND were at pains to point out we were not welcome to play at. . . . CND felt that our presence at a rally would merely create trouble. They had a point, but nevertheless, it was one that we found galling."[86]

In his article on the innovative subcultures the CND helped to foster, George McKay finds the CND was often resistant, ambivalent, or embarrassed when nuclear protest was conveyed in nonmainstream forms, like punk rock.[87]

Another problem with political messages expressed through punk music has to do with the DIY aesthetics of the style. Punk music often stresses immediacy and emotion over articulation and precision. A vital element of the punk aesthetic is that anyone can play it. Like Tony Moon's illustration in *Sideburns*, mentioned at the beginning of this chapter, all you have to know is how to play three chords on guitar or a fast, basic beat on the drums. You don't even need to know how to sing; shouting will do. The same goes for the lyrics—they need not be grammatically correct, follow a specific form, or even present a logical flow of ideas. These elements often make punk music utterly incoherent to mainstream audiences. The messages are just for those within the scenes where they were generated and don't translate well to the broader culture. For example, Henry Rollins is very articulate and intelligent, but the harshness of Black Flag's music does not allow the messages to reach the mainstream, no matter how valuable those messages may be. Thus, punks and their songs about the nuclear-arms race remained underground.

Ironically, these violent sounding songs promoted peace and sought to understand the suffering of the Japanese victims in Hiroshima and Nagasaki, even if they were the enemy during World War II. It is remarkable that the most compassionate and empathetic sentiments about the effects of nuclear warfare came out of a musical style regarded by many as simply foulmouthed, brutal, and barbaric.

NOTES

1. Jon Savage, *England's Dreaming: Anarchy, Sex Pistols, Punk Rock, and Beyond* (New York: St. Martin's Griffin, 2002), 280–281.
2. Johnny Ramone, *End of the Century: The Story of the Ramones* (Rhino R2 970399, 2005, DVD), 1:29:46–1:29:56.
3. Marky Ramone with Rich Herschlag, *Punk Rock Blitzkrieg* (New York: Touchstone, 2015), 134.
4. Johnny Ramone, *Commando: The Autobiography of Johnny Ramone*, ed. John Cafiero with Steve Miller and Henry Rollins (New York: Abrams, 2012), 167.
5. Johnny Ramone, "Ramones Accept Rock and Roll Hall of Fame Awards," 1:03–1:07, https://www.youtube.com/watch?v=ekyI5ZsjTPk.
6. Johnny Ramone, *Commando*, 158.
7. Monte A. Melnick and Frank Meyer, *On the Road with the Ramones* (London: Bobcat, 2007), 163.

8. Melnick and Meyer, *On the Road with the Ramones,* 43.

9. Mickey Leigh, with Legs McNeil, *I Slept with Joey Ramone: A Family Memoir* (New York: Simon and Schuster, 2009), 47, 42, 48.

10. Legs McNeil and Gillian McCain, *Please Kill Me: The Uncensored Oral History of Punk* (New York: Penguin Books, 1997), 177.

11. Leigh, *I Slept with Joey Ramone,* 247–248.

12. Joey Ramone, in the music video for "Sun City" at 2:37–2:43, https://www.youtube.com/watch?v=bY3w9gLjEV4.

13. Leigh, *I Slept with Joey Ramone,* 285.

14. C. J. Ramone, in *End of the Century,* 1:29:40–1:29:46.

15. Tommy Ramone, "Tommy Ramone: His Story as Told to Legs McNeil," interview by Legs McNeil, *Hollywood Reporter,* July 14, 2014, http://www.hollywoodreporter.com/news/tommy-ramone-his-story-as-718469.

16. Dee Dee Ramone, *Lobotomy: Surviving the Ramones,* 3rd ed. (Boston: DaCapo, 2016), 8–9.

17. Ramone, *Lobotomy,* 24–25; McNeil and McCain, *Please Kill Me,* 235–236.

18. Ramone, *Lobotomy,* 25.

19. Nicholas Rombes, *Ramones* (New York: Continuum, 2005), 88.

20. Ramone, *Commando,* 155.

21. Richard J. Jensen, *Reagan at Bergen-Belsen and Bitburg* (College Station: Texas A&M University Press, 2007), 17.

22. Jensen, *Reagan at Bergen-Belsen and Bitburg,* 54.

23. Legs McNeil and John Holmstrom, "We're a Happy Family," *Spin* 2 no. 5 (August 1986): 78.

24. Ramone, *Commando,* 158.

25. Melnick and Meyer, *On the Road with the Ramones,* 163.

26. Jim Bessman, *Ramones: An American Band* (New York: St. Martin's, 1993), 39.

27. Bessman, *Ramones,* 39.

28. Leigh, *I Slept with Joey Ramone,* 141.

29. John Holmstrom, email interview with Tim Smolko on March 23, 2013.

30. Ramone, *Commando,* 153.

31. Bob Gruen, *New York Dolls: Photographs* (New York: Abrams Image, 2008), 14, 148.

32. Nina Antonia, *Too Much, Too Soon: The Makeup and Breakup of the New York Dolls* (London: Omnibus, 1998), 163.

33. Malcolm McLaren, "Dirty Pretty Things," interview by Dave Simpson and Dorian Lynskey, *Guardian,* May 27, 2004, http://www.theguardian.com/music/2004/may/28/2.

34. Bergen-Belsen was a Nazi concentration camp in northern Germany where over fifty thousand people died during World War II. The Sex Pistols refer to the camp in another song sardonically titled "Belsen Was a Gas."

35. Pat Gilbert, *Passion Is a Fashion: The Real Story of the Clash* (London: Da Capo, 2005), 6–7. Thank you to Rachel Cabaniss for this information.

36. George Orwell, "Politics and the English Language," in *Selected Essays* (Middlesex: Penguin Books, 1957), 153.

37. William C. Gay, "The Language of War and Peace," in *Encyclopedia of Violence, Peace, and Conflict* (San Diego: Academic Press, 1999), 2:303–312.

38. Harry Truman, "The President's News Conference of June 29, 1950," Teaching American History, https://teachingamericanhistory.org/library/document/the-presidents-news-conference-of-june-29-1950/.

39. Dave Thompson, *1000 Songs That Rock Your World* (Iola, WI: Krause, 2011), 171.

40. Arata Osada, *Children of the A-bomb: Testament of the Boys and Girls of Hiroshima*, trans. Jean Dan and Ruth Sieben-Morgen (Tokyo: Uchida Rokakuho, 1959); Takashi Nagai, ed., *Living Beneath the Atomic Cloud: The Testimony of the Children of Nagasaki*, trans. by a volunteer group, compiled by Frank Zenisek (Nagasaki: Nagasaki Appeal Committee, 1979); "The Voice of Hibakusha," Atomic Archive, https://www.atomicarchive.com/resources/documents/hibakusha/index.html.

41. Takashi Nagai, *We of Nagasaki: The Story of Survivors in an Atomic Wasteland*, trans. Ichiro Shirato and Herbert B. L. Silverman (London: Victor Gollancz, 1951), 19.

42. Some noteworthy Cold War songs by American punk bands are "Kill the Poor" by Dead Kennedys, "Limited Nuclear War" by Toxic Reasons, "Deadly Skies" by Hüsker Dü, "Paranoid Chant" by Minutemen, and the album *International P.E.A.C.E. Benefit Compilation.*

43. David Fairhall, "£5 Billion Trident Deal Is Agreed," *Guardian*, July 16, 1980, http://www.theguardian.com/century/1980-1989/Story/0,,108170,00.html; Kristan Stoddart, *Facing Down the Soviet Union: Britain, the USA, NATO and Nuclear Weapons, 1976–1983* (Houndmills, Basingstoke, Hampshire: Palgrave Macmillan, 2014), 112–153.

44. Julian Haviland, "Britain to Buy 'Bargain' US Trident 2 for £7,500m," *Times*, March 12, 1982; Claire Mills, "Replacing the UK's 'Trident' Nuclear Deterrent." Briefing Paper Number 7353, July 12, 2016, House of Commons Library, 20–21, http://researchbriefings.files.parliament.uk/documents/CBP-7353/CBP-7353.pdf.

45. "Securing Britain in an Age of Uncertainty: The Strategic Defence and Security Review" (London: Her Majesty's Stationary Office, 2010), 5, 38, http://www.globalsecurity.org/military/library/report/2010/uk-mod_strategic-defense-review_101019.pdf.

46. Francis Pym, "Cruise Missile Sites," House of Commons Hansard Archives, Commons Sitting of June 17, 1980, http://hansard.millbanksystems.com/commons/1980/jun/17/cruise-missile-sites.

47. Brian Roe, drummer of the Varukers, demonstrating "D-beat" drumming. "Brian Roe—D-beat," https://www.youtube.com/watch?v=fQwCVBQN10M; Ian Glasper, *Burning Britain: The History of UK Punk, 1980–1984* (Oakland, CA: PM Press, 2014), 75–76, 189.

48. Ian Glasper, *The Day the Country Died: A History of Anarcho Punk, 1980–1984* (London: Cherry Red Books, 2006), 6.

49. Glasper, *The Day the Country Died*, 9.

50. Jim Donaghey, "Bakunin Brand Vodka: An Exploration into Anarcho-punk and Punk-anarchism," *Anarchist Developments in Cultural Studies* 1: Blasting the Canon (2013):140–141, 144, 164.

51. George Berger, *The Story of Crass* (Oakland, CA: PM Press, 2009), 129.

52. Matt Worley, "Youth Subcultures: An Alternative History," University of Reading Department of History, 6:27–7:02, https://www.youtube.com/watch?v=l8fPaevWpQk.

53. Penny Rimbaud, *Shibboleth: My Revolting Life* (San Francisco: AK Press, 1998), 109.

54. One side of the poster included with Crass's "Nagasaki Nightmare" can be viewed online here: https://livingwiththebomb.files.wordpress.com/2013/04/foldout_nagasaki.jpg and both sides can be viewed here: http://punkygibbon.co.uk/bands/c/crass_nagasaki_7_images.html.

55. Matthew Worley, "One Nation under the Bomb: The Cold War and British Punk to 1984," *Journal for the Study of Radicalism* 5, no. 2 (Fall 2011): 73.

56. Rupert Jenkins, ed., *Nagasaki Journey: The Photographs of Yosuke Yamahata, August 10, 1945* (Rohnert Park, CA: Pomegranate, 1995), 85.

57. Jenkins, *Nagasaki Journey*, 98–99.

58. Yuki Tanaka and Marilyn B. Young, eds., *Bombing Civilians: A Twentieth-Century History* (New York: New Press, 2009).

59. James Brown Scott, ed., *The Hague Conventions and Declarations of 1899 and 1907: Accompanied by Tables of Signatures, Ratifications and Adhesions of the Various Powers and Texts of Reservations* (New York: Oxford University Press, 1915), 157–161, http://avalon.law.yale.edu/20th_century/hague09.asp.

60. Franklin D. Roosevelt, "An Appeal to Great Britain, France, Italy, Germany, and Poland to Refrain from Air Bombing of Civilians," September 1, 1939, American Presidency Project, https://www.presidency.ucsb.edu/documents/appeal-great-britain-france-italy-germany-and-poland-refrain-from-air-bombing-civilians.

61. Harry S. Truman, "August 6, 1945: Statement by the President Announcing the Use of the A-bomb at Hiroshima," Presidential Speeches, Harry S. Truman, University of Virginia, Miller Center, https://millercenter.org/the-presidency/presidential-speeches/august-6-1945-statement-president-announcing-use-bomb.

62. The Committee for the Compilation of Materials on Damage Caused by the Atomic Bombs in Hiroshima and Nagasaki, *Hiroshima and Nagasaki: The Physical, Medical, and Social Effects of the Atomic Bombings*, trans. Eisei Ishikawa and David L. Swain (New York: Basic, 1981), 363–367; Barton J. Bernstein, "Truman and the A-Bomb: Targeting Noncombatants, Using the Bomb, and His Defending the 'Decision,'" *Journal of Military History* 62, no. 3 (July 1998): 562–566.

63. Mark Vallen, "Discharge: Hear Nothing See Nothing Say Nothing." Art for a Change, http://www.art-for-a-change.com/Punk/punk6a.htm.

64. Makoto Ueda, *Modern Japanese Poets and the Nature of Literature* (Stanford, CT: Stanford University Press, 1983), 170.

65. Monica Braw, *The Atomic Bomb Suppressed: American Censorship in Occupied Japan* (Armonk, NY: M. E. Sharpe, 1991), 35–36.

66. Ann Sherif, "Hiroshima, or Peace in a 'City of Cruelty and Bitter Bad Faith': Japanese Poetry in the Cold War," in *Global Cold War Literature: Western, Eastern and Postcolonial Perspectives*, ed. Andrew Hammond (New York: Routledge, 2012), 75.

67. Sherif, "Hiroshima," 75.

68. Kurihara Sadako, *When We Say "Hiroshima": Selected Poems*, trans. with an introduction by Richard H. Minear (Ann Arbor: Center for Japanese Studies, University of Michigan, 1999); Chad Diehl, *And the River Flowed as a Raft of Corpses: The Poetry of Yamaguchi Tsutomu: Survivor of Both Hiroshima and Nagasaki* (New York: Excogitating over Coffee, 2010); Atsuyuki Matsuo, *A-Bomb Haiku*, trans. Masumi Midorikawa (Tokyo: Shinjusha, 1995); Jiro Nakano, ed. and trans., *Outcry from the Inferno: Atomic Bomb Tanka Anthology* (Honolulu, HI: Bamboo Ridge, 1995).

69. William Howard Cohen, *To Walk in Seasons: An Introduction to Haiku* (Rutland, VT: Charles E. Tuttle, 1972), 20.

70. *Protect and Survive* (London: Her Majesty's Stationary Office, 1980).

71. E. P. Thompson, *Protest and Survive* (Nottingham: Campaign for Nuclear Disarmament, 1980).

72. Matthew Israel, *Kill for Peace: American Artists against the Vietnam War* (Austin: University of Texas Press, 2013), 130–135.

73. Kendrick Oliver, *The My Lai Massacre in American History and Memory* (Manchester: Manchester University Press, 2006); James S. Olson and Randy Roberts, *My Lai: A Brief History with Documents* (Boston: Bedford, 1998).

74. "Transcript of Interview of Vietnam War Veteran on His Role in Alleged Massacre of Civilians at Songmy," *New York Times*, November 25, 1969, 16, https://archive.org/stream/MeadloWallaceInterviewNov241969/Meadlo-Wallace%20interview%20Nov%2024%201969#page/n0/mode/1up.

75. The poem first appeared in the collection *Penguin Modern Poets 2: Kingsley Amis, Dom Moraes, Peter Porter* (Middlesex, England: Penguin Books, 1962), 108–109.

76. Bruce Bennett, *Spirit in Exile: Peter Porter and His Poetry* (New York: Oxford University Press, 1991), 67–68.

77. "Peter Porter: What I Have Written," https://www.youtube.com/watch?v=sDGz3eY5WZU.

78. *Peter Porter: What I Have Written.* Directed by Richard Kelly Tipping (Third Millennium Pictures, 1985), 3:11–3:26.

79. Robert S. Norris and Hans M. Kristensen, "Global Nuclear Stockpiles, 1945–2006," *Bulletin of the Atomic Scientists* 62, no. 4 (July 2006): 66, http://bos.sagepub.com/content/62/4/64.full.pdf+html.

80. "Postpunk" is a nebulous term used to describe bands that adopted the sensibilities of early punk but eschewed its rawness by experimenting with new sounds.

81. Matthew Guerrieri, *The First Four Notes: Beethoven's Fifth and the Human Imagination* (New York: Knopf, 2012), 46–48.

82. Anton Schindler, *The Life of Beethoven: Including His Correspondence with His Friends, Numerous Characteristic Traits, and Remarks on His Musical Works*, ed. and trans. Ignace Moscheles (London: Henry Colburn, 1841), 2:150.

83. "V for Victory," *CBS News Sunday Morning*, Sunday Morning Almanac segment, July 19, 2015, narrated by Jane Pauley, https://www.youtube.com/watch?v=T6eIkamRsO8.

84. For more on the Doomsday Clock, see the section in chapter 7 on the Iron Maiden song "2 Minutes to Midnight."

85. Stephen Huggins argues that aerial bombardment of civilians is terrorism in *America's Use of Terror: From Colonial Times to the A-bomb* (Lawrence: University Press of Kansas, 2019). Eric Markusen and David Kopf argue that aerial bombardment of civilians, especially with nuclear weapons, is genocide in *The Holocaust and Strategic Bombing: Genocide and Total War in the Twentieth Century* (Boulder, CO: Westview, 1995).

86. Rimbaud, *Shibboleth*, 109–110.

87. George McKay, "Subcultural Innovations in the Campaign for Nuclear Disarmament," *Peace Review* 16, no. 4 (December 2004): 436.

NINE

ELECTRONIC AND NEW WAVE

The Cold War in a Synthesizer

LIKE THE ELECTRIC GUITAR, THE synthesizer can easily conjure up the sounds of war. According to Trevor Pinch and Frank Trocco, "Explosions, sirens, and rockets were some of the easiest sounds to create on the early synthesizers."[1] An event that took place in San Francisco in 1966 demonstrates this. Don Buchla, an early synthesizer pioneer, was invited to play his "Buchla Box" synthesizer on October 1, 1966, at an event called the Awareness Festival or the Whatever It Is Festival at San Francisco State College. The Grateful Dead jammed, Bill Ham provided a psychedelic light show, hippies danced and swirled, and LSD was in plentiful supply—it was legal until October 1968. Stewart Brand, a member of the Merry Pranksters who laid the foundation for the counterculture movement in San Francisco, organized the "happening." As Charles Perry recounts, "Around midnight, Brand staged an atomic apocalypse with Don Buchla, the sound synthesizer inventor. They announced to the crowd in the auditorium that Russian missiles, presumably carrying nuclear warheads, had been detected on their way to the West Coast; they evaded our antiballistic missile defenses; they were now two and one half minutes away; two minutes; one minute; fifteen seconds; ten, nine, eight, seven, six, five, four, three, two, one—and all at once hundreds of flashbulbs went off as the house lights were cut. All good fun among acidheads."[2]

Journalist and author Tom Wolfe described the experience of listening to Buchla and his synthesizer while tripping on LSD in this lively way, "The music suddenly submerges the room from a million speakers . . . a soprano tornado of it . . . all-electric, plus the Buchla electronic music machine screaming like a logical lunatic."[3] Buchla, who played at several of these events in the mid-1960s, said nonchalantly, "I just showed up at the places with my instruments, took some acid, played some music."[4] Oddly enough, the instrument producing such explosive sounds was crafted from parts that came straight out of military technology.

This chapter begins with a section on how military technology from World War II and the Cold War, especially in electronics, spawned the synthesizer and other innovations in music technology. We then look at Kraftwerk, the German band that played an important role in bringing electronic music into the mainstream. Lastly, we analyze songs by electronic, new wave, and synthpop bands about Cold War issues.

MILITARY TECHNOLOGY BECOMES MUSIC TECHNOLOGY

War technology and music technology rarely crossed paths before the twentieth century. Since then, war history and music history, and their associated technological advancements, have been bound up with one another.[5] During World War I, for example, radio technology came into full bloom due to its use in military communications, which then impacted the commercial-music industry in profound ways. By the mid-1930s, most American homes had a radio. This section will show how instrument and recording technologies can often be traced back to innovations stemming from military research and development in the interwar years (1919–1939), World War II, and the Cold War.

A perfect example of the overlap between the military and music worlds is Lev Termen (1896–1993). A Russian physicist, engineer, and inventor, he had one foot in military surveillance technology and the other in musical instrument technology. In 1920, he invented the radio watchman, which according to Hans-Joachim Braun is an "alarm device which produces a whistle over headphones whenever anyone entered the area under surveillance."[6] It was essentially the first motion detector. In the same year, Termen built his first theremin, which he called an "etherphone." Both inventions operated on the same principle: they generate an electromagnetic field and respond audibly to intrusions into that field. One of the most intriguing musical instruments ever invented, the theremin is played without actually touching it. Musicians (thereminists) manipulate the electromagnetic field with their hands to control the pitch and volume. The field is then amplified and sent to a speaker that produces a haunting sound with a whistling, wailing timbre.[7] As Albert Glinsky eloquently writes, "This was electricity singing . . . pure and simple. No friction of physical soundmakers rubbing against each other. No mechanical energy. Just the free voice of electrons."[8] Termen amazed audiences when he played his theremin in the Soviet Union, Europe, and the United States. For the rest of his life, Termen's career continued down dual paths, military and musical; he worked on surveillance technology and covert listening devices ("bugs") for the KGB and performed around the world on his theremin.

He even played for Vladimir Lenin in the Kremlin in 1922. Dmitri Shostakovich was the first major composer to write a part for it in his score for the film *Odna* from 1931. In the 1950s, before the synthesizer boom of the sixties and seventies, soundtrack composers for science fiction films used the theremin to generate creepy space sounds, such as in *The Day the Earth Stood Still* (1951) and *It Came from Outer Space* (1953). The most well-known use of the theremin in popular music is the wailing theme in the chorus of "Good Vibrations" by the Beach Boys (1966), although it was played on a variant, the Electro-Theremin developed by Bob Whitsell and Paul Tanner. Another good example is during "Whole Lotta Love" in Led Zeppelin's concert film *The Song Remains the Same*. Jimmy Page can be seen crafting weird and wild sounds from his Sonic Wave theremin with the help of a Maestro echoplex tape-delay unit.[9]

Like Lev Termen, inventor Laurens Hammond (1895–1973) had parallel careers in music and military R & D. In the 1930s, he invented the Hammond organ and one of the first synthesizers, the Novachord. During World War II, he helped pioneer the technology of missile guidance. Also during the war, his organ factory completely stopped making organs and instead manufactured radio transmitters for use in airplanes. As soon as the war ended, he converted his factory back to manufacturing organs.[10] The Novachord never caught on with the public, but the Hammond organ, often paired with a Leslie speaker cabinet, was a ubiquitous instrument in 1960s and 1970s popular music. It can be heard prominently in songs such as Booker T. & the M.G.'s "Green Onions" (1962), Procol Harum's "A Whiter Shade of Pale" (1967), Sugarloaf's "Green-Eyed Lady" (1970), and Jon Lord's solo on Deep Purple's "Highway Star" (1972).

Military technology really started affecting music technology during the 1940s and 1950s. The vast scale of armament production in America during World War II and the building of planes, ships, tanks, bombs, trucks, and other munitions transformed countless industries. Even if one narrows the focus to just one factory, the scale of production is still mind-boggling. For example, from 1942 to 1945, the Willow Run factory in Michigan produced 8,685 B-24 Liberator heavy bombers. The assembly line was over a mile long and a quarter-mile wide. At peak production in March 1944, it churned out one of these massive bomber planes every sixty-three minutes.[11] As Sarah Jo Peterson writes, "The entire Willow Run complex consumed nearly 3 square miles. . . . More than 80,000 men and women . . . worked at Willow Run between January 1, 1942 and June 30, 1945. . . . Workers could park their cars in one of 15,300 parking spaces, punch in on one of 220 time clocks, and down their midshift meals in one of 44 eating places while listening to broadcasts out of the B-24 Studio, Willow Run's own radio station."[12]

When the war ended, a flood of scrap material poured out of the factories and into the marketplace, making the early years of the Cold War a golden age for the electronics enthusiast. Tony Turrell writes, "With the end of World War Two, the ready availability of electronic surplus war stock and industrial stock such as vacuum tubes, capacitors, and scrap metals were enabling an electronic hobbyist craze, especially in America."[13] Magazines like *Popular Electronics, Electronics World,* and *Electronics Illustrated* showed that anyone with a trusty soldering iron by their side could make their own ham radio, Geiger counter, miniature rocket, or even synthesizer. Robert Moog, one of the founding fathers of the synthesizer and an avid thereminist, did his first experiments on cheap vacuum tubes and capacitors he bought from war-surplus stores that were popping up in the 1950s near his house in Queens, New York.[14] Don Buchla, another founding father of the synthesizer, did the same in California. The synthesizers invented in the 1950s and 1960s were made from the electronic flotsam and jetsam of World War II. According to Nick Collins, Margaret Schedel, and Scott Wilson, "The electronics boom from the mid-twentieth century onward was sparked by intensive war research and fed by post-war economic activity; the availability of war surplus to hobbyists after the Second World War was also a factor in enabling many early electronic music studios and synthesizer experiments to get off the ground."[15]

The war machine gave birth to the ultimate music machine, the synthesizer.

When one builds a synthesizer from scratch in the basement, as Robert Moog did, a key ingredient is transistors. Transistors magnify an electric current and turn it on and off. In the late 1940s, William Shockley and other engineers at Bell Labs were the first to recognize transistors were good replacements for inefficient and cumbersome vacuum tubes. At first, the technology was disclosed exclusively to military R & D scientists and defense contractors. The US government came close to classifying the research and withholding it from the private sector because it had great potential military applications. For example, due to their small size, transistors were used in intercontinental ballistic missiles (ICBMs), like the Minuteman I, to make their guidance systems more efficient and precise. In 1951 and 1952, the technology was disclosed to entrepreneurs and manufacturers in the private sector. It went on to revolutionize electronics.[16] Transistors became the beating heart of the computer industry since they made integrated circuits (microchips) possible.

By the early 1960s, cheap transistors were plentiful, and they made the invention of the synthesizer possible. As Robert Moog excitedly said in an interview, "Now I can't tell you how important it was that I could buy a silicon junction transistor for 25 cents. *That's amazing*. . . . In 1957 this is $1000 for the transistors. And there they were [in 1964] for 25 cents."[17] The development of the transistor also led to the invention of the portable transistor radio in 1954, just in time for Elvis Presley and the rock and roll boom in the mid- to late 1950s.

Keyboard instruments besides the synthesizer were invented as a direct result of World War II technology: the vocoder, the Fender Rhodes, and the Mellotron. The vocoder will be covered in depth in the next section on Kraftwerk. Harold Rhodes made his first electric pianos from hydraulic aluminum pipes salvaged from the wings of a B-17 "Flying Fortress," the American bomber that dropped the most bombs in World War II.[18] The Fender Rhodes piano was one of the most popular keyboard instruments of the 1970s and featured on hit songs, like the Doors' "Riders on the Storm" (1971), Minnie Riperton's "Lovin' You" (1975, played by Stevie Wonder), Billy Joel's "Just the Way You Are" (1977), Styx's "Babe" (1979), and Chick Corea's albums with his jazz-fusion band, Return to Forever, such as *Light as a Feather* (1972). Keyboards that employed magnetic tape were invented. Magnetic tape was another World War II military invention. Tape is the primary sound-producing element in the Mellotron, heard in the Beatles's "Strawberry Fields Forever" (1967), the Moody Blues's "Nights in White Satin" (1969), and Led Zeppelin's "The Rain Song" (1973). Two other tape-driven keyboards were the Chamberlin, featured in the Moody Blues's "I'm Just a Singer (In a Rock and Roll Band)" (1972) and the Birotron, played by Yes's Rick Wakeman in the late 1970s.

In fact, magnetic tape came to be the World War II invention that had the greatest impact on twentieth-century music history. It was pioneered by the German-Austrian engineer Fritz Pfleumer in the 1930s. Adolf Hitler's speeches were recorded onto magnetic tape using Pfleumer's *Magnetophon*. The Nazis used it to store military intelligence and transmit classified information.[19] Shortly after the war, US Army intelligence officials, such as John Herbert Orr, Jack Mullin, and Richard H. Ranger, adopted the German technology and developed it for American commercial use.[20] This was part of Operation Paperclip, in which the United States brought over more than 1,600 Nazi military and intelligence officials, scientists, technicians, and engineers to divulge their expertise to American scientists. This was done in the early Cold War years to ensure Germany would not rise again to be a superpower and to prevent the Soviets from obtaining such a wealth of Nazi scientific knowledge. In the 1950s, French composer Pierre Schaeffer used magnetic tape to create *musique concrete,* one of the first major developments in electronic music. In the same decade, magnetic tape began to be used to record music in studios—reel-to-reel. This caused a revolution in the audio-recording industry and led naturally to video recording, producing another revolution in television and film. By the 1980s, compact cassette tapes vied with vinyl records as the primary format for commercial recordings. Compact discs would eclipse both in the 1990s. Not only tapes but tape players benefited from war technology. Research on the atomic bomb "Fat Man" circuitously gave birth over thirty years later to Sony's portable cassette player, the Walkman.[21]

The two world wars and the Cold War generated so much technological advancement in the twentieth century that few fields of human activity were unaffected. As seen in this section, music significantly changed, particularly the field of electronic music. The technology we've developed to cure diseases, connect globally, put a man on the moon, and invent new musical instruments is interwoven with the technology we've developed to build hydrogen bombs, which can kill millions of people in a minute. America, which currently spends more on national defense and military R & D than the next eight countries combined, is still coming to terms with the military-industrial complex and how it both benefits and jeopardizes our well-being as a nation. As David Hambling writes, "If you want to know where the technology of the future will come from and what the twenty-first century will look like, then the military labs of today offer some valuable clues."[22] For good and for ill, the military-industrial complex will continue to influence our lives and our music for the foreseeable future. This is especially so for popular music, which is generated by and enveloped in modern technology. The next section shows how the German band Kraftwerk became emblematic of modern technology in popular music and helped to bring electronic music into the mainstream.

KRAFTWERK: WERE THEY MEN OR MACHINES?

With their mastery of synthesizers and drum machines, the German band Kraftwerk played a huge role in shaping the soundscape of Western popular music from the late 1970s to the present day. Aspects of their music can be heard in pop, new wave, techno, funk, indie, electro, industrial, and hip hop. Pascal Bussy neatly summarizes their legacy when he writes, "Spawning legions of imitators and influencing music far beyond the experimental or electronic, Kraftwerk provided the natural link between the German avant-garde and pop music."[23] In assessing their wide-ranging influence, some music journalists have placed them in the same league as the Beatles.[24]

Ralf Hütter and Florian Schneider formed Kraftwerk in Düsseldorf in 1969 and 1970. They were schooled in the classics of the great composers but were most inspired during their formative years by the electronic experimentation of Karlheinz Stockhausen, who worked in nearby Köln. As students they studied his music at the Robert Schumann Hochschule in Düsseldorf.[25] They were also fans of American and British rock since the German popular music scene was uninspiring at the time. Lightweight *Schlager* music (sweet, sentimental love songs) dominated German popular music from the end of World War II into the 1950s and 1960s. By the late 1960s, German musicians like Hütter and Schneider were looking for a uniquely German style of popular music that was more modern, experimental, and edgy. They achieved this on their first three albums (*Kraftwerk, Kraftwerk 2, Ralf und Florian*) on which they played a wide array of traditional, electronic, and self-made instruments. These albums were almost entirely instrumental and relied heavily on studio experimentation with long passages of improvised soloing. Kraftwerk built a following in Germany, yet mainstream success eluded them. They released a more accessible album, *Autobahn,* in late 1974. In 1975, a three-minute edit of the twenty-two-minute title song became a surprise hit in several European countries and America. By that year, Wolfgang Flür and Karl Bartos had joined the group on electronic percussion, giving the band its classic four-member lineup. They toured France, England, and the United States in 1975 and were well received and critically acclaimed. They had everything going for them except two things: the Cold War was on and they were German.

In the decades after World War II, Americans and Britons tended to gloat excessively about the Allied victory over Germany and did their best to make sure the country would never become a superpower during the Cold War. British and American popular culture often stereotyped Germans as evil scientists (Peter Sellers's Dr. Strangelove character from the film of the same name), goose-stepping Neo-Nazis ("The Germans" episode of *Fawlty Towers*), or cold, detached automatons (the "Sprockets" sketches from *Saturday Night Live*).[26] These stereotypes plagued Kraftwerk as well. When Lester Bangs, an American rock critic known for his acerbic wit, interviewed the group in 1975 for *Creem* magazine, he slipped in several not-so-subtle Nazi references. For example, Bangs described Kraftwerk's fresh, modern sound and embrace of technology as "the final solution to the music problem."[27] This was obviously a play on the phrase "The Final Solution to the Jewish Question" ("Die Endlösung der Judenfrage"), the Nazi euphemism for the Holocaust. When the British music magazine *New Musical Express* reprinted Bangs's interview, the phrase was put right into the title: "Kraftwerk: The Final Solution to the Music Problem?"[28] To drive the point home, the *NME* editors manipulated a photograph of the band seated at a café table by superimposing the four of them in front of ranks of Nazi soldiers at a Nuremburg rally. As if that weren't enough, a large monument with a swastika was placed in the center of the photograph. Kraftwerk percussionist Karl Bartos remembered seeing it and thinking, "This was really mean and awful. We didn't [have] anything to do with it."[29] These allusions and images would follow Kraftwerk throughout their career. David Buckley sums up such stereotyping when he writes, "Political correctness was unheard of in 1975. Ralf, Florian, Karl and Wolfgang had been turned into Adolf, Hermann, Rudolf and Heinrich."[30] Although the band took it all in stride, attitudes such as this caused them to do few interviews, which in turn made them even more mysterious and prone to be stereotyped by anglophone audiences. In many ways, the legacy of World War II and the reality of the Cold War shaped the American and British reception of Kraftwerk's music, lyrics, album covers, videos, and concerts. They couldn't escape the stereotypes, so as we will see, they embraced and exaggerated them for a laugh.

Kraftwerk's engagement with Cold War issues can be traced back to their first album, *Kraftwerk*, recorded in the summer and early fall of 1970 and released that November. The beginning of the last song, "Vom Himmel Hoch," which can be translated variously as "From the Sky Above" or "From Heaven High," begins with a synthesizer imitating the hum of a bomber engine. Ralf Hütter created the sound on a Tubon, a rare, guitar-shaped synthesizer invented in 1966 by Joh Mustad AB, a Swedish manufacturer of electronic tube organs.[31] The sound pans between the left and right channels and slight pitch bends emulate the Doppler effect as the plane flies by. Later on, engine hums are heard at different pitches and volumes, as if multiple planes are flying by at different altitudes. Massive explosions interrupt the engine hums three times. Mark Prendergast suggests these sounds summon up images of the Allied bombs dropped on Germany in World War II and the bombs Germany dropped on Allied countries.[32] From 1968 to 1970, Jimi Hendrix had been coaxing similar sounds out of his Stratocaster in numerous renditions of "The Star-Spangled Banner." His guitar pyrotechnics, emulating "bombs bursting in air," were often interpreted as a commentary on the aerial bombing of civilians during the Vietnam War. (This is covered in chap. 7.) Hendrix died in September 1970. At the time Kraftwerk was working on their first album. It is impossible to know if Kraftwerk's bomb sounds were influenced by Hendrix, but it is probable since he had played concerts in Köln and Düsseldorf in January 1969, and his influence was felt all over Western Europe at the time.

As the 1970s progressed, Kraftwerk's music leaned more heavily toward the programmatic and representational. They created sounds to represent specific things, like motorways, comets, and robots. On their fifth album, *Radio-Activity* (1975), they found ways to paint aural pictures of a variety of objects related to radios, such as transistors, antennas, and news broadcasts. The song "Transistor" is played on a Minimoog, an instrument made possible by the invention of the transistor. The album is not only about activity on the radio but radioactivity itself. It has songs like "Geiger Counter," "Radioactivity," and "Uranium." The first song, "Geiger Counter," lasts but one minute and features just two sound elements. The first is a steady stream of pulses that slowly increase in tempo. The second, which appears thirty-one seconds in, is the sound of an actual Geiger counter; its beats come at the ear in short spasms of energy. The initial pulses become the steady sixteenth-note rhythm of the next song, "Radioactivity." As "Radioactivity" begins, a third series of pulsating beats is heard. In fact, it is the Morse code pattern for the word *radioactivity* (.-. .- -.. .. --- .- -.-. - .. ...- .. - -.--) played on an actual Morse code machine. The machine itself "sings" the lyrics of the song in Morse code while simultaneously mimicking the ticking of a Geiger counter.

In order to evoke strange and extraordinary phenomena, like radioactive decay, the band experimented with strange and extraordinary instruments. The eerie background texture of "Radioactivity" and "Uranium" was achieved by playing chords on a Vako Polyphonic Orchestron with a "vocal choir" optical disc. The Orchestron was a keyboard instrument that used optical discs imprinted with waveforms of various instruments (violin, French horn, flute, pipe organ, etc.) that a light beam read and turned into sound. It was a successor to the Mellotron, which used magnetic tapes instead of discs. The Orchestron gives the two songs an aural representation of the "strange glow" often associated with radioactivity. The vocal of "Uranium" was spoken through a Votrax speech synthesizer.[33] This was a keyboard that turned typed words into speech, aiding people with impaired vocal cords, such as Cambridge physicist Stephen Hawking. These songs portray radioactivity as a fascinating phenomenon, something to be celebrated and enjoyed for its own sake. This is quite a different perspective from songwriters discussed earlier in the book, who viewed radioactivity either as a great danger or a humorous metaphor for sexual attraction.

Like scientists in a laboratory experimenting with chemicals and test tubes, Kraftwerk saw themselves as scientists experimenting with sound. In their private studio in Düsseldorf, called Kling Klang, they fashioned their own sounds through trial and error. They altered their equipment, hired audio engineers to make custom-built components, combined different keyboard modules with patch cords, and employed devices outside the realm of what most musicians would call "musical instruments," like Geiger counters and Morse code machines. Today's synthesizers are digitized and often come with a preset menu of 500 sounds and 150 rhythms. The analog synthesizers from the 1960s and 1970s that Kraftwerk toyed with were quite different. They still had moving parts, like rotating tape reels or optical discs, a dizzying array of knobs and switches, and plugs and jacks based on 1940s-era telephone switchboard technology. Hütter said of Kraftwerk's compositional method, "We make compositions from everything. All is permitted, there is no working principle, there is no system. . . . We are playing the machines, the machines play us."[34] David Bowie recounts that one of the most interesting things in working with early synthesizers was "throwing the manuals away, so that we had no idea how the damn things worked. And it was the mistakes that they made that we found more interesting. . . . If you get the wrong circuits going you get all these crackles and farts coming out of those things . . . the most extraordinary sounds and different range of textures."[35]

While the band experimented with the Tubon, the Votrax, the Orchestron, the Minimoog, and many other electronic gizmos and gadgets, one of their favorites was the vocoder. Kraftwerk played a huge role in making it a popular electronic instrument in the late 1970s and early 1980s. Because of the ubiquity of the vocoder in this period, robots seemed to be taking over the airwaves. The robotic sound of the vocoder was embraced by disco and funk groups, like Lipps, Inc. ("Funkytown"), Midnight Star ("Freak-a-Zoid" and "No Parking (On the Dance Floor)"), and Earth, Wind & Fire ("Let's Groove"); early rappers Grandmaster Flash and the Furious Five ("Scorpio"); arena-rock groups Styx ("Mr. Roboto") and Electric Light Orchestra ("Sweet Talkin' Woman," "Mr. Blue Sky," and "The Diary of Horace Wimp"); and progressive rock groups Alan Parsons Project ("The Raven") and Pink Floyd ("Dogs" and "Sheep").

Robotic voice effects, whether they were generated by a vocoder or some other device, were all over the pop culture map in late 1970s and early 1980s. The first time the vocoder was heard in mainstream media was 1971, when Stanley Kubrick used a vocoderized version of the last movement of Beethoven's Ninth Symphony in his film *A Clockwork Orange*. The cylons in the *Battlestar Galactica* television series (1978–1980) spoke in robotic voices. Vocoders were heard in cartoons, such as in the *Transformers* theme ("robots in disguise") from the animated series that first aired in 1984. One heard robotic voices when playing video games like Berzerk ("Intruder alert! Intruder alert!") in the arcade or at home on the Atari. Kids learned how to speak and spell like a robot by playing Speak & Spell, which first appeared in 1978. In that year Kraftwerk released their seventh album, *The Man-Machine*, in which they turned themselves into robots. But before we explore this album, it is important to uncover the surprising backstory of the vocoder. It is another excellent example, like the theremin and synthesizer, of how military technology spawned musical technology.

While most people recognize the robotic sound of the vocoder from hearing it in popular songs, video games, films, and TV shows, few people know how large a role the device played in World War II and the Cold War. Before pop singers sang into it, Winston Churchill, Franklin D. Roosevelt, Dwight D. Eisenhower, and John F. Kennedy spoke into it. Before the vocoder turned Kraftwerk into robots, it did the same to world leaders. As Dave Tompkins writes, "During World War II, the vocoder reduced the voice to something cold and tactical . . . dehumanizing the larynx, so to speak, for some of man's more dehumanizing moments: Hiroshima, the Cuban Missile Crisis, Soviet gulags, Vietnam."[36] Let us take a brief look at the role of the vocoder in these four instances.

Bell Labs engineer Homer Dudley invented the vocoder, short for "voice coder" or "voice encoder," in the 1930s. In 1943 engineers at Bell Labs, with the help of British mathematician and cryptanalyst Alan Turing, built the SIGSALY system, which incorporated Dudley's vocoder. The purpose of SIGSALY was to scramble speech in order to make it unintelligible to eavesdroppers in Germany and Japan during World War II. According to Ralph Miller, a Bell Labs scientist who worked with Dudley, the vocoder was "based on the syllabic nature of speech. It tore the speech signal apart resulting in a number of very low frequency signals, and then the voice was reconstructed at the receiving end."[37] The development of SIGSALY was shrouded in secrecy and referred to as "Project X," "The X System," or "The Green Hornet." Although SIGSALY was cumbersome to use and took up an entire room, it was able to send high-level, securely encrypted messages between continents. The Germans and Japanese never cracked it. The US Army Signal Corps installed several SIGSALY consoles. One was housed in the newly built Pentagon with an extension to the White House for Presidents Roosevelt and Truman. For Winston Churchill, there was one in the basement of Selfridges department store with an extension to the Cabinet war rooms. A ship on the Pacific Ocean housed one for General Douglas McArthur to use. Others were installed around the globe in Paris, North Africa, Australia, Guam, and Hawaii. SIGSALY also played a role in the climactic event of World War II; Manhattan Project director Leslie Groves used it to discuss the logistics of the Hiroshima and Nagasaki bombings.[38] Roosevelt and Churchill, who conversed about the war on a regular basis, employed it most often.

After World War II, the vocoder played a role in the Cold War. Joseph Stalin heard of America's new toy and wanted one for himself. At the Marfino prison camp outside Moscow, he ordered prisoners who were audio engineers to build one. Russian writer Alexander Solzhenitsyn, who was also imprisoned at Marfino from 1947 to 1950, knew some of these prisoners and wrote of them in his novel *In the First Circle* as they frantically tried to develop the vocoder. Solzhenitsyn would go on to write *One Day in the Life of Ivan Denisovich* and *The Gulag Archipelago,* which revealed to the Western world the brutality of the Soviet gulag prison system. Stalin never did get his vocoder, but he did catch up to the United States in a more significant way when the Soviet Union detonated its first atomic bomb in 1949. His successor, Nikita Khrushchev, managed to plant atomic bombs in Cuba thirteen years later. Here the vocoder pops up again in Cold War history. John F. Kennedy used it during the Cuban Missile Crisis in October 1962. During the crisis, Kennedy sought the advice of British Prime Minister Harold MacMillan using the KY-9 voice scrambler, a successor to SIGSALY, which also used vocoder technology.[39] A few years later during the Vietnam War, the HY-2 vocoder (coupled with the KG-13 cryptographic machine) was used to send messages between the Pentagon and the US Navy stationed in the Gulf of Tonkin.[40] Outside of the Cold War, the vocoder and SIGSALY would go on to play a foundational role in the digital revolution. Ralph Miller said, "The X System had at times linked 5 continents, the first Internet."[41] Thus, long before the vocoder became a groovy musical instrument, it had lived a completely different life encrypting fateful messages during World War II and the Cold War and paving the way for the instantaneous global communication we enjoy today.

Like a Cold War spy going undercover, the vocoder turned itself into a musical instrument in 1950s and 1960s. One of the first people to use the vocoder for musical purposes was Werner Meyer-Eppler, a Belgian-born German physicist and experimental acoustician. His 1949 book, *Elektronische Klangerzeugung* (*Electronic Sound Generation*), laid the groundwork for German electronic music.[42] With his assistance, the *Studio für elektronische Musik des Nordwestdeutscher Rundfunk* (NWDR Electronic Music Studio) opened in Köln in 1953. Some of the first synthesizers were invented there, and the studio became a major center for avant-garde music. One of Meyer-Eppler's students was Karlheinz Stockhausen, who at this studio in 1955 and 1956 created *Gesang der Jünglinge*, the first internationally well-known piece of electronic music. Stockhausen greatly influenced Kraftwerk, and their private recording studio, Kling Klang, in Düsseldorf could well have been modeled on the NWDR Electronic Music Studio in Köln, which was just an hour drive away.

While several composers and musicians used the vocoder before Kraftwerk, they made the instrument known among other popular musicians. They played a large role in changing the vocoder's reputation from an encryption device into a musical one. The vocoder appears briefly in the song "Ananas Symphonie" from their third album, *Ralf und Florian* (1973), and then prominently on *Autobahn* (1974), *Trans-Europe Express* (1977), and especially *The Man-Machine* (1978). On this record, Kraftwerk used the vocoder in the most obvious way possible, to portray themselves as robots in the songs "The Robots" and "The Man-Machine." *The Man-Machine* played a part in shaping the sound of early 1980s American and British popular music with its synthesizers, drum machines, and vocoded vocals.

Were Kraftwerk or any of the other dozens of musicians who used the vocoder aware of its intriguing backstory and how it played a role in World War II and the Cold War? Most likely they were not. They were interested in the sounds they could get out of it. The robotic sound of the vocoder fit right in with the robotic image Kraftwerk began projecting around 1977. After 1975's *Radio-Activity*, the band put more emphasis on their appearance and how they were perceived by audiences. The songs they wrote about Cold War topics shifted away from objects and instruments (bombs, transistors, Geiger counters, uranium) to themselves. This shift can be seen vividly on their albums covers. On the first five albums, their faces appear prominently on the front cover of just one, *Ralf und Florian* (1973). On their next four albums, from 1977 to 1986, their faces are featured prominently on all. The four members all have similar facial expressions, haircuts, and clothes, emphasizing a uniform, collectivist image—a far cry from the individualistic image most American and British popular rock stars projected. They referred to themselves not as "musicians" or "artists" but as "musical workers." They worked regular hours at Kling Klang, as if they were blue-collar employees. Mark Duffett writes that the band "willingly became read in relation to Anglo-American *stereotypes* of the German people. The group itself played up that role, constantly toying with its image as a cold, disinterested and soulless neo-Teutonic collective."[43]

On *The Man-Machine*, Kraftwerk turned up the communist connotations. The inside sleeve of the album contains the phrase "Inspired by El Lissitzky." Lissitzky was a Russian artist who created procommunist propaganda posters in the 1920s and 1930s. As David Cunningham says, "*The Man-Machine*'s restricted colour scheme of black, white, grey, and red visually alludes to the 1919 poster *Beat the Whites with the Red Wedge*, a Bolshevik propaganda work produced during the Russian Civil War."[44] In the poster, the "red wedge" (symbolizing communism) infiltrates a white circle (symbolizing the Whites, a coalition of anticommunist forces). Kraftwerk's allusion to such artwork shows how intentional they were in projecting a collectivist mentality. David Buckley writes, "The dehumanisation inherent in the concept shadowed the rise of dehumanisation in reality, on a wide scale, as Nazi Germany, Communist Russia, and other totalitarian regimes of the mid-twentieth century either classified and/or treated certain ethnic groups as sub-human, disposable drones."[45]

Perhaps the members of Kraftwerk felt like "sub-human, disposable drones" because of the incessant stereotyping by British and American rock journalists. While the meaning and history behind these symbols were most likely beyond the ken of the average popular music fan, it is striking that such obvious communist allusions did not raise many eyebrows or provoke any censorship, especially in America.

Lyrics became more prominent in Kraftwerk's music in the late 1970s, and the subject matter in their songs often emphasized collectivism.[46] One would think the greater role given to vocals would make their music sound more "human," but their use of the vocoder and other devices often made them sound robotic. The first-person plural pronoun "we" dominates the groupthink lyrics of "Showroom Dummies" and "The Robots." Even when the first-person singular pronoun "I" appears in the lyrics, as in the line "ya tvoy sluga, ya tvoy rabotnik" ("I am your worker, I am your servant") in "The Robots," it still expresses subordination rather than assertiveness. The presence of Russian lyrics in "The Robots" adds even another level of stereotype. Like Germans, Westerners portrayed Russians during the Cold War as emotionless automatons or mindless, subservient sheep trapped in oppressive communism. Cyndy Hendershot states that "the Soviet Communist was typically stereotyped as an unemotional robot."[47] It's as if Kraftwerk wrapped up all the stereotypes associated with communists into a nice, neat package for Western consumers to feast on.

Yet Kraftwerk were quite clever with their image as communists. In fashioning themselves as a collective unit of carbon copies, they were hailed as original and unique. They spawned numerous synthpop, new wave, and new-romantic bands in the 1980s, who replicated aspects of their drum patterns, synthesizer sounds, and image. Proving they were fine capitalists, Kraftwerk earned millions from record sales and licensing fees as musicians from a wide variety of musical styles sampled their beats. Perhaps the business suits they wore on their album covers and in their concerts weren't just for show.

In the 1990s and 2000s, Kraftwerk became outspoken antinuke proponents. On their 1991 album, *The Mix,* a collection of their hits with new arrangements, they refashioned "Radioactivity" into an explicitly antinuke song. The original version from 1975 centered on the wordplay between "radioactivity" and "radio activity," or listening to music on a radio. It offered no critique of nuclear energy or weapons and simply acknowledged the existence of radioactivity as a natural phenomenon. The 1991 version makes no allusion to radios, focusing solely on the negative aspects of radioactivity. The song begins by naming Chernobyl, Harrisburg, Sellafield, and Hiroshima, four locations where nuclear disasters occurred. The Morse code for "SOS," the universally known distress signal, is added to the song, alluding to the danger inherent in radioactivity. Most noticeably, the recurring hook "radioactivity" has been changed to "stop radioactivity." The band performed the song at the Stop Sellafield concert organized by Greenpeace on June 19, 1992, in Manchester, England. In 2005, on their live CD and DVD *Maximum-Minimum,* Kraftwerk refashioned the song again. This version included a spoken, vocoded introduction about the dangers a proposed Sellafield 2 nuclear power plant would cause. In 2012, Kraftwerk performed yet another new version of "Radioactivity" for the No Nukes 2012 concert held in Tokyo to commemorate the Fukushima nuclear power plant disaster caused by the March 2011 tsunami. They sang portions in Japanese and added Fukushima to the list of nuclear disaster sites.

With Kraftwerk, we see a band that played synthesizers crafted from World War II and Cold War military technology, used Cold War devices as musical instruments, wrote songs about Cold War devices, parodied Western stereotypes of communists, and even fashioned their bodies into those communist stereotypes. They were the ultimate Cold War music machine.

NEW WAVE AND SYNTHPOP

Synthesizers were all over the popular music map in the 1970s. British progressive rock bands were especially enamored by them. Keith Emerson of Emerson Lake & Palmer, Rick Wakeman of Yes, and Tony Banks of Genesis made them as important an instrument in rock music as the guitar, bass, or drums. Yet, they did not usurp the other essential rock instruments. Kraftwerk and other electronic bands of the 1970s that used only synthesizers were on the fringe. By the late 1970s and early 1980s, thanks in part to Kraftwerk's influence, the synthesizer became the usurper. With the advent of new wave and synthpop, synthesizers often replaced the lead guitar, rhythm guitar, bass, drums, and strings, creating a drastic shift in popular music instrumentation. While watching MTV in the early 1980s, one saw and heard plenty of guitars and drums, but one also saw and heard the Sequential Circuits Prophet-5, the Roland Jupiter-8, the Oberheim OB-X, the Yamaha DX7, the Minimoog, the Linn LM-1 drum machine, and the Roland TR-808 drum machine. "Don't You Want Me" by the Human League (1982) exemplified this shift in instrumentation. It was the first *Billboard* number one song consisting exclusively of vocals, synthesizers, and a drum machine.

New wave was one of the dominant styles of mainstream popular music during the years 1979–1985, when Cold War tension was peaking. One reason why new wave was an apt medium to convey Cold War fears was its quality of nervousness, which Theo Cateforis devotes a whole chapter to in his book, *Are We Not New Wave?*[48] He discusses how the members of Devo and David Byrne of the Talking Heads projected a sense of unease with themselves and modern society and with the frightening pace of technology. Cateforis links this unease to the Cold War, saying nervousness is "symptomatic of the underlying tensions in the post-World War II suburbs, not only as a reflection of the pressures of modern living but as a measure of the pervasive anxiety linked with Cold War panic and societal paranoia."[49] Dozens of songs and album titles not just from new wave but from all genres of popular music in the early 1980s projected nervousness. For instance, songs and albums about pressure include "Pressure" by Billy Joel (1982 song), "Under Pressure" by Queen and David Bowie (1981 song), *Grace under Pressure* by Rush (1984 album), "Got Me Under Pressure" by ZZ Top (1983 song), *Pressure Points* by Anne Clark (1985 album), and "Too Much Pressure" by the Selecter (1980 song and album).

New wave overlapped with other categories of rock in the early 1980s, such as postpunk, synthpop, power pop, and the new romantics. The bands most closely associated with these interrelated styles are Blondie, the Cars, the Knack, Gary Numan, Talking Heads, the B-52's, the Pretenders, the Fixx, the Human League, Eurhythmics, Soft Cell, and Devo. Since several new wave bands evolved out of the punk scenes of the 1970s—Blondie, the Police, the Pretenders, Talking Heads, Billy Idol, Adam Ant—one might expect the same large number of songs about the Cold War; yet there are relatively few well-known new wave songs about the subject. A major reason for this is many of these bands left behind the abrasive protest songs and political ideology of punk.[50] Their lyrics reflected the anxiety and overall feeling of doom the arms race produced in the 1980s but did not address it nearly as specifically as the punk bands did. Yet what is missing in

Table 9.1 New Wave Songs about Cold War Issues

Song	Songwriter
"Eighth Day"	Hazel O'Connor
"Breathing" and "Army Dreamers"	Kate Bush
"Enola Gay"	Andy McCluskey
"Stand or Fall" and "Red Skies"	The Fixx
"So Afraid of the Russians"	Tom Lyon
"Poem for a Nuclear Romance"	Anne Clark
"99 Luftballons" / "99 Red Balloons"	Jörn-Uwe Fahrenkrog-Petersen, Carlo Karges, and Kevin McAlea
"Dancing with Tears in My Eyes"	Ultravox
"People Are People"	Martin Gore
"Peace in Our Time"	Elvis Costello
"P.O.E."	Adam Ant and Marco Pirroni
"Let's Go All the Way"	Gary Cooper

the lyrics is present in the music. The textures and sounds musicians coaxed out of their synthesizers were often dark, thick, and heavy. Speaking of the morose Moog sounds created by Wendy Carlos for *A Clockwork Orange* (1971), Simon Reynolds says, "There was a . . . linkage made there between those sounds and the idea of a cold future, a bleak future, and that . . . sunk quite deeply into the psyche of a lot of young musicians at that time."[51] This idea of a bleak future was articulated well by Cy Curnin, lead singer and songwriter of the Fixx in an interview with rock radio host Redbeard. Curnin said of the band's song "Stand or Fall,"

> The news going on in England [was about the government] bringing in the Trident missiles and treating Germany like a theatre for a small controllable nuclear war. This is how they were talking. . . . The term "Eurotheatre" came up and we felt like Euro-puppets. A sense of impotence was there because you couldn't really control it, and it was almost like some antichrist growing up and overtaking your imagination. All of a sudden, young kids weren't thinking about what they would be doing in their sixties. They'd be thinking about what they were going to do with the last six months of their lives. It became a sense of despair because your horizon, when you're young, is normally broad, and political conversations like "Eurotheatre" and "limited warfare" is really disturbing and crushing to young people's minds. It was written in that sort of environment.[52]

Table 9.1 shows some of the new wave songs about the Cold War. Besides the female folk singers discussed in chapter 2, new wave is the only style of popular

Performer	Album/Single	Year
Hazel O'Connor	*Breaking Glass*	1980
Kate Bush	*Never for Ever*	1980
Orchestral Manoeuvres in the Dark	*Organisation*	1980
The Fixx	*Shuttered Rooms*	1982
Made for TV	single	1983
Anne Clark	*Changing Places*	1983
Nena	*Nena, 99 Luftballons*	1983–1984
Ultravox	*Lament*	1984
Depeche Mode	*Some Great Reward*	1984
Elvis Costello and the Attractions	*Goodbye Cruel World*	1984
Adam Ant	*Vive le Rock*	1985
Sly Fox	*Let's Go All the Way*	1985

music where we've found a strong feminist perspective on nuclear war. Three of the songwriters are female and one song is sung by a female.

In "Eighth Day," Hazel O'Connor casts her lyrics into the form of a creation narrative that mirrors the first chapter of Genesis. This song is also similar in construction to Zager & Evans's number one hit from 1969, "In the Year 2525 (Exordium & Terminus)," yet the timeline is greatly compressed from thousands of years to eight days. Instead of God creating the world, it is man who is the creator, and he fashions a world full of weapons. He starts out with poison gas on the second day, and by the fifth, he's created rockets and submarines. On the sixth day he creates robots and computers to work as slaves. He rests on the seventh day, leaving the machines in charge of all the technology and weapons. The music builds up in intensity to the seventh day but then the instruments drop out—except for lonely chords on a synthesizer that create a sense of eerie foreboding. There is one more day, and man saw that it was not good. On the eighth day, the machines wage nuclear war on man and destroy all life on earth.

While O'Connor's song presents a global scenario in which nuclear weapons affect all of humankind, three songs from the table show how they affect two people in an intimate relationship. Anne Clark speaks the lyrics to "Poem for a Nuclear Romance" over arpeggios on synthesizer, a simple drum machine rhythm, and male background singers. The lyrics disregard the outside world, focusing on the loss of two lovers' youth, beauty, and dreams. Radiation burns render their bodies incapable of physical contact or even any notion of closeness. "Dancing with Tears in My Eyes" by Ultravox begins with a man driving home from work. On the way he hears on the wireless that a nuclear catastrophe has occurred. He makes it home to his wife. They share a drink, make love, and wait for the inevitable. Their only comfort is they can die together rather than alone. The setting for both of these songs is a bedroom, traditionally a place of intimacy, comfort, and security. The invasion of toxic radiation into such a cherished space is unnerving. The setting of the third song is even more intimate than the other two. In "Breathing," Kate Bush writes about nuclear war from the point of view of a baby still in the womb. The fetus is conscious of the destruction outside and is breathing in the same radioactive fallout as her mother. This is reflected in the line, "Chips of plutonium are twinkling in every lung." Halfway through the song, a stark, scientific voice states facts about the flash of a nuclear explosion. The scientist's monotonous voice contrasts greatly with the expressiveness of Bush's singing and John Giblin's fretless bass guitar lines. Of her inspiration for political songs, Bush says, "My motivations are not social or political. It's an emotional motivation, where I'm so moved by something that's happening that I have to write. . . . nuclear war is a political thing, but it's also incredibly emotional."[53]

Continuing the theme of relationships, or lack thereof, two songs reflect the cultural divide between Westerners and Russians. The Washington, DC, band Made for TV released "So Afraid of the Russians" in 1983. John Cale, famous for creating the Velvet Underground with Lou Reed and for his collaborations with a number of experimental musicians, produced the song. The protagonist is enmeshed in the conundrum of whether the US government should spend more money on social security or national security. He would like to see more funds allocated for hungry children, disease research, crumbling cities, the ecology, college education, the arts, space exploration, and job growth. On the other hand, there are the Russians. They have ships, missiles, tanks, and "spies everywhere." Tom Lyon speaks the lyrics, and his voice has been treated with a filter stripping it of its high and low frequencies. This gives it a nervous, yet somewhat emotionless, tone. The instrumental backing on the verses features a two-measure riff with a shuffling rhythm in 4/4 time. On the last beat of every other measure, the band cuts out, except for the drummer, who plays a triplet on a timbale. Thus, the music continuously starts and stops, as if it is tripping on its own shoelaces. When Lyon speaks of the Russian ships, missiles, tanks, and spies, the band strips the music down to just chords on beats one and four, sounding much like heart palpitations. The song oozes with the nervousness Theo Cateforis identifies as a characteristic of new wave music.

Included with the single of "So Afraid of the Russians" came a promotional insert stating that the song addressed "the state's apparent inability to reconcile traditional social service spending with a perceived need to re-establish a credible military deterrent to potential Soviet aggression within the constraints posed by a post-Keynesian fiscal and monetary policy." Here, tucked inside the sleeve of an obscure new wave song, is a cogent summary of the political, military, and economic climate of the Cold War in early 1980s America.

Depeche Mode's "People Are People" (1984) also encapsulates the suspicion between the superpowers. The lyrics question why peoples of different colors and creeds should fear and hate each other when we all share a common humanity. The song appeals to common decency and understanding as a solution to the mistrust; people shouldn't feel enmity for those they haven't even met. Yet the clamorous music accompanying the lyrics reflects reality; hatred, fear, and violence are as much a part of the human character as graciousness and understanding. They recorded the song at Hansa Tonstudio in Berlin, which was situated five hundred yards from the Wall. They recorded in a city that felt acutely the division between peoples. This is the same studio David Bowie recorded "Heroes" in 1977 and U2 would later record "One" in 1990 and1991, both songs with similar themes to "People Are People."

The most distinctive feature of the song is its sampled metallic sounds. Ned Raggett writes that the song sounds "like a factory coming to life . . . overstuffed with clatter and clangs."[54] The song assaults the ear with the din of metal on metal. It resonates with the Italian Futurist Luigi Russolo and his 1913 book, *The Art of Noises*, explored more fully in chapter 7. Russolo stressed that the musical arts should move beyond sweet, harmonious sounds and embrace what he called "noise-sounds," the sounds of the industrial age and warfare. While Depeche Mode may not have known much about Russolo, they were inspired by the German industrial band Einstürzende Neubauten ("Collapsing New Buildings"), who turned Russolo's ideas into sonic reality. Einstürzende Neubauten made music by generating earsplitting feedback with guitars, screaming into microphones, banging on metal sheets with hammers and pipes, breaking up concrete with jackhammers, and wielding chain saws and power drills. "People Are People" songwriter, Martin Gore, saw the band live in London and said, "The power and excitement of it was brilliant!"[55]

While Jimi Hendrix and other electric guitarists of the 1960s and 1970s conjured up the noises of industry and war using electric guitars, Depeche Mode used synthesizers and samplers. Sampling was new to mainstream popular music in this period. As discussed previously in this chapter, early synthesizers easily approximated the sounds of warfare. The samplers of the early 1980s took this further by allowing musicians to manipulate actual found sounds (*musique concrete*), not just approximate them. In 1980, Kate Bush used a Fairlight CMI to sample the sound of a rifle being cocked in "Army Dreamers."[56] Filling the role of handclaps or finger snaps, the sound is used as a percussive element throughout the song, bolstering its theme of the trials of being a soldier. With "People Are

People," Depeche Mode created a song filled with industrial and warlike sounds. They used an Emulator II and a Synclavier, two other sampling keyboards besides the Fairlight CMI available in the early 1980s.[57] Producer Gareth Jones says the band created some of the sounds with "drumsticks and hammers beating steel plates, pipes and various other metal objects, as recorded at a disused train station in Shoreditch, East London, with a cassette machine and assorted mics. . . . We could sample almost [any] sound and turn it into a rhythm or melody, or even use the intrinsic rhythm within a sound."[58]

The lyrics of the song make no mention of particular nations or groups of people, but the music video, directed by Clive Richardson, has much to do with World War II and the Cold War. The video places the lyrics into the context of the confrontation between superpowers. It was filmed in the World War II battleship HMS Belfast. Jones says, "In the 'People are People' video that was shot on HMS Belfast, we felt that banging metal was a very brutal and intense noise, and so a lot of that was built into the song."[59] The band turns the warship itself into an instrument by ringing its bells, turning its wheels, and banging on it with metal pipes. Interspersed and crossfaded with scenes of the band members "playing" various parts of the ship is black-and-white footage of battleships at sea, sailors working on ships, deck canons blasting, Soviet soldiers marching in Red Square, and paratroopers jumping from planes. There are also short clips of vinyl records being pressed in a factory, making the connection (addressed in the first section of this chapter) between the industry of war and the industry of music production. Like the heavy metal and punk bands discussed in the previous chapters, Depeche Mode used abrasive, warlike music to accompany lyrics about peace and understanding.

Other synthpop groups turned this paradigm on its head by using bright keyboard sounds and catchy dance rhythms to accompany dark lyrics. One example of this is "Enola Gay" by Orchestral Manoeuvres in the Dark, a British synthpop band founded by Paul Humphreys and Andy McCluskey. The song addresses the atomic bombing of Hiroshima but has a synthesizer melody that can only be described as bouncy and jolly. It was played on a Korg Micro-Preset, which according to Paul Humphreys was "bought from a mail order catalogue—the cheapest one you could buy."[60] Rarely has there been a song about war that has such a divergence between its music and its lyrics. As Andy McCluskey explains, "I was always uneasy about the fact that 'Enola Gay' was a bright, perky pop song about a nuclear holocaust, but it was insanely catchy. It referenced the fact that the plane was named after the pilot's mother, and the bomb was codenamed 'little boy'—while also asking whether a mother would be proud of what her son was doing. I was ambivalent about this: would you fly a plane to kill all those people because you thought you were going to save even more?"[61]

McCluskey explains further,

> I wasn't interested in the politics of it or the morals of it. It isn't an anti-nuclear song, nor is it a celebration. . . . I was fascinated that this aeroplane had the capability to do that and I was also fascinated that the guy [Brigadier General Paul Tibbets] could name the aeroplane after his mother and then go and do that!. . . . My classic defence when people said, "How can you write such a twee song about something so disgusting?" was always, "Well, if you think that's perverse, what about naming a bomber plane after your mother in the first place!"[62]

The song also shows how ignorant some people were at the time about one of the most significant events of the twentieth century. The problem with "Enola Gay" was that it had the word *gay* in it. Andy McCluskey said, "Many people simply don't know what it's actually about. Some even thought it was a coded message that we were gay."[63] The popular BBC1 children's program *Swap Shop* even banned the song. The producers thought it might corrupt young listeners simply because the title had the word *gay* in it.[64]

The final song we will look at in this chapter is "99 Luftballons/99 Red Balloons" by Nena from 1984. Rarely does a German singer or band, or a song sung in German, reach the upper echelons of the US *Billboard* singles chart. Despite this, the German language version reached number two on the *Billboard* chart on March 3, 1984. The English version of the song ("99 Red Balloons") was also a hit, reaching number one on the British singles chart. It was a hit in many European countries, as well as Canada, Australia, and Japan. Yes, the synthesizer riff wears out its welcome halfway through the song and labels it as a product of the 1980s, like a gelatin mold epitomizes a 1950s cookbook. Nevertheless, the song is a pop music gem. If any one song is emblematic of the Cold War in the 1980s, it is surely this one.

Nena was a five-member band that formed in West Berlin in 1981. The group named itself after their female lead singer's childhood nickname, Nena. Her real name is Gabriele Susanne Kerner. Carlo Karges, the guitarist for Nena, wrote the lyrics for "99 Luftballons." He based them on an experience he had at a Rolling Stones concert in June 1982 in West Berlin. Helium balloons were released during the show, and he imagined what might happen if East Berliners saw them floating over the Berlin Wall.[65] The lyrics tell a compelling story in five verses. The first invites the listener to hear a tale about 99 balloons and how something like a protracted world war could be caused by something as innocuous as balloons. The next three verses describe the bulk of the story. Someone sees the balloons in the sky, thinks they are UFOs, and notifies a general. The general assumes that, whatever they are, they are hostile and sends out 99 jet fighters. The pilots see that they are only balloons, but imagining they are war heroes on an important mission, they decide to shoot down the balloons. Ninety-nine war ministers take this as an opportunity to declare war. A world war ensues. The war lasts 99 years and results in total devastation on all sides. In the end, there are no victors, no war ministers, and no jet fighters. In the final verse, the singer walks among the ruins, sees a balloon, picks it up, and lets it fly away. Regarding the swift escalation from balloons to world war the lyrics describe, Karges said in 1984, "Paranoia determines our lives. Fear of each other brings us to deal more cruelly with each other than is necessary."[66] Such escalation from balloons to ballistics is not as farfetched as one might imagine. Numerous false alarms and accidents ("bugs in the software") with atomic bombs during the Cold War could have resulted in escalation to nuclear war. In documents obtained through the Freedom of Information Act while researching his book *Command and Control,* Eric Schlosser found hundreds of accidents involving nuclear weapons. He writes, "The fallibility of human beings guarantees that no technological system will ever be infallible."[67]

Nena asked Irish keyboardist and songwriter Kevin McAlea to write English lyrics to the song, which he did. McAlea's lyrics are not a direct translation of the German lyrics. They are a slightly different retelling of the story. Kevin McAlea says, "I took the tape and first thing I did was record my own backtrack. I asked a German speaking friend what the general gist was and wrote the English version. I didn't really pay much attention to the meaning of the song as it had to sound good as a lyric in its own right. . . . I was more interested in the sound the lyrics were making than anything else."[68]

The German and English lyrics are shown below.

German lyrics to "99 Luftballons" by Carlo Karges

Verse 1:
Hast du etwas Zeit für mich
Dann singe ich ein Lied für dich
Von 99 Luftballons
Auf ihrem Weg zum Horizont
Denkst du vielleicht g'rad an mich
Dann singe ich ein Lied für dich
Von 99 Luftballons
Und dass sowas von sowas kommt

Verse 2:
99 Luftballons
Auf ihrem Weg zum Horizont
Hielt man für UFOs aus dem All
Darum schickte ein General
'ne Fliegerstaffel hinterher
Alarm zu geben, wenn's so wär

Dabei war'n dort am Horizont
Nur 99 Luftballons

Verse 3: 99 Düsenflieger
Jeder war ein großer Krieger
Hielten sich für Captain Kirk
Das gab ein großes Feuerwerk
Die Nachbarn haben nichts gerafft
Und fühlten sich gleich angemacht
Dabei schoss man am Horizont
Auf 99 Luftballons

Verse 4: 99 Kriegsminister
Streichholz und Benzinkanister
Hielten sich für schlaue Leute
Witterten schon fette Beute
Riefen Krieg und wollten Macht
Mann, wer hätte das gedacht
Dass es einmal soweit kommt
Wegen 99 Luftballons

Verse 5: 99 Jahre Krieg
Ließen keinen Platz für Sieger
Kriegsminister gibt's nicht mehr
Und auch keine Düsenflieger
Heute zieh' ich meine Runden
Seh' die Welt in Trümmern liegen
Hab' 'nen Luftballon gefunden
Denk' an dich und lass' ihn fliegen

English lyrics to "99 Red Balloons" by Kevin McAlea.

Verse 1: You and I in a little toy shop
Buy a bag of balloons with the money we've got
Set them free at the break of dawn
'Til one by one, they were gone
Back at base, bugs in the software
Flash the message, "Something's out there"
Floating in the summer sky
99 red balloons go by

Verse 2: 99 red balloons
Floating in the summer sky

Panic bells, it's red alert
There's something here from somewhere else
The war machine springs to life
Opens up one eager eye
Focusing it on the sky
99 red balloons go by

Verse 3: 99 Decision Street
99 ministers meet
To worry, worry, super-scurry
Call the troops out in a hurry
This is what we've waited for
This is it boys, this is war
The president is on the line
As 99 red balloons go by

Verse 4: 99 knights of the air
Ride super high-tech jet fighters
Everyone's a superhero
Everyone's a Captain Kirk
With orders to identify
To clarify and classify
Scramble in the summer sky
99 red balloons go by

Verse 5: 99 dreams I have had
In every one a red balloon
It's all over and I'm standing pretty
In this dust that was a city
If I could find a souvenir
Just to prove the world was here
And here is a red balloon
I think of you, and let it go

99 Red Balloons (99 Luftballons)
Music by Joern Uwe Fahrenkrog-Peterson
Original Words by Carlo Karges
English Lyrics by Kevin McAlea

Besides the lyrics, the song's most distinctive feature is the two keyboard riffs played on an Oberheim OB-X synthesizer. Yet what makes the song a classic is how its ABA form complements and frames the story in the lyrics. In the first and last verses (the A sections), the musical accompaniment has no rhythm and no riff, just a simple progression in E major of the chords E major, F-sharp minor seventh, A major, and B major. The chords in the first verse prepare the listener for the story; the chords in the last verse allow the listener to reflect on the aftermath. The two synthesizer riffs and syncopated dance rhythms in the middle three verses (the B section) provide the "action music" for the escalation to world war. This ABA structure is simple and has been used countless times in popular, jazz and classical music but is still very effective as a vehicle to tell a "before and after" story such as this, about how children's balloons drifting innocently in the sky could cause World War III.

CONCLUSION

As we quoted Trevor Pinch and Frank Trocco at the beginning of this chapter, "Explosions, sirens, and rockets were some of the easiest sounds to create on the early synthesizers."[69] With a little noodling around on a Minimoog, one can generate the hum of a bomber plane, the whistling descent of an atomic bomb, and a massive explosion. Any kid can do it. Isn't it eerie that instruments constructed from the electronic residue of World War II and the Cold War can so easily reproduce the sounds of war? We've grown accustomed to such sounds because the twentieth century produced the most bloodshed in human history. If we have not heard the sounds of war in real life, we are sure to hear them in our news programs, films, TV shows, music, and video games. Even when we are at peace, military expenditures are a permanent, ever-increasing component of our modern economy.[70] Since the major world powers spent so much on military R & D in the twentieth century, many everyday consumer goods that we use were, and still are, made by companies that have close connections with the military. The US economy is so enmeshed in the war industry that cuts in defense spending would affect millions of people who depend on those jobs for their livelihood. Nick Turse, in his book *The Complex*, writes, "The high-level of military-civilian interpenetration in a heavily consumer-driven society means that almost every American (aside, perhaps, for a few determined anarcho-primitivists) is, at least passively, supporting the [military-industrial complex] every time he or she shops for groceries, sends a package, drives a car, or watches TV."[71]

Hans-Joachim Braun rightly cautions us not to take this thinking too far: "This does not mean that military interests were lurking behind all this."[72] Technology developed through military R & D has benefited humankind in countless ways too, making our lives easier, longer, and safer. Yet the "military-civilian interpenetration" is disquieting. Open up the console of a Minimoog, one of the most well-known synthesizers used in popular music, and in the jumble of transistors, circuits, and other gizmos, you will see the technology of World War II and the Cold War. Warfare is the ghost in the machine.

NOTES

1. Trevor Pinch and Frank Trocco, *Analog Days: The Invention and Impact of the Moog Synthesizer,* foreword by Robert Moog (Cambridge, MA: Harvard University Press, 2002), 101.

2. Charles Perry, *The Haight-Ashbury: A History* (New York: Random House/ Rolling Stone, 1984), 94.

3. Tom Wolfe, *The Electric Kool-Aid Acid Test* (New York: Farrar, Straus and Giroux, 1968), 393.

4. Don Buchla, quoted in *The San Francisco Tape Music Center: 1960s Counterculture and the Avant-garde,* ed. David W. Bernstein (Berkeley, CA: University of California Press, 2008), 173.

5. Hans-Joachim Braun, "Introduction: Technology and the Production and Reproduction of Music in the 20th Century," in *Music and Technology in the Twentieth Century,* ed. Hans-Joachim Braun (Baltimore: The Johns Hopkins University Press, 2002), 9–10, 17–18.

6. Hans-Joachim Braun, "'Strange Bedfellows': The Relationship between Music Technology and Military Technology in the First Half of the Twentieth Century," in *Global Village—Global Brain—Global Music, KlangArt–Kongreß 1999,* ed. Bernd Enders and Joachim Stange-Elbe (Osnabrück: Electronic Publishing Osnabrück, 2003), 138.

7. Albert Glinsky, *Theremin: Ether Music and Espionage* (Urbana: University of Illinois Press, 2000), 23–24.

8. Ibid., 24.

9. *Led Zeppelin: The Song Remains the Same* (1976), directed by Peter Clifton and Joe Massot, produced by Peter Grant (Two-disc Special Edition. Warner Bros. 72654, 2007), 1:56:33–1:58:28.

10. Stuyvesant Barry, "Chapter XVII—After World War II," from *Hammond as in Organ: The Laurens Hammond Story.* Unpublished manuscript, 1974, http://thehammondorganstory.com/chapterxvii.asp.

11. Sarah Jo Peterson, *Planning the Home Front: Building Bombers and Communities at Willow Run* (Chicago: University of Chicago Press, 2013), xiv, 235.

12. Ibid., 236–237.

13. Tony Turrell, "The History & Impact of the Synthesizer: The Real Symbol of the Western Popular Music Revolution?," in *Popscript: Graduate Research in Popular Music Studies,* ed. Simone Krüger and Ron Moy (Raleigh, NC: Lulu, 2014), 35.

14. Pinch and Trocco, *Analog Days*, 13.

15. Nick Collins, Margaret Schedel, and Scott Wilson, *Electronic Music* (New York: Cambridge University Press, 2013), 65.

16. Gerald W. Brock, *The Second Information Revolution* (Cambridge, MA: Harvard University Press, 2003), 83–84; Steven Klepper, *Experimental Capitalism: The Nanoeconomics of American High-Tech Industries* (Princeton, NJ: Princeton University Press, 2016), 164–169.

17. Trevor Pinch and Frank Trocco, "The Social Construction of the Early Electronic Music Synthesizer," in *Music and Technology in the Twentieth Century*, ed. Hans-Joachim Braun (Baltimore: The Johns Hopkins University Press, 2002), 69.

18. Freddie "Freddan" Adlers, "Fender Rhodes: The Piano That Changed the History of Music," Fenderrhodes.com, http://www.fenderrhodes.com/history/narrative.html.

19. Aaron Foisi Nmungwun, *Video Recording Technology: Its Impact on Media and Home Entertainment* (Hillsdale, NJ: Erlbaum, 1989), 58–65.

20. David L. Morton, "'The Rusty Ribbon': John Herbert Orr and the Making of the Magnetic Recording Industry, 1945–1960," *Business History Review* 67, no. 4 (Winter 1993): 589–622.

21. David Hambling, *Weapons Grade: How Modern Warfare Gave Birth to Our High-Tech World* (New York: Carroll and Graf, 2005), 135–136.

22. Ibid., 1–2.

23. Pascal Bussy, *Kraftwerk: Man, Machine and Music*, 3rd ed. (London: SAF, 2005), 17–18.

24. Jude Rogers, "Why Kraftwerk Are Still the World's Most Influential Band," *Guardian*, January 27, 2013, https://www.theguardian.com/music/2013/jan/27/kraftwerk-most-influential-electronic-band-tate.

25. Karl Bartos, from *Kraftwerk and the Electronic Revolution* (Sexy Intellectual SIDVD541, 2008, DVD), 26:57–27:20.

26. In fact, the theme song for the "Sprockets" sketches was a sped-up and looped version of Kraftwerk's 1986 song "Electric Café."

27. Lester Bangs, "Kraftwerkfeature: Or How I Learned to Stop Worrying & Love the Balm," *Creem*, September 1975, 30, reprinted in *Psychotic Reactions and Carburetor Dung*, ed. Greil Marcus (New York: Knopf, 1987), 159.

28. Lester Bangs, "Kraftwerk: The Final Solution to the Music Problem?" *New Musical Express*, September 6, 1975, 20–21.

29. Karl Bartos, from "I Was a Robot" interview included with *Kraftwerk and the Electronic Revolution* (Sexy Intellectual SIDVD541, 2008, DVD), 3:00–3:17.

30. David Buckley, *Kraftwerk Publikation*, in collaboration with Nigel Forrest, foreword by Karl Bartos (New York: Overlook Omnibus, 2015), 74.

31. Kraftwerk can be seen playing "Von Himmel Hoch" (Ralf Hütter is playing the Tubon) at the beginning of their set from a 1970 concert in Soest, Germany, shown on the German television rock program *Rockpalast*, https://www.youtube.com

/watch?v=vNoFHdlMrtI. (A screen title names the song "Stratovarius," but this is an error.)

32. Mark Prendergast, from *Kraftwerk and the Electronic Revolution* (Sexy Intellectual SIDVD541, 2008, DVD), 56:30–58:30.

33. Dave Tompkins, *How to Wreck a Nice Beach: The Vocoder from World War II to Hip-Hop: The Machine Speaks* (Brooklyn, NY: Stop Smiling, 2010), 185–186; Carsten Brocker, "Kraftwerk: Technology and Composition," in *Kraftwerk: Music Non-Stop*, ed. Sean Albiez and David Pattie, trans. Michael Patterson (New York: Continuum, 2011), 107.

34. Bussy, *Kraftwerk*, 99.

35. David Bowie, from the episode "The '70s: Have a Nice Decade" in *The History of Rock 'n' Roll*. Created and produced by Jeffrey Peisch (Time-Life Video & Television, Warner Home Video 34991, c1995, 2004, DVD 4), 24:17–25:00.

36. Tompkins, *How to Wreck a Nice Beach*, 20.

37. Ralph Miller, "Project X—The Beginning of the Digital Transmission Age," 1, http://ralph-miller.org/docs/Project_X_The_Beginning_of_the_Digital_Age.pdf.

38. Tompkins, *How to Wreck a Nice Beach*, 77.

39. Ibid., 152–154.

40. Ibid., 170–173.

41. Miller, "Project X," 4.

42. Werner Meyer-Eppler, *Elektrische Klangerzeugung; Elektronische Musik und synthesische Sprache* (Bonn: F. Dümmler, 1949).

43. Mark Duffett, "Average White Band: Kraftwerk and the Politics of Race," in *Kraftwerk: Music Non-Stop*, 198.

44. David Cunningham, "Kraftwerk and the Image of the Modern," in *Kraftwerk: Music Non-Stop*, 44.

45. Buckley, *Kraftwerk Publikation*, 139.

46. John T. Littlejohn, "Kraftwerk: Language, Lucre, and Loss of Identity," *Popular Music and Society* 32, no. 5 (December 2009): 635–653.

47. Cyndy Hendershot, *Anti-Communism and Popular Culture in Mid-Century America* (Jefferson, NC: McFarland, 2003), 86.

48. Theo Cateforis, *Are We Not New Wave? Modern Pop at the Turn of the 1980s* (Ann Arbor: University of Michigan Press, 2011), 71–94.

49. Cateforis, *Are We Not New Wave?*, 77.

50. "VH1 Presents the Eighties," VH1, 2001, 8:30–16:00, https://www.youtube.com/watch?v=gfQMBGyTnsI.

51. Simon Reynolds in "Synth Britannia." BBC 4 documentary. Produced and directed by Ben Whalley. Uploaded April 18, 2020, YouTube. https://www.youtube.com/watch?v=JuQz8fHB7iw.

52. Cy Curnin in "In the Studio 30 Years Ago: The Fixx *Reach the Beach*," Redbeard's *In the Studio* radio show. 6:58–8:00, https://www.inthestudio.net/online-only-interviews/fixx-reach-beach/.

53. Kate Bush, "Kate Bush: From Piano to Fairlight with Britain's Exotic Chanteuse," interview by John Diliberto, *Keyboard*, July 1985, 73.

54. Ned Raggett, "Thirty Years On: Depeche Mode's *Some Great Reward* Revisited," *Quietus* (September 15, 2014), http://thequietus.com/articles/16246-depeche-mode-some-great-reward.

55. Dave Thompson, *Depeche Mode: Some Great Reward* (New York: St. Martin's, 1994), 123.

56. Graeme Thomson, *Under the Ivy: The Life & Music of Kate Bush* (New York: Omnibus, 2010), 164–165.

57. Jonathan Miller, *Stripped: Depeche Mode* (New York: Omnibus, 2008), 180–182.

58. Gareth Jones, "Classic Tracks: Depeche Mode 'People Are People,'" interview by Richard Buskin, *Sound on Sound*, February 2007, http://www.soundonsound.com/people/classic-tracks-depeche-mode-people-are-people.

59. Ibid.

60. Paul Humphreys, "How We Made: Orchestral Manoeuvres in the Dark on 'Enola Gay,'" interview by Jack Watkins, *Guardian*, January 7, 2013, https://www.theguardian.com/music/2013/jan/07/orchestral-manoeuvres-dark-enola-gay; Andy McCluskey and Paul Humphreys are shown speaking about and playing the melody in "Synth Britannia." BBC 4 documentary. Produced and directed by Ben Whalley. Uploaded April 18, 2020, YouTube. https://www.youtube.com/watch?v=JuQz8fHB7iw.

61. Andy McCluskey, "How We Made: Orchestral Manoeuvres in the Dark on 'Enola Gay,'" interview by Jack Watkins, *Guardian*, January 7, 2013.

62. Johnny Waller and Mike Humphreys, *Messages: Orchestral Manoeuvres in the Dark: An Official Biography* (London: Sidgwick and Jackson, 1987), 78.

63. Andy McCluskey, "Enola Gay," interview by Garin Pirnia, *Rolling Stone*, June 12, 2012, http://www.rollingstone.com/music/news/enola-gay-orchestral-manoeuvres-in-the-dark.

64. Waller and Humphreys, *Messages*, 80.

65. Carlo Karges, "Nena's '99 Luftballons' Soars up U.S. Charts," interview by Kurt Loder, *Rolling Stone*, March 15, 1984, 41.

66. Carlos Karges, "99 Luftballons und das Chaos der Gefühle," *Der Spiegel* 38 no. 13 (March 26, 1984): 221. Translated from the German: "Daß Paranoia unser Leben bestimmt. Die Angst voreinander bringt uns dazu, grausamer miteinander umzugehen, als es nötig wäre."

67. Eric Schlosser, *Command and Control: Nuclear Weapons, the Damascus Accident, and the Illusion of Safety* (New York: Penguin, 2013), 461.

68. Kevin McAlea, "99 Red Balloons—Interview with the Writer, Kevin McAlea," Eighty-Eightynine, http://www.eightyeightynine.com/music/99luftballoons-english.html.

69. Pinch and Trocco, *Analog Days*, 101.

70. Rebecca U. Thorpe, *The American Warfare State: The Domestic Politics of Military Spending* (Chicago: University of Chicago Press, 2014), 3–12.

71. Nick Turse, *The Complex: How the Military Invades Our Everyday Lives* (New York: Metropolitan Books, 2008), 18.

72. Hans-Joachim Braun, "Introduction: Technology and the Production and Reproduction of Music in the 20th Century," 18.

TEN

WIND OF CHANGE

The Fall of the Wall and the End of the Cold War

AS WE SAW IN THE first few chapters, the early years of the Cold War were strange days indeed. There was the bomb, *Sputnik*, fallout shelters, and fears of communists lurking everywhere. Popular songs reflected how strange those days were. In "Tic Tic Tic," Doris Day sang cheerfully about being a Geiger counter. In "Fallout Shelter," Peter Scott Peters bragged about how comfy and cozy his bomb shelter was. In "A Bomb Bop," Mike Fern urged listeners to get up and dance to that "wonderful A-bomb beat."

The last years of the Cold War were strange as well. This chapter will show how popular musicians were caught up in some odd circumstances occurring between 1989 and 1991. The Ramones did a black market deal through a hole in the Berlin Wall. David Hasselhoff, perched in a bucket crane and wearing a jacket covered in motion lights, stole the show from Beethoven at a celebration at the wall. Pink Floyd's Roger Waters rebuilt the wall and then knocked it down. Shirley Temple, who sang "On the Good Ship Lollipop," became the official US Ambassador to Czechoslovakia during the Velvet Revolution. Frank Zappa was the unofficial ambassador. German metal band Scorpions met with Mikhail Gorbachev in the Kremlin. Before recounting these strange collisions between politics and popular music, we must tell perhaps the strangest tale, the role Western popular music played in the breakdown of the Soviet Union.

THE ROLE OF WESTERN POPULAR MUSIC IN THE FALL OF COMMUNISM

Although there is no quantifiable way to gauge the impact Western popular music had in the fall of communism, it surely had one. Throughout the Cold War, citizens and government authorities throughout the Eastern Bloc saw music as a medium of free speech and therefore a possible threat to the established order. In the 1950s and 1960s, the generation of older Soviets who formulated communism in the 1920s and 1930s under Lenin and Stalin began losing political power to a younger generation that craved more avenues of free speech, more scrutiny of the government, and more consumer opportunities.[1] To many Soviets in this younger generation, Western popular music embodied these desires. In his 1976 book *The Russians,* Hedrick Smith observed that "the hunger for Western music and the paraphernalia of the pop culture is evidence enough of a generation gap in Russia, a generation gap in reverse, at least among the middle-class and the establishment youth. Whereas the American youth rebelliously turned to jeans, copping out, and the folk-rock ambience in defiant rejection of parental affluence, precisely what Soviet youth want is affluence and the good life. They are in the vanguard of the new materialism."[2]

Thus, a generation gap grew during the Khrushchev and Brezhnev administrations, although revolution never threatened the established order. In 1985, a revolution did emerge from within when Mikhail Gorbachev became the leader of the Soviet Union. He exemplified the aspirations of this younger generation. His policies of perestroika ("restructuring") and glasnost ("openness") not only allowed but actively encouraged scrutiny of the government, freedom of the press, a semifree market economy, and democratic elections. All of this resulted in the fall of Soviet communism from 1989 to 1991.

Cultural exchange was an important factor in creating the conditions for someone like Gorbachev to arise. It allowed people to see what the Soviet Union and the United States had in common culturally, rather than what divided them politically. Cultural exchange between the two superpowers flourished during World War II but remained strong during the Cold War as well. Yale Richmond writes, "Despite the chill winds of the Cold War . . . the performing arts were one of the most visible of U.S.-Soviet exchanges. . . . The Soviet dance groups, symphony orchestras, operas, ice shows, and circuses . . . visited the United States each year. American ensembles and soloists that went to the Soviet Union in exchange invariably played to full houses and were likewise appreciated by both the intelligentsia and the general public."[3]

Cultural exchange allowed citizens of both countries to view each other as individual people with individual talents. It slowly hacked away at the rampant stereotyping and propaganda that portrayed one country as good and the other as bad. Classical music and jazz played a huge role. Classical musicians traveled frequently between America and the Soviet Union. When Texan pianist Van Cliburn won the first International Tchaikovsky Competition in Moscow in 1958, he received adulation not only from the Soviet public but from Premier

Nikita Khrushchev himself. Balalaika orchestras were a big hit in America. Dmitri Shostakovich made the cover of *Time* magazine in 1942. He and four other preeminent Soviet composers traveled to the United States in 1959. American jazz musicians Dave Brubeck, Duke Ellington, Benny Goodman, and Louie Armstrong made well-publicized tours in Eastern Bloc countries from the 1950s on. The US State Department sent both classical and jazz musicians as "good will ambassadors" to shine a positive light on American culture.[4]

What about popular musicians? In July and August 1957, folk musician Peggy Seeger performed in Moscow, China, and Warsaw. Her half brother, Pete Seeger, played concerts in Czechoslovakia, Poland, and the Soviet Union in the spring of 1964. The Soviet Union also invited several country artists. Roy Clark (host of the variety show *Hee Haw*) and the Oak Ridge Boys (famous for their 1981 song "Elvira") were the first country musicians to perform there, in January 1976. The Nitty Gritty Dirt Band, another country group, toured the Soviet Union in May 1977. Bluesman B. B. King toured there in 1979, playing twenty-two sold out concerts. John Denver went in 1984, 1985, and again in October 1986. He played at benefit concerts in Kiev and Moscow for the victims of the Chernobyl accident. Two British superstars made it over, Cliff Richard in 1976 and Elton John in 1979. Cliff played mostly his pop hits and Elton played mostly his ballads. Although Elton had numerous rock hits, he brought just percussionist Ray Cooper with him instead of his entire band. Table 10.1 lists the popular musicians who played in Eastern Bloc countries during the Cold War.

The case was quite different for rock musicians. British bands Manfred Mann, the Animals, the Hollies, and the Rolling Stones made it as far as Prague and Warsaw in the mid- to late 1960s but not as far as Moscow. Because many rock bands were unpredictable and impulsive—and had reputations as purveyors of social protest, degenerate morality, and unruly crowd behavior at concerts—they were not fit for cultural exchange. The US State Department had little interest in sending American rock bands to the Soviet Union, and Soviet officials detested Western rock bands, especially the Beatles. Why would Soviet officials be so concerned about a rock and roll band from Liverpool? As Leslie Woodhead, author of *How the Beatles Rocked the Kremlin*, deftly puts it, "They instinctually understood that there was something about the spirit of the music that threatened central control. That's what it came down to."[5]

Even though the Beatles and other early rockers never entered the Soviet Union, they still caused problems for Soviet authorities. In the late 1950s, young Soviet music fans began to make their own copies of rock records that were smuggled behind the Iron Curtain. In hidden studios, they copied music onto discarded x-ray plates of bones, a process called *roentgenizdat*.[6] It was *samizdat* for sounds.[7] For Russian music lovers, these records were a breath of fresh air despite

Table 10.1 Western Popular Musicians Who Performed in the Eastern Bloc

Musician	Style
Paul Robeson	spirituals, folk songs, musicals, popular standards
Peggy Seeger	folk
Paul Anka	pop
Pete Seeger	folk
Manfred Mann	early rock
Animals	rock, pop
Hollies	pop, rock
Paul Anka	pop
Joan Baez	folk
Pete Seeger	folk
The Rolling Stones	rock
Traffic	rock
Beach Boys	pop, rock
Blood, Sweat & Tears	rock, jazz
Pete Seeger	folk
Joan Baez	folk
Roy Clark, Oak Ridge Boys	country
Cliff Richard	pop
ABBA	pop
Nitty Gritty Dirt Band	country, rock
Elton John	pop, rock
B. B. King	blues
Elton John	pop, rock
Iron Maiden	heavy metal
John Denver	pop, country
Bob Dylan	folk, rock
Queen	rock
UB40	reggae, pop
July Fourth Disarmament Festival with Bonnie Raitt, James Taylor, Santana, and the Doobie Brothers	country, rock
Billy Joel	rock
Bob Dylan / Tom Petty and the Heartbreakers	rock
Uriah Heep	hard rock
Depeche Mode	new wave
Scorpions	heavy metal
Joe Cocker	rock, soul
Peace Week of the Berlin Youth concert with Bryan Adams, James Brown, Marillion, Fischer-Z, and Big Country	rock, soul
Bruce Springsteen	rock
Human Rights Now! concert with Bruce Springsteen, Sting, Peter Gabriel, Tracy Chapman, Youssou N'Dour, Hobo Blues Band, and János Bródy	rock, pop
Moscow Music Peace Festival with Cinderella, Scorpions, Skid Row, Mötley Crüe, Ozzy Osbourne, Bon Jovi, Gorky Park, Brigada S, and Nuance	hard rock, heavy metal

Date	Location
1934, 1936, 1949, 1958, 1959, 1960, 1961, 1963	Moscow, Prague, Warsaw, East Berlin
July–August 1957	Moscow, China, Warsaw
1963	Warsaw
March 1964	Prague, Warsaw, Moscow
1965	Prague
1966	Warsaw
1966	Warsaw
1966	Prague
1966	East Berlin
January 1967	East Berlin
April 13, 1967	Warsaw
July 1968	Budapest
1969	Prague
June-July 1970	Yugoslavia, Romania, Poland
March 1972	Hanoi
December 1972	Hanoi
January 1976	Moscow, Leningrad, Riga
1976	Leningrad, Moscow
October 1976	Warsaw
May 1977	Armenia, Soviet Union
May 1979	Leningrad, Moscow
1979	Soviet Union
1984	Yugoslavia, Hungary, Czechoslovakia, Poland
1984	Poland, Hungary, Yugoslavia
November 1984, June 1985, October 1986	Soviet Union
July 1985	Moscow
July 27, 1986	Budapest
October 1986	Leningrad, Moscow
July 4, 1987	Moscow
August 1987	Tbilisi, Leningrad, Moscow
September 17, 1987	East Berlin
December 1987	Moscow
March 1988	East Berlin
April 1988	Leningrad
June 1, 1988	East Berlin
June 16–19, 1988	East Berlin
July 19, 1988	East Berlin
September 6, 1988	Budapest
August 12–13, 1989	Moscow

their poor quality, which collector Kolya Vasin describes as "listening through sand. It was like you had music playing in one ear and someone crunching biscuits in the other."[8] Stephen Coates expands,

> They are images of pain and damage inscribed with the sound of forbidden pleasure; fragile photographs of the interiors of Soviet citizens, layered with the ghostly music that they secretly loved. . . . Bone bootlegs are about 15 cm to 30 cm in diameter. Each is an edition of one, unique from all others. The quality of the recordings varies considerably. The source material, the lathe used, the particular x-ray sheet and the skill of the bootlegger would all affect the final sound. . . . The x-ray bootlegs are palimpsests: objects made for one purpose but reused for another; skin-thin slivers of plastic compressed with deep layers of time, oppression, culture and hope. These records were made in a time when music mattered so much that people were prepared to go to prison for it.[9]

This subversive production of records—and later reel-to-reel and cassette tape recordings—led to the formation of hundreds of Soviet rock bands in the 1960s and 1970s. Yet they were forced to remain underground. The state-owned record label, Melodiya, treated the bands with indifference, they were harassed by officials from the Ministry of Culture, and their lyrics were scrutinized for objectionable content.

Mikhail Gorbachev, Vladimir Putin, and Sergei Ivanov (Putin's minster of defense and deputy prime minister) listened to the Beatles in their youth. When Paul McCartney performed in the Soviet Union for the first time in 2003, he got to meet all three, and they were thrilled.[10] Gorbachev said on the occasion, "I do believe the music of the Beatles has taught the young people of the Soviet Union that there is another life, that there is freedom elsewhere, and of course this feeling has pushed them towards *perestroika*, towards the dialogue with the outside world. . . . I don't think this is just pop music. This is something much greater."[11] Putin invited McCartney into the Kremlin and told him the Beatles' music was "a gulp of freedom . . . an open window to the world."[12] Ivanov became a Beatles' fan in 1963 at the age of ten when he heard "Love Me Do" through the static on the partially jammed Radio Luxembourg.[13] In an interview included with the DVD *Paul McCartney in Red Square,* he waxed poetic about first hearing that song and how in 1984 he was finally able to fulfill a lifetime wish to buy all the Beatles' records.[14] Here we have three of the most influential men in recent Russian history unashamedly acknowledging the impact of the Beatles, a band their predecessors thought of as a menace. Pavel Palazhchenko, Gorbachev's chief English-language interpreter, who attended all the nuclear-arms reduction summits between him and Ronald Reagan, put it best when he wrote, "I am sure that the impact of the

Beatles on the generation of young Soviets in the 1960s will one day be the object of studies. We knew their songs by heart.... In the dusky years of the Brezhnev regime, they were not only a source of musical relief. They helped us create a world of our own, a world different from the dull and senseless ideological liturgy that increasingly reminded us of Stalinism.... The Beatles were our quiet way of rejecting 'the system' while conforming to most of its demands."[15]

When young Soviets in the 1960s, 1970s, and 1980s listened to scratchy x-ray records or smuggled Beatles records or tuned in to Radio Luxembourg and Voice of America on their radios, they were not listening for the messages in the lyrics. Few of them would have understood English anyway. They simply heard freedom of expression, and they craved it for themselves. In 1987, four years before the official collapse of Soviet communism, Russian rock musician Boris Grebenshchikov said, "Everybody in Russia has been listening to American and English rock n' roll for all these years since Elvis Presley, and nobody understood a word. But still it changed everything. Russia is not the same."[16] Summing up the rise of Russian rock, journalist Artemy Troitsky writes,

> The generation gap (here we call it "the problem of fathers and children") ... began to widen in response to the Beatles. The cherished and fostered "commonality" of cultural identity suddenly started breaking up. Now it was not just an isolated gang of hipsters, but an enormous mass of the "children" who said goodbye to arias and operettas, athletic marches, tearjerker romances and other formalistic popular music and surrendered to the power of alien electric rhythms.... And the new language was so enticing and accessible that listening wasn't enough—people wanted to express something for themselves.... Young people for the first time felt the right to their own, independent self-expression. Russian rock had lifted off.[17]

As Timothy W. Ryback, Sabrina Petra Ramet, William Jay Risch, and others have shown, young musicians in the satellite countries of the Eastern Bloc each created their own unique music scenes.[18] In Ukraine, "Deep Purple Mania" was as fervent as Beatlemania.[19] In East Germany, punk rock contributed a noisy soundtrack to the civil unrest that eventually brought down the wall.[20] In Poland, heavy metal fans greeted Iron Maiden as if they were liberators when they played there in 1984.[21] Although these scenes were thriving, few groups had opportunities to play to large crowds. In March 1980, the state-sanctioned Spring Rhythms festival, a competition between the top Soviet bands held in Tbilisi, Georgia, finally gave Soviet rock music a place in mainstream Russian culture. In the 1980s, Eastern Bloc bands began releasing albums and touring beyond their local scenes. By 1987, Gorbachev's policy of glasnost was having a tangible effect, allowing young musicians to bring their own musical cultures up from the underground.

On July 4, 1987, Soviet music fans got their first real taste of a truly international rock concert. Bonnie Raitt, James Taylor, Santana, and the Doobie Brothers joined several Russian rock bands in Moscow for the July Fourth Disarmament festival. The concert was a success, but at least two hundred armed security guards kept the crowd at a healthy distance from the stage. Journalist Philip Taubman was there and wrote in the *New York Times* that there were "enough soldiers and plainclothes security agents on hand to secure a small city. Thousands of army troops ringed the large outdoor stadium where the concert took place."[22] Three weeks later, Billy Joel came and opened the floodgates. During his seven concerts, discussed in chapter 6, there were no barriers between him and twenty thousand roaring Soviet fans. Summing up the role of Western rock at the end of the Cold War, Tony Mitchell writes, "Rock music has represented probably the most widespread vehicle of youth rebellion, resistance and independence behind the Iron Curtain, both in terms of providing an enhanced political context for the often banned sounds of British and American rock, and in the development of home-grown musics built on western foundations but resonating within their own highly charged political contexts."[23]

Now that we've provided a context for popular music's role at the end of the Cold War, we can recount a number of uncommon events from that time involving the Ramones, David Hasselhoff, Roger Waters, Shirley Temple, Frank Zappa, and the Scorpions.

THE RAMONES AND THE HOLE IN THE WALL

Two-and-a-half weeks after the border between East and West Berlin opened on November 9, 1989, the four Ramones were at the Berlin Wall. The significance was not lost on them. Drummer Marky Ramone said,

> Our tour of Germany brought us to Berlin on November 27. . . . German citizens from both sides started showing up with picks and sledgehammers and busting through the concrete. The guards had orders but just gave up. They probably would have joined in if they were off duty. People were hacking at the wall, smiling, taking pictures, and walking away with little concrete souvenirs. . . . I walked over to a hole about a foot and a half in diameter and put my hand clear through to the other side. Someone in East Berlin—not more than two feet away—shook my hand. . . . What an amazing way this was to experience history.[24]

Bass player CJ Ramone recounts his experience, "It was wild. We were at the wall one day with MTV and there was a small hole the size of a basketball, and there were two guards standing on the other side. They offered to sell me a belt buckle and a military hat, and I bought them off them and shook their hands through the wall. It was so weird to be part of a situation where you're part of history."[25]

Such experiences show how strange and surreal life was in Berlin in 1989 and 1990. The handshake highlights the miraculous shift from division to unity. The selling of the military hat highlights the abrupt change from communism to consumerism. Here we have an East German guard selling government property as merchandise to someone in the west: free market capitalism right through a hole in the Berlin Wall.

DAVID HASSELHOFF'S "LOOKING FOR FREEDOM"

What piece of music did the German crowds sing as they celebrated the fall of the Berlin Wall in November and December 1989? Surely it must have been the stirring "Ode to Joy" chorus from Beethoven's Ninth Symphony, with its fitting phrase "Alle Menschen werden Brüder" ("all people become brothers"). Yet another piece of music is cited just as often for capturing the spirit of the time. It is none other than "Looking for Freedom" by all-American hunk and heartthrob David Hasselhoff, star of *Knight Rider* and *Baywatch*.

How did such an unremarkable song become associated with such a remarkable event? The story begins in 1978 when British songwriter Gary Cowtan wrote the lyrics to "Looking for Freedom" and German songwriter and producer Jack White wrote the music. German/English singer Marc Seaberg released an English version of the song, while German singer Tony Marshall recorded a German version with different lyrics titled "Auf Der Strasse Nach Suden." The song was a minor hit in West Germany but soon forgotten. About ten years later, White recruited Hasselhoff, a celebrity in Germany because of the *Knight Rider* TV series, to record a new version. White released the song on the German label BMG Ariola in March 1989.[26] It was the right place and the right time for an anthem about freedom. The song hit number one in West Germany (on the GfK Entertainment / Media Control chart) on March 31, 1989, and stayed there for eight weeks. It became the top single in Germany for 1989. It was an underground hit in East Germany as well, due to copies smuggled in on cassette tapes. In the latter half of 1989, German television variety shows invited Hasselhoff to sing the song. He did a tour of both East and West Germany. On November 9, the border between East and West Germany opened. Around this time, the German TV station Zweites Deutsches Fernsehen (ZDF) invited Hasselhoff to perform "Looking for Freedom" for a New Year's Eve celebration concert at the Berlin Hilton hotel. Hasselhoff said, "Sure I'll come, but I want to sing on the Berlin Wall."[27]

He got his wish. He was at the Brandenburg Gate on New Year's Eve 1989, less than two months after the wall became null and void, singing "Looking for

Freedom."[28] Perched in a bucket crane high above a massive crowd that numbered in the hundreds of thousands, he sang along to a recording of the song while wearing a piano keyboard scarf and a leather jacket with motion lights. In subsequent years, Hasselhoff has been criticized often by American and British journalists for shamelessly stealing the spotlight that night.[29] One might wish such a momentous occasion as the fall of the Berlin Wall would be memorialized with a more substantial piece of music. But Cold War historians and music fans should not be put off by "The Hoff." He forthrightly admitted he was simply in the right place at the right time with the right anthem. He said, "I didn't have anything to do with bringing down the wall. I just happened to have a song about freedom."[30]

Beethoven was hovering in the Berlin air at this time, or perhaps rolling over in his grave, as Chuck Berry famously sang. Leonard Bernstein conducted two performances of the Ninth Symphony on December 23 and Christmas Day 1989, the first in West Berlin and the second in East Berlin.[31] Bernstein even changed the words of Friedrich Schiller's poem "An die Freude" ("Ode to Joy") to "An die Freiheit" ("Ode to Freedom") to give the text more relevance to the fall of the wall. David B. Dennis writes, "No product of German art, whether painting, sculpture, essay, novel, poem, film, or song, could capture the emotion of the 'reunification' as well as Beethoven's Ninth Symphony—especially its finale."[32] A recording of Beethoven's "Ode to Joy" was played to the Berlin crowds on that most auspicious New Year's Eve, but like it or not, Hasselhoff's "Looking for Freedom" was the song to sing on that night. Bernstein did have Beethoven, but what he didn't have was a hit TV show about a talking car, a bucket crane, a piano keyboard scarf, and a leather jacket decked out with motion lights.

THE WALL AT THE WALL

On July 21, 1990, between Potsdamer Platz and the Brandenburg Gate in Berlin, Roger Waters and a host of guest musicians played Pink Floyd's *The Wall*.[33] A more meaningful and significant location could not have been chosen for such a concert. This site was part of the Berlin Wall's death strip, the no-man's-land of guard towers, tank traps, electric fences, and beds of nails between the actual Berlin Wall, which faced West Berlin, and the inner wall, which faced East Berlin. The concert, called The Wall Live in Berlin, was not initially conceived as an event to celebrate the fall of the Berlin Wall. In September 1989, two months before the East and West Berlin border opened, Waters agreed to play *The Wall* as the initial fundraising effort for the Memorial Fund for Disaster Relief created by World War II hero and philanthropist Leonard Cheshire. Waters and Cheshire first thought about staging the concert on Wall Street in New York or near the Grand

Canyon. After the extraordinary events of November 1989, they both agreed that Berlin would be the perfect place to build *The Wall* and then demolish it. Although the album was not written with the Berlin Wall specifically in mind, it had the potential to translate well to the German audience. As Philip Jenkins writes, "It is striking that so quintessentially British a work should have appeared so thoroughly and immediately applicable to Germany. The original album had drawn heavily on German experiences such as the rise of Nazism . . . the inheritance of 1945 is a central theme of the work."[34]

Preparing the space for such an event was a massive undertaking. Planning began in January 1990, six months before the concert. Waters and his production team had difficulty gaining permits because the East and West German governments, no longer divided but not yet officially reunified, were in such disorder. Enough space had to be cleared to accommodate a large concert stage and room for hundreds of thousands of concertgoers. Not only were the construction workers and excavators uncovering Cold War history by clearing what remained of the Berlin Wall at Potsdamer Platz but World War II history as well. Before the Berlin Wall was constructed in 1961, the area housed the *Führerbunker*, the underground bunker where Adolf Hitler and Eva Braun committed suicide on April 30, 1945. The *Führerbunker* had been cleared out decades before, but excavators uncovered another Nazi bunker with ammunition, daggers with swastika emblems, and well-executed murals of Nazi SS (*Schutzstaffel*) guards.[35] Thus, on the stage above these remains of Nazism, Waters would sing "In the Flesh," "Run Like Hell," and "Waiting for the Worms," in which the title character Pink imagines he is a Hitleresque dictator leading a fascist rally. Excavators also found a five-hundred-pound, unexploded Soviet bomb from World War II.[36] Songs like "Goodbye Blue Sky," "What Shall We Do Now?," and "Mother," which reference World War II and Cold War bombs, become even more chilling in light of the sleeping giant that had been lurking beneath the concert site.

The Berlin Wall played not only a symbolic role in the concert but a tangible and practical one. It helped out with security. Set designer, Jonathan Park, recounts, "As we were building up our show over a number of weeks, the Wall was gradually disappearing. We actually asked [the demolition workers] if they would leave the bit of Wall in the backstage area because it meant that we didn't have to put a security fence up."[37] So for a concert celebrating the fall of the wall, it served one last time as a wall, protecting rock stars from their meddlesome fans. Estimates of the size of the crowd were between two hundred and four hundred thousand people, comparable to the 1969 Woodstock concert. In fact, the Berlin show was referred to at the time as the "German Woodstock."[38] The show was also broadcast on television to a worldwide audience of hundreds of millions of people.

The stage design consisted of a wall of fire-retardant polystyrene bricks with a large gap in the middle. As with the original 1980–1981 tour, the rest of the wall was slowly built during the first half of the concert. This created a barrier between the musicians and the audience. It measured 550 feet (170 meters) long and 82 feet (25 meters) high, seven times the height of the actual Berlin Wall. The last brick, of twenty-five hundred, was placed after Waters sang, "Goodbye," the last word of "Goodbye Cruel World." During the second half of the show, the musicians performed either behind the wall, in small openings in it, on top of it, or in front of it. Of course, the wall came crashing down at the end of "The Trial" to thunderous applause from the audience.

The stage wall was used not only as a prop but as a massive projection screen. The production team found photographs of certain sections of the western side of the Berlin Wall, which were covered with colorful graffiti. These were then projected onto the much wider and taller stage wall, making the Berlin Wall seem many times larger. Additionally, scenes from Pink Floyd's 1982 film, *The Wall*, were shown on the stage wall throughout the concert.[39] The 1982 film is an extremely intense viewing experience not only because of the lyrics, the music, and Bob Geldof's acting but because of Gerald Scarfe's animation. Scarfe drew unforgettable sequences of copulating flowers, marching hammers, the trial scene, and of course, the wall itself in its many manifestations. During the 1990 concert, his animation of the wall from the film projected onto the stage wall at the site of the actual Berlin Wall must have boggled the minds of the concertgoers.

Gerald Scarfe himself had a chilling experience at the Berlin Wall in August 1962, just one year after its construction began. For one of his earliest assignments as a professional illustrator, *Esquire* magazine sent him to Berlin to draw the Berlin Wall. He arrived there just after eighteen-year-old East German Peter Fechter tried to climb the wall, was shot in the hip by East German border guards, and bled to death over a span of one hour on August 17, 1962.[40] Scarfe drew an illustration of the memorial (crosses and bouquets of flowers) that West Berliners placed on the ground across from where the incident took place.[41] This occurred near Checkpoint Charlie, just a few blocks from Potsdamer Platz, where the concert was held.

Journalist Marc Fisher, trying to summarize how the concert was awash in symbolism writes,

> It was a semiotician's bonanza. Pink, a tormented, lonely rock star, breaks down the wall he has built between himself and his audience. A people break down the wall their oppressors erected to keep them prisoner. Finally, [Roger Waters] returns to the scene of history, charging $25 a head so the people can watch the bricks tumble once more. . . . [After the concert,] Waters' Wall—bigger, taller, cleaner, prettier than the one the Communists

> built—was being stacked for a recycling company. Sixty yards away, the real sound of Berlin could be heard once more. Sharing hammers and chisels, Germans and foreign visitors got back to the work that has united the city, the hollow clink of metal against concrete, the destruction of the Wall.[42]

Besides the wall, another potent symbol used in the concert was rife with allusion and meaning: Scarfe's animation of the marching hammers during "Waiting for the Worms."[43] In the film, the hammers are a haunting image of relentless, unfeeling, mechanical evil. The allusion to the goose-stepping march of Nazi troops in newsreels and in Leni Riefenstahl's 1935 German propaganda film, *Triumph des Willens* (*Triumph of the Will*), is obvious. Yet, ironically, the marching hammers projected onto the stage wall in the 1990 concert can be seen as a positive, celebratory image.[44] It reminds the viewer that even as the concert was occurring, Germans on both sides were out having the time of their lives breaking off pieces of the Berlin Wall with their own hammers, picks, and chisels. In fact, sometime in the late 1980s, a graffiti artist painted Scarfe's marching hammers on the Berlin Wall, where it followed the Ebertstraße between the Brandenburg Gate and Potsdamer Platz, the location of the concert.[45] This painting of marching hammers would eventually be obliterated by actual hammers.

The concert itself was a great success, a star-studded affair. Since Pink Floyd had split into two camps in the 1980s (with Waters going solo and David Gilmour, Nick Mason, and Richard Wright continuing on as Pink Floyd), Waters and his team found their own musicians to play the music, calling them the Bleeding Hearts Band. To help him with the singing, he recruited well-known rock stars, such as Joni Mitchell, Van Morrison, Cyndi Lauper, Sinéad O'Connor, Scorpions, the Band, and Bryan Adams. He also managed to get the Berlin Radio Symphony Orchestra and Choir from East Berlin and the Marching Band of the Combined Soviet Forces in Germany for the numbers that required orchestral, martial, and choral accompaniment.

Although the music, lyrics, and overall narrative of the Berlin show are the same as the original 1979 album, Waters used stagecraft and props to expand the scope of the show, making it broader in conception and more relevant to the situation. Waters said, "The symbolic connotations were more important than the rock and roll show."[46] Executive producer Tony Hollingsworth expanded on this, saying, "We could see that there was this very direct, simple analogy between *The Wall* and the Wall, and that one dealt with the personal alienation and the other dealt with the political alienation."[47] There are moments in the show where the personal and the political mesh very well, where stage props emphasize both Pink's meltdown and the fall of the Berlin Wall. One of these moments is during "Comfortably Numb." In the original 1979 song and the 1982 film, a doctor injects Pink with a stimulant to bring him out of his mad and depressed state so he can perform on stage. In the 1990 Berlin show, Pink is not the one who is injected; it is the wall. Waters emerges from an ambulance dressed as the doctor himself, wielding a giant syringe. He plunges it into the stage wall at the line "okay, just a little pin prick."[48] This suggests the wall itself, and the political condition that erected it, is mad and sick and in need of remedy. What Waters said of *The Wall* tour from 2010 to 2013 is pertinent to the 1990 Berlin show: "It's now much less about that simple personal narrative, and much more of a kind of geopolitical piece about the walls that separate us nation from nation and ideology from ideology, walls between nations and religions, and all those other walls between north and south, rich and poor . . . It's a much more direct anti-war statement."[49]

Roger Waters's antiwar stance dates back to his early childhood. His grandfather (George Henry Waters) was killed in World War I at the Battle of the Somme in 1916. His father (Eric Fletcher Waters) was two years old at the time. He was killed at the Battle of Anzio in World War II in 1944. Roger Waters was five months old. So he and his father became fatherless as babies in the two world wars. Unsurprisingly, the legacy of World War II is a major theme of *The Wall*. In the late 1950s and early 1960s, Roger's mother participated in CND (Campaign for Nuclear Disarmament) rallies and antibomb Aldermaston marches. Waters did the same. At the age of fifteen, Waters became chairman of the Cambridge Youth Campaign for Nuclear Disarmament (YCND).[50] The CND turns up in the 1982 film, when Pink's wife falls in love with a CND organizer during the latter half of "Mother." *The Wall* is full of such allusions to World War II and the Cold War because they shaped so many aspects of Waters's life.[51] For the German concertgoers familiar with the album and film, The Wall Live in Berlin must have been a profoundly moving experience. In a location steeped in German history, they saw enacted before them World War II bombers, a Hitleresque dictator, the construction of a massive wall, and climactically, the destruction of the wall.

VELVET REVOLUTIONARIES: SHIRLEY TEMPLE AND FRANK ZAPPA

What did Shirley Temple and Frank Zappa have in common? Surely it wasn't their music; it wasn't their image either. Temple was the lovable sweetheart who brought some light to the dark days of the Great Depression, while Zappa was the freak who made the sixties and seventies even freakier. What did they have in common? The surprising answer is they both played a part in the Velvet Revolution, the emancipation of Czechoslovakia from the Soviet Union in late 1989.

While Shirley Temple is well-known as a child actress, singer, and dancer in the 1930s and 1940s, she is not well-known as an international ambassador. After appearing in dozens of films, she left Hollywood in 1950, married Charles Alden

Black, raised children, and made a few appearances in films and television.[52] In the 1960s, she cofounded the International Federation of Multiple Sclerosis Societies and happened to be in Prague on its behalf in August 1968. Here she witnessed firsthand the brutal end of Prague Spring, when on August 20 and 21, 1968, over two hundred thousand Soviet and Eastern Bloc troops with over one thousand tanks invaded Czechoslovakia. Their mission was to squash the reforms in First Secretary Alexander Dubček's "Action Programme," a blueprint for Czechoslovakia's own brand of socialism within the Warsaw Pact but without the heavy-handed control of the Soviets. For a precious seven months, Prague Spring granted freedom of speech, assembly, and movement to Czech citizens, a glimpse of glasnost seventeen years before Gorbachev. Temple arrived in Prague on August 17, 1968, and was scheduled to meet with Dubček a few days later. She never met with him. She was stranded in a hotel as the tanks rolled by. As she recounts,

> A secretary came in and told me, "Your meeting with Mr. Dubček in 15 minutes is canceled—he is all tied up." Those were the exact words. . . . It wasn't until the next day that my guide came back and told me: "You will not see Mr. Dubček, and you will not leave from the airport today. We have been invaded." There were tears in her eyes. . . . On the way up to the roof of the hotel to try to see what was happening . . . I looked down and saw tanks all around the hotel, and their guns were pointing up. That night, after curfew, in the lobby looking out at the street, I saw a Czech middle-aged woman shaking her fist at the soldiers. She was shot in the stomach and went down. That was a bad sight. Nothing crushes freedom as substantially as a tank.[53]

Temple was secretly escorted out of the country two days later.

After her short-lived and precarious trip to Czechoslovakia, Temple became active in politics in the late 1960s. In 1974 President Gerald Ford appointed her US ambassador to Ghana. In August 1989, when Czechoslovakia was still under Soviet influence, President George Bush appointed her US ambassador to the country. Three months later, Czechoslovakia achieved a peaceful transferal of power (the Velvet Revolution) from a one-party, communist-controlled government to a parliamentary republic. Alexander Dubček was elected chairman of the federal assembly and Václav Havel was elected president. Temple was overjoyed to see democracy come to Czech citizens. US Deputy Secretary of State Lawrence Eagleberger quipped that Temple's accomplishments as ambassador heralded "the end of the ship of state and the beginning of the Good Ship Lollipop."[54] On January 20, 1990, she was at the Prague airport when she saw a crowd of people. She soon realized they were there not to greet her but to greet Frank Zappa on his first trip to the country. He had been personally invited by Václav Havel. Although Zappa had been well-known in both the United States and

Czechoslovakia for over two decades, Temple confessed to interviewers at the airport that she had "never heard him."[55]

Václav Havel was a Czechoslovakian playwright and philosopher, and during the Soviet invasion of Czechoslovakia in August 1968, he became a political dissident. In the 1970s and 1980s, he was imprisoned several times for his writings against Soviet communism and his participation in the anticommunist/human rights group Charter 77. In 1989, he found himself in the position of being the spokesman for the country and, during the Velvet Revolution, elected president. Havel greatly admired Shirley Temple, but it is not known what he thought of her acting, dancing, or singing. What is certain is he loved American rock music. Since the late 1960s, he had been a fan of Lou Reed, the Velvet Underground, the Rolling Stones, and Captain Beefheart. He admired Frank Zappa and his music above all.

Zappa's outspoken nature, outrageous personality, and fierce defense of freedom of speech inspired Havel and the anticommunist movement in Czechoslovakia. According to Milan Hlavsa, a founder of the Czech underground band the Plastic People of the Universe, named after the song "Plastic People" on the 1967 Mothers of Invention album *Absolutely Free*, "Zappa was quite well known in Czechoslovakia [in the late 1960s] thanks perhaps to his pervasive irony, which is the cornerstone of the Czech mentality."[56] In 1976, communist officials arrested members of the Plastic People, DG 307, and other underground groups and put them on trial.[57] Their songs did not have any overt political or anticommunist content, nor did the bands align themselves with any oppositional organizations.[58] They were simply playing rock music. Writing of this in one of his most famous essays, "The Power of the Powerless" from 1978, Havel wrote, "Everyone understood that an attack on the Czech musical underground was an attack on a most elementary and important thing. . . . The freedom to play rock music was understood as a human freedom and thus as essentially the same as the freedom to engage in philosophical and political reflection, the freedom to write, the freedom to express and defend the various social and political interests of society."[59]

Zappa said, "I had no idea that song ['Plastic People'] made the impact it did there. . . . We were touring heavily in Europe at the time [1977], and a few Czechs had come across the Austrian border to hear our concert in Vienna. I talked with them after the show, and they told me that 'Plastic People' was responsible for a whole movement of dissidents within Czechoslovakia."[60]

Zappa said further in 1990, "In Czechoslovakia, for twenty years, they've been smuggling my records in, and translating the lyrics into Czech, and people were arrested and beaten by the secret police for owning the albums, and the same thing was true with the secret police in East Germany."[61]

Thus Zappa became an emblem of free speech for those suffering under the oppressive Soviet regime. By the time of the Velvet Revolution, many Czechs considered him a cult hero. As president, Havel sought out Zappa for advice on ways to modernize Czechoslovakia and integrate it into mainstream European culture. He made Zappa "special ambassador" to the West on trade, culture, and tourism. Of his relationship to Havel and the Czechoslovakian government, Zappa said, "What I do goes through the Ministry of Culture in Czechoslovakia, but I have no official government title. I am not a member of their government . . . [just] . . . a private individual trying to do something to help them."[62] Thus, on January 20, 1990, "special ambassador" Zappa arrived at the Prague airport to the befuddlement of the official US ambassador to Czechoslovakia, Shirley Temple Black.

Zappa did not hold his position for long. Later in 1990, US Secretary of State James Baker learned of Zappa's position and told Havel, "You can either do business with the United States or you can do business with Frank Zappa. What'll it be?"[63] Baker had little patience or respect for Zappa since Zappa mercilessly ridiculed his wife, Susan, and other senators' wives during the 1985 PMRC (Parents Music Resource Center) Senate Commerce Committee hearings.[64] Czechoslovakia greatly needed US economic support, so Havel was compelled to conduct politics in the more traditional way—with politicians instead of rock stars. Nevertheless, he remained friends with Zappa until the musician's death in 1993. Havel wrote,

> He was the first rock celebrity I had ever met, and, to my great delight, he was a normal human being, with whom I could carry on a normal conversation. He was eager to learn everything he could about the radical changes taking place in the countries of the former Soviet bloc. Meeting him was like entering a different world from the one I live in as President. He gave serious thought to offering unofficial assistance to our country, in both cultural and economic spheres, and I later learned that he discussed the matter in detail with several ministers. . . . What fascinated and excited him was the idea that the artist had a role to play in active politics.[65]

Why did Havel and the dissident Czechs take to Zappa so easily? Zappa himself is a tough nut to crack; his music is difficult, at times impenetrable. Most Americans did not know what to make of him. They saw him simply as a freak who made crazy music—he "played" a bicycle on the Steve Allen Show in 1963, gave his albums and songs vulgar titles (*Weasels Ripped My Flesh*, "Hot Poop"), and bestowed his children with wacky names (Moon Unit and Dweezil). Yet he greatly inspired the Czechs. Why? As we shall see, the answer is absurd, literally absurd.

In their twentieth-century literature, theater, and art, the Czechs had a proclivity toward the absurd, the surreal, and the ironic. Reflecting the European trend of moving away from the naturalism of the nineteenth century, the Czechs embraced satire and Dadaism. Václav Havel's plays, such as *The Garden Party* and

The Memorandum, incorporate these elements. Czechoslovakia's most famous writer is Franz Kafka, although he wrote in German. His unsettling novels and short stories defined the absurdist literary style. As quoted before, Plastic People founder, Milan Hlavsa, admired Zappa's "pervasive irony, which is the cornerstone of the Czech mentality."[66]

Reading Zappa's autobiography, *The Real Frank Zappa Book*, one is struck by how Kafkaesque it is.[67] It is a tale told by someone who is trying to make sense of an absurd world. Martin Esslin's definition of "Theatre of the Absurd" could be a description of Frank Zappa's book, as well as his songs, album covers, and concerts:

> The Theatre of the Absurd attacks the comfortable certainties of religious or political orthodoxy. It aims to shock its audience out of complacency, to bring it face to face with the harsh facts of the human situation. . . . It is a challenge to accept the human condition as it is, in all its mystery and absurdity, and to bear it with dignity, nobly, responsibly; precisely because there are no easy solutions to the mysteries of existence, because ultimately man is alone in a meaningless world. The shedding of easy solutions, of comforting illusions, may be painful, but it leaves behind it a sense of freedom and relief. And that is why, in the last resort, the Theatre of the Absurd does not provoke tears of despair but the laughter of liberation.[68]

Havel and the other dissident Czechs recognized the absurd in Zappa and adopted him as one of their own. His music, like their absurd literature, was a foil against the absurdity of Soviet communist oppression.

Frank Zappa has another connection to the Cold War, a gruesome one that is quite different from being special ambassador to Czechoslovakia. It is no surprise he turned out to be a satirist and an absurdist since he experienced things in his childhood that can only be described as absurd. For example, as a child, he had a radioactive radium pellet inserted into his nose by his pediatrician. Zappa (born in 1940) came into a world enthralled with radioactivity but clueless about its immediate and long-term effects on the human body. As Pulitzer Prize–winning journalist Eileen Welsome reports in her groundbreaking work, *The Plutonium Files*, physicians in collaboration with the US Department of Defense and the Atomic Energy Commission subjected millions of US citizens to unethical and inhumane radiation experiments.[69] Ill-informed as to the potential harm done to them, and often without their consent, pregnant women were given radioactive iron "cocktails," mentally disabled children were fed radioactive oatmeal, cancer patients were injected with plutonium, prisoners had their testicles irradiated, and American soldiers were stationed less than two miles from hydrogen bomb blasts and burned by fallout.[70] Sometime in the 1940s, Zappa was subjected to nasopharyngeal radium irradiation (NRI) for sinus trouble. Estimates of how many Americans (mostly children) received this "treatment" from the 1940s to the late 1960s reach 2.5 million.[71] One researcher, Stewart Farber, referred to it as "Nagasaki up the nose."[72] Zappa describes it in his autobiography this way, "There was some 'new treatment' for this ailment [sinus trouble] being discussed in the neighborhood. It involved stuffing *radium* into your sinus cavities. . . . The doctor had a long wire thing—maybe a foot or more, and on the end was a pellet of radium. He stuffed it up my nose and into my sinus cavities on both sides. (I should probably check to see if my handkerchief is glowing in the dark.)"[73]

Zappa was a lifelong chain-smoker, so it is more likely that his smoking habit, not the radium treatment, caused his premature death from prostate cancer at fifty-three. Scientific studies have not conclusively linked NRI to early onset of cancer.[74] Nevertheless, like millions of other US citizens, Frank Zappa was an unknowing participant in the scientific community's infatuation with radioactivity during the Cold War.

SCORPIONS

David Hasselhoff's "Looking for Freedom" was heard throughout West and East Germany in 1989 and captured the spotlight on New Year's Eve night in Berlin, but the song that's become the finest encapsulation of the hope and euphoria of that time is "Wind of Change" by the German band Scorpions. Their roots go back to 1965 when guitarist Rudolf Schenker, born on August 31, 1948, started the band in Hanover, West Germany. In 1970 lead singer Klaus Meine joined, and they released their first album, *Lonesome Crow*, in 1972. Seeking international acclaim, they chose to record all their songs in English. Of this Schenker said, "We wanted to get away from this German history. From the Holocaust, from our parents' generation being at war with all the world. We wanted to be musicians and hopefully join the international family of music. That was one of the reasons for us to sing in English, to leave behind the German history that of course you couldn't be proud of."[75]

Constant touring and recording in the 1970s paid off, and by the early 1980s, they were one of the most popular hard rock/heavy metal bands in the world. Along with Schenker and Meine, the band's lineup during the years of their greatest success included Matthias Jabs on guitar, Francis Buchholz on bass, and Herman Rarebell on drums. Their 1984 album, *Love at First Sting*, was a breakthrough thanks to the hit song "Rock You Like a Hurricane." Another hit from the album, "Still Loving You," has subtle Cold War overtones, although few rock journalists or fans picked up on them when the song was climbing the charts. The lyrics describe a man trying to mend a broken relationship with a woman. A wall is used as a metaphor to describe their division. The chorus has the line "your pride has built a wall," while the second stanza of the first verse has the line "love, only love, can break down the wall someday." In retrospect, they were somewhat prophetic of the events of 1989.

In April 1988, they played ten sold out concerts in Leningrad, eight months after Billy Joel. Schenker remembers, "It was a dream come true to play in Russia because, from our point of view, because of our German history, we did so many bad things in Russia that we wanted to do something good. We wanted to show the people in Russia that here is a new generation of Germans growing up."[76] These concerts led a year later to the Moscow Music Peace Festival, a two-day concert that took place on August 12 and 13, 1989. It featured Scorpions, Mötley Crüe, Bon Jovi, Cinderella, Skid Row, Ozzy Osbourne, and Russian rock bands Gorky Park, Brigada S, and Nuance. The bands played in Lenin Stadium in Moscow to over one hundred thousand Soviet fans each day. Concertgoers were allowed to stand up, jump around, and cheer—something they did with trepidation during Billy Joel's concerts. Although the festival was scarred by the musicians' drug use and skirmishes between bands about the billing, it showed by the sheer magnitude of the crowds and the publicity it generated that the Soviet youth were ready for the freedom of expression granted by Gorbachev's policy of glasnost. It also inspired the greatest song about the end of the Cold War. Scorpions' lead singer, Klaus Meine, wrote "Wind of Change" during the festival, three months before the border between East and West Germany was opened. It was recorded in 1990 and released in January 1991. Meine shared his memories of this with rock historian Redbeard on the radio show *In the Studio*,

> There were so many kids from East Germany, from the GDR, at this Moscow show. [They were seeing us] for the first time. . . . We talked to many of them. They travelled all the way. We had the feeling [that it was] all loosening up. . . . Everybody could sense it was changing. That was the whole inspiration for "Wind of Change." That's why the song was written before the Berlin Wall came down. But it was what we all experienced in Moscow in those days. . . . We had a jam session, somebody gave me a balalaika as a present, a Russian guy, and we were playing for German television [the Beatles'] "Back in the U.S.S.R." It was an amazing vibe. It was a spirit of hope, because the Russians were always for us, when we grew up, the bad guys. But when we played there first in '88, we had a wonderful experience. And coming back there a year later [at the Moscow Music Peace Festival], . . . it had an impact on the youth, the young generation. They wanted to be a part of the whole world. . . . This inspiration was so strong. "I follow the Moskva, down to Gorky Park, listening to the wind of change," because that's what we just did. We were all on a boat on the Moskva, staying at the Ukraina which is

> a big hotel there. And there was a barbeque one night at the Gorky Park . . . [with] all those bands from America, from England, from Germany, from Russia, journalists from all over the world, and Russian soldiers, the Red Army. . . . And when we went up on stage, 100,000 people were singing "Still Loving You" with us. The Russian Army, they were supposed to be security, they went crazy like the audience. It makes your hair stand up. It gives you goosebumps all over your body just to think about it. . . . It was so exciting because of this whole Russian adventure for us as a German band, because of the history. . . . ["Wind of Change"] hit a certain nerve, and it became, in a way, a soundtrack to the politics of Gorbachev.[77]

The song was indeed indicative of changes sweeping through the Eastern Bloc countries in 1989 and 1990. Meine said, "One thing that was important to 'Wind of Change' was that we were not just a band singing about these things; we were a *part* of these things."[78] The lyrics are below.

Lyrics to "Wind of Change" by Scorpions (1990)

Verse 1:
I follow the Moskva
Down to Gorky Park
Listening to the wind of change
An August summer night
Soldiers passing by
Listening to the wind of change

The world is closing in
Did you ever think
That we could be so close, like brothers?
The future's in the air
I can feel it everywhere
Blowing with the wind of change

Chorus 1:
Take me to the magic of the moment
On a glory night
Where the children of tomorrow dream away
In the wind of change

Verse 2:
Walking down the street
Distant memories
Are buried in the past forever
I follow the Moskva
Down to Gorky Park
Listening to the wind of change

Chorus 2: Take me to the magic of the moment
On a glory night
Where the children of tomorrow share their dreams
With you and me

Take me to the magic of the moment
On a glory night
Where the children of tomorrow dream away
In the wind of change

Bridge: The wind of change
Blows straight into the face of time
Like a stormwind that will ring the freedom bell
For peace of mind
Let your balalaika sing
What my guitar wants to say

Chorus 3: Take me to the magic of the moment
On a glory night
Where the children of tomorrow share their dreams
With you and me

Take me to the magic of the moment
On a glory night
Where the children of tomorrow dream away
In the wind of change

The opening lines, "I follow the Moskva down to Gorky Park," place Meine, and us, in a boat on the Moskva River on its way to Gorky Park, an amusement park. The imposing icons of the Soviet Union, the Kremlin, and Red Square are not mentioned in the song. They have been replaced by the river and the amusement park. Red Army soldiers are passing by the singer, but they are not threatening figures. They too listen to the wind. The second stanza of verse one speaks of the world "closing in," getting smaller, more integrated, and more unified. It expresses wonder that Soviets and Westerners could be so close, like brothers.

The bridge of the song contains some remarkable imagery, using a storm wind, a bell, and a balalaika. First, it likens the wind of change to a "stormwind," bringing to mind not only the strong winds of a thunderstorm but the blast wave of a nuclear explosion and the scorching radioactive winds it produces. This wind, however, does not produce destruction and death. This storm wind "will ring the freedom bell for peace of mind." The ringing of bells has been a common trope for freedom in numerous countries around the world, but the term "freedom bell" implies a more specific reading, one packed with Cold War history. In October 1950, the United States gave West Berlin a massive ten-ton bell called "the Freedom Bell," or in German *die Freiheitsglocke*. Based on the one-ton Liberty Bell in Philadelphia, it was a sign of America's commitment to help West Berlin (surrounded on all sides by communist East Germany) remain free from Soviet influence and encroachment. The United States demonstrated this commitment in the 1948 to 1949 Berlin Airlift, which ended the Berlin Blockade. Installed in the tower at the *Rathaus Schöneberg*, which was the seat of the state senate of West Berlin from 1949 to 1990, the Freedom Bell has been rung every day at noon. It was also rung on occasions of historical significance, such as the East German Uprising in 1953, the Hungarian Uprising in 1956, the construction of the Berlin Wall in 1961, and the reunification of Germany in 1990. Thus, the storm wind that causes catastrophe in a storm or nuclear explosion has been transformed into a wind of change that rings out freedom, peace, and the end of the Cold War. Another remarkable line in the bridge is "let your balalaika sing what my guitar wants to say." Like the Kremlin, vodka, matryoshka (nesting dolls), and Tchaikovsky, the balalaika is an enduring symbol of Russia. The triangular-shaped, three-stringed instrument dates back at least to the seventeenth century and has become well-known outside Russia since the late nineteenth century thanks to traveling balalaika orchestras. The line in "Wind of Change" speaks of a dialogue between the iconic rock instrument, the guitar, and the iconic Russian instrument, the balalaika. Although language barriers make communication and understanding difficult between Soviets and Westerners, the language of music is a common tongue, one that both guitars and balalaikas speak. The line takes on additional meaning when one realizes Rudolf Schenker's Gibson "Flying V" guitar has the same triangular shape as a balalaika. During the Moscow Music Peace Festival, as mentioned above, a Russian fan gave Klaus Meine a balalaika as a gift. On the sleeve of the Russian version of the "Wind of Change" single, Klaus Meine is shown holding the balalaika over his shoulder. The open dialogue between the two instruments represents glasnost, the open dialogue between the West and the Soviet Union.

Although the band wrote several ballads before "Wind of Change," the song was quite a departure for them. It begins with Klaus Meine whistling and Matthias Jabs playing bluesy riffs on guitar. Pop, folk, and country musicians often employ whistling, but heavy metal bands rarely come on stage and start whistling a tune. The whistling projects a feeling of peace, gentleness, and calm, emotions rarely associated with hard rock and heavy metal. Of the whistling, Klaus Meine said, "When we first talked about the song, I wasn't sure if it was strong enough; it was a little different. We even spoke about not including the whistling."[79] As Schenker recalls, "The record company came and said, 'You know, guys, the song "Wind of Change," it's great . . . but maybe you can cut the whistling out?' And we tried it a few different ways, but we noticed immediately that when the whistling was out of the song, the song lost something."[80] The whistling was left in, and it has become a trademark of the song.

"Wind of Change" became a massive hit, reaching number one in over ten countries. The band then made a video for the song focusing on the historical significance of the Berlin Wall. The video begins with black-and-white footage of Soviet tanks roaring through Potsdamer Platz in 1953 during the people's uprising against the East German government. Moments later, more black-and-white footage of Potsdamer Platz is shown. This time a barbed wire fence is being put up in 1961, the first iteration of the Berlin Wall. Later in the video, color footage of the Berlin Wall being demolished is shown, as well as the toppling of the polystyrene brick wall at the end of Roger Waters's The Wall Live in Berlin concert in 1990, in which the Scorpions participated, again at Potsdamer Platz.

Eager to make the song available to Russians in their own language, Klaus Meine recorded a version of the song with Russian lyrics. It became a big hit in Russia. Gorbachev heard the song, loved it, and invited the band to meet him in the Kremlin. On meeting Gorbachev, Meine recounts,

> When we got this invitation from Gorbachev, [that] he wanted to see us in the Kremlin, we just couldn't believe it. . . . In December '91 we went to Moscow and we met him and his wife for one hour. He sent all the press out, after all the pictures were taken. He just wanted to spend time with us. . . . It was amazing. At this big conference table, he took me by the arm and said, "you're sitting next to me, forget the protocol." He started talking about *glasnost* and *perestroika*, and we were talking about rock and roll and music.[81] . . . The most memorable moment probably is when I said to him, "Mr. Gorbachev, when I was a kid, Nikita Khrushchev was in power and he took out his shoe and hit the table at the United Nations.[82] We were all in shock that there would be another war." And Gorbachev looked at me and he said, "I think that was rock & roll, wasn't it?"[83]

CONCLUSION

This chapter has shown how Western rock had an impact on the Eastern Bloc and played a role in ending the Cold War. Two questions related to this remain to be answered. First, did Russian popular music have any effect on America and England during the Cold War? It appears not. The winds of popular music culture blew from the West to the East, with little blowing the other way. There were no Russian language popular songs on the mainstream American or British charts during the Cold War. There was no widespread underground culture of Russian popular music either. The only Russian band to tour the United States and appear on MTV was the metal band Gorky Park in 1989 and 1990. During the Cold War, Russian bands did not have the means to record or distribute their music, let alone travel outside the Soviet Union. Even after the Cold War, there was not much interest in Russian rock in the West. To the West, Russian music meant Russian symphonic music, like Tchaikovsky or Shostakovich. Thomas Cushman, who interviewed numerous Russian rock musicians before and after the dissolution of the Soviet Union in December 1991, astutely observed,

> Unfortunately, as long as [Russian] rock music was seen in the West as a battle with the Soviet state instead of a more general commentary on Soviet existence, Western attention to Russian rock depended on the existence of a Soviet state and, more particularly, on a state which had been demonized in the consciousness of the Western public. The disappearance of the Soviet state produced a crisis for Russian rock musicians, for without a state which supposedly thwarted musicians at every juncture, the battles of musicians themselves would be seen as superfluous. Of what use could rockers be if they no longer had a state to fight against? Since most Westerners had little or no knowledge of the local meanings of rock music . . . their attention waned almost as soon as the Soviet state dissolved. Many members of the [Saint Petersburg] musical community were deeply aware and resentful of the superficiality and even banality of the Western perception of Soviet rock.[84]

Thus, the narrative of "the West is the best" dictated that Russian rock was thought of as simply a pale imitation of Western rock. Russian rock musicians were never granted a "human" face, just a mask of defeated communists trying to be Western rock stars.

The second question is, Did British and American popular musicians play a part in ending the Cold War in their own countries? Again, it appears they did not. As discussed in the section "Geopolitics in a Song" in the introductory chapter, there were organizations protesting against the nuclear-arms race, but the songs associated with these protests received little mainstream attention and did not reach iconic status. There was no anthem that caught the attention of world leaders for nuclear disarmament or harmony between the superpowers in the way "We Shall Overcome" caught the attention of President Lyndon Johnson for civil rights. The role American and British popular music played in the Cold War came not in the West but in the Eastern Bloc.

NOTES

1. Donna Bahry, "Politics, Generations, and Change in the USSR," in *Politics, Work, and Daily Life in the USSR: A Survey of Former Soviet Citizens*, ed. James R. Millar (Cambridge, MA: Cambridge University Press, 1987), 61–99; George W. Breslauer, "Is There a Generation Gap in the Soviet Political Establishment? Demand Articulation by RSFSR Provincial Party First Secretaries," *Soviet Studies* 36, no. 1 (January 1984): 1–25.

2. Hedrick Smith, *The Russians* (New York: Quadrangle/New York Times, 1976), 178.

3. Yale Richmond, *Cultural Exchange and the Cold War: Raising the Iron Curtain* (University Park: Pennsylvania State University Press, 2003), 123.

4. For more on this, see Danielle Fosler-Lussier, *Music in America's Cold War Diplomacy* (Oakland: University of California Press, 2015); Lisa E. Davenport, *Jazz Diplomacy: Promoting America in the Cold War Era* (Jackson: University Press of Mississippi, 2009); Penny M. Von Eschen, *Satchmo Blows Up the World: Jazz Ambassadors Play the Cold War* (Cambridge, MA: Harvard University Press, 2004).

5. Leslie Woodhead, "The Beatles: Bringing Down the Soviet Union," *CBS News This Morning* interview, May 18, 2013, 1:28–1:38, https://www.youtube.com/watch?v=UDWUJkWnaJQ.

6. Wilhelm Conrad Röntgen (1845–1923) was a German/Dutch physicist who was the first to investigate electromagnetic radiation in the wavelength range known as x-rays. Thus, the production of x-ray records (*roentgenizdat*) was named after him.

7. *Samizdat* was the practice during the Soviet era of self-publishing or copying literature that was forbidden by Soviet censorship.

8. Stephen Coates, ed., *X-Ray Audio* (London: Strange Attractor, 2015), 14.

9. Ibid., 9, 13, 14. Coates has also created a website that explores Soviet x-ray records called X-Ray Audio, https://x-rayaudio.squarespace.com/x-rayaudioproject/.

10. Leslie Woodhead, *How the Beatles Rocked the Kremlin: The Untold Story of a Noisy Revolution* (New York: Bloomsbury, 2013), 2, 151–155.

11. Mikhail Gorbachev, interview in *Paul McCartney in Red Square: A Concert Film* (A&E AAE-71104, 2005, DVD), 48:26–48:42, 49:12–49:16.

12. Vladimir Putin, speaking to McCartney in *Paul McCartney in Red Square*, 1:09:45–1:09:56.

13. Woodhead, *How the Beatles Rocked the Kremlin*, 153.

14. Sergei Ivanov, interview in *Paul McCartney in Red Square*, 53:03–53:40, 28:28–28:38.

15. Pavel Palazhchenko, *My Years with Gorbachev and Shevardnadze: The Memoir of a Soviet Interpreter* (University Park: Pennsylvania State University Press, 1997), 3.

16. Boris Grebenshchikov, interviewed by Alan Hunter in the 1987 MTV documentary "Tell Tchaikovsky the News: Rock in Russia," 50:16–50:31.

17. Artemy Troitsky, *Back in the USSR: The True Story of Rock in Russia* (Boston: Faber and Faber, 1987), 24.

18. Timothy W. Ryback, *Rock around the Bloc: A History of Rock Music in Eastern Europe and the Soviet Union* (New York: Oxford University Press, 1990); Sabrina Petra Ramet, ed., *Rocking the State: Rock Music and Politics in Eastern Europe and Russia* (Boulder, CO: Westview, 1994); William Jay Risch, ed., *Youth and Rock in the Soviet Bloc: Youth Cultures, Music, and the State in Russia and Eastern Europe* (Lanham, MD: Lexington Books, 2015).

19. Sergei I. Zhuk, *Rock and Roll in the Rocket City: The West, Identity, and Ideology in Soviet Dniepropetrovsk, 1960–1985* (Washington, DC: Woodrow Wilson Center, 2010), 171–179.

20. Tim Mohr, *Burning Down the Haus: Punk Rock, Revolution, and the Fall of the Berlin Wall* (Chapel Hill, NC: Algonquin, 2018).

21. "Iron Maiden Behind the Iron Curtain," *Iron Maiden: Live After Death* (Columbia Music Video 88697227379, 2008, DVD 2).

22. Philip Taubman, "At Soviet Rock Concert, the Beat of Security," *New York Times*, July 5, 1987, http://www.nytimes.com/1987/07/05/world/at-soviet-rock-concert-the-beat-of-security.html.

23. Tony Mitchell, "Mixing Pop and Politics: Rock Music in Czechoslovakia before and after the Velvet Revolution," *Popular Music* 11, no. 2 (May 1992): 187.

24. Marky Ramone, *Punk Rock Blitzkrieg* (New York: Touchstone, 2015), 337–338.

25. Everett True, *Hey Ho Let's Go: The Story of the Ramones* (New York: Omnibus, 2005), 253.

26. David Hasselhoff, with Peter Thompson, *Don't Hassel the Hoff: The Autobiography* (New York: Thomas Dunne, 2007), 122.

27. Ibid., 139.

28. "David Hasselhoff 1989," https://www.youtube.com/watch?v=MQ5rIbnD_P4.

29. Hasselhoff, *Don't Hassel the Hoff*, 140–141.

30. David Hasselhoff in *Hasselhoff vs. the Berlin Wall* (National Geographic, 2014, DVD), 3:48–3:53.

31. "The Berlin Celebration Concert 1989 - Leonard Bernstein - Beethoven Symphony No 9." Uploaded February 18, 2017, YouTube. https://www.youtube.com/watch?v=HnoIS-vlwCI.

32. David B. Dennis, *Beethoven in German Politics, 1870–1989* (New Haven, CT: Yale University Press, 1996), 198.

33. For an introduction to the story and themes of the album, which are far too complex to summarize here, see the opening page of Bret Urick's website, Pink Floyd The Wall: A Complete Analysis, http://www.thewallanalysis.com/.

34. Philip Jenkins, "Bricks in the Wall: An Interpretation of Pink Floyd's *The Wall*," in *Berlin Wall: Representations and Perspectives*, ed. Ernst Schürer, Manfred Keune, and Philip Jenkins (New York: Peter Lang, 1996), 210.

35. "Berliners Find Nazi Bunker with Arms, Murals Intact." *Los Angeles Times*, June 11, 1990, http://articles.latimes.com/1990-06-11/news/mn-146_1_east-berlin-border.

36. Michael Walsh, "Roger Waters' 'Wall.'" *Entertainment Weekly*, August 3, 1990, http://ew.com/article/1990/08/03/roger-waters-wall/.

37. Jonathan Park, from documentary on Roger Waters, *The Wall Live in Berlin*, written and directed by Roger Waters (Universal Music B0000369-09, 2003, DVD), 7:13–7:25.

38. Michael Walsh, "Roger Waters' 'Wall,'" *Entertainment Weekly*, August 3, 1990, http://ew.com/article/1990/08/03/roger-waters-wall/.

39. *Pink Floyd The Wall*, directed by Alan Parker, screenplay by Roger Waters (Sony BMG Music Entertainment CVD 58163, 2005, DVD).

40. Christine Brecht, "Peter Fechter," in *The Victims at the Berlin Wall 1961–1989: A Biographical Handbook*, ed. Hans-Hermann Hertle and Maria Nooke, trans. Miriamne Fields (Berlin: Ch. Links, 2011), 102–105.

41. Gerald Scarfe, *The Making of Pink Floyd The Wall* (London: Weidenfeld and Nicholson, 2010), 6, 11.

42. Marc Fisher, "Wall to Wall in Berlin," *Washington Post*, July 23, 1990, https://www.washingtonpost.com/archive/lifestyle/1990/07/23/wall-to-wall-in-berlin/0cc6b636-b780-4e9f-b8c7-67b1a9e137ff/?utm_term=.94d71622a3f3.

43. *Pink Floyd The Wall*, 1:20:08–1:21:19.

44. Roger Waters, *The Wall Live in Berlin*, written and directed by Roger Waters (Universal Music B0000369-09, 2003, DVD), 1:30:42–1:31:48.

45. "Juggling on the Berlin Wall," photograph by Yann Forget, November 16, 1989, https://commons.wikimedia.org/wiki/File:Juggling_on_the_Berlin_Wall.jpg.

46. Roger Waters, from documentary on Roger Waters, *The Wall Live in Berlin*, written and directed by Roger Waters (Universal Music B0000369-09, 2003, DVD), 5:37–5:43.

47. Tony Hollingsworth, from documentary on Roger Waters, *The Wall Live in Berlin*, written and directed by Roger Waters (Universal Music B0000369-09, 2003, DVD), 5:00–5:11.

48. Ibid., 1:12:27.

49. Roger Waters, from 2011 interview with Russ Williams on Absolute Radio, 5:44–6:14, https://www.youtube.com/watch?v=HaaVdpMrEyY.

50. Nick Mason, *Inside Out: A Personal History of Pink Floyd*, ed. Philip Dodd (London: Weidenfeld and Nicolson, 2004), 13.

51. Roger Waters and David Gilmour wrote other Cold War–themed songs, too numerous to analyze here, for Pink Floyd and solo albums. Some include "Two Suns in the Sunset" (Pink Floyd's *The Final Cut* [1983]), "Cruise" (David Gilmour's *About Face* [1984]), "Four Minutes" and "The Tide Is Turning (After Live Aid)" (Roger Wa-

ters's *Radio K.A.O.S.* [1987]), and "A Great Day for Freedom" (Pink Floyd's *The Division Bell* [1994]).

52. Shirley Temple changed her name to Shirley Temple Black when she married Charles Alden Black in 1950.

53. Shirley Temple Black, "Prague Journal: Shirley Temple Black Unpacks a Bag of Memories," interview by Craig R. Whitney, *New York Times*, September 11, 1989, A4.

54. John Swaine, "Shirley Temple Silenced Critics with Successful Roles in US Diplomacy," *Guardian*, February 11, 2014, https://www.theguardian.com/film/2014/feb/11/shirley-temple-ambassador-us-diplomacy.

55. Shirley Temple Black in the Czech documentary "Frank Zappa in Prague / Frank Zappa v Praze (20. - 24. 01. 1990)," 0:41–0:50, https://www.youtube.com/watch?v=1qF4fhWJR5s.

56. Richie Unterberger, *Unknown Legends of Rock 'n' Roll: Psychedelic Unknowns, Mad Geniuses, Punk Pioneers, Lo-fi Mavericks & More* (San Francisco: Backbeat, 1998), 191.

57. Jonathan Bolton, *Worlds of Dissent: Charter 77, the Plastic People of the Universe, and Czech Culture under Communism* (Cambridge, MA: Harvard University Press, 2012), 115–151.

58. Unterberger, *Unknown Legends*, 190–194.

59. Václav Havel, "The Power of the Powerless," in *Václav Havel or Living in Truth: Twenty-Two Essays Published on the Occasion of the Award of the Erasmus Prize to Václav Havel*, ed. Jan Vladislav (Boston: Faber and Faber, 1987), 64.

60. Kevin Courrier, *Dangerous Kitchen: The Subversive World of Zappa* (Toronto: ECW, 2002), 111–112.

61. Frank Zappa from "Frank Zappa - TV Interview, 1990." Interview from *The Today Show*, with Bryant Gumbel, Venice Beach, California, March 1990, 0:55–1:10, https://www.youtube.com/watch?v=m6w6KsQgWOs.

62. Ibid., 1:19–1:32, https://www.youtube.com/watch?v=m6w6KsQgWOs.

63. Neil Slavin, *Electric Don Quixote: The Definitive Story of Frank Zappa* (New York: Omnibus Press, 2003), 372; J. Y. Smith, "Czech Writer, President was Symbol of Freedom," *Washington Post*, December 19, 2011, A9.

64. Jack Anderson and Michael Binstein, "Baker Zaps Rocker Critical of His Wife," *Washington Post*, February 6, 1992, B11. The Parents Music Resource Center was headed up by Tipper Gore, the wife of Senator Al Gore (later vice president under Bill Clinton). Their objective was to place warning labels on recordings to inform buyers of explicit content. Along with Dee Snider of Twisted Sister and John Denver, Frank Zappa testified during the hearing against the labels and gave numerous interviews on the subject.

65. Richard Kostelanetz, ed., *The Frank Zappa Companion: Four Decades of Commentary* (New York: Schirmer, 1997), 247.

66. Unterberger, *Unknown Legends*, 191.

67. Frank Zappa, with Peter Occhiogrosso, *The Real Frank Zappa Book* (New York: Poseidon, 1989).

68. Martin Esslin, *Absurd Drama* (New York: Penguin, 1965), 23.

69. Eileen Welsome, *The Plutonium Files: America's Secret Medical Experiments in the Cold War* (New York: Dial, 1999); Eileen Welsome, "The Plutonium Files: How the U.S. Secretly Fed Radioactivity to Thousands of Americans," interview by Amy Goodman, "Democracy Now," May 5, 2004, https://www.democracynow.org/2004/5/5/plutonium_files_how_the_u_s.

70. "U.S. Radiation Experiments," Alliance for Human Research Protection (AHRP), http://ahrp.org/category/scientific-racism/us-radiation-experiments-atomic-energy-commission/.

71. Alice Cherbonnier, "Nasal Radium Irradiation of Children Has Health Fallout," *Baltimore Chronicle and Sentinel,* October 1, 1997, http://www.baltimorechronicle.com/rupnose.html.

72. Mark Maramont, "One Crusader's Effort to Publicize a Health Risk Finds Little Success," *Wall Street Journal,* July 26, 1999, http://www.wsj.com/articles/SB932939277927490585.

73. Zappa, *Real Frank Zappa Book*, 20.

74. Danielle Gordon, "The Verdict: No Harm, No Foul," *Bulletin of the Atomic Scientists* 52, no. 1 (January/February 1996): 32–40; "Nasopharyngeal Radium Irradiation (NRI) and Cancer: Fact Sheet," National Cancer Institute, https://stacks.stanford.edu/file/druid:st370yg4366/Fs3_87.pdf.

75. Rudolf Schenker, "Scorpions' 'Wind of Change': The Oral History of 1990's Epic Power Ballad," interview by Richard Bienstock, *Rolling Stone,* September 2, 2015, http://www.rollingstone.com/music/features/scorpions-wind-of-change-the-oral-history-of-1990s-epic-power-ballad-20150902.

76. Ibid.

77. Klaus Meine, "Scorpions—Moscow Music Peace Fest 30th Anniversary—Klaus Meine, Rudolph Schenker," interview by Redbeard, *In the Studio,* https://www.inthestudio.net/online-only-interviews/scorpions-love-first-sting-klaus-meinerudolph-schenker/.

78. Schenker, "Scorpions' 'Wind of Change.'"

79. Garry Sharpe-Young, *Metal: The Definitive Guide* (London: Jawbone, 2007), 63.

80. Schenker, "Scorpions' 'Wind of Change.'"

81. Meine, "Scorpions—Moscow Music Peace Fest."

82. For more on the hilarious and hotly debated incident of Khrushchev banging his shoe at the United Nations in 1960, see William Taubman's, *Khrushchev: The Man and His Era* (New York: W. W. Norton, 2003), 657–658; "Did He Bang It? Nikita Khrushchev and the Shoe," *New York Times,* July 26, 2003, http://www.nytimes.com/2003/07/26/opinion/did-he-bang-it-nikita-khrushchev-and-the-shoe.html.

83. Schenker, "Scorpions' 'Wind of Change.'"

84. Thomas Cushman, *Notes from the Underground: Rock Music Counterculture in Russia* (Albany, NY: State University of New York Press, 1995), 298–299.

CONCLUSION

IN THIS BOOK, WE HAVE shown how popular songs reveal deep and substantial insights into the social history of the Cold War. Like Cold War films, TV shows, and novels, the songs remind the listener how great a threat nuclear weapons were (and are!) and how utterly catastrophic World War III could be. The songs reflect the shifting and sometimes contradictory attitudes of the populace throughout the course of the conflict not only about nuclear weapons but about the proxy wars, the threat posed by communism, fear of the Soviet Union and China, civil defense, the Berlin Wall, the space race, uranium mining, and espionage. Songwriters expressed their opinions not only through lyrics and music but through album covers, live performances, interviews, and political activism. The songs are time capsules, capturing and preserving Cold War history in detail.

In looking broadly at the history of popular songs about warfare in the twentieth century, one can see a shift in sentiment and tone occurring during the Cold War. The popular songs that came out of World War I, World War II, and the Korean War were, for the most part, patriotic and sentimental. At the time, these wars were perceived as "good wars," and songwriters wrote more prowar than antiwar songs, with the notable exception of folk and protest singers. A shift occurred during the Vietnam War, when protest songs took the forefront across most genres. Many Americans perceived this war, as well as the nuclear-arms race, negatively. Thus, most of the songs in the latter half of the Cold War were antiwar.

This shift was spurred most urgently by the folk musicians of the 1940s and 1950s, who wrote many antiwar songs and were closely aligned with the labor movement, the civil rights movement, and other left-wing political stances. This viewpoint was then infused into the early rock of the 1950s and 1960s, mainstream rock from the 1960s to the 1980s, punk rock, heavy metal, reggae, and new wave. Few right-wing songs became hits, and when they did, they often became fodder for parody. For example, Janet Greene's anticommunist songs never reached beyond the anticommunist crusade from which they originated. We have found hundreds of songs about the dangers nuclear weapons pose to humankind but only a few songs advocating for more weapons or arguing that more weapons equal more deterrence. This book shows that popular music about politics in the latter half of the twentieth century was clearly antiestablishment. It was much more common to criticize than it was to praise the government. Songs expressing patriotism tended to be regarded as trite, sentimental, manipulative, and jingoistic, while songs protesting against government policy tended to be taken more seriously. Songs addressing political issues have been written for centuries, but the protest song as we know it today came to fruition during the Cold War.

Besides giving a bird's-eye view of Cold War music, we've also explored how songwriters in specific genres of popular music expressed their different views. Country musicians stand out here as the lone conservative voice applauding America's actions among a sea of liberal dissenters. Most country songwriters saw the United States as a shining city on a hill, a beacon of democracy, and the world's policeman, keeping communist dictators at bay. Manifesting their beliefs rooted in southern Christian traditions, country musicians filled their lyrics with Bible quotations, patriotic sentiments, and warnings of retribution for America's enemies. While they expressed fear of the atomic bomb and questioned its use in warfare, they also saw it as America's best defense against communist encroachment. On the other side of the political spectrum, folk musicians were passionate about free speech, ending McCarthyism, banning the bomb, stopping the proxy wars, and giving certain aspects of socialism a try. While most folk singers did not see communism as a viable solution to America's problems, some did. Paul Robeson and Peggy Seeger traveled to the Soviet Union to see for themselves what life in a communist country might be like.

While country and folk songwriters were passionately for or against the Cold War, comedy songwriters passionately made fun of it. They made the horror of a nuclear apocalypse all the more real not by describing it in detail but by satirizing it. They showed comedy can be used as incisive and persuasive political commentary. They poked fun at communist leaders, such as Stalin, Khrushchev, and Castro, and even US presidents. Bomb shelters were a favorite target, and songwriters were fond of quipping that they would be better used as love shacks than as protection against B-52 bombers. One of the most well-known songs that came out of the Cold War, "Bert the Turtle (The Duck and Cover Song)," has come to be regarded as a joke, even though it was intended in the 1950s to convey sober advice about preserving lives during a nuclear attack.

Like the novelty and comedy songwriters, the early rock stars from the 1950s made light of the atomic bomb. Yet these songs often lack the social commentary and wit found in the satirical songs. They were intended to amuse and shock the listener. Bombs, missiles, atomic energy, and mushroom clouds were used as sexual metaphors in dozens of early rock songs. On the other hand, African American and Latin American musicians wrote songs in the styles of doo-wop, calypso, musicals, blues, and spirituals that asked substantive questions about the bomb and other Cold War issues. Songs from minority groups such as these pushed back against the frivolity and therefore have much in common with the folk songs covered in the first two chapters.

Moving into the 1970s and 1980s, we find songwriters wrote fewer humorous songs or songs expressing wonder about the glorious future promised by harnessing the atom. As the superpowers pushed the number of nuclear weapons into the tens of thousands, dread of nuclear war became the dominating theme. We also see the number of songs written by British songwriters becomes greater than those written by Americans. The Brits felt more threatened by the escalation of the arms race since they didn't have a substantial stockpile of weapons or the buffer of the Atlantic Ocean, which America enjoyed. Another trend we see in post-Vietnam era music is musicians traveling abroad to Cold War hotspots. Joan Baez (North Vietnam), Sting (Chile), U2 (El Salvador and Nicaragua), Billy Joel (Soviet Union), David Bowie (West Berlin), and Bruce Springsteen (East Berlin) wrote songs about their firsthand experiences of Cold War places and events.

The styles of music that produced the greatest number of Cold War–themed songs in the 1970s and 1980s were mainstream rock, hard rock/heavy metal, punk rock, and electronic/new wave. Hard rock and heavy metal bands expressed Cold War angst through their instrumentation just as much as through their lyrics. The actual sounds generated by their drums and distorted guitars allowed listeners to "feel" the tumult of warfare and contemplate the consequences of a nuclear apocalypse in a way earlier styles of music could not. Likewise, electronic musicians, especially Kraftwerk, used synthesizers to mimic the sounds of war, emphasizing the close relationship between war technology and instrument technology. They even turned Cold War technology (Geiger counters, for example) into musical instruments. Punk musicians dispensed with anything peripheral and wrote short, direct songs laser-focused on the perils of the nuclear-arms race. Some, such as Crass, were involved in the Campaign for Nuclear Disarmament. The final chapter of the book shows how musicians were caught up in some odd circumstances in Czechoslovakia, Berlin, and Moscow as the Cold War came to its close.

Did popular musicians engage with Cold War issues after the conflict ended? Several did. Even before the official dissolution of the Soviet Union in December 1991, songwriters reflected the optimism and euphoria of the end of the Cold

War. The music video for Jesus Jones's "Right Here, Right Now" (1990) captures how quickly the events enfolded—"at the blink of an eye"—with the Berlin Wall falling and several nations breaking free from the Soviet Union. Even country songwriters, those who expressed the most vehement anti-Soviet sentiments, changed their tune. When Iraq invaded Kuwait in August 1990, the event that precipitated the first Gulf War, Mikhail Gorbachev joined George Bush in condemning Saddam Hussein's actions. Hank Williams Jr. wrote "Don't Give Us a Reason" (1990). The lyrics have the line "the eagle and the bear make a mighty strong pair." The Russian bear and the American eagle now joined together as allies against Saddam, even before the Soviet Union had dissolved.

Songs about Cold War topics became scarcer in the late 1990s and 2000s. The songs written then took on a historical tone, looking back at certain events with a somewhat detached perspective. Nuclear war continued to be addressed, such as in "Brighter Than a Thousand Suns" by Iron Maiden (2006) and Linkin Park's concept album, *A Thousand Suns* (2010). Kitschy humor about the bomb, difficult to find in the 1980s, made a return with the Killers' "Miss Atomic Bomb" (2012). The cover of the promotional CD single features Las Vegas dancer Lee Merlin, a model who wore a mushroom cloud made of cardboard and cotton balls over her swimsuit on the occasion of a nuclear-bomb test in 1957 at the Nevada Test Site. Songs about communism were rare after the Cold War since the Soviet Union collapsed and the Chinese were not perceived as a threat. One example would be "Stranger in Moscow" (1995) by Michael Jackson, with its brooding lines about the KGB, "Stalin's tomb," and the "Kremlin's shadow." Space race songs were also rare since there was no space race to write about. There were scarcely any songs about civil defense, bomb shelters, or Geiger counters since they had been dismissed as useless as early as the 1960s.

Since the songs discussed in this book are decades old, some readers—especially the younger sort—may regard them as relics of a foregone age and question what relevance they have today. Some may wonder at all the controversy and commotion about nuclear weapons and communism in the twentieth century, as represented in these songs. After all, nuclear war never happened. The Soviet Union collapsed. Wasn't the Cold War simply a nuclear-arms race that fizzled out and an ideological battle between communism and capitalism? Writing about his course on the Cold War at Yale University, professor John Lewis Gaddis observed, "When I talk about Stalin and Truman, even Reagan and Gorbachev, it could as easily be Napoleon, Caesar, or Alexander the Great. . . . My students sign up for this course with very little sense of how the Cold War started, what it was about, or why it ended in the way that it did. For them it's history: not all that different from the Peloponnesian War."[1]

The songs discussed in this book show why the Cold War was one of the monumental events of the twentieth century. Oppressive communism and nuclear weapons were more than just threats. They were reality. Several scholars assert that the actions of communist dictators (executions, forced labor camps, famines, economic dispossession) caused even more deaths than the seventy million who perished in World War II.[2] Additionally, the proxy wars resulted in over five million deaths. Thousands of people also died in radiation experiments, nuclear-bomb tests, and nuclear accidents. Several incidents, such as the Cuban Missile Crisis and accidents or false alerts with nuclear missiles, came close to starting World War III.

One of the most frightening aspects of the Cold War is the fact, in some ways, it is still ongoing. The probing, disquieting questions Vern Partlow's "Old Man Atom" raises are just as relevant today as they were when he wrote the song in 1945. As long as nuclear weapons exist in the world, we cannot say the danger of nuclear war is over. In fact, according to many prominent nuclear-war theorists, the risk has never been greater. In January 2020, the Doomsday Clock moved to 100 seconds to midnight, the closest it has ever been. It is closer now than it was in 1984 (then at three minutes) when there were approximately seventy thousand nuclear weapons in the world and arms-reduction talks between the superpowers had ceased for two years. It appears nuclear weapons will always be a part of human civilization. Even if through some miracle all nations disarm themselves and ban nuclear weapons, the knowledge and potential to construct weapons of mass destruction will always be there. What countries in the future will develop nuclear weapons? Might terrorists or rogue states obtain them through subterfuge?

There has been a noticeable rise in the number of songs about Cold War issues in recent years as a result of Russia's invasion of Ukraine, Donald Trump being elected president of the United States, and the desire of Iran and North Korea to join the nuclear club. As with the Cold War–era songs, their tone varies from comedy to condemnation. In "Putin," Randy Newman melodramatically portrays the Russian leader as the man who will put Russia back on top again, sitting in the "comfy chair." Musicians such as Billy Bragg ("The Times They Are A-Changing Back") have voiced negative opinions about President Trump. Many of the anti-Trump songs have been written by hip-hop artists, such as Eminem. In "North Korea Polka (Please Don't Nuke Us)," "Weird Al" Yankovic tries to convince Kim Jong-un that Americans aren't evil and aren't worth bombing. They're just a "bunch of simple fidget-spinning goofy dorks."

Regardless of musical style, popular music will continue to be a medium through which citizens express their political views. If deterrence theory fails and nuclear weapons become more of a palpable threat to our planet, what new songs will be written? What will their effect be? From what styles of popular music will songs emerge? We can surmise songwriters will write what their conscious dictates. They will also look to the songs discussed in this book for inspiration and insight. Popular songs will continue to reflect, and perhaps change, the way society thinks about the continuing Cold War.

NOTES

1. John Lewis Gaddis, *The Cold War: A New History* (New York: Penguin, 2005), ix.
2. Steven Rosefielde, *Red Holocaust* (New York: Routledge, 2010); Benjamin A. Valentino, *Final Solutions: Mass Killing and Genocide in the Twentieth Century* (Ithaca, NY: Cornell University Press, 2004).

BIBLIOGRAPHY

Adlers, Freddie "Freddan." "Fender Rhodes: The Piano That Changed the History of Music." Fenderrhodes.com. Accessed October 7, 2020. http://www.fenderrhodes.com/history/narrative.html.

Allen, Philip W., and Lester Machta. "Transport of Radioactive Debris from Operations Buster and Jangle." Washington, DC: US Department of Commerce, Weather Bureau, Armed Forces Special Weapons Project, 1952.

Alliance for Human Research Protection (AHRP). "U.S. Radiation Experiments." Accessed October 7, 2020. http://ahrp.org/category/scientific-racism/us-radiation-experiments-atomic-energy-commission/.

Alonso, Harriet Hyman. *Peace as a Women's Issue: A History of the U.S. Movement for World Peace and Women's Rights*. Syracuse: Syracuse University Press, 1993.

———. *Yip Harburg: Legendary Lyricist and Human Rights Activist*. Middletown, CT: Wesleyan University Press, 2012.

American Business Consultants. *Red Channels: The Report of Communist Influence in Radio and Television*. New York: American Business Consultants, 1950.

"American Icons: Jimi Hendrix's Star-Spangled Banner." Studio 360 radio show, produced by David Krasnow, November 19, 2010. http://www.studio360.org/story/96239-jimi-hendrixs-star-spangled-banner/.

Americas Watch. *El Salvador's Decade of Terror: Human Rights since the Assassination of Archbishop Romero*. New Haven, CT: Yale University Press, 1991.

———. *Human Rights in Nicaragua: Reagan, Rhetoric, and Reality*. New York: Americas Watch Committee, 1985.

———. *Violations of the Laws of War by Both Sides in Nicaragua, 1981–1985*. New York: Americas Watch Committee, 1985.

Amnesty International. *Chile*. London: Amnesty International Publications, 1988.

———. *El Salvador: "Death Squads"; A Government Strategy*. London: Amnesty International, 1988.

———. *Nicaragua: The Human Rights Record*. London: Amnesty International Publications, 1986.

Amundson, Michael A. *Yellowcake Towns: Uranium Mining Communities in the American West*. Boulder: University Press of Colorado, 2002.

Anderson, Jack, and Michael Binstein. "Baker Zaps Rocker Critical of His Wife." *Washington Post*, February 6, 1992.

Ansari, Emily Abrams. "Shaping the Policies of Cold War Musical Diplomacy: An Epistemic Community of American Composers." *Diplomatic History* 36 (January 2012): 41–52.

Anschel, Eugene. *American Appraisals of Soviet Russia, 1917–1977*. Metuchen, NJ: Scarecrow, 1978.

Antonia, Nina. *Too Much, Too Soon: The Makeup and Breakup of the New York Dolls*. London: Omnibus, 1998.

Apodaca, Clair. *Understanding U.S. Human Rights Policy: A Paradoxical Legacy*. New York: Routledge, 2006.

Arbel, David, and Ran Edelist. *Western Intelligence and the Collapse of the Soviet Union, 1980 1990: Ten Years That Did Not Shake the World*. Portland, OR: Frank Cass, 2003.

Armbruster, Gary. "Geddy Lee of Rush." *Keyboard* 10, no. 9 (September 1984): 52–65.

Arnson, Cynthia J. "Window on the Past: A Declassified History of Death Squads in El Salvador." In *Death Squads in Global Perspective: Murder with Deniability*, edited by Bruce B. Campbell and Arthur D. Brenner, 85–124. New York: St. Martin's, 2000.

Artists United Against Apartheid. "Sun City." Uploaded July 7, 2010, YouTube. https://www.youtube.com/watch?v=bY3w9gLjEV4.

Atomic Archive. "The Voice of Hibakusha." Accessed October 7, 2020. https://www.atomicarchive.com/resources/documents/hibakusha/index.html.

Baade, Christina L. *Victory through Harmony: The BBC and Popular Music in World War II*. New York: Oxford University Press, 2012.

Babiuk, Andy. *Beatles Gear*. Foreword by Mark Lewisohn. Edited by Tony Bacon. San Francisco: Backbeat, 2001.

Baez, Joan. *And a Voice to Sing With: A Memoir*. New York: Simon and Schuster, 2009.

———. "Playboy Interview: Joan Baez." Interview by Nat Hentoff. *Playboy*, July 1970, 54–62.

Bahry, Donna. "Politics, Generations, and Change in the USSR." In *Politics, Work, and Daily Life in the USSR: A Survey of Former Soviet Citizens*, edited by James R. Millar, 61–99. New York: Cambridge University Press, 1987.

Bangs, Alan. "U2—Interview, 20 Aug 83." Uploaded August 21, 2009, YouTube. http://www.youtube.com/watch?v=dfdsoIlGH9s.

Bangs, Lester. "Kraftwerk: The Final Solution to the Music Problem? *New Musical Express*, September 6, 1975.

———. "Kraftwerkfeature: or How I Learned to Stop Worrying & Love the Balm." *Creem* (September 1975): 30.

———. *Psychotic Reactions and Carburetor Dung*. New York: Knopf, 1987.

"Barbara Is Moscow Molly to U.S. Soldiers in Berlin." *Reading Eagle*, January 11, 1962. http://news.google.com/newspapers?nid=1955&dat=19620111&id=wBIrAAAAIBAJ&sjid=oZsFAAAAIBAJ&pg=5712,3789556.

Barry, Stuyvesant. "Chapter XVII—After World War II." *Hammond as in Organ: The Laurens Hammond Story*. Unpublished manuscript, 1974. http://thehammondorganstory.com/chapterxvii.asp.

Bartrop, Paul R. *A Biographical Encyclopedia of Contemporary Genocide: Portraits of Evil and Good*. Santa Barbara, CA: ABC-CLIO, 2012.

Beeber, Steven Lee. *The Heebie Jeebies at CBGB's: A Secret History of Jewish Punk*. Chicago: Chicago Review, 2006.

Belz, Carl. *The Story of Rock*. New York: Oxford University Press, 1969.

Benarde, Scott R. *Stars of David: Rock 'n' Roll's Jewish Stories*. Hanover, NH: Brandeis University Press, 2003.

Bennett, Bruce. *Spirit in Exile: Peter Porter and His Poetry*. New York: Oxford University Press, 1991.

Bentley, Eric, ed. *Thirty Years of Treason: Excerpts from Hearings before the House Committee on Un-American Activities, 1938–1968*. New York: Viking, 1971.

Berger, George. *The Story of Crass*. Oakland, CA: PM Press, 2009.

"The Berlin Celebration Concert 1989 - Leonard Bernstein - Beethoven Symphony No 9." Uploaded February 18, 2017, YouTube. https://www.youtube.com/watch?v=HnoIS-vlwCI.

"Berliners Find Nazi Bunker with Arms, Murals Intact." *Los Angeles Times*, June 11, 1990. http://articles.latimes.com/1990-06-11/news/mn-146_1_east-berlin-border.

Bernstein, Barton J. "Truman and the A-Bomb: Targeting Noncombatants, Using the Bomb, and His Defending the 'Decision.'" *Journal of Military History* 62, no. 3 (July 1998): 547–570.

Bernstein, David W., ed. *The San Francisco Tape Music Center: 1960s Counterculture and the Avant-Garde*. Berkeley: University of California Press, 2008.

Bessman, Jim. *Ramones: An American Band*. New York: St. Martin's, 1993.

Bienstock, Richard. "Scorpions' 'Wind of Change': The Oral History of 1990's Epic Power Ballad." *Rolling Stone*, September 2, 2015. http://www.rollingstone.com/music/features/scorpions-wind-of-change-the-oral-history-of-1990s-epic-power-ballad-20150902.

Black, Earl, and Merle Black. *The Rise of Southern Republicans*. Cambridge, MA: Belknap, 2002.

"'Black Stalin' Aim Is Laid to Robeson: Ex-Red Official Says Singer, a Communist, Suffered 'Delusions of Grandeur.'" *New York Times*, July 15, 1949.

Bloch, Avital H. "Joan Baez: A Singer and Activist." In *Impossible to Hold: Women and Culture in the 1960s*, edited by Avital H. Bloch and Lauri Umansky, 126–151. New York: New York University Press, 2005.

The Blue Book of the John Birch Society. Boston: Western Islands, 1959.

Bogart, Humphrey. "I'm No Communist." *Photoplay*, March 1948.

Bogle, Lori Lyn. *The Pentagon's Battle for the American Mind: The Early Cold War*. College Station: Texas A&M University Press, 2004.

Bolton, Jonathan. *Worlds of Dissent: Charter 77, the Plastic People of the Universe, and Czech Culture under Communism*. Cambridge, MA: Harvard University Press, 2012.

Bono. *Bono: In Conversation with Michka Assayas*. New York: Riverhead, 2005.

Bordo, Susan. *Unbearable Weight: Feminism, Western Culture, and the Body*. 10th anniversary ed. Berkeley: University of California Press, 2003.

Boswell, Matthew. *Holocaust Impiety in Literature, Popular Music and Film*. New York: Palgrave Macmillan, 2012.

Bourke, Joanna. *Fear: A Cultural History*. Emeryville, CA: Shoemaker and Hoard, 2006.

Bowie, David. "David Bowie: Let's Dance 30th Anniversary." Redbeard's *In the Studio* radio show.

Bowman, Durrell. "More Than They Bargained For." In *Rush and Philosophy: Heart and Mind United*, edited by Jim Berti and Durrell Bowman, 169–188. Chicago: Open Court, 2011.

Boyer, Paul. *By the Bomb's Early Light: American Thought and Culture at the Dawn of the Atomic Age*. Chapel Hill: University of North Carolina Press, 1994.

Bradley, Doug, and Craig Werner. *We Gotta Get Out of This Place: The Soundtrack of the Vietnam War*. Amherst: University of Massachusetts Press, 2015.

Braestrup, Peter. "Joan Baez and the Interpreter, or What Japanese Didn't Hear." *New York Times*, February 21, 1967.

Branstetter, Leah. "Wanda Jackson Goes to Japan: The Hidden Histories of 'Fujiyama Mama.'" Paper presented at the EMP Pop Conference, Seattle, WA, April 24–27, 2014.

Braun, Hans-Joachim. "Introduction: Technology and the Production and Reproduction of Music in the 20th Century." In *Music and Technology in the Twentieth Century*, edited by Hans Joachim Braun, 9–32. Baltimore: The Johns Hopkins University Press, 2002.

———. "'Strange Bedfellows': The Relationship between Music Technology and Military Technology in the First Half of the Twentieth Century." In *Global Village—Global Brain—Global Music, KlangArt-Kongreß 1999*, edited by Bernd Enders and Joachim Stange-Elbe, 137–152. Osnabrück: Electronic Publishing Osnabrück, 2003.

Braw, Monica. *The Atomic Bomb Suppressed: American Censorship in Occupied Japan*. Armonk, NY: M. E. Sharpe, 1991.

Brelis, Dean. *Run, Dig or Stay? A Search for an Answer to the Shelter Question*. Boston: Beacon, 1962.

Breslauer, George W. "Is There a Generation Gap in the Soviet Political Establishment?: Demand Articulation by RSFSR Provincial Party First Secretaries." *Soviet Studies* 36, no. 1 (January 1984): 1–25.

Britten, Loretta, and Sarah Brash, eds. *Our American Century: The American Dream: The 50s*. Richmond, VA: Time-Life, 1998.

Broadside #1 (February 1962). https://singout.org/downloads/broadside/b001.pdf.

Broadside #18 (late December 1962). https://singout.org/downloads/broadside/b018.pdf.

Brock, Gerald W. *The Second Information Revolution*. Cambridge, MA: Harvard University Press, 2003.

Brocker, Carsten. "Kraftwerk: Technology and Composition." In *Kraftwerk: Music Non-Stop*, edited by Sean Albiez and David Pattie and translated by Michael Patterson, 97–118. New York: Continuum, 2011.

Brookfield, Tarah. *Cold War Comforts: Canadian Women, Child Safety, and Global Insecurity, 1945–1975*. Waterloo, Ontario: Wilfrid Laurier University Press, 2012.

Broscious, S. David. "Longing for International Control, Banking on American Superiority: Harry S. Truman's Approach to Nuclear Weapons." In *Cold War Statesmen Confront the Bomb: Nuclear Diplomacy since 1945*, edited by John Lewis Gaddis, Philip H. Gordon, Ernest R. May, and Jonathan Rosenberg, 15–38. Oxford: Oxford University Press, 1999.

Brugge, Doug, Timothy Benally, and Esther Yazzie-Lewis, eds. *The Navajo People and Uranium Mining*. Albuquerque: University of New Mexico Press, 2006.

Brune, Lester, and Richard Dean Burns. *Chronology of the Cold War, 1917–1992*. New York: Routledge, 2006.

Buckley, David. *Kraftwerk Publikation*. New York: Overlook Omnibus, 2015.

———. "Revisiting Bowie's Berlin." In *David Bowie: Critical Perspectives*, edited by Eoin Devereux, Aileen Dillane, and Martin J. Power, 215–229. New York: Routledge, 2015.

Bulletin of the Atomic Scientists. "Purpose." Accessed October 7, 2020. http://thebulletin.org/purpose/.

Buskin, Richard. "Classic Tracks: Depeche Mode 'People Are People.'" *Sound on Sound*, February 2007. http://www.soundonsound.com/people/classic-tracks-depeche-mode-people-are-people.

Bussy, Pascal. *Kraftwerk: Man, Machine and Music*. 3rd ed. London: SAF, 2005.

Cahill, Tim. "Joan Baez in Hanoi: 12 Days under the Bombs." *Rolling Stone*, February 1, 1973.

Calamur, Krishnadev. "'Heroes' at the Wall." *Atlantic*, January 11, 2016. http://www.theatlantic.com/notes/2016/01/bowie-berlin-1987/423564/.

Cantor, Joanne. "Fear Reactions and the Mass Media." In *The Routledge Handbook of Emotions and Mass Media*, edited by Katrin Döveling, Christian von Scheve, and Elly A. Konijn, 148–165. New York: Routledge, 2011.

Carawan, Guy and Candie, eds. *Sing for Freedom: The Story of the Civil Rights Movement through Its Songs*. Bethlehem, PA: Sing Out, 1990.

Cash, W. J. *The Mind of the South*. New York: Knopf, 1941.

Castro, Fidel, and Ignacio Ramonet. *Fidel Castro: My Life; A Spoken Autobiography*. Translated by Andrew Hurley. New York: Scribner, 2008.

Cateforis, Theo. *Are We Not New Wave? Modern Pop at the Turn of the 1980s*. Ann Arbor: University of Michigan Press, 2011.

CBS News Sunday Morning. "V for Victory." Sunday Morning Almanac. Uploaded July 19, 2015, YouTube, narrated by Jane Pauley. https://www.youtube.com/watch?v=T6eIkamRsO8.

Chase, Jennifer. "'87 Concert Was a Genesis of East German Rebellion." *Deutsche Welle*, July 4, 2007. http://www.dw.com/en/87-concert-was-a-genesis-of-east-german-rebellion/a-2663850.

Cherbonnier, Alice. "Nasal Radium Irradiation of Children Has Health Fallout." *Baltimore Chronicle & Sentinel*, October 1, 1997. http://www.baltimorechronicle.com/rupnose.html.

Churchill, Winston. *Never Give In! The Best of Winston Churchill's Speeches*. New York: Hyperion, 2003.

"Civil Defense: The Sheltered Life." *Time*, October 20, 1961.

Clague, Mark. "'This Is America': Jimi Hendrix's Star Spangled Banner Journey as Psychedelic Citizenship." *Journal of the Society for American Music* 8, no. 4 (November 2014): 435–478.

Clarke, Eric F. *Ways of Listening: An Ecological Approach to the Perception of Musical Meaning*. Oxford: Oxford University Press, 2005.

Clausewitz, Karl von. *On War*. Translated by O.J. Matthijs Jolles. Washington, DC: Combat Forces, 1953.

Clover, Joshua. *1989: Bob Dylan Didn't Have This to Sing About*. Berkeley: University of California Press, 2009.

Coates, Stephen. *X-Ray Audio*. London: Strange Attractor, 2015.

Cohen, William Howard. *To Walk in Seasons: An Introduction to Haiku*. Rutland, VT: Charles E. Tuttle, 1972.

Cohn, Carol. "Sex and Death in the Rational World of Defense Intellectuals." In *Exposing Nuclear Phallacies*, edited by Diana E. H. Russell, 127–159. New York: Pergamon, 1989; *Signs* 12, no. 4, Within and Without: Women, Gender, and Theory (Summer 1987): 687–718. http://genderandsecurity.org/sites/default/files/carol_cohn_sex_and_death_in_the_world_of_rational_defense_intellectuals.pdf.

Collins, Nick, Margaret Schedel, and Scott Wilson. *Electronic Music*. New York: Cambridge University Press, 2013.

Committee for the Compilation of Materials on Damage Caused by the Atomic Bombs in Hiroshima and Nagasaki. *Hiroshima and Nagasaki: The Physical, Medical, and Social Effects of the Atomic Bombings*. Translated by Eisei Ishikawa and David L. Swain. New York: Basic, 1981.

———. *The Impact of the A-Bomb, Hiroshima and Nagasaki, 1945–85*. Translated by Eisei Ishikawa, and David L. Swain. Tokyo: Iwanami Shoten, 1985.

Communist Interrogation, Indoctrination, and Exploitation of Prisoners of War. Pamphlet no. 30-101. Washington, DC: US Department of the Army, 1956.

CONELRAD. Website created by Ken Sitz, Bill Geerhart, and Curtis Samson. Accessed October 7, 2020. http://www.conelrad.com/index.php.

———. "Anti-Baez: The Ballad of Janet Greene." Accessed October 7, 2020. http://www.conelrad.com/greene/index.php.

———. "Anti-Baez: The Janet Greene Songbook." Accessed October 7, 2020. http://www.conelrad.com/greene/janetgreene_songbook.php.

———. "Atomic Honeymooners: 'Well-Sheltered Love May Last a Lifetime.'" Accessed October 7, 2020. http://www.conelrad.com/atomic_honeymooners.html.

———. "The Freewheelin' Janet Greene: The CONELRAD Interview." Accessed October 7, 2020. http://www.conelrad.com/greene/interview.php.

CONELRAD Adjacent. "Atomic Goddess Revisited: Rita Hayworth's Bomb Image Found!" August 19, 2013. http://conelrad.blogspot.com/2013/08/atomic-goddess-revisited-rita-hayworths.html.

"'Conscientious Objector' Stays at School during Test." *Palo Alto Times*, February 7, 1958.

Cope, Andrew L. *Black Sabbath and the Rise of Heavy Metal Music*. Burlington, VT: Ashgate, 2010.

Cott, Jonathan, ed. *Bob Dylan: The Essential Interviews*. New York: Wenner, 2006.

Cotten, Lee. *The Elvis Catalog: Memorabilia, Icons, and Collectibles Celebrating the King of Rock 'n' Roll*. Garden City, NY: Doubleday and Company, 1987.

Courrier, Kevin. *Dangerous Kitchen: The Subversive World of Zappa*. Toronto: ECW, 2002.

Covach, John. "Form in Rock Music: A Primer." In *Engaging Music: Essays in Music Analysis*, edited by Deborah Stein, 65–76. New York: Oxford University Press, 2005.

Cross, Charles R. *Room Full of Mirrors: A Biography of Jimi Hendrix*. New York: Hyperion, 2005.

Crossland, David. "Chimes of Freedom: How Springsteen Helped Tear Down the Wall." *Spiegel Online*, June 19, 2013. http://www.spiegel.de/international/germany/book-says-springsteen-concert-helped-bring-down-berlin-wall-a-906236-2.html.

Cunningham, David. "Kraftwerk and the Image of the Modern." In *Kraftwerk: Music Non-Stop*, edited by Sean Albiez and David Pattie, 44–62. New York: Continuum, 2011.

Curnin, Cy. "In the Studio 30 Years Ago: The Fixx *Reach the Beach*." Redbeard's *In the Studio* radio show. Accessed October 7, 2020. https://www.inthestudio.net/online-only-interviews/fixx-reach-beach/.

Cushman, Thomas. *Notes from the Underground: Rock Music Counterculture in Russia.* Albany: State University of New York Press, 1995.

Daisley, Bob. *For Facts Sake.* Moonee Ponds, Victoria, Australia: Thompson Music, 2013.

Daniels, Charlie. "Peace through Strength." *Soapbox* on the Charlie Daniels Band website. Accessed March 21, 2014. http://www.charliedaniels.com/soap-box?b_id=366&pg=31.

Darden, Robert F. "The Other Berlin Wall—and What It Can Teach Us Today." *Huffington Post.* Last updated January 5, 2015. http://www.huffingtonpost.com/robert-f-darden/the-other-berlin-walland-_b_6102746.html.

Davenport, Lisa E. *Jazz Diplomacy: Promoting America in the Cold War Era.* Jackson: University Press of Mississippi, 2009.

Davies, Dave. *Kink: An Autobiography.* New York: Hyperion, 1996.

Davies, Hunter, and Giles Smith. "Sting: How We Mock Our Most Serious Star, Our National Friend of the Earth. Shouldn't He Be a Protected Species? Or at Least a Respected One?" *Independent,* May 1, 1993. http://www.independent.co.uk/life-style/interview—sting-how-we-mock-our-most-serious-star-our-national-friend-of-the-earth-shouldnt-he-be-a-protected-species-or-at-least-a-respected-one-2320343.html.

Dawson, Jim, and Steve Propes. *What Was the First Rock 'n' Roll Record?* Boston: Faber and Faber, 1992.

DeGroot, Gerard J. *The Bomb: A Life.* Cambridge, MA: Harvard University Press, 2005.

Delgado, James P. *Nuclear Dawn: The Atomic Bomb, from the Manhattan Project to the Cold War.* New York: Osprey, 2009.

Deloria, Philip J. *Indians in Unexpected Places.* Lawrence: University Press of Kansas, 2004.

DeMain, Bill. "The Sound and Vision of David Bowie." *Performing Songwriter* 11, no. 72 (September–October 2003): 44–52.

Denisoff, R. Serge. "Protest Songs: Those on the Top Forty and Those of the Streets." *American Quarterly* 22, no. 4 (Winter 1970): 807–823.

Dennis, David B. *Beethoven in German Politics, 1870–1989.* New Haven, CT: Yale University Press, 1996.

Denver, John. *The Complete Lyrics.* New York: Cherry Lane Music, 2002.

Di Salvatore, Bryan. "Profiles Ornery [Merle Haggard]." *New Yorker,* February 12, 1990. http://www.newyorker.com/magazine/1990/02/12/ornery.

"Did CIA Seek to Change Quotes of Folk Singer?" *Washington Star,* February 21, 1967. Declassified from Central Intelligence Agency. https://www.cia.gov/library/readingroom/document/cia-rdp75-00001r000300040002-9.

Diehl, Chad. *And the River Flowed as a Raft of Corpses: The Poetry of Yamaguchi Tsutomu: Survivor of Both Hiroshima and Nagasaki.* New York: Excogitating over Coffee, 2010.

Diliberto, John. "Kate Bush: From Piano to Fairlight with Britain's Exotic Chanteuse." *Keyboard*, July 1985.

Doerschuk, Robert L. "Billy Joel: The Piano Man Rocks On." In *Keyboard Presents Classic Rock*, edited by Ernie Rideout, 60–75. New York: Backbeat, 2010.

Donaghey, Jim. "Bakunin Brand Vodka: An Exploration into Anarcho-punk and Punk-anarchism." *Anarchist Developments in Cultural Studies* 1, Blasting the Canon (2013): 138–170.

Douglas, Susan J. *Where the Girls Are: Growing Up Female with the Mass Media*. New York: Times Books, 1994.

Dregni, Michael, ed. *Rockabilly: The Twang Heard 'Round the World: The Illustrated History*. Minneapolis: Voyageur, 2011.

Drott, Eric. *Music and the Elusive Revolution: Cultural Politics and Political Culture in France, 1968–1981*. Berkeley: University of California Press, 2011.

Duberman, Martin. *Paul Robeson*. New York: New Press, 2005.

Duffett, Mark. "Average White Band: Kraftwerk and the Politics of Race." In *Kraftwerk: Music Non-Stop*, edited by Sean Albiez and David Pattie, 194–213. New York: Continuum, 2011.

Dunaway, David King. *How Can I Keep From Singing? The Ballad of Pete Seeger*. New York: Villard, 2008.

Dylan, Bob. *Chronicles: Volume One*. New York: Simon and Schuster, 2004.

———. "Talking John Birch," *Broadside #1*, February 1962. https://singout.org/downloads/broadside/b001.pdf.

Easlea, Brian. *Fathering the Unthinkable: Masculinity, Scientists and the Nuclear Arms Race*. Suffolk: Pluto, 1983.

———. "Patriarchy, Scientists, and Nuclear Warriors." In *Beyond Patriarchy: Essays by Men on Pleasure, Power, and Change*, edited by Michael Kaufman, 195–215. New York: Oxford University Press, 1987.

Ehrlich, Robert. *Waging Nuclear Peace: The Technology and Politics of Nuclear Weapons*. Albany: State University of New York Press, 1985.

Einstein, Albert. "A Statement: Emergency Committee of Atomic Scientists." *Bulletin of the Atomic Scientists* 3, no. 6 (June 1947): 136.

Eisenhower, Dwight D. "Farewell Address, Reading Copy." Dwight D. Eisenhower Presidential Library, Museum, and Boyhood Home. Accessed October 7, 2020. https://www.eisenhowerlibrary.gov/sites/default/files/research/online-documents/farewell-address/reading-copy.pdf.

Elliot, Rona. "Billy Joel '87 intvw ussr part 1." *Today Show*. Uploaded May 8, 2008, YouTube. https://www.youtube.com/watch?v=YIVrrof6ODA.

———. "Billy Joel '87 intv ussr part 2." *Today Show*. Uploaded May 8, 2008, YouTube. https://www.youtube.com/watch?v=tDLSWR4akB4.

———. "Interview with U2, 1987, Part 4/6." U2 interview September 11, 1987. Uploaded July 29, 2007, YouTube. https://www.youtube.com/watch?v=nNmROSiqb7U.

English, Robert, and Jonathan J. Halperin. *The Other Side: How Soviets and Americans Perceive Each Other*. New Brunswick, NJ: Transaction, 1987.

Eno, Brian. *A Year with Swollen Appendices*. London: Faber and Faber, 1996.

Erickson, Robert. *Sound Structure in Music*. Berkeley: University of California Press, 1975.

Esslin, Martin, ed. *Absurd Drama*. New York: Penguin, 1965.

Etcoff, Nancy L. *Survival of the Prettiest: The Science of Beauty*. New York: Doubleday, 1999.

Etheridge, Brian C. *Enemies to Allies: Cold War Germany and American Memory*. Lexington: University Press of Kentucky, 2016.

Facts about Fallout. Washington, DC: Federal Civil Defense Administration, 1955. http://research.archives.gov/description/306714.

Fairhall, David. "£5 Billion Trident Deal Is Agreed." *Guardian*, July 16, 1980. http://www.theguardian.com/century/1980-1989/Story/0,,108170,00.html.

Fallout Protection: What to Know and Do about Nuclear Attack. Washington, DC: Office of Civil Defense, 1961. http://www.dahp.wa.gov/sites/default/files/Fallout%20Protection%20What%20to%20Know%20and%20Do.pdf.

Farber, Paul M. "Boundaries of Freedom: An American History of the Berlin Wall." PhD diss., University of Michigan, 2013.

Fedorak, Shirley. *Pop Culture: The Culture of Everyday Life*. Toronto: University of Toronto Press, 2009.

Feininger, Andreas. "History's Greatest Metal Hunt." *Life* 38, no. 21 (May 23, 1955): 25–35.

Feldman, Glenn, ed. *Painting Dixie Red: When, Where, Why, and How the South Became Republican*. Gainesville: University Press of Florida, 2011.

Fisher, Marc. "Wall to Wall in Berlin." *Washington Post*, July 23, 1990. https://www.washingtonpost.com/archive/lifestyle/1990/07/23/wall-to-wall-in-berlin/0cc6b636-b780-4e9f-b8c7-67b1a9e137ff/?utm_term=.94d71622a3f3.

Florek, Neil A. "Free Wills and Sweet Miracles." In *Rush and Philosophy: Heart and Mind United*, edited by Jim Berti and Durrell Bowman, 139–155. Chicago: Open Court, 2011.

Flynt, Wayne. *Alabama Baptists: Southern Baptists in the Heart of Dixie*. Tuscaloosa: University of Alabama Press, 1998.

Fontenot, Kevin S. "'Dear Ivan': Country Music Perspectives on the Soviet Union and the Cold War." In *Country Music Goes to War*, edited by Charles K. Wolfe and James E. Akenson, 143–151. Lexington: University Press of Kentucky, 2005.

Forget, Yann. "Juggling on the Berlin Wall." Photograph, November 16, 1989. https://commons.wikimedia.org/wiki/File:Juggling_on_the_Berlin_Wall.jpg.

Fosler-Lussier, Danielle. *Music in America's Cold War Diplomacy*. Oakland: University of California Press, 2015.

Freedman, Jean R. *Peggy Seeger: A Life of Music, Love, and Politics*. Urbana: University of Illinois Press, 2017.

Freedman, Lawrence. *The Cold War: A Military History*. London: Cassell, 2001.

Friedman, Jonathan C., ed. *The Routledge History of Social Protest in Popular Music*. New York: Routledge, 2013.

Frith, Simon. *Taking Popular Music Seriously: Selected Essays*. Burlington, VT: Ashgate, 2007.

Fuss, Charles J. *Joan Baez: A Bio-Bibliography*. Westport, CT: Greenwood, 1996.

Gaddis, John Lewis. *The Cold War: A New History*. New York: Penguin, 2005.

Garofalo, Reebee. *Rockin' the Boat: Mass Music and Mass Movements*. Boston: South End, 1992.

Gay, William C. "The Language of War and Peace." In *Encyclopedia of Violence, Peace, and Conflict*. Vol. 2. San Diego: Academic Press, 1999.

Gilbert, Pat. *Passion Is a Fashion: The Real Story of the Clash*. London: Da Capo, 2005.

Gimarc, George. *Post Punk Diary: 1980–1982*. New York: St. Martin's Griffin, 1997.

Glasper, Ian. *Burning Britain: The History of UK Punk, 1980–1984*. Oakland, CA: PM Press, 2014.

———. *The Day the Country Died: A History of Anarcho Punk, 1980–1984*. London: Cherry Red Books, 2006.

Glinsky, Albert. *Theremin: Ether Music and Espionage*. Urbana: University of Illinois Press, 2000.

Goldberg, Marv. "The Chords." *Marv Goldberg's R&B Notebook*. Accessed October 7, 2020. http://www.uncamarvy.com/Chords/chords.html.

Golsan, Richard J., ed. *Fascism's Return: Scandal, Revision, and Ideology since 1980*. Lincoln: University of Nebraska Press, 1998.

Goodman, Jon. "Dave's Gone By." Interview by Dave Lefkowitz, December 8, 2012. Uploaded February 24, 2013, YouTube. http://www.youtube.com/watch?v=RkMBeqRppJs.

———. *The King of Novelty, Dickie Goodman*. Bloomington, IN: Xlibris, 2000.

Goodman, Jordan. *Paul Robeson: A Watched Man*. London: Verso, 2013.

Gordon, Danielle. "The Verdict: No Harm, No Foul." *The Bulletin of the Atomic Scientists* 52, no. 1 (January/February 1996): 32–40.

Graham, Billy. "Christianism vs. Communism," Minneapolis, MN, 1951. Billy Graham Evangelistic Association, September 16, 1951. http://billygraham.org/audio/christianism-vs-communism/.

———. "Does a Religious Crusade Do Any Good?" *U.S. News & World Report*, September 27, 1957.

———. "Satan's Religion." *American Mercury*, August 1954.

Green, Abel. "A Warning to the Music Business." *Variety*, February 23, 1955.

Gregory, Ross. *Cold War America, 1946 to 1990*. New York: Facts on File, 2003.

Grossman, Andrew D. *Neither Dead nor Red: Civilian Defense and American Political Development during the Early Cold War*. New York: Routledge, 2001.

Gruen, Bob. *New York Dolls: Photographs*. New York: Abrams Image, 2008.

Guerrieri, Matthew. *The First Four Notes: Beethoven's Fifth and the Human Imagination.* New York: Knopf, 2012.

Gyorgy, Anna, and friends. *No Nukes: Everyone's Guide to Nuclear Power.* Boston: South End, 1979.

Hacker, Barton C. *Elements of Controversy: The Atomic Energy Commission and Radiation Safety in Nuclear Weapons Testing, 1947–1974.* Berkeley: University of California Press, 1994.

Halloran, Richard. "Weinberger Denies U.S. Plans for a 'Protracted' War." *New York Times,* June 21, 1982. http://www.nytimes.com/1982/06/21/world/weinberger-denies-us-plans-for-protracted-war.html.

Hambling, David. *Weapons Grade: How Modern Warfare Gave Birth to Our High-Tech World.* New York: Carroll and Graf, 2005.

Hare, Nathan. "Can Negroes Survive a Nuclear War? *Negro Digest* 12, no. 7 (May 1963): 26–33.

Hasselhoff, David. "David Hasselhoff 1989." Uploaded November 7, 2007, YouTube. https://www.youtube.com/watch?v=MQ5rIbnD_P4.

———, with Peter Thompson. *Don't Hassel the Hoff: The Autobiography.* New York: Thomas Dunne, 2007.

Havel, Václav. *Václav Havel or Living in Truth: Twenty-Two Essays Published on the Occasion of the Award of the Erasmus Prize to Václav Havel.* Boston: Faber and Faber, 1987.

Haviland, Julian. "Britain to Buy 'Bargain' US Trident 2 for £7,500m." *Times,* March, 12 1982, quoted in Adam Suddaby's *The Nuclear War Game.* London: Longman, 1983.

Hein, Laura, and Mark Selden. "Commemoration and Silence: Fifty Years of Remembering the Bomb in American and Japan." In *Living with the Bomb: American and Japanese Cultural Conflicts in the Nuclear Age,* edited by Laura Hein and Mark Selden, 3–34. Armonk, NY: M. E. Sharpe, 1997.

Hendershot, Cyndy. *Anti-Communism and Popular Culture in Mid-Century America.* Jefferson, NC: McFarland, 2003.

Hendershot, Heather. *What's Fair on the Air?: Cold War Right-wing Broadcasting and the Public Interest.* Chicago: University of Chicago Press, 2011.

Henriksen, Margot A. *Dr. Strangelove's America and Culture in the Atomic Age.* Berkeley: University of California Press, 1997.

Hersey, John. "A Reporter at Large, Hiroshima." *New Yorker,* August 31, 1946.

———. *Hiroshima.* New York: Knopf, 1946.

Hertle, Hans-Hermann, and Maria Nooke, eds. *The Victims at the Berlin Wall 1961–1989: A Biographical Handbook.* Berlin: Ch. Links, 2011.

Herzog, Jonathan P. *The Spiritual-Industrial Complex: America's Religious Battle against Communism in the Early Cold War.* New York: Oxford University Press, 2011.

Heylin, Clinton. *Bob Dylan: A Life in Stolen Moments; Day by Day: 1941–1995.* London: Book Sales, 1996.

Hijiya, James A. "The *Gita* of J. Robert Oppenheimer." *Proceedings of the American Philosophical Society* 144, no. 2 (June 2000): 123–167.

Hilburn, Robert. "How Does It Feel? Don't Ask." *Los Angeles Times*, September 16, 2001. https://www.latimes.com/archives/la-xpm-2001-sep-16-ca-46189-story.html.

Hildebrandt, Alexandra. *The Wall: Figures, Facts*. Berlin: Haus am Checkpoint Charlie, 2002.

Hill, Michael, and George M. Walsh. "FBI Files: Military Questioned Pete Seeger's Wartime Loyalty." *AP News*, December 19, 2015. https://apnews.com/dc9d717fba864fef80ba36fe224d6846/fbi-files-military-questioned-pete-seegers-wartime-loyalty.

Hodgson, Jay. *Understanding Records: A Field Guide to Recording Practice*. New York: Continuum, 2010.

Hornblum, Allen M., Judith L. Newman, and Gregory J. Dober. *Against Their Will: The Secret History of Medical Experimentation on Children in Cold War America*. New York: Palgrave Macmillan, 2013.

Horvitz, Leslie Alan, and Christopher Catherwood. *Encyclopedia of War Crimes and Genocide*. New York: Facts on File, 2006.

"How to Hunt for Uranium." *Popular Science*, February 1946.

Huggins, Stephen. *America's Use of Terror: From Colonial Times to the A-Bomb*. Lawrence: University Press of Kansas, 2019.

Hunter, Edward. *Brain-washing in Red China: The Calculated Destruction of Men's Minds*. New York: Vanguard, 1951.

"Impresarios: The Man Who Sold Parsley." *Time*, May 16, 1960.

Iommi, Tony, with T. J. Lammers. *Iron Man: My Journey through Heaven and Hell with Black Sabbath*. Cambridge, MA: Da Capo, 2011.

Israel, Matthew. *Kill for Peace: American Artists against the Vietnam War*. Austin: University of Texas Press, 2013.

Jablonski, Edward. *Harold Arlen: Rhythm, Rainbows, and Blues*. Boston: Northeastern University Press, 1996.

Jacobs, Robert A. *The Dragon's Tail: Americans Face the Atomic Age*. Amherst: University of Massachusetts Press, 2010.

Jäger, Markus. *Popular Is Not Enough: The Political Voice of Joan Baez; a Case Study in the Biographical Method*. Stuttgart: Ibidem, 2010.

Janssen, David, and Edward Whitelock. *Apocalypse Jukebox: The End of the World in American Popular Music*. Brooklyn: Soft Skull, 2009.

Jenkins, Philip. "Bricks in the Wall: An Interpretation of Pink Floyd's *The Wall*." In *Berlin Wall: Representations and Perspectives*, edited by Ernst Schürer, Manfred Keune, and Philip Jenkins, 205–213. New York: Peter Lang, 1996.

———, ed. *Nagasaki Journey: The Photographs of Yosuke Yamahata, August 10, 1945*. Rohnert Park, California: Pomegranate, 1995.

Jensen, Richard J. *Reagan at Bergen-Belsen and Bitburg*. College Station: Texas A&M University Press, 2007.

"Joan Baez in Palo Alto: Her First Protest." Palo Alto History.Org. Accessed October 7, 2020. http://www.paloaltohistory.org/joan-baez-in-palo-alto.php.

Johnson, Chad. *Jimi Hendrix Volume 2*. Guitar Signature Licks. Milwaukee, WI: Hal Leonard, 2006.

Johnson, Lyndon Baines. "President Johnson's Special Message to the Congress: The American Promise." Lyndon Baines Johnson Library and Museum, March 15, 1965. http://www.lbjlibrary.org/lyndon-baines-johnson/speeches-films/president-johnsons-special-message-to-the-congress-the-american-promise/.

Johnson Reagon, Bernice. "Let the Church Sing 'Freedom.'" *Black Music Research Journal* 7 (1987): 105–118.

Jorgensen, Timothy J. *Strange Glow: The Story of Radiation*. Princeton, NJ: Princeton University Press, 2016.

Jungk, Robert. *Brighter Than a Thousand Suns: A Personal History of the Atomic Scientists*. New York: Harcourt Brace, 1958.

Kahn, Herman. *On Thermonuclear War*. Princeton, NJ: Princeton University Press, 1960.

Kajzer, Jackie, and Roger Lotring. *Full Metal Jackie Certified: The 50 Most Influential Heavy Metal Songs of the '80s and the True Stories behind Their Lyrics*. Boston: Course Technology, 2010.

Kälin, Walter, and Jörg Künzli. *The Law of International Human Rights Protection*. New York: Oxford University Press, 2009.

Kaplan, Mike. "Mdse. Swells Record Take." *Variety*, October 24, 1956.

Kaufman, Will. *Woody Guthrie, American Radical*. Urbana: University of Illinois Press, 2011.

———. *Woody Guthrie's Modern World Blues*. Norman: University of Oklahoma Press, 2017.

Kaufmann, Eric P. *The Rise and Fall of Anglo-America*. Cambridge, MA: Harvard University Press, 2004.

Kearney, David Daithí. "'I Can't Believe the News Today': Music and the Politics of Change." *Chimera* 24 (2009): 122–140.

Kemp, Mark. *Dixie Lullaby: A Story of Music, Race, and New Beginnings in a New South*. Athens: University of Georgia Press, 2006.

Kennaway, James. *Bad Vibrations: The History of the Idea of Music as Cause of Disease*. Burlington, VT: Ashgate, 2012.

Kennedy, John F. "A Message to You from the President." *Life*, September 15, 1961.

———. "Radio and Television Report to the American People on the Berlin Crisis, July 25, 1961." John F. Kennedy Presidential Library and Museum, July 25, 1961. https://www.jfklibrary.org/archives/other-resources/john-f-kennedy-speeches/berlin-crisis-19610725.

"Kennedy Denounces Reagan for 'Voodoo Arms Control.'" *New York Times*, June 22, 1982. http://www.nytimes.com/1982/06/22/world/kennedy-denouces-regan-for-voodoo-arms-control.html.

Keyes, Jimmy. "The Chords." *Marv Goldberg's R&B Notebook*. Accessed October 7, 2020. http://www.uncamarvy.com/Chords/chords.html.

———. "How Sh Boom Originated." Uploaded February 26, 2009, YouTube. http://www.youtube.com/watch?v=3dUK9j5X7Zw.

Khrushchev, Sergei. *Khrushchev in Power: Unfinished Reforms, 1961–1964*. Translated by George Shriver. Boulder, CO: Lynne Rienner, 2014.

King, Martin Luther, Jr. "Address at the Conclusion of the Selma to Montgomery March." The Martin Luther King, Jr. Research and Education Institute, March 25, 1965. https://kinginstitute.stanford.edu/king-papers/documents/address-conclusion-selma-montgomery-march.

———. *The Papers of Martin Luther King, Jr., Volume VI: Advocate of the Social Gospel, September 1948–March 1963*. Berkeley: University of California Press, 1992.

Kirschbaum, Erik. *Rocking the Wall: Bruce Springsteen: The Berlin Concert That Changed the World*. New York: Berlinica, 2013.

Kizer, Elizabeth J. "Protest Song Lyrics as Rhetoric." *Popular Music and Society* 9, no. 1 (1983): 3–11.

Klare, Michael T., and Cynthia Arnson with Delia Miller and Daniel Volman. *Supplying Repression: U.S. Support for Authoritarian Regimes Abroad*. Washington, DC: Institute for Policy Studies, 1981.

Klepper, Steven. *Experimental Capitalism: The Nanoeconomics of American High-Tech Industries*. Princeton, NJ: Princeton University Press, 2016.

Kostelanetz, Richard, ed. *The Frank Zappa Companion: Four Decades of Commentary*. New York: Schirmer, 1997.

"Kraftwerk." Documentary directed by Malik Bendjelloul for Swedish music program "Pop I Fokus," 2001. Uploaded February 10, 2009, YouTube. https://www.youtube.com/watch?v=vYeuPWOQM44.

Kraftwerk. "Kraftwerk live Soest, Winter 1970." *Rockpalast*. Uploaded May 19, 2018, YouTube. https://www.youtube.com/watch?v=vNoFHdlMrtI.

———. "Kraftwerk—Roboter 1978." Music video. Uploaded November 18, 2012, YouTube. https://www.youtube.com/watch?v=5DBc5NpyEoo.

Kramer, Mark, ed. *The Black Book of Communism: Crimes, Terror, Repression*. Cambridge, MA: Harvard University Press, 1999.

Kramer, Michael J. "The Multitrack Model: Cultural History and the Interdisciplinary Study of Popular Music." In *Music and History: Bridging the Disciplines*, edited by Jeffrey H. Jackson and Stanley C. Pelkey, 220–255. Jackson: University Press of Mississippi, 2005.

———. *The Republic of Rock: Music and Citizenship in the Sixties Counterculture*. New York: Oxford University Press, 2013.

Kristensen, Hans M., and Robert S. Norris. "Status of World Nuclear Forces." Federation of American Scientists. Updated September 2020. http://fas.org/issues/nuclear-weapons/status-world-nuclear-forces/.

Kurihara, Sadako. *When We Say "Hiroshima": Selected Poems*. Translated with an introduction by Richard H. Minear. Ann Arbor: Center for Japanese Studies, University of Michigan, 1999.

Lacina, Bethany, and Nils Petter Gleditsch. "Monitoring Trends in Global Combat: A New Dataset of Battle Deaths." *European Journal of Population* 21, no. 2–3 (June 2005): 145–166. http://www.prio.org/Global/upload/CSCW/Data/Monitoring%20trends%20in%20global%20combat%20EJP.pdf.

Larson, Deborah Welch. *Anatomy of Mistrust: U.S.-Soviet Relations During the Cold War*. Ithaca, NY: Cornell University Press, 1997.

Lautz, Terry. *John Birch: A Life*. New York: Oxford University Press, 2016.

Lech, Raymond B. *Tortured into Fake Confession: The Dishonoring of Korean War Prisoner Col. Frank H. Schwable, USMC*. Jefferson, NC: McFarland, 2011.

Lehrer, Tom. *Too Many Songs*. New York: Pantheon, 1981.

Leigh, Mickey, with Legs McNeil. *I Slept with Joey Ramone: A Family Memoir*. New York: Simon and Schuster, 2009.

Lens, Sidney. "Revive the Ban-the-Bomb Movement." In *Apocalyptic Premise: Nuclear Arms Debated: Thirty-one Essays by Statesmen, Scholars, Religious Leaders, and Journalists*, edited by Ernest W. Lefever and E. Stephen Hunt, 93–104. Washington, DC: Ethics and Public Policy Center, 1982.

Leonard, Richard D. *Call to Selma: Eighteen Days of Witness*. Boston: Skinner House, 2002.

Lester, Paul. "Black Sabbath: 'We Used to Have Cocaine Flown in by Private Plane.'" *Guardian*, June 6, 2013. http://www.guardian.co.uk/music/2013/jun/06/black-sabbath-cocaine-private-plane.

Lieberman, Robbie. "'Does That Make Peace a Bad Word?' American Responses to the Communist Peace Offensive, 1949–1950." *Peace and Change* 17, no. 2 (April 1992): 198–228.

———. *"My Song Is My Weapon": People's Songs, American Communism, and the Politics of Culture, 1930–1950*. Urbana: University of Illinois Press, 1989.

Lippy, Charles H. *Bibliography of Religion in the South*. Macon, GA: Mercer, 1985.

Littlejohn, John T. "Kraftwerk: Language, Lucre, and Loss of Identity." *Popular Music and Society* 32, no. 5 (December 2009): 635–653.

Loder, Kurt. "Nena's '99 Luftballons' Soars Up U.S. Charts." *Rolling Stone*, March 15, 1984, 41.

Lott, Tim. "The Thin White Duke Has Gone. Here's the New David Bowie." *Record Mirror*, September 24, 1977. https://timlottwriter.wordpress.com/2016/01/11/my-interview-with-bowie-1977/.

Lowery, Tamara C. *Your Chance to Live*. San Francisco: Far West Laboratory for Educational Research and Development, 1972.

Lubasch, Arnold H. *Robeson: An American Ballad*. Lanham, MD: Scarecrow, 2012.

Lund, Jens. "Fundamentalism, Racism, and Political Reaction in Country Music." In *Sounds of Social Change: Studies in Popular Culture*, edited by R. Serge Denisoff and Richard A. Peterson, 79–91. Chicago: Rand McNally, 1972.

Lynch, Edward A. *The Cold War's Last Battlefield: Reagan, the Soviets, and Central America*. Albany: State University of New York Press, 2011.

Lynskey, Dorian. *33 Revolutions per Minute: A History of Protest Songs, from Billie Holiday to Green Day*. New York: Ecco, 2011.

McMahon, Robert J., ed. *The Cold War in the Third World*. New York: Oxford University Press, 2013.

Malloy, Sean L. "'A Very Pleasant Way to Die': Radiation Effects and the Decision to Use the Atomic Bomb against Japan." *Diplomatic History*, 36, no. 3 (June 2012): 515–545.

Malone, Bill C. *Don't Get above Your Raisin': Country Music and the Southern Working Class*. Urbana: University of Illinois Press, 2002.

Malvina Reynolds: Song Lyrics and Poems. Website created by Charles H. Smith and Nancy Schimmel. Last modified March 24, 2019. http://malvinareynolds.com/.

Mangano, Joseph J., and Janette D. Sherman. "Elevated In Vivo Strontium-90 from Nuclear Weapons Test Fallout among Cancer Decedents: A Case-Control Study of Deciduous Teeth." *International Journal of Health Services* 41, no. 1 (2011): 137–158.

Maramont, Mark. "One Crusader's Effort to Publicize a Health Risk Finds Little Success." *Wall Street Journal*, July 26, 1999. http://www.wsj.com/articles/SB932939277927490585.

Mariner, Rosemary B., and G. Kurt Piehler, eds. *The Atomic Bomb and American Society: New Perspectives*. Knoxville: University of Tennessee Press, 2009.

Markusen, Eric, and David Kopf. *The Holocaust and Strategic Bombing: Genocide and Total War in the Twentieth Century*. Boulder, CO: Westview, 1995.

Marqusee, Mike. *Wicked Messenger: Bob Dylan and the 1960s; Chimes of Freedom*. New York: Seven Stories, 2005.

Marsden, George M. *Reforming Fundamentalism: Fuller Seminary and the New Evangelicalism*. Grand Rapids, MI: Eerdmans, 1987.

Marshall, Wolf. "Introduction." *Metallica, Ride the Lightning*. Port Chester, NY: Cherry Lane Music, 1990.

Martin, Spider. *Selma 1965: The Photographs of Spider Martin*. Austin: University of Texas Press, 2015.

Martinelli, Dario. *Give Peace a Chant: Popular Music, Politics and Social Protest*. Cham, Switzerland: Springer, 2017.

Mason, Nick. *Inside Out: A Personal History of Pink Floyd*. Edited by Philip Dodd. London: Weidenfeld and Nicolson, 2004.

Masters, Dexter, and Katharine Way, eds. *One World or None*. New York: McGraw-Hill, 1946.

Matsuo, Atsuyuki. *A-Bomb Haiku.* Translated by Masumi Midorikawa. Tokyo: Shinju-sha, 1995.

Matthews, Melvin E. Jr., *Duck and Cover: Civil Defense Images in Film and Television from the Cold War to 9/11.* Jefferson, NC: McFarland, 2012.

May, Elaine Tyler. *Homeward Bound: American Families in the Cold War Era.* 20th anniversary ed. New York: Basic, 2008.

"Mayor Rejects Request from Civil Rightists." *Selma Times-Journal,* March 12, 1965.

McAlea, Kevin. "99 Red Balloons—Interview with the Writer, Kevin McAlea." Eighty Eightynine. Accessed October 7, 2020. http://www.eightyeightynine.com/music/99luftballoons-english.html.

McBride, Donald. "Broadcast News Coverage of the Korean War." In *Korean War: An Encyclopedia,* edited by Stanley Sandler, 56. New York: Garland, 1995.

McCarthy, James R., and Robert E. Rayfield. *Linebacker II: A View from the Rock.* Washington, DC: US Air Force, Office of Air Force History, 1985.

McCarthy, Joseph. Quoted in "Pusey vs. McCarthy," *Congressional Quarterly Almanac, 83rd Congress 1st Session-1953, Volume IX.* Washington, DC: Congressional Quarterly News Features, 1953.

McDonald, Chris. *Rush, Rock Music and the Middle Class: Dreaming in Middletown.* Bloomington: Indiana University Press, 2009.

McEnaney, Laura. *Civil Defense Begins at Home: Militarization Meets Everyday Life in the Fifties.* Princeton, NJ: Princeton University Press, 2000.

McGee, Matt. *U2: A Diary.* New York: Omnibus, 2011.

McKay, George. "Subcultural Innovations in the Campaign for Nuclear Disarmament." *Peace Review* 16, no. 4 (December 2004): 429–438.

McLaren, Malcolm. "Dirty Pretty Things." Interview by Dave Simpson and Dorian Lynskey. *Guardian,* May 28, 2004. http://www.theguardian.com/music/2004/may/28/2.

McLaurin, Melton A. "Proud to Be an American: Patriotism in Country Music." In *America's Musical Pulse: Popular Music in Twentieth-Century Society,* edited by Kenneth J. Bindas, 23–32. New York: Greenwood, 1992.

McNeil, Legs. "Tommy Ramone: His Story as Told to Legs McNeil." *Hollywood Reporter,* July 14, 2014. http://www.hollywoodreporter.com/news/tommy-ramone-his-story-as-718469.

McNeil, Legs, and John Holmstrom. "We're a Happy Family." *Spin* 2, no. 5 (August 1986): 66, 70, 78.

McNeil, Legs, and Gillian McCain. *Please Kill Me: The Uncensored Oral History of Punk.* New York: Penguin, 1997.

Meine, Klaus. "Scorpions—Moscow Music Peace Fest 30th Anniversary—Klaus Meine, Rudolph Schenker." Interview by Redbeard, *In the Studio.* Accessed October 8, 2020. https://www.inthestudio.net/online-only-interviews/scorpions-love-first-sting-klaus-meinerudolph-schenker/.

Melnick, Monte A., and Frank Meyer. *On the Road with the Ramones*. London: Bobcat, 2007.

Menjívar, Cecilia, and Néstor Rodríguez, eds. *When States Kill: Latin America, the U.S., and Technologies of Terror*. Austin: University of Texas Press, 2005.

Meyer-Eppler, Werner. *Elektrische Klangerzeugung; Elektronische Musik und synthesische Sprache*. Bonn, Germany: F. Dümmler, 1949.

Meyerowitz, Joanne. *Not June Cleaver: Women and Gender in Postwar America, 1945–1960*. Philadelphia: Temple University Press, 1994.

Miers, Jeff. "The Road Less Traveled: A Conversation with Neil Peart of Rush." *Metro Weekend*, October 17–23, 1996. http://www.2112.net/powerwindows/transcripts/19961017metroweekend.htm.

Miles, Barry. *Paul McCartney: Many Years from Now*. New York: Holt, 1997.

Miller, Jonathan. *Stripped: Depeche Mode*. New York: Omnibus, 2008.

Miller, Ralph. "Project X—The Beginning of the Digital Transmission Age." Accessed October 8, 2020. http://ralph-miller.org/docs/Project_X_The_Beginning_of_the_Digital_Age.pdf.

Mills, Claire. "Replacing the UK's 'Trident' Nuclear Deterrent." Briefing Paper Number 7353, July 12, 2016, House of Commons Library. http://researchbriefings.files.parliament.uk/documents/CBP-7353/CBP-7353.pdf.

Mitchell, Tony. "Mixing Pop and Politics: Rock Music in Czechoslovakia before and after the Velvet Revolution." *Popular Music* 11, no. 2 (May 1992): 187–203.

Mohr, Tim. *Burning Down the Haus: Punk Rock, Revolution, and the Fall of the Berlin Wall*. Chapel Hill, NC: Algonquin, 2018.

Mondak, Jeffrey J. "Protest Music as Political Persuasion." *Popular Music and Society* 12, no. 3 (Fall 1988): 25–38.

Monteyne, David. *Fallout Shelter: Designing for Civil Defense in the Cold War*. Minneapolis: University of Minnesota Press, 2011.

Morrison, Joan and Robert K. Morrison. *From Camelot to Kent State: The Sixties Experience in the Words of Those Who Lived It*. Oxford: Oxford University Press, 2001.

Morton, David L. "'The Rusty Ribbon': John Herbert Orr and the Making of the Magnetic Recording Industry, 1945–1960." *Business History Review* 67, no. 4 (Winter 1993): 589–622.

Moynihan, Michael. "The Death of 'Stalin's Songbird' Pete Seeger." *Daily Beast*, January 29, 2014. https://www.thedailybeast.com/the-death-of-stalins-songbird.

Murray, Bruce T. *Religious Liberty in America: The First Amendment in Historical and Contemporary Perspective*. Amherst, MA: University of Massachusetts Press in association with Foundation for American Communications, 2008.

Murray, Charles Shaar. "Who Was That (Un)masked Man?" *New Musical Express*, November 12, 1977.

Muzzey, David Saville. *An American History*. Boston: Ginn and Company, 1911.

Nagai, Takashi, ed. *Living beneath the Atomic Cloud: The Testimony of the Children of Nagasaki*. Nagasaki: Nagasaki Appeal Committee, 1979.

———. *We of Nagasaki: The Story of Survivors in an Atomic Wasteland.* Translated by Ichiro Shirato and Herbert B. L. Silverman. London: Victor Gollancz, 1951.

Nakamura, Masako. "'Miss Atom Bomb' Contests in Nagasaki and Nevada: The Politics of Beauty, Memory, and the Cold War." *U.S.-Japan Women's Journal* 37 (2009): 117–143.

Nakano, Jiro, ed. and trans. *Outcry from the Inferno: Atomic Bomb Tanka Anthology.* Honolulu, HI: Bamboo Ridge, 1995.

"Nasopharyngeal Radium Irradiation (NRI) and Cancer: Fact Sheet." National Cancer Institute. Accessed October 8, 2020. https://stacks.stanford.edu/file/druid:st370yg4366/Fs3_87.pdf.

"National Radiation Instrument Catalog, 1920–1960." Accessed October 8, 2020. http://national-radiation-instrument-catalog.com/new_page_34.htm.

Nickerson, Michelle M. *Mothers of Conservatism: Women and the Postwar Right.* Princeton, NJ: Princeton University Press, 2012.

"99 Luftballons und das Chaos der Gefühle." *Der Spiegel* 38 no. 13 (March 26, 1984): 218–226.

Nmungwun, Aaron Foisi. *Video Recording Technology: Its Impact on Media and Home Entertainment.* Hillsdale, NJ: Erlbaum, 1989.

Noebel, David A. *Communism, Hypnotism and the Beatles.* Tulsa, OK: Christian Crusade, 1965.

Norris, Robert S., and Hans M. Kristensen. "Global Nuclear Stockpiles, 1945–2006." *Bulletin of the Atomic Scientists* 62, no. 4 (July 2006): 64–66. http://bos.sagepub.com/content/62/4/64.full.pdf+html.

O'Hare, Colm. "The Secret History of 'The Joshua Tree' (Part 2)." *Hot Press,* November 21, 2007. http://www.atu2.com/news/the-secret-history-of-the-joshua-tree-part-2.html.

Oliver, Kendrick. *The My Lai Massacre in American History and Memory.* Manchester: Manchester University Press, 2006.

Olson, James S., and Randy Roberts. *My Lai: A Brief History with Documents.* Boston: Bedford, 1998.

O'Neill, Patrick. "The Comedy of Entropy: The Contexts of Black Humour." *Canadian Review of Comparative Literature* 10, no. 2 (June 1983): 145–166.

Onkey, Laura. "Voodoo Child: Jimi Hendrix and the Politics of Race in the Sixties." In *Imagine Nation: The American Counterculture of the 1960s and '70s,* edited by Peter Braunstein and Michael William Doyle, 189–214. New York: Routledge, 2002.

Orwell, George. *Selected Essays.* Middlesex: Penguin, 1957.

Osada, Arata. *Children of the A-Bomb: Testament of the Boys and Girls of Hiroshima.* Translated by Jean Dan and Ruth Sieben-Morgen. Tokyo: Uchida Rokakuho, 1959.

Osbourne, Ozzy. "Off the Record with Mary Turner." Westwood One Radio, Part 4, 1985.

———. "Ozzy Osbourne Interview 1982." Uploaded May 12, 2007, YouTube. https://www.youtube.com/watch?v=Vpvo-FppQ-8.

Osbourne, Ozzy, with Chris Ayres. *I Am Ozzy*. New York: Grand Central, 2010.

Otfinoski, Steven. *The Golden Age of Novelty Songs*. New York: Billboard, 2000.

Paas, John Roger, ed. *America Sings of War: American Sheet Music from World War I*. Wiesbaden: Harrassowitz, 2014.

Palazhchenko, Pavel. *My Years with Gorbachev and Shevardnadze: The Memoir of a Soviet Interpreter*. University Park: Pennsylvania State University Press, 1997.

Parenti, Michael. *The Anti-Communist Impulse*. New York: Random House, 1969.

Pasternak, Judy. *Yellow Dirt: An American Story of a Poisoned Land and a People Betrayed*. New York: Free Press, 2010.

Peart, Neil. *Far and Away: A Prize Every Time*. Toronto: ECW, 2011.

———. "Pressure Release." *Grace under Pressure* Tour Book, 1984.

———. *Roadshow: Landscape with Drums: A Concert Tour by Motorcycle*. Cambridge, MA: Rounder, 2006.

———. "Shunpikers in the Shadowlands." Neil Peart website, June 2013. http://www.neilpeart.net/index.php/space-for-news-items/june-2013-shunpikers-shadowlands1/.

———. *Traveling Music: The Soundtrack to My Life and Times*. Toronto: ECW, 2004.

Pegg, Nicholas. *The Complete David Bowie*. 6th ed. London: Titan, 2011.

Penguin Modern Poets 2: Kingsley Amis, Dom Moraes, Peter Porter. Middlesex: Penguin, 1962.

The People's Song Book. Foreword by Alan Lomax. Preface by B. A. Botkin. New York: Boni and Gaer, 1948.

Perone, James E. *Music of the Counterculture Era*. Westport, CT: Greenwood, 2004.

Perry, Charles. *The Haight-Ashbury: A History*. New York: Random House/Rolling Stone, 1984.

Perucci, Tony. *Paul Robeson and the Cold War Performance Complex: Race, Madness, Activism*. Ann Arbor: University of Michigan Press, 2012.

Peterson, Sarah Jo. *Planning the Home Front: Building Bombers and Communities at Willow Run*. Chicago: University of Chicago Press, 2013.

Philbin, Marianne, ed. *Give Peace a Chance: Music and the Struggle for Peace: A Catalog of the Exhibition at the Peace Museum, Chicago*. Chicago: Chicago Review, 1983.

Phillips, Christopher, and Louis and P. Masur, eds. *Talk about a Dream: The Essential Interviews of Bruce Springsteen*. New York: Bloomsbury, 2013.

Phinney, Kevin. *Souled America: How Black Music Transformed White Culture*. New York: Billboard, 2005.

Pichaske, David. *Song of the North Country: A Midwest Framework to the Songs of Bob Dylan*. New York: Continuum, 2010.

Pillsbury, Glenn T. *Damage Incorporated: Metallica and the Production of Musical Identity*. New York: Routledge, 2006.

Pinch, Trevor, and Frank Trocco. *Analog Days: The Invention and Impact of the Moog Synthesizer*. Foreword by Robert Moog. Cambridge, MA: Harvard University Press, 2002.

———. "The Social Construction of the Early Electronic Music Synthesizer." In *Music and Technology in the Twentieth Century*, edited by Hans-Joachim Braun, 67–83. Baltimore: Johns Hopkins University Press, 2002.

Pirnia, Garin. "Enola Gay." *Rolling Stone*, June 12, 2012. http://www.rollingstone.com/music/news/enola-gay-orchestral-manoeuvres-in-the-dark.

Porter, Peter. "Peter Porter: What I Have Written." Uploaded October 30, 2015, YouTube. https://www.youtube.com/watch?v=sDGz3eY5WZU.

Postman, Neil. *Amusing Ourselves to Death: Public Discourse in the Age of Show Business*. New York: Viking, 1985.

Prokofieff, Sergei. *Lieutenant Kijé, Suite Symphonique, op. 60*. Boca Raton, FL: Kalmus, 1980.

Prospecting for Uranium. Washington, DC: United States Atomic Energy Commission and the United States Geological Survey, 1949. http://babel.hathitrust.org/cgi/pt?id=mdp.39015003999797#view=1up;seq=4.

Protect and Survive. London: Her Majesty's Stationary Office, 1980.

Protzman, Ferdinand. "A Day of Celebrations and a Bit of Shopping." *New York Times*, November 11, 1989.

Przybys, John. "50 Years Ago, the King Came Back." *Las Vegas Review-Journal*, July 22, 2019. https://www.reviewjournal.com/entertainment/shows/elvis-came-to-las-vegas-50-years-ago-and-history-was-made-1807088/.

Raggett, Ned. "Thirty Years On: Depeche Mode's *Some Great Reward* Revisited." *Quietus*, September 15, 2014. http://thequietus.com/articles/16246-depeche-mode-some-great-reward.

Ramet, Sabrina Petra, ed. *Rocking the State: Rock Music and Politics in Eastern Europe and Russia*. Boulder, CO: Westview, 1994.

Ramone, Dee Dee, with Veronica Kofman. *Lobotomy: Surviving the Ramones*. 3rd ed. Boston: DaCapo, 2016.

Ramone, Johnny. *Commando: The Autobiography of Johnny Ramone*. New York: Abrams, 2012.

Ramone, Marky, with Rich Herschlag. *Punk Rock Blitzkrieg*. New York: Touchstone, 2015.

Ramones. "Ramones Accept Rock and Roll Hall of Fame Awards." Uploaded September 5, 2012, YouTube. https://www.youtube.com/watch?v=ekyI5ZsjTPk.

Rarebell, Herman, and Michael Krikorian. *And Speaking of Scorpions . . . The Autobiography of Herman "ze German" Rarebell*. Herman Rarebell and Michael Krikorian, 2011.

Reagan, Ronald. "Address to the Nation on Strategic Arms Reduction and Nuclear Deterrence," November 22, 1982. Ronald Reagan Presidential Library and Museum. https://www.reaganlibrary.gov/archives/speech/address-nation-strategic-arms-reduction-and-nuclear-deterrence.

———. *An American Life*. New York: Simon and Schuster, 1990.

———. *Greatest Speeches of Ronald Reagan*. West Palm Beach, FL: NewsMax, 2002.

———. "Remarks at the Annual Convention of the National Association of Evangelicals in Orlando, Florida," March 8, 1983. Ronald Reagan Presidential Library and Museum. https://www.reaganfoundation.org/library-museum/permanent-exhibitions/berlin-wall/from-the-archives/remarks-at-the-annual-convention-of-the-national-association-of-evangelicals-in-orlando-florida/.

———. "Remarks on Central America and El Salvador at the Annual Meeting of the National Association of Manufacturers," March 10, 1983. Ronald Reagan Presidential Library and Museum. https://www.reaganlibrary.gov/research/speeches/31083a.

Regis, Louis. *The Political Calypso: True Opposition in Trinidad and Tobago, 1962–1987*. Gainesville: University Press of Florida, 1999.

Russell Reising, "Iron Curtains and Satin Sheets: 'Strange Loves' in Cold War Popular Music," *Cultural Logic* 10 (2003). https://ojs.library.ubc.ca/index.php/clogic/article/view/191911/188872.

———. "Covering and Un(covering) the Truth with 'All Along the Watchtower': From Dylan to Hendrix and Beyond." In *Play It Again: Cover Songs in Popular Music*, edited by George Plasketes, 153–175. Farnham: Ashgate, 2010.

Reuss, Richard A., with JoAnne C. Reuss. *American Folk Music and Left-Wing Politics, 1927–1957*. Lanham, MD: Scarecrow, 2000.

Reynolds, Glenn Harlan. "The Unexpected Return of 'Duck and Cover.'" *Atlantic*, January 4, 2011. http://www.theatlantic.com/national/archive/2011/01/the-unexpected-return-of-duck-and-cover/68776/.

Reynolds, Malvina. "Billy Boy." *Broadside #18*, late December 1962. http://singout.org/downloads/broadside/b018.pdf.

———. "The H.U.A.C." *Broadside #18*, late December 1962. https://singout.org/downloads/broadside/b018.pdf.

———. *Little Boxes and Other Handmade Songs*. New York: Oak Publications, 1964.

Reynolds, Mardelle L. and Francis X. Lynch. "Atomic Bomb Injuries among Survivors in Hiroshima." *Public Health Reports* 70, no. 3 (March 1955): 261–270.

Richmond, Yale. *Cultural Exchange and the Cold War: Raising the Iron Curtain*. University Park: Pennsylvania State University Press, 2003.

Rimbaud, Penny. *Shibboleth: My Revolting Life*. San Francisco: AK Press, 1998.

Risch, William Jay, ed. *Youth and Rock in the Soviet Bloc: Youth Cultures, Music, and the State in Russia and Eastern Europe*. Lanham, MD: Lexington Books, 2015.

Robeson, Paul. *Paul Robeson Speaks: Writings, Speeches, Interviews, 1918–1974*. New York: Brunner/Mazel, 1978.

Robinson, Earl, with Eric A. Gordon. *Ballad of an American: The Autobiography of Earl Robinson*. Lanham, MD: Scarecrow, 1998.

Roby, Steven. *Black Gold: The Lost Archives of Jimi Hendrix*. New York: Billboard, 2002.

Roby, Steven, and Brad Schreiber. *Becoming Jimi Hendrix: From Southern Crossroads to Psychedelic London, the Untold Story of a Musical Genius*. Philadelphia: Da Capo, 2010.

Roe, Brian. "Brian Roe—D-beat." Uploaded October 20, 2012, YouTube. https://www.youtube.com/watch?v=fQwCVBQN1oM.

Rogers, Jude. "Why Kraftwerk Are Still the World's Most Influential Band." *Guardian*, January 27, 2013. https://www.theguardian.com/music/2013/jan/27/kraftwerk-most-influential-electronic-band-tate.

Rogovoy, Seth. *Bob Dylan: Prophet, Mystic, Poet*. New York: Scribner, 2009.

Roland, Charles P. *The Improbable Era: The South since World War II*. Lexington: University Press of Kentucky, 1975.

Rombes, Nicholas. *Ramones*. New York: Continuum, 2005.

Roosevelt, Franklin D. "An Appeal to Great Britain, France, Italy, Germany, and Poland to Refrain from Air Bombing of Civilians," September 1, 1939. American Presidency Project. https://www.presidency.ucsb.edu/documents/appeal-great-britain-france-italy-germany-and-poland-refrain-from-air-bombing-civilians.

Rose, Kenneth D. *One Nation Underground: The Fallout Shelter in American Culture*. New York: New York University Press, 2001.

Rosefielde, Steven. *Red Holocaust*. London; New York: Routledge, 2010.

Roselle, Laura. *Media and the Politics of Failure: Great Powers, Communication Strategies, and Military Defeats*. New York: Palgrave Macmillan, 2006.

Russolo, Luigi. *The Art of Noises*. Translated from the Italian with an introduction by Barclay Brown. New York: Pendragon, 1986.

Rüther, Tobias. *Heroes: David Bowie and Berlin*. Translated by Anthony Matthews. London: Reaktion, 2014.

Ryan, Thomas. *American Hit Radio: A History of Popular Singles from 1955 to the Present*. Rocklin, CA: Prima, 1996.

Ryback, Timothy W. *Rock around the Bloc: A History of Rock Music in Eastern Europe and the Soviet Union*. New York: Oxford University Press, 1990.

Rydell, Randy. "Nuclear Weapon State Transparency, the Nuclear Non-Proliferation Treaty, and the United Nations." New York: United Nations Office for Disarmament Affairs, 2013. http://www.un.org/disarmament/content/speeches/oda-ny/rydell/2013-10-22_RR_IPFM_side_event.

Sagolla, Lisa Jo. *Rock 'n' Roll Dances of the 1950s*. Santa Barbara, CA: Greenwood, 2011.

Samuels, Gertrude. "Why They Rock 'n' Roll—And Should They?" *New York Times Magazine*, January 12, 1958.

San Roman, Gabriel. "The Life and Times of Malvina Reynolds: Long Beach's Most Legendary (and Hated) Folk Singer." *OC Weekly*, August 31, 2016. http://www.ocweekly.com/music/the-life-and-times-of-malvina-reynolds-long-beachs-most-legendary-and-hated-folk-singer-7474438.

Santa Barbara, Joanna. "Living in the Shadow: The Effects of Continual Fear." In *Nuclear War: The Search for Solutions: Proceedings of a Conference held at the University of British Columbia, October 19–21, 1984, with Special Essays by Major-General Leonard V. Johnson, and Dr. Helen Caldicott*. Preface by the Hon. Walter L. Gordon.

Edited by Thomas L. Perry and Dianne DeMille, 93–104. Vancouver, BC: Physicians for Social Responsibility, 1985.

Saturday Night Live. "Wayne's World" sketch. February 17, 1990. *Saturday Night Live* transcripts. http://snltranscripts.jt.org/89/89mwaynesworld.phtml.

Savage, Jon. *England's Dreaming: Anarchy, Sex Pistols, Punk Rock, and Beyond.* New York: St. Martin's Griffin, 2002.

Scarfe, Gerald. *The Making of Pink Floyd The Wall.* London: Weidenfeld and Nicholson, 2010.

Schimmel, Nancy. "1959–1965: March for Peace, Sit in for Civil Rights and Free Speech." Unpublished manuscript.

———. "Let's Go Dancing Til the Break of Day: A Remembrance of Malvina Reynolds." Harvard Square Library. Accessed October 8, 2020. http://www.harvardsquarelibrary.org/biographies/malvina-reynolds/.

Schindler, Anton. *The Life of Beethoven: Including his Correspondence with His Friends, Numerous Characteristic Traits, and Remarks on His Musical Works.* 2 vol. Edited and translated by Ignace Moscheles. London: Henry Colburn, 1841.

Schlosser, Eric. *Command and Control: Nuclear Weapons, the Damascus Accident, and the Illusion of Safety.* New York: Penguin, 2013.

Schlosser, Nicholas J. "The Berlin Radio War: Broadcasting in Cold War Berlin and the Shaping of Political Culture in Divided Germany 1945–1961." PhD diss., University of Maryland, College Park, 2008.

Schmelz, Peter J. "Introduction: Music in the Cold War." *Journal of Musicology* 26, no. 1 (Winter 2009): 3–16.

Schmidt, Dana Adams. "Castro Stresses Land Reform Aid." *New York Times*, April 21, 1959.

Schwartz, Richard Alan. *Cold War Culture: Media and the Arts, 1945–1990.* New York: Facts on File, 1998.

Schwebel, Sara L. *Child-Sized History: Fictions of the Past in U.S. Classrooms.* Nashville: Vanderbilt University Press, 2011.

Scott, James Brown, ed. *The Hague Conventions and Declarations of 1899 and 1907: Accompanied by Tables of Signatures, Ratifications and Adhesions of the Various Powers and Texts of Reservations.* New York: Oxford University Press, 1915.

Seabrook, Thomas Jerome. *Bowie in Berlin: A New Career in a New Town.* London: Jawbone, 2008.

"Securing Britain in an Age of Uncertainty: The Strategic Defence and Security Review." London: Her Majesty's Stationary Office, 2010. http://www.globalsecurity.org/military/library/report/2010/uk-mod_strategic-defense-review_101019.pdf.

Seeger, Peggy. *First Time Ever: A Memoir.* London: Faber and Faber, 2017.

———. *The Peggy Seeger Songbook: Warts and All: Forty Years of Songmaking.* New York: Oak Publications, 1998.

Seeger, Pete. *Pete Seeger in His Own Words*. Edited by Rob Rosenthal and Sam Rosenthal. Boulder, CO: Paradigm, 2012.

———. *Where Have All the Flowers Gone: A Singer's Stories, Songs, Seeds, Robberies*. Edited by Peter Blood. Bethlehem, PA: A Sing Out Publication, 1993.

Seegmiller, Janet Burton. "Nuclear Testing and the Downwinders." Utah Division of State History. Accessed October 8, 2020. https://historytogo.utah.gov/downwinders/.

Seligson, Mitchell A., and Vincent McElhinny. "Low-Intensity Warfare, High-Intensity Death: The Demographic Impact of the Wars in El Salvador and Nicaragua." *Canadian Journal of Latin American and Caribbean Studies* 21, no. 42 (1996): 211–241.

Shapiro, Harry, and Caesar Glebbeek. *Jimi Hendrix: Electric Gypsy*. New York: St. Martin's, 1991.

Sharpe-Young, Garry. *Metal: The Definitive Guide*. London: Jawbone, 2007.

Shearman, Peter. *The Soviet Union and Cuba*. London: Routledge and Kegan Paul, 1987.

Sheehan, Thomas. "Friendly Fascism: Business as Usual in America's Backyard." In *Fascism's Return: Scandal, Revision, and Ideology since 1980*," edited by Richard J. Golsan, 260–300. Lincoln: University of Nebraska Press, 1998.

"Shelter Boom." *Newsweek*, September 18, 1961.

Shelton, Robert. *No Direction Home: The Life and Music of Bob Dylan*. Rev. and updated ed. Milwaukee, WI: Backbeat, 2011.

Sherif, Ann. "Hiroshima, or Peace in a 'City of Cruelty and Bitter Bad Faith': Japanese Poetry in the Cold War." In *Global Cold War Literature: Western, Eastern and Postcolonial Perspectives*, edited by Andrew Hammond, 72–86. New York: Routledge, 2012.

Sherry, Michael S. *The Rise of American Air Power: The Creation of Armageddon*. New Haven, CT: Yale University Press, 1987.

Silvey, Anita. *Let Your Voice Be Heard: The Life and Times of Pete Seeger*. New York: Houghton Mifflin Harcourt, 2016.

Simpson, Kim. "Riley Walker, Uranium Minstrel (redux)." Boneyard Media. Accessed October 8, 2020. http://www.boneyardmedia.com/?p=1275.

Simpson, Philip L. "Hiroshima-Nagasaki, August 1945." In *The Concise Routledge Encyclopedia of the Documentary Film*, edited by Ian Aitken, 367–369. New York: Routledge, 2013.

Slavin, Neil. *Electric Don Quixote: The Definitive Story of Frank Zappa*. New York: Omnibus, 2003.

Smith, Charles H., and Nancy Schimmel. Notes to "What Have They Done to the Rain?" Malvina Reynolds: Song Lyrics and Poems. Accessed October 8, 2020. http://people.wku.edu/charles.smith/MALVINA/mr183.htm.

Smith, Hedrick. *The Russians*. New York: Quadrangle/New York Times, 1976.

Smith, J. Y. "Czech Writer, President Was Symbol of Freedom." *Washington Post*, December 19, 2011.

Smith, Kyle. "'Only One Way to Fight a Toxin': The Poison and Progress of Radioactivity in *The Incredible Shrinking Man*." In *Containing America: Cultural Production and Consumption in Fifties America*, edited by Nathan Abrams and Julie Hughes, 105–124. Birmingham: University of Birmingham Press, 2000.

Smith, Robert Freeman. *The Caribbean World and the United States: Mixing Rum and Coca-Cola*. New York: Twayne, 1994.

Smith, Wilbur M. *This Atomic Age and the Word of God*. Boston: W. A. Wilde, 1948.

Smolko, Joanna. "Politics and Protest in Springsteen's 'Born in the U.S.A.'" *Avid Listener*, September 19, 2016. https://theavidlistenerblog.com/2020/07/27/politics-and-protest-in-springsteens-born-in-the-u-s-a/.

———. "Springsteen and Human Rights: 'Chimes of Freedom.'" *Avid Listener*. Accessed November 14, 2018. http://www.theavidlistener.com/2016/11/springsteen-and-human-rights-chimes-of-freedom-embed-video-httpswwwyoutubecomwatchvg3onnjubs18-caption-b.html.

Spencer, Steven M. "Fallout: The Silent Killer." *Saturday Evening Post* 232, no. 9 (August 29, 1959): 26–27, 87, 89–90.

———. "Fallout: The Silent Killer: How Soon Is Too Late." *Saturday Evening Post* 232, no. 10 (September 5, 1959): 25, 84–86.

Springsteen, Bruce. *Born to Run*. New York: Simon and Schuster, 2016.

———. "Bruce Springsteen—Chimes of Freedom." Live in Copenhagen, July 25, 1988. YouTube. https://www.youtube.com/watch?v=G3onnJuBS18.

———. "Bruce Springsteen—Chimes Of Freedom" [audio]. Detroit, September 1, 1978. Uploaded September 1, 2019, YouTube. https://www.youtube.com/watch?v=ybFC3lhn9QU.

Stauffer, John, and Benjamin Soskis. *The Battle Hymn of the Republic: A Biography of the Song That Marches On*. Oxford: Oxford University Press, 2013.

Stephen, Lynn. *Women and Social Movements in Latin America: Power from Below*. Austin: University of Texas Press, 1997.

Stewart, Sean. *It's Russia, My Son! A (Partial) Roadmap of the Russian Soul*. Indianapolis, IN: Dog Ear, 2015.

Sting. "Sting in Russia." Interview by Vladimir Pozner. *Pozner*, Channel One Russia, December 26, 2010. Uploaded October 28, 2011, YouTube. http://www.youtube.com/watch?v=GHcsGZzJWds.

———. "Sting–Behind the Music (September 26 1999)." Uploaded December 6, 2019, YouTube. https://www.youtube.com/watch?v=xAcxTOfD3RE.

———. "Sting Good Rockin' Tonight 4/88 Interview." Interview by Paul McGrath. *Good Rockin' Tonite*, CBC Television, April 1988. Uploaded January 14, 2011, YouTube. https://www.youtube.com/watch?v=y5ZIp_DL4VE.

Stoddart, Kristan. *Facing Down the Soviet Union: Britain, the USA, NATO and Nuclear Weapons, 1976–1983*. Houndmills, Basingstoke, Hampshire: Palgrave Macmillan, 2014.

Stratton, Jon. "Jews, Punk and the Holocaust: From the Velvet Underground to the Ramones the Jewish-American Story." *Popular Music* 24, no. 1 (January 2005): 79–105.

Street, John. "Rock, Pop and Politics." In *The Cambridge Companion to Pop and Rock*, edited by Simon Frith, Will Straw, and John Street, 243–255. Cambridge, UK: Cambridge University Press, 2001.

Suddaby, Adam. *The Nuclear War Game*. London: Longman, 1983.

Survival under Atomic Attack. Washington, DC: Civil Defense Office, 1950. http://www.orau.org/ptp/Library/cdv/Survival%20Under%20Atomic%20Attack.pdf.

Swaine, Jon. "Shirley Temple Silenced Critics with Successful Roles in US Diplomacy." *Guardian*, February 11, 2014. https://www.theguardian.com/film/2014/feb/11/shirley-temple-ambassador-us-diplomacy.

Swerdlow, Amy. *Women Strike for Peace: Traditional Motherhood and Radical Politics in the 1960s*. Chicago: University of Chicago Press, 1993.

"Synth Britannia." BBC 4 documentary. Produced and directed by Ben Whalley. Uploaded April 18, 2020, YouTube. https://www.youtube.com/watch?v=JuQz8fHB7iw.

Tanaka, Yuki, and Marilyn B. Young, eds. *Bombing Civilians: A Twentieth-Century History*. New York: New Press, 2009.

Taubman, Philip. "At Soviet Rock Concert, the Beat of Security." *New York Times*, July 5, 1987. http://www.nytimes.com/1987/07/05/world/at-soviet-rock-concert-the-beat-of-security.html.

Taubman, William. "Did He Bang It? Nikita Khrushchev and the Shoe." *New York Times*, July 26, 2003. http://www.nytimes.com/2003/07/26/opinion/did-he-bang-it-nikita-khrushchev-and-the-shoe.html.

———. *Khrushchev: The Man and His Era*. New York: W. W. Norton, 2003.

Tempey, Nathan. "Helter Shelter: NYC's Fallout Shelters Basically Don't Exist Anymore." *Gothamist*, March 9, 2017. http://gothamist.com/2017/03/09/fallout_shelters_nyc.php.

Thompson, Dave. *Depeche Mode: Some Great Reward*. New York: St. Martin's, 1994.

———. *1000 Songs That Rock Your World*. Iola, WI: Krause, 2011.

Thompson, Dorothy. "Greenham Common Peace Camp, 1981–1993." In *Protest, Power, and Change: An Encyclopedia of Nonviolent Action from ACT-UP to Women's Suffrage*, edited by Roger S. Powers and William B. Vogele, 219–220. New York: Garland, 1997.

Thompson, E. P. *Protest and Survive*. Nottingham: Campaign for Nuclear Disarmament, 1980.

Thompson, Stephen. "Tom Lehrer." *A.V. Club*, May 24, 2000. http://www.avclub.com/article/tom-lehrer-13660.

Thomson, Graeme. *Under the Ivy: The Life and Music of Kate Bush*. New York: Omnibus, 2010.

Thorpe, Rebecca U. *The American Warfare State: The Domestic Politics of Military Spending*. Chicago: University of Chicago Press, 2014.

Titus, A. Costandina. *Bombs in the Backyard: Atomic Testing and American Politics*. Reno: University of Nevada Press, 2001.

———. "The Mushroom Cloud as Kitsch." In *Atomic Culture: How We Learned to Stop Worrying and Love the Bomb*, edited by Scott C. Zeman and Michael A. Amundson, 101–123. Boulder: University Press of Colorado, 2004.

Tompkins, Dave. *How to Wreck a Nice Beach: The Vocoder from World War II to Hip-Hop: The Machine Speaks*. Brooklyn, NY: Stop Smiling, 2010.

"Transcript of Interview of Vietnam War Veteran on His Role in Alleged Massacre of Civilians at Songmy." *New York Times*, November 24, 1969. https://archive.org/stream/MeadloWallaceInterviewNov241969/Meadlo-Wallace%20interview%20Nov%2024%201969#page/no/mode/1up.

Troitsky, Artemy. *Back in the USSR: The True Story of Rock in Russia*. Boston: Faber and Faber, 1987.

True, Everett. *Hey Ho Let's Go: The Story of the Ramones*. New York: Omnibus, 2005.

Truman, Harry S. "August 6, 1945: Statement by the President Announcing the Use of the A-Bomb at Hiroshima." Presidential Speeches, Harry S. Truman, University of Virginia, Miller Center. Accessed October 8, 2020. https://millercenter.org/the-presidency/presidential-speeches/august-6-1945-statement-president-announcing-use-bomb.

———. "August 9, 1945: Radio Report to the American People on the Potsdam Conference." Presidential Speeches, Harry S. Truman, University of Virginia, Miller Center. Accessed October 8, 2020. https://millercenter.org/the-presidency/presidential-speeches/august-9-1945-radio-report-american-people-potsdam-conference.

———. *Off the Record: The Private Papers of Harry S. Truman*. Edited by Robert H. Ferrell. New York: Harper and Row, 1980.

———. "The President's News Conference of June 29, 1950." Teaching American History, June 29, 1950. https://teachingamericanhistory.org/library/document/the-presidents-news-conference-of-june-29-1950/.

Turse, Nick. *The Complex: How the Military Invades Our Everyday Lives*. New York: Metropolitan Books, 2008.

Turrell, Tony. "The History & Impact of the Synthesizer: The Real Symbol of the Western Popular Music Revolution?" In *Popscript: Graduate Research in Popular Music Studies*, edited by Simone Krüger and Ron Moy, 25–58. Raleigh, NC: Lulu, 2014.

U2 by U2: Bono, the Edge, Adam Clayton, Larry Mullen Jr. With Neil McCormick. London: HarperCollins, 2006.

U2: The Best of Propaganda: 20 Years of the Official U2 Magazine. New York: Thunder's Mouth, 2003.

Ueda, Makoto. *Modern Japanese Poets and the Nature of Literature*. Stanford, CT: Stanford University Press, 1983.

United States Congress. Senate. Subcommittee of the Committee on Armed Services. "Nomination of Millard Frank Caldwell, Jr. to be Federal Civil Defense Administrator." Eighty-second Congress, first session. January 15, 1951. Washington, DC: United States Government Printing Office, 1951.

United States Department of Justice. "Justice Department, EPA and the Navajo Nation Announce Settlement for Cleanup of 94 Abandoned Uranium Mines on the Navajo Nation." January 17, 2017. https://www.justice.gov/opa/pr/justice-department-epa-and-navajo-nation-announce-settlement-cleanup-94-abandoned-uranium.

United States War Department. *Cavalry Drill Regulations, United States Army*. Washington, DC: Government Printing Office, 1918.

Unterberger, Richie. *Unknown Legends of Rock 'n' Roll: Psychedelic Unknowns, Mad Geniuses, Punk Pioneers, Lo-fi Mavericks & More*. San Francisco: Backbeat, 1998.

Urick, Bret. "Pink Floyd The Wall: A Complete Analysis." Accessed October 8, 2020. http://www.thewallanalysis.com/.

Vale, Lawrence J. *The Limits of Civil Defence in the USA, Switzerland, Britain, and the Soviet Union: The Evolution of Policies since 1945*. New York: St. Martin's, 1987.

Valentino, Benjamin A. *Final Solutions: Mass Killing and Genocide in the Twentieth Century*. Ithaca, NY: Cornell University Press, 2004.

Vallen, Mark. "Discharge: Hear Nothing See Nothing Say Nothing." Art for a Change. http://www.art-for-a-change.com/Punk/punk6a.htm.

VH1. "VH1 Presents the Eighties." Uploaded November 6, 2012, YouTube. https://www.youtube.com/watch?v=gfQMBGyTnsI.

Vivinetto, Gino. "Off-duty from Men at Work." *St. Petersburg Times*, April 26, 2001.

Vogel, Peter. "Uranium Miners Have a Blast: Rockin-R-Rangers Lay Down a Boogie Beat." *New Mexico*, January 1989.

Vogel, Shane. "*Jamaica* on Broadway: The Popular Caribbean and Mock Transnational Performance." *Theatre Journal* 62, no. 1 (March 2010): 1–21.

Von Eschen, Penny M. *Satchmo Blows Up the World: Jazz Ambassadors Play the Cold War*. Cambridge, MA: Harvard University Press, 2004.

Waksman, Steve. *Instruments of Desire: The Electric Guitar and the Shaping of Musical Experience*. Cambridge, MA: Harvard University Press, 1999.

Waldenburg, Harmann. *The Berlin Wall*. New York: Abbeville, 1990.

Waldman, Tom. *We All Want to Change the World: Rock and Politics from Elvis to Eminem*. Foreword by Donovan Leitch. Lanham, MD: Taylor Trade, 2003.

Wall, Mick. *Bono: In the Name of Love*. New York: Thunder's Mouth, 2005.

Wallace, Rich, and Sandra Neil Wallace. *Blood Brother: Jonathan Daniels and His Sacrifice for Civil Rights*. Honesdale, PA: Calkins Creek, 2016.

Waller, Johnny, and Mike Humphreys. *Messages: Orchestral Manoeuvres in the Dark: An Official Biography*. Foreword by Andy McCluskey and Paul Humphreys. London: Sidgwick and Jackson, 1987.

Walser, Robert. *Running with the Devil: Power, Gender, and Madness in Heavy Metal Music*. Hanover, NH: Wesleyan University Press, 1993.

Walsh, Michael. "Roger Waters' 'Wall.'" *Entertainment Weekly*, August 3, 1990. http://ew.com/article/1990/08/03/roger-waters-wall/.

Waters, Roger. "Roger Waters—Berlin Wall Pre & Post Concert Reports 1990." Uploaded August 15, 2013, YouTube. https://www.youtube.com/watch?v=ZQgP6zZrmhE.

Watkins, Jack. "How We Made: Orchestral Manoeuvres in the Dark on 'Enola Gay.'" *Guardian*, January 7, 2013. https://www.theguardian.com/music/2013/jan/07/orchestral-manoeuvres-dark-enola-gay.

Webb, Sheyann, and Rachel West Nelson. *Selma, Lord, Selma: Girlhood Memories of the Civil Rights Days as told to Frank Sikora*. Tuscaloosa: University of Alabama Press, 1980.

Weinstein, Deena. "Rock Protest Songs: So Many and So Few." In *The Resisting Muse: Popular Music and Social Protest*, edited by Ian Peddie, 3–16. Aldershot: Ashgate, 2006.

Weinstein, Deena, and Michael A. Weinstein. "Neil Peart versus Ayn Rand." In *Rush and Philosophy: Heart and Mind United*, edited by Jim Berti and Durrell Bowman, 273–285. Chicago: Open Court, 2011.

Weissman, Dick. *Talkin' 'bout a Revolution: Music and Social Change in America*. New York: Backbeat, 2010.

Welch, Chris. *Complete Guide to the Music of the Police & Sting*. New York: Omnibus, 1996.

Welch, Robert. *The Politician*. Belmont, MA: Robert Welch, 1963.

Welles, Chris. "The Angry Young Folk Singer." *Life*, April 10, 1964.

Wells, Rufus. "What Would Happen If the Bomb Falls?" *Sepia*, January 1962.

Welsome, Eileen. *The Plutonium Files: America's Secret Medical Experiments in the Cold War*. New York: Dial, 1999.

———. "The Plutonium Files: How the U.S. Secretly Fed Radioactivity to Thousands of Americans." Interview by Amy Goodman. "Democracy Now," May 5, 2004. https://www.democracynow.org/2004/5/5/plutonium_files_how_the_u_s.

"When Atom Bomb Struck—Uncensored." *Life* 33, no. 13 (September 29, 1952): 19–25.

Whitney, Craig R. "Prague Journal: Shirley Temple Black Unpacks a Bag of Memories." *New York Times*, September 11, 1989.

Wilcken, Hugo. *David Bowie's Low*. London: Continuum, 2005.

Wissner, Reba A. "Pop Music and the Bomb." *Bulletin of the Atomic Scientists*, December 14, 2018. https://thebulletin.org/2018/12/pop-music-and-the-bomb/.

Wolfe, Charles K. *In Close Harmony: The Story of the Louvin Brothers*. Jackson: University Press of Mississippi, 1996.

———. "'Jesus Hits Like an Atom Bomb': Nuclear Warfare in Country Music 1944–56." In *Country Music Goes to War*, edited by Charles K. Wolfe and James E. Akenson, 102–125. Lexington: University Press of Kentucky, 2005.

Wolfe, Charles K., and James E Akenson, eds. *Country Music Goes to War*. Lexington: University Press of Kentucky, 2005.

Wolfe, Tom. *The Electric Kool-Aid Acid Test*. New York: Farrar, Straus and Giroux, 1968.

Woodhead, Leslie. "The Beatles: Bringing Down the Soviet Union." *CBS News This Morning* interview. Uploaded May 18, 2013, YouTube. https://www.youtube.com/watch?v=UDWUJkWnaJQ.

———. *How the Beatles Rocked the Kremlin: The Untold Story of a Noisy Revolution*. New York: Bloomsbury, 2013.

Worley, Matthew. "One Nation under the Bomb: The Cold War and British Punk to 1984." *Journal for the Study of Radicalism* 5, no. 2 (Fall 2011): 65–83.

———. "Youth Subcultures: An Alternative History." University of Reading Department of History. Uploaded September 29, 2015, YouTube. https://www.youtube.com/watch?v=l8fPaevWpQk.

"Youth from 102 Lands Swarms over Moscow: U.S.S.R. Teaches—and Is Taught." *Life* 43, no. 7 (August 12, 1957): 22–27.

Zappa, Frank. "Frank Zappa in Prague / Frank Zappa v Praze (20.—24. 01. 1990)." Uploaded December 9, 2015, YouTube. https://www.youtube.com/watch?v=1qF4fhWJR5s.

———. "Frank Zappa—TV Interview, 1990." Interview by Bryant Gumbel. *Today Show*, March 1990. Uploaded May 14, 2013, YouTube. https://www.youtube.com/watch?v=m6w6KsQgWOs.

Zappa, Frank, with Peter Occhiogrosso. *The Real Frank Zappa Book*. New York: Poseidon, 1989.

Zarlengo, Kristina. "Civilian Threat, the Suburban Citadel, and Atomic Age American Women." *Signs* 24, no. 4 (Summer 1999): 925–958.

Zeman, Scott C., and Michael A. Amundson, eds. *Atomic Culture: How We Learned to Stop Worrying and Love the Bomb*. Boulder, CO: University Press of Colorado, 2004.

Zhuk, Sergei I. *Rock and Roll in the Rocket City: The West, Identity, and Ideology in Soviet Dniepropetrovsk, 1960–1985*. Baltimore: The Johns Hopkins University Press, 2010.

Zoellner, Tom. *Uranium: War, Energy, and the Rock that Shaped the World*. New York: Viking, 2009.

DISCOGRAPHY

Atomic Platters: Cold War Music from the Golden Age of Homeland Security. Liner notes by Bill Geerhart and Ken Sitz. Hambergen, Germany: Bear Family Records BCD 16065 FM, 2005, five-CD/one-DVD box set.

Baez, Joan. *Joan Baez in Concert*. Vanguard VRS-9112, 1962, LP.

———. *Where Are You Now, My Son?* A&M Records SP-4390, 1973, LP.

Battleground Korea: Songs and Sounds of America's Forgotten War. Program notes by Hugo Keesing and Bill Geerhart. Bear Family Records BCD 17518, 2018, four-CD box set.

Bowie, David. *A New Career in a New Town [1977–1982].* Parlophone Records, 2017, eleven-CD set.

Country Music Goes to War. Starday Records, SLP 374, 1966, LP.

Dylan, Bob. *The Bootleg Series, Volumes 1–3 (Rare & Unreleased), 1961–1991.* Columbia C3K 65302, 1991, three-CD set.

———. *The Freewheelin' Bob Dylan.* Columbia CS 8786, 1963, LP.

Freedom Is a Hammer: Conservative Folk Revolutionaries of the Sixties. Liner notes by Bill Geerhart. Australia: Omni Recording OMNI-167, 2012, CD.

Freedom Songs: Selma, Alabama: A Documentary Recording by Carl Benkert. Folkways Records FH 5594, 1965, LP. Smithsonian Folkways Recordings, 2006, CD.

Joel, Billy. *A Matter of Trust: The Bridge to Russia.* Columbia 88883759762, 2014, two-CD/one-DVD set.

Next Stop Is Vietnam: The War on Record, 1961–2008. Foreword by Country Joe McDonald. Liner notes by Hugo A. Keesing, Lois T. Vietri, Doug Bradley, and Craig Werner. Hambergen, Germany: Bear Family Records BCD 16070 MS, 2010, thirteen-CD box set.

People Take Warning! Murder Ballads & Disaster Songs, 1913–1938. Tompkins Square TSQ1875, 2007, three-CD set.

Songs Against the Bomb. Topic 12001, 1959, LP.

Songs for Political Action: Folk Music, Topical Songs and the American Left, 1926–1953. Liner notes by Ronald D. Cohen and Dave Samuelson. Hambergen, Germany: Bear Family Records BCD 15720 JL, 1996, ten-CD box set.

Songs of the Selma-Montgomery March. Folkways Records FH 5595, 1965, LP. Smithsonian Folkways Recordings, 2007, CD.

Sting. *The Dream of the Blue Turtles.* A&M Records SP-3750, 1985, LP.

Schwarz, Fred. *What Is Communism?* Cantico Records, 1966, four-LP set.

The Weavers. *Wasn't That a Time.* Liner notes by Mary Katherine Aldin. Vanguard VCD4-147/50, 1993, four-CD set.

VIDEOGRAPHY

The Atomic Café. 20th anniversary edition. Produced and directed by Kevin Rafferty, Jayne Loader, Pierce Rafferty. New Video Group NVG-9496, 2002, DVD.

Black Sabbath: Paranoid. Classic Albums. New York: Eagle Vision EV302959, 2010, DVD.

Cold War: The Complete Series. A Jeremy Isaacs Production for Turner Original Productions. Narrated by Kenneth Branagh. Warner Home Video 3000042713, 2012, six-DVD set.

David Bowie: Under Review, 1976—1979: The Berlin Trilogy. Films Media Group 49263, 2006, DVD.

End of the Century: The Story of the Ramones. Rhino R2 970399, 2005, DVD.

The Fever of '57: The Sputnik Movie. Varied Directions International MVD5321D, 2007, two-DVD set.

Hasselhoff vs. the Berlin Wall. National Geographic, 2014, DVD.

The History of Rock 'n' Roll. Created and produced by Jeffrey Peisch. Time-Life Video and Television, Warner Home Video 34991, c1995, 2004, five-DVD set.

Jimi Hendrix: Live at Woodstock. Experience Hendrix B0005283-09, 2005, two-DVD set.

Iron Maiden: Live after Death. Columbia Music Video 88697227379, 2008, two-DVD set.

Kraftwerk and the Electronic Revolution. Sexy Intellectual SIDVD541, 2008, DVD.

Led Zeppelin: The Song Remains the Same (1976). Directed by Peter Clifton and Joe Massot. Produced by Peter Grant. Two-disc Special Edition. Warner Bros. 72654, 2007, two-DVD set.

Love It Like a Fool: A Film about Malvina Reynolds. Directed and edited by Susan Wengraf. Red Hen Films, 1977, DVD.

Paul McCartney in Red Square: A Concert Film. A&E AAE-71104, 2005, DVD.

Paul Robeson: Here I Stand. WinStar Home Entertainment, Fox Lorber Home Video WHE71177, 1999, VHS.

Pete Seeger: The Power of Song. Weinstein Company and Live Nation Artists 81411, 2007, DVD.

Peter Porter: What I Have Written. Directed by Richard Kelly Tipping. Third Millennium Pictures, 1985.

Pink Floyd The Wall. Directed by Alan Parker. Screenplay by Roger Waters. Sony BMG Music Entertainment CVD 58163, 2005, DVD.

Released! The Human Rights Concerts, 1986–1998. Shout! Factory, Amnesty International 826663135562, 2013, six-DVD set.

Sting. *Bring On the Night*. Directed by Michael Apted. A & M Records 9880428, 2005, DVD.

———. *Live in Berlin*. Deutsche Grammophon BOO14981-59, 2010, Blu-Ray.

U2. *Rattle and Hum* (1988). Paramount Home Video 32228, 1999, DVD.

———. *The Joshua Tree*. Classic Albums. Eagle Rock Entertainment ID9074ERDVD, 1999, DVD.

Waters, Roger. *The Wall Live in Berlin*. Written and directed by Roger Waters. Universal Music B0000369-09, 2003, DVD.

Woodstock: 3 Days of Peace and Music. The Director's Cut. Two-disc 40th anniversary edition. Warner Bros. Pictures 2000007993-2000007994, 2009, two-DVD set.

INDEX

TIM SMOLKO holds master's degrees in musicology and library science and is monographs original cataloger at the University of Georgia. He is author of *Jethro Tull's Thick as a Brick and A Passion Play: Inside Two Long Songs* (2013), which won the 2014 Award for Excellence in Historical Recorded Sound Research in Recorded Rock Music from the Association for Recorded Sound Collections.

JOANNA SMOLKO holds a PhD in musicology and is Adjunct Professor of Music at the Hugh Hodgson School of Music at the University of Georgia. She has published journal articles and book chapters and was a contributing editor for the second edition of *The Grove Dictionary of American Music* (2013).

Tim and Joanna live in Athens, Georgia.
They have thirteen-year-old twins, Ian and Elanor.

CPSIA information can be obtained
at www.ICGtesting.com
Printed in the USA
JSHW051925220722
28431JS00002B/96

9 780253 024466